'EVERY SOUND THERE IS'

'Every Sound There Is':

The Beatles' *Revolver* and the transformation of rock and roll

Edited by
RUSSELL REISING

Ashgate

Published by
Ashgate Publishing Limited
Gower House
Croft Road
Aldershot
Hants GU11 3HR
England

Ashgate Publishing Company
131 Main Street
Burlington
Vermont, 054011–5600
USA

Ashgate website: http://www.ashgate.com

British Library Cataloguing in Publication Data

'Every Sound There Is': The Beatles' *Revolver* and the Transformation of Rock and Roll– (Ashgate Popular and Folk Music Series)
    1. Beatles. Revolver. 2. Beatle—Influence. 3. Rock music—1961–1970—History and criticism. I. Reising, Russell.
    782.4'2'166'0922

US Library of Congress Cataloging in Publication Data

'Every Sound There Is': The Beatles' *Revolver* and the Transformation of Rock and Roll/edited by Russell Reising.
    p.–cm. – Ashgate Popular and Folk Music Series)
    Includes bibliographical references and index.
    1. Beatles. Revolver. 2. Rock music—History and criticism. I. Title: Beatles' *Revolver* and the Transformation of Rock and Roll. II. Reising, Russell. III. Series.
    ML421.134E94 2002
    782.42166'092'2–dc21   2001055338

ISBN 0 7546 0556 6 (hbk)
ISBN 0 7546 0557 4 (pbk)

This book is printed on acid free paper.

Typeset by Q3 Bookwork, Loughborough, Leicestershire

Printed and bound in Great Britain by TJ International Ltd., Padstow, Cornwall

Contents

General Editor's preface

The upheaval that occurred in musicology during the last two decades of the twentieth century has created a new urgency for the study of popular music alongside the development of new critical and theoretical models. A relativistic outlook has replaced the universal perspective of modernism (the international ambitions of the 12-note style); the grand narrative of the evolution and dissolution of tonality has been challenged; and emphasis has shifted to cultural context, reception and subject position. Together, these have conspired to eat away at the status of canonical composers and categories of high and low in music. A need has arisen, also, to recognize and address the emergence of crossovers, mixed and new genres, to engage in debates concerning the vexed problem of what constitutes authenticity in music and to offer a critique of musical practice as the product of free, individual expression.

Popular musicology is now a vital and exciting area of scholarship, and the Ashgate Popular and Folk Music series aims to present the best research in the field. Authors will be concerned with locating musical practices, values and meanings in cultural context, and may draw upon methodologies and theories developed in cultural studies, semiotics, poststructuralism, psychology and sociology. The series will focus on popular musics of the twentieth and twenty-first centuries. It is designed to embrace the world's popular musics from Acid Jazz to Zydeco, whether high tech or low tech, commercial or non-commercial, contemporary or traditional.

Professor Derek B. Scott
Chair of Music
University of Salford

Visit Project Pop:
http://www.music.salford.ac.uk/music2/web/projects/FDTLpop/welcome.htm

Introduction: 'Of the beginning'

Don Wargowsky, one of my oldest and dearest friends and one of the world's ultimate Beatles fans, has always claimed there are two answers to the question 'What is your favorite Beatles album?': the 'snooty' answer and the right answer. For him, the right answer has always been *Sgt Pepper's Lonely Hearts Club Band*, the snooty answer *Revolver*. Don and I are very frequently 'on the same page' when it comes to musical preferences, and our obsessive lists of 'Greatest Songs of All Time', 'Greatest Albums of All Times', and even 'Greatest Songs Beginning Album Side Twos' usually tickle us with their superimposability. However, I never quite bought the distinction, nor did I accept the implications for the evolution of the Beatles' music encoded within Donald's evaluation of *Revolver*. Since the first day I heard it, *Revolver* has always been the right answer, as it increasingly seems to be for Beatles and rock and roll fans around the world. *Revolver* has been shocking, provoking, frightening and delighting listeners with its lyrical beauty and sonic wonders – spoken, sung, wailed, archaic, pop, atmospheric, acoustic, electronic, impossible, and some almost terrifyingly futuristic – for over thirty-five years, and, if the contemporary reviews I cite below are any indication, its grip on our collective imaginations shows no signs of loosening. *Revolver* remains a haunting, soothing, confusing, grandly complex and ambitious *statement* about the possibilities of popular music; it also still stands as a testament to the force a group of minds – the Beatles, George Martin, and all their performing and producing collaborators – can exert when they merge in some mystical space both deeply embedded in the culture of their times and simultaneously freed from the trammels of time and space. Part tribute, part labor of love, part inquiry into the mysteries of *Revolver*'s many sounds, '*Every Sound There Is*' collects fourteen attempts to define just what it is about *Revolver* that has exerted such enduring joy and magic for its millions of fans and casual listeners.

The specific inspiration and origins of this collection date back to the 'Beatles 2000' conference held in Jyväskylä, Finland in June 2000. I had organized, along with three friends and colleagues, a panel which we called 'Happiness is a Warm Gun: *Revolver* and the Transformation of Rock and Roll'. Our four papers were well received, and Derek Scott of Ashgate encouraged us to propose a book project on *Revolver*. Since we were spending the gloriously nightless midsummer in Central Finland mingling with Beatles scholars and fanatics from around the world, it didn't take a 'long, long, long time' to assemble the roster of scholars who wrote '*Every Sound There Is*'. Our merry band includes citizens of Canada, England, Israel, the Netherlands, New Zealand, South Africa, and the United States. We range in age from twenty to sixty-something, and, in experience, from some of the world's foremost Beatles scholars to second-generation Beatles fans currently in college. We are students, literary scholars, librarians, musicians, musicologists, nurses, social scientists, and cultural studies specialists. Some of us have already published on the Beatles, most of us on popular music. However broad our backgrounds and from however many corners of the world we come, the contributors to '*Every Sound There Is*' are united in their shared passion for the Beatles' revolutionary 1966 release.

As we basked in that Finnish midnight sun, little did most of us then know that *Q* magazine had, in its June 2000 issue, ranked *Revolver* as the #1 album in its survey of the '50 Greatest British Albums Ever!' Since Radiohead's *OK Computer* was the only album to surpass *Revolver* in *Q*'s 1998 list of 'The 100 Greatest Albums of All Time', we can infer that *Revolver* now stands at the absolute top of the heap for any *Q* list. In his commentary on *Revolver*, *Q*'s David Quantick captured much of the album's original and enduring appeal. Referring to it as 'the most shocking Beatles record, the one that makes a quantum leap even from the brilliantly developed super pop of *Rubber Soul*', Quantick quite rightly suggests that, for many historico-cultural reasons, '1966 was the only year that The Beatles' album *Revolver* could have been recorded.' Carefully balanced in his assessment of each Beatle's contribution to *Revolver*, Quantick nonetheless characterizes the 'grand vision' which the album's canvas created, noting '*Revolver* combines an astonishing mix of styles with a weirdly consistent sense of purpose (it doesn't meander like *Sgt Pepper*).' By way of conclusion, Quantick offers something like a definition of *Revolver*'s essence: 'more than a collection of tunes, *Revolver* is six loaded chambers of contemporary British culture at a point when contemporary British culture reverberated around the world' (Quantick, 2000, pp. 92–93). Of course, the contributors to this book all took tremendous heart and pleasure in the *Q* ranking, especially since it boded well for the timing and importance of our collective work.

Revolver's rise to the absolute top of the heap, however, was long in coming. We should recall that, as recently as 1987, *Rolling Stone* ranked *Revolver* a significant, but still comparatively modest #17 in its list of the '100 Greatest Albums of the Rock Era', behind *Sgt Pepper* (#1), *The Beatles* (#10), *Abbey Road* (#13), and just ahead of *Rubber Soul* (#21). Even by 1995, a substantial entry for the Beatles in their *Encyclopedia of Rock & Roll* mentions *Revolver* only in passing, their sole remark being 'With "Taxman" and "Love You To" on *Revolver*, Harrison began to emerge as a songwriter' (Romanowski and George-Warren, 1995, p. 61; see Matthew Bannister's essay in this collection for a thorough discussion of Harrison's emergence on *Revolver*). More recently, the multi-hour public television special *Rock and Roll* jumped from a few remarks about the classical breakthroughs on 'Eleanor Rigby' to 1967 and the release of *Sgt Pepper's Lonely Hearts Club Band* without so much as mentioning the album *Revolver*, any of its songs other than 'Eleanor Rigby,' and none of its thematic, musical, or technological revolutions. Like so many accounts, the producers rushed to get to *Sgt Pepper*. *Revolver* does get slightly more attention during that series' 'Blues in Technicolor' segment focusing on the psychedelic revolution in music, although the only song discussed is 'Tomorrow Never Knows'. Phil Lesh comments on *Revolver* signaling the Beatles' joining of the psychedelic avant-garde, and we get a few minutes on the exotic elements of the record, including interview footage with George Martin about the technical advances integral to recording 'Tomorrow Never Knows', and some footage of George Harrison studying the sitar with Ravi Shankar. The *Q* ranking, then, signals a sea-change in our understanding of and response to *Revolver*.

This change in our sense of *Revolver*'s significance impacts musical culture at every level, from academic scholarship to the popular reception of the album. In one of the many insights of his excellent *Tell Me Why: The Beatles: Album by Album, Song by Song, The Sixties and After*, Tim Riley notes that '*Revolver* single-handedly made Beatlemania irrelevant – there was no longer any need for touring to keep the idea of the Beatles alive. It is so clearly the work of *recording* artists that the idea of them running through their hits on that last tour now seems ridiculous, a compromise of all the creative progress they had made in the studio' (Riley, 1988, p. 176). One can infer Riley's deep appreciation for *Revolver* from this passage, but he delivers an absolute coup de grace in the first sentence of his chapter on *Sgt Pepper's Lonely Hearts Club Band*: '*Sgt Pepper* is the Beatles' most notorious record for the wrong reasons – a flawed masterpiece that can only echo the strength of *Revolver*' (Riley, 1988, p. 203). *Sgt Pepper* defenders will, of course, bristle at Riley's position, but his perspective does foreshadow much of the current '*Revolver* Revival'.

The *Q* ranking was only the beginning of what appears to be a full-scale, mass media reevaluation of *Revolver*'s significance within the Beatles' corpus as well as within the entire history of rock and roll. A few months after *Q*'s deification of *Revolver*, in September 2000, *Virgin All Time Top 1,000 Albums*, a study which compiled nearly a quarter million votes cast by record buyers, music enthusiasts and journalists, also ranked it as the greatest album of all time. And, just a few months later in February 2001, VH1, the popular cable television music channel, jumped on board this yellow submarine, declaring *Revolver* as its all-time greatest album of rock 'n' roll. Said Bill Flanagan, VH1 executive producer, '*Revolver* is just invulnerable. Every track is great. Every track is like a polished jewel.' The Associated Press release accompanying the VH1 ranking adds that 'the album's reputation has grown recently, particularly when its CD re-release restored songs left off the original American record' (*Toledo Blade*, 5 January, 2001, Section D 11).[1] Amidst its generally hyperbolic tone and effusive praise, the VH1 commentary echoes and expands upon the *Q* commentary from a year earlier when it makes this particularly compelling point: 'If pop music were destroyed tomorrow, we could re-create it from this album alone', the editors remark. 'There's Paul's song for all the lonely people ("Eleanor Rigby"), George's beef with the IRS ("Taxman"), Ringo's jocular "Yellow Submarine", and John's existential opus "Tomorrow Never Knows".'[2] What a stunning remark: the entire history of pop music encoded within a single album.

Many cuts from *Revolver* also top many lists of favorite individual Beatles songs. In the July 2001 issue of *Uncut* magazine, songs from *Revolver* figure significantly in their 'All-Star' Panel's votes for the 50 Greatest Beatles Songs. 'And Your Bird Can Sing' came in as number 40, 'Eleanor Rigby' at number 34, 'I'm Only Sleeping' at number 32, 'She Said She Said' at number 30, 'Paperback Writer' and 'Rain' from the *Revolver* sessions at numbers 11 and 8 respectively, and 'Tomorrow Never Knows' managed number 4, resulting in five cuts actually from *Revolver* and two more from the same recording sessions occupying an inordinate number of places in the Beatles' 50 greatest.[3] Most of the 'All Star' panel chime in at some point or other during the rankings, but several comments on *Revolver* are noteworthy. Of 'Eleanor Rigby', Jerry Lieber (of the famous songwriting team Lieber and Stoller) remarks, 'Eleanor Rigby is a beautiful piece of work. It makes you feel the geographic area is in the song. You can smell it, like grass. It's like something out of the 19th century. ... It's evocative and it's complete. Everything is intact. It's together, lyrically and musically, and the arrangement, production and vocals are all integrated' (p. 36). Jackie Leven (Doll By Doll) loves 'the confusion ['She Said She Said'] sets up, and the way the singer resolves it when he says, "No, no, no you're wrong, when I was a boy ..." I was intrigued by the complexity of emotion it expressed' (p. 40). Of 'Tomorrow Never Knows', Andy Bell (Oasis) remarks, 'Words can't describe how great this is, so I'm not going to try. I heard it when I was 13 and have never been the same since. It got me into playing music really loud and losing myself in the sounds' (p. 60).

Recent on-line media has proven no less effusive in their response to this trend. Consider, for example, *Ink Blot Magazine*'s compelling case for *Revolver*'s centrality:

> It is nearly impossible to overestimate this record. *Revolver* straddles with steady legs the divide between the exuberant pop of the '60s beat boom and the experimental outlands that followed. And then pisses over it all. ... *Revolver* stands at the summit of western pop music, partly by virtue of its centrality to the musical revolution of the '60s, and partly because its songs have endured as well as any ever written. On cuts like 'Taxman' (featuring a fantastically ferocious guitar solo from, of all people, Paul McCartney) and 'Doctor Robert', The Beatles' harmony-rich R&B is on such masterful form, the only question remaining is what they would do for act two. The answer: Change Everything.

A random sampling of Reader's Reviews from the popular UK and North American 'Amazon.com' web-sites suggests the degrees of enthusiasm to which contemporary listeners are still propelled by *Revolver*. Posted in calendar year 2001, these unsolicited on-line reviews indicate the depths of passion *Revolver* still triggers in younger listeners. Ricky Wright's 'Editorial Review' of *Revolver* as an 'essential recording' makes a powerful case for the album's popularity:

> *Revolver* wouldn't remain the Beatles' most ambitious LP for long, but many fans – including this one – remember it as their best. An object lesson in fitting great

songwriting into experimental production and genre play, this is also a record whose influence extends far beyond mere they-was-the-greatest cheerleading. Putting McCartney's more traditionally melodic 'Here, There and Everywhere' and 'For No One' alongside Lennon's direct-hit sneering ('Dr. Robert') and dreamscapes ('I'm Only Sleeping,' 'Tomorrow Never Knows') and Harrison's peaking wit ('Taxman') was as conceptually brilliant as anything *Sgt Pepper* attempted, and more subtly fulfilling. A must.

'Regular readers' add to Wright's evaluation. John Jones from Boston, Massachusetts, provides elaborate and thoughtful commentary:

After 1965's adventurous *Rubber Soul*, The Beatles upped the ante and released an album that branched out even further in both writing and production. At once highly artistic and commercially accessible, *Revolver* starts the era most modern rock artists are surely referring to when they cite a Beatles influence.

Stylistically fearless, the Fab Four break new ground with the greatest of ease: the lovely, Gothic 'Eleanor Rigby' flows like a concerto, 'I'm Only Sleeping' could just as easily be cited as blues as it could be country, and 'Love You To' was an early glimpse of World Pop. Also ahead of its time was 'Tomorrow Never Knows' ... who'd have guessed that the rhythms of the drum-&-bass movement in 90's dance music was experimented with over thirty years ago by Ringo Starr? (And let's not forget the track's trippy sonic boom, either, falling somewhere between World Music and acid trip.) *Revolver* is also responsible for the genre-busting, sea-shanty-on-hallucinogens 'Yellow Submarine,' the granddaddy of far-out rock fiction that still remains a relentlessly singable treasure.

The changes within the Beatles cache that subtly began on *Rubber Soul* were forwarded here, and also dropped hints at what was to come on the likes of *Sgt Pepper* and *The White Album*. As fresh as it is classic, *Revolver* remains one of rock's standout recordings.

Seattlean Jay Thompson believes that *Revolver*

is, more or less, everything people say *Sgt Pepper* was – a terrific fusion of strong songs and imaginative production in a pioneering way, driven by two intensely competitive songwriters. ... I know that I *should* like *Sgt Pepper* more – after all, it's the Record That Broke All the Rules – I think this record's subtler pleasures are more enjoyable. I listen to it much more than I listen to *Sgt Pepper*.

Finally, Willie A. Young II from Houston, Texas reiterates the shocking revelations *Revolver* provided for many of its listeners, from 1966 to the present:

No other band was able to sound completely new on each release, yet still sound like The Beatles! *Revolver* is my personal favorite because it caught me completely off guard the first time I heard it 16 years ago, and it still unveils something new every time I listen to it now. (Special Musical Note: Ringo is the star of ['Tomorrow Never Knows'], his low, repetitive, thudding drums anchor the piece from start to finish, and

he NEVER falters.) I consider this the group's greatest album because of its stunning
diversity and effortless eclecticism, nothing here sounds forced or out of place and
they were still a band, a situation that would change drastically over the next 2 to 3
years. *Sgt Pepper* was more excessive and artsy, but song for song, *Revolver* is a
stronger effort. A True Classic!

Amazon.com reviewers from the United Kingdom communicate the same exuberance as do their on-line peers from the United States, revisiting, in fact, many
of the specific points common to those comments. 'Nostromed' from Leicester,
England offers this over-the-top commentary: 'Anyone who says they don't like
this album either hasn't heard it or is in serious need of some psychiatric help (No
offence Dad!). It is guaranteed to appeal to everyone, everywhere with consistently varied, brilliant songs. Still as revolutionary and jaw-droppingly fresh as it
was in the sixties ... Mind-blowing stuff!' An anonymous 'music fan from London'
struggles to situate *Revolver* as an album at the cusp of a transformation in dance
culture. *Revolver*, s/he says,

> is where the Beatles really began to move away from the early 60's 'rock n roll dance'
> sound, as can be witnessed in the haunting orchestral piece 'Eleanor Rigby'. I'm
> slightly surprised that many reviewers here consider the McCartney songs 'superior'.
> I love them, but Its John (backed by George) that are truely innovative here. The
> proof? – witness the finale 'Tomorrow never knows', perhaps the worlds first Dance
> track (in the modern sense) with F/X laden Trippy haunting lyrics, sitars [sic], what
> sounds like deranged seagulls in the background, backwards guitar, and a beat that
> the Chemical Brothers would have been proud of (in fact they copied it for 'setting
> sun'). God only knows what the Beatlemania hoard of teeny-boppers made of this.

Timmo@mi6-agent.co.uk, also from England, similarly focuses *Revolver* in the
context of contemporary dance scene: '"Tomorrow Never Knows" is an astonishing song, a true delight with backwards guitars, weird voices and strange
samples filling your ears. This song is a pre-cursor to dance music and influenced
artists such as The Chemical Brothers. Plus I am 18 years of age, this music is too
good … gotta go to have another listen.' 'Krichardson', from Northern England,
summarizes the general drift of most of the amazon.com amateur reviews: 'This
is by far the greatest and most influential album in the history of music; from the
haunting themes of "Eleanor Rigby" and "For No One" to the fun time tracks of
"Dr Robert" and "Yellow Submarine" this is one cd you have to have in your
collection.'

Finally, a web-site advertising a *Revolver* Boxed Set encapsulates much of the
enthusiasm that has characterized the recent reevaluation of the 1966 release:

> This is The Beatles just past the mid-point in their journey, young of body but
> wizened of soul. *Revolver* is a mélange of style and substance that allowed The
> Beatles to lay claim to their title as The Greatest Of All-Time. The album contains
> everything from baroque medievalisms to the intoxicating forbidden sounds of the
> mysterious East, as well as nursery rhyme singalongs and the very music of

Beelzebub himself. Rock and Roll. Vacillating between perfect pop jewelry and the din of the impending apocalypse, *Revolver* ripped a hole in the time/space continuum offering a snapshot of the era for all-time and rendering itself utterly timeless. (superfly.home.texas.net/revolver/)

As many will recall, of course, whether from those bracing initial encounters with *Revolver* itself or from its initial press, the album began its revolutionary work of shaking up the musical world, and changing everything, at the moment of its release in 1966. In one representative early review published soon after the release of *Revolver* in 1966, Jules Siegel suggested:

> Now the fate of the Beatles lies in the hands of those who someday will prepare the poetry textbooks of the future, in which songs of unrequited love and psychedelic philosophy will appear stripped of their music, raw material for doctoral dissertations, just as the songs of John Donne, William Shakespeare, and John Milton, once a special kind of 17th century Top 40, are now locked inside the groves of the academy, armored in footnotes and frozen out flat on the dry, cold paper of expensive variorum editions. (Siegel, 1966, p. 14)

The Beatles had finally made it, rubbing shoulders with Shakespeare, Milton, and their ilk. Equally hyperbolic in his tone, Richard Goldstein in the *Village Voice* review (1966) felt that 'it seems now that we will view this album in retrospect as a key work in the development of rock 'n' roll into an artistic pursuit' and called *Revolver* 'a revolutionary record'. In a recent letter, Sam Andrew, guitar player from Big Brother and the Holding Company, remembers his initial reaction to *Revolver*'s release in similar terms, albeit with the added cachet of a musician's insider angle:

> When *Revolver* came out, I was living with Big Brother and the Holding Company in Lagunitas, California, out among the redwoods, glorying in our new counterculture life. I had a little cabin, precious privacy, out in back of the mainhouse where the rest of the band lived. I wrote songs all night in that cabin and then came back into the house to rehearse them with the band for eight hours or so. I listened to *Revolver* over and over again and realized that the Beatles had definitely 'come on board'. It was obvious from the songs and from the treatment of the songs that the four lads had grown up. Every track on the album was a revelation and a revolution. There was a wild, intoxicating sense of promise in listening to this latest Beatles collection. The name '*Revolver*' said it all. (personal correspondence, August, 2001)

It is important to note that this wave whose crest *Revolver* seems to be riding is not universally acknowledged. A recent search of the World Wide Web for 'Top 100 Albums of All Time' reveals that *Revolver*'s fate is still quite mixed. The 'Rock N World' list for 1999 and 2000 has *Revolver* coming in at #55 on the 2000 list, down significantly from its #35 placing on the 1999 chart. *Revolver* trailed behind *Sgt Pepper* and *The Beatles* both years. *The Melody Maker* All Time Top 100 list, compiled in 2000, lists The Smiths' *The Queen is Dead* as #1, with

Revolver charting at #6, just behind *The Beatles* at #4 (*Abbey Road* managed only #93). At 'netscape.net/strajnic/top100albums' (last checked update, 5 July 2001), an interesting list updated weekly, *Sgt Pepper* and *Revolver* come in at Number 1 and 2 respectively, ahead of Nirvana's *Nevermind* at #3. A site labeled as 'GLR,' which scores votes for the greatest 100 albums of all time, had Van Morrison's *Astral Weeks* topping the list in September 2000, with *Abbey Road* at #3, *Revolver* at #5, and *Sgt Pepper*, *The Beatles*, and *Rubber Soul* listed at #8, 14, and 74 respectively.

Revolver has generally received enthusiastic kudos in specialized evaluations and rankings of 'psychedelic music', but, even in those discussions, the album's fate has been mixed. *MOJO*'s list of the greatest psychedelic songs of all time also enshrined 'Tomorrow Never Knows' atop the list of British psychedelia (Savage, 1997, p. 61). *I Want to Take You Higher*, the companion book to the special exhibit on the psychedelic era at The Rock and Roll Hall of Fame and Museum, barely mentions *Revolver* and, in one of the two brief remarks about the album, inexplicably refers to it as 'protopsychedelic', while also hailing it as the Beatles' 'most daring album yet' (Henke and Puterbaugh, 1997, pp. 40, 80). The authors of *Rhino's Psychedelic Trip* are so eager to move on to *Sgt Pepper* that they barely even mention *Revolver*, referring to it as 'transitional' and grudgingly admitting that it, along with *Rubber Soul*, 'represented an artful step forward', and the remainder of their Beatles commentary suffers accordingly (Bisbort and Puterbaugh, 2000, p. 79). Finally, the wildly flawed and almost pointlessly theorized list in *20th Century Rock and Roll: Psychedelia* ranks 'Tomorrow Never Knows' as the Number 1 psychedelic song one should put on a tape of the '200 Greatest Psychedelic Songs' and perches the Beatles atop its list of the '50 Most Influential Artists', but then relegates *Revolver* to number 32 on its list of 'The 100 Best Psychedelic Albums', behind such obviously legitimate offerings as *Sgt Pepper's Lonely Hearts Club Band*, *Magical Mystery Tour*, Pink Floyd's *The Piper at the Gates of Dawn*, and Jimi Hendrix's *Are You Experienced?* and such genuinely interesting albums as the Thirteenth Floor Elevators' *Psychedelic Sounds of the 13th Floor Elevators* and The Music Machine's *(Turn On) The Music Machine*, but also far behind such absurdities as Iron Butterfly's *In-A-Gadda-Da-Vida* and Strawberry Alarm Clock's *Incense & Peppermints* (Belmo, pp. 135, 21, 133).

What is this thing called *Revolver*? It originally existed in two different forms, the British release and the American bowdlerized version, three forms if we count segments of the American *Yesterday … and Today*. Is it mono or stereo? Is it the LP or the CD? Does it include 'Rain' and 'Paperback Writer', the two other noteworthy songs recorded during the so-called '*Revolver* sessions'? Does, or should it, include the alternative takes recently made available on the Beatles *Anthology 2* releases? There is now a *Revolver* magazine, claiming to be 'the world's loudest rock magazine' (www.revolvermag.com), a Revolver film company, and Revolver Records (www.revolvermusic.com). Cover and tribute bands abound, including

The Revolvers, a British Beatles tribute band, a Chicago-based Beatles tribute band – Revolver (www.revolver909.com) – and a band called Revolver, whose web slogan reads 'Become part of the band before the band becomes part of you'. Antelope Valley, California's 'hottest country cover band', also call themselves Revolver, but I have a sneaking suspicion they tend more toward the six-shooter variety of the term. There are also Beatles cover bands named Revolver in Japan (moz.co.jp/revolver/mokuji) and Italy (revolveronline.it), and a Brazilian site (www.revolver.com.br) that features a Portugese language-based tribute, including a link to a radio station that plays *Revolver* twenty-four hours a day! Another Japanese site features 'Revolver: A Golden 60/70s Music Bar'. One can buy Revolver lunch boxes at 'lunchboxshop.com' ('Your One Stop Lunchbox Shop'!), *Revolver* t-shirts at numerous sites, and even 'Beatles *Revolver* novelty neck ties' graced with the original album cover art in either the original black and white or in Ralph Marlin's colorized version. Canasailcraft.com, a web-site purveying various recreational sailing craft, sells the 'F-One TT Revolver 142 Kiteboard', but since it includes 'no flotation', it probably wouldn't be appropriate for floating up- or downstream. Like few other rock and roll recordings, *Revolver* has assumed the status of cultural icon, approaching in its many avatars, its impact and its endurance the status of some of the definitive works of Anglo-American culture such as Herman Melville's *Moby-Dick* and James Joyce's *Ulysses*.

Needless to say, numerous other *Revolver* sites exist, many of them functioning as tribute pages (see, for example, 'www.clixto/Revolver'). One even offers 'the Zen interpretation' of the album (http://pages.cthome.net/tobelman/page08), along with Buddhist-based readings of several of Brian Wilson's accomplishments. Here follows a brief list of the best and most informative web-sites devoted to *Revolver*:

1. 'Graham Calkin's Beatles Pages' (jpgr.co.uk/pcs7009) includes excellent recording information, pictures, charts outlining the differences between the mono and stereo versions as well as among different pressings, and the amazing cover from a Russian release of *Revolver*, featuring a different cover collage.
2. 'Erek's Beatles Page' (whose banner reads: 'where nothing is real'), (embers.nbci.com/revolver_66/revolver_sessions.htm), features information on the *Revolver* recording sessions and plenty of good graphics.
3. John T. Marck's site, 'www.iamthebeatles.com/article1008', entitled 'Oh Look Out! Part 7. *Revolver*', includes Marck's insights on each song, a complete list of lyrics, and excerpts from important statements on the album.
4. For information on a *Revolver* boxed set (including the contents of this multi-disc collection), consult 'superfly.home.texas.net/revolver/'.

We can only guess at what the now-defunct Slovenian on-line magazine '*Revolver*: an online magazine for homoerotic cultural and political issues' was all about!

Perhaps more than any of these other phenomena, Ann Dyer's brilliantly conceived and performed 'cover' version, *Revolver: A New Spin* (Premonition Records – a subsidiary of Mr. Brown Records – 2000), celebrates *Revolver*'s genius as much as it projects and complicates its status. Dyer rearranges, both musically and sequentially, most of the original cuts from *Revolver* and reimagines them within a jazz context, a testament to *Revolver*'s flexible and resilient core. As '*Every Sound There Is*' contributor Jacqueline Warwick wrote to me, 'It's interesting that a musician invested in perpetuating free jazz would be attracted to *Revolver*; both free jazz and *Revolver* can be understood as efforts to break up and shake up mainstream styles in the sixties.' Stunningly original and ambitious, Dyer's recording achieves much of the Beatles' original diversity, and coherence, while quite clearly reinterpreting many of the album's cuts. Dyer doesn't include 'Love You To', 'Yellow Submarine', 'Got to Get You Into My Life' or 'Doctor Robert', but she does add her shimmering interpretation of 'Rain' to the mix, all with the variety, exuberance and glowing musical complexity of the Beatles' release. Again, as Warwick commented on Dyer's inclusion of 'Rain': 'Well first of all it's a damn good song! More to the point, it fits in very well with the overall mood of mystery, exoticism, spookiness and philosophising [of *Revolver*] not to mention the fact that its vocal melody refers a bit to classical North Indian styles, especially on the word "rain" in the chorus.' Moreover, Dyer's treatments of other songs smuggle significant moments from these missing numbers, resulting in their absence seeming less significant. Her version of 'Good Day Sunshine', for example, sounds to have been recorded on a beach, and the sounds of waves and beach frolicking that form the background to her spirited remake echo the ambient oceanic soundscape from 'Yellow Submarine'. Similarly, Dyer's loosely Asiatic-sounding version of several numbers (most especially the exotic rendition of 'Taxman' and the sitar-heavy 'Tomorrow Never Knows') imports those first realizations of George Harrison's other-worldliness into the album without actually including 'Love You To'. Moreover, throughout *Revolver: A New Spin* Dyer and her backing band, 'No Goodtime Fairies', sing and play like they've sampled Doctor Robert's special cup on more than one occasion.

Dyer's CD begins with her version of 'She Said She Said', and the first sung words from that cut: 'She said' make it amply clear that this is a woman's response to and retelling of *Revolver* and its narratives. What does it mean for a woman artist to remake *Revolver*? What does it mean for 'She Said She Said' to be the album's first cut, for 'Tomorrow Never Knows' to occupy a position near its middle, and for 'And Your Bird Can Sing' to conclude her interpretation? Her 'Eleanor Rigby' pulses with an unnerving synergy of elegiac somberness and plaintively seductive moaning. (Readers interested in these questions will certainly find great pleasure and provocation in Jacqueline Warwick's chapter in this collection.) Moreover, with its astonishing range of musical styles and sounds, Dyer's version captures and contemporarizes the original heterogeneity of the Beatles' original, virtually giving voice to the VH1 commentary that the entire history of pop music could be reconstructed from *Revolver* alone. Fusing dreamy soundscapes, acid-zydeco, Sheila Chandra-esque subcontinental vocalese, and hard rocking, Dyer and her No Goodtime Fairies venture boldly into a sonic arena where few have gone before. Indeed, as I argue in my own contribution to '*Every Sound There Is*', such diversity and integration constitute two of the essential hallmarks of psychedelic song-writing and album composition.

However one defines and wherever one ranks *Revolver*, no one can deny that *Revolver*'s impact was, by any standard of measurement, massive and transformative. The contributors to '*Every Sound There Is*' believe that *Revolver* invented musical expressions and initiated trends and motifs that would chart the path not only of the Beatles and a cultural epoch, but of the subsequent history of rock and roll as well. *Revolver* is, in many ways, an album of 'firsts' and 'onlies' in the Beatles' canon. Let us just consider some of the innovations encoded within those fourteen songs and their collective impact as an album. *Revolver* represents the first song on which no Beatles play instruments ('Eleanor Rigby'), the first Beatles song adapted from a literary source (in penning 'Tomorrow Never Knows', John borrowed heavily from Timothy Leary's *Psychedelic Experience*), the first album opened with a George Harrison composition (and perhaps the only George Harrison song on which Paul McCartney plays the guitar solo!), and first songs influenced by LSD ('Tomorrow Never Knows', 'She Said She Said', and 'Got To Get You Into My Life'). As Tim Riley points out, 'Love You To' is 'the first Beatles track where traditional Western instruments aren't even alluded to' (Riley, 1988, p. 186). In terms of recording studio techniques, *Revolver* includes the first recorded use of reverse tape effects (thanks to Jim LeBlanc and Steve Valdez for reminding me that 'Rain,' while released earlier than *Revolver*, was recorded on 16 April, 1966, ten days after recording began on 'Tomorrow Never Knows'), the first examples both of ambient background sounds (cocktail party and ship sounds in 'Yellow Submarine', and the seagull sounds in 'Tomorrow Never Knows' that get echoed near the conclusion of Pink Floyd's 'Set the Controls for the Heart of the Sun'), and the first heavily altered vocal effects ('Eleanor Rigby', 'I'm Only Sleeping', 'And Your Bird Can Sing' and 'Tomorrow Never Knows'). In one of our email discussions during the preparation of this book, Walter Everett noted that one could argue that vocal tracks had always been subject to electronic EQ/compression, revert, balancing, and other mixing board magic, but then noted that such modifications pale in comparison to what is attempted and how it is achieved on *Revolver*. Klaus Voormann's cover art even represents the Beatles' first use of animated and drawn, rather than photographic, art. George's strangely exotic and studio-produced count-in of 'One, Two, Three, Four' takes us up to another kind of level from that peppiest and most famous of Beatles introductory countdowns to 'I Saw Her Standing There' in much the same way that 'A Day In The Life' psychedelicizes their first statement of desire from 'I Want To Hold Your Hand' with 'I'd love to turn you on.' With the exception of Phish's live version of *The Beatles* and the bootleg copies of those performances floating around, *Revolver* is also the first and only Beatles album to be released in a cover version (nearly in its entirety), by Ann Dyer. In my own contribution to this volume, I go so far as to propose that *Revolver* is the first album to initiate and maintain an intra-album dialogue; an album's songs speak meaningfully to each other for the first time in rock and roll history. Whether we define these and other innovations as 'evolutions' or 'revolutions', *Revolver* signaled massive rupture from the moment it began revolving on any turntable. In short, *Revolver* is rock and roll's first 'album'.

Many commentators have noted the range of human concerns encoded within *Revolver*'s lyrics. The chapters collected in '*Every Sound There Is':* The Beatles' Revolver *and the Transformation of Rock and Roll* assess the Beatles' accomplishment on their 1966 masterpiece from a variety of perspectives, angles of vision crucial to the album's contemporary creation and reception as well as to those for listeners in the twenty-first century. While our fourteen chapters duplicate the number of cuts on *Revolver*, no correlation links individual chapters to specific songs, except for Cy Schleifer's engaging discussion of Paul McCartney's bass work on 'For No One'. I have organized our contributions according to the most obvious drifts of their discussions. We begin with ' "When I'm in the middle of a dream": the contributors Remember *Revolver*', an introduction to each of the contributors, in which each provides both the usual professional information and one of their most memorable associations with *Revolver*.' The first group of chapters, ' "Where do they all come from?": *Revolver*'s influences', collects various perspectives on the question of 'influence', both influences on *Revolver* as well as *Revolver*'s influence on subsequent music. The second collection, ' "It is shining": *Revolver*'s musicality', offers more technical discussions of various elements of *Revolver*'s musicality, i.e., its chords, harmonies, and tonal relationships. While some of the terminology in these essays might be daunting for many readers, each chapter's main idea is developed in very accessible language, with useful examples and references to specific passages in *Revolver*'s songs. Part III, ' "And our friends were all aboard": *Revolver*'s players', contains five chapters, focusing separately on how each of the Beatles and George Martin (along with his production team) contributed to the album. ' "Here, there, and everywhere": *Revolver*'s themes', our last grouping, features chapters which offer thematic interpretations of *Revolver* in its entirety. Finally, a bibliography lists early reviews and the subsequent critical and scholarly reception of *Revolver*. So, taken all together, *Every Sound There Is* devotes extensive attention to the cultural and musical contexts, to the musical texts themselves, to the performers and to the large themes of *Revolver*. While this may not exactly constitute 'every perspective there is' on the album, we hope that the sum total adds to our appreciation and understanding of this remarkable record.

A bit more on the organizational scheme of *Every Sound There Is*. I would like to stress that, while I have organized these chapters according to the reasonably rational scheme outlined above, the divisions I have chosen are in no way fixed or impermeable. As I have just discussed, *'Every Sound There Is'* includes sections on influences (on and by *Revolver*), musicological analyses of different facets of the album, the performers, and, finally, on thematic overviews. While the individual chapters are arranged in groupings under section titles, most of these discussions could have been placed in several different categories. For example, I placed Kari McDonald and Sarah Hudson Kaufman's chapter on the contributions of George Martin and his entire production team in the section devoted to the performers, largely because of all the talk about the so-called 'Fifth Beatle', but also because, as McDonald and Kaufman reveal, Martin and his mates turned the recording studio into a musical instrument in ways that no one had endeavored or succeeded at before. I could just as easily have positioned their chapter in the section on technical analyses of the music. So, in order to suggest the section-breaking scope of their chapter, I place it first in the section on performers, immediately after the musicological discussions. Similarly, Jim LeBlanc focuses on the impact of John Lennon's songs having been deleted from the initial American version. I have included his chapter, 'Premature turns: thematic disruption in the American version of *Revolver*', in the section containing chapters on each Beatle's contribution to the album. But, since his chapter is equally an overview of *Revolver* with much to say about its production, marketing, and coherence as a work of art, I placed LeBlanc's contribution as the last chapter in that section, positioning it on the cusp with the thematic chapters. In fact, much of the enjoyment of being involved in a project such as this is the challenge of arranging the various contributions in hopes of maximizing their originality, scholarship, coherence and impact.

While almost all of the chapters collected in this volume approach and analyze *Revolver* from thematic, non-technical perspectives, a few draw heavily on the specialized jargon of musicological analysis. *Every Sound There Is* should be accessible to the general reader, the Beatles fan without specialized musical knowledge, and to lovers of rock and roll everywhere. We have tried, when possible, to include brief explanations and helpful examples of some of the more specialized musical terms and concepts addressed in these chapters. What is most important to remember, of course, is that, when we swoon to the vocal, instrumental and technological synergy creating the magic of the line 'You tell me that you've heard every sound there is' from 'And Your Bird Can Sing', we are responding in multiple and subtle ways to some of the most complex, coherent, and beautiful products of the human imagination wedded with sophisticated studio technologies. And that's what, in the final analysis, music appreciation is all about. We, the authors of *'Every Sound There Is': The Beatles' Revolver and the Transformation of Rock and Roll*, offer these fourteen chapters in the hopes that they will help all our readers appreciate and understand this landmark recording in new and important ways.

The inspiration for '*Every Sound There Is*': *The Beatles'* Revolver *and the Transformation of Rock and Roll* began at the Beatles 2000 Interdisciplinary Conference held in Jyväskylä, Finland in June 2000. For this opportunity, the contributors collected here wish to recognize and thank Yrjö Heinonen, Terhi Nurmesjärvi, Jouni Koskimäki, and Seppo Niemi, all of the University of Jyväskylä, Finland, and collectively known for their project, Beatles 2000. This Finnish Fab Four not only organized and hosted the highly successful conference out of which this book grew, but they have, themselves, contributed immensely to our knowledge of many facets of the Beatles' career. We would also like to acknowledge the important role IASPM (the International Association for the Study of Popular Music) has had in advancing the cause of popular music studies in universities around the world.

I would personally like to thank all the contributors to '*Every Sound There Is*' for their excellent chapters as well as for the many times they came to my assistance while I was putting this volume together and writing this introduction. On behalf of all of us, I would also like to dedicate this book to the Beatles and to George Martin and his production team, with a special dedication to the memories of John Lennon and George Harrison. Their work during those days in 1966 altered the course of popular music, enriching and elevating the lives of millions of people all over the world. This might not exactly be what Donovan meant when he sang 'happiness runs in a circular motion', but I think we can all agree that happiness is, indeed, a spinning *Revolver*.

Notes

1. Readers of the present volume will find Jim LeBlanc's essay particularly illuminating on this latter point.
2. George's 'beef', of course, was certainly not with the United States IRS! While the catalogue of individual contributions doesn't begin to assess the scope or the brilliance of *Revolver*, the VH1 remarks do hint at the range and the scope of *Revolver*'s integrative themes and music. In a bizarre twist, however, one of the largest preparation companies in the United States aired commercials in early 2002 using 'Taxman' as their theme song. So many the VH1 commentary was merely prophetic in its sensititvity to the appeal of George's song.
3. On the other hand, *Revolver* cuts also figure hugely in some witheringly snotty ranking provided by one Luke Haines in his '10 Most Hated Tracks'. 'Tomorrow Never Knows' tops his list, with 'all of George's' coming in second place, 'Doctor Robert' and 'And Your Bird Can Sing' in sixth and seventh places respectively, and 'Rain' coming in at Number 9, just above 'Hey Jude'.

'When I'm in the middle of a dream': the contributors remember *Revolver*

Matthew Bannister, University of Auckland, New Zealand

'When I was a boy', I went through phases of liking different Beatles records. At first I liked *Sgt Pepper*, because it sounds like a record for children – it's got all those weird effects and barnyard noises. As I got a bit older I preferred the early Beatles because it was so joyous and innocent. *Revolver* for me then was the one where they started to get weird. I guess I intuitively sensed this was 'adult' music, and felt excluded. Now I'm an adult (at least I think I am) and I love it all. 'Long live the Beatles.'

I am currently completing a PhD on white masculinities and indie guitar rock at the University of Auckland, New Zealand. I've loved the Beatles since I was five, and all the music I've made has been inspired by them. I've played in many bands – Sneaky Feelings, Dribbling Darts of Love and the Weather, in ascending order of obscurity. My book, *Positively George Street*, recounts my experiences in the Flying Nun/Dunedin scene. Together with my wife, Alice, who plays violin, and two sons, whose 'instruments' are recorders and cricket bats, I live in Auckland, New Zealand.

Steven Baur, UCLA, USA

One of the earliest experiences that remains accessible to my memory took place when I was about five years old. An alluring cartoon came on the television, revolving around four male characters, each bedecked in polychromatic clothing, sporting fanciful facial hair, and speaking in a captivating exotic dialect. Reeled in by the sights and sounds unfolding before me, I followed the four protagonists on a fantastical voyage through variegated land- and seascapes and witnessed their encounters with multifarious creatures and monsters of all colors, sizes, and physiognomies, all undertaken in the name of love and music. Indeed the accompanying music made the deepest impression upon my budding consciousness, particularly the animated film's title track, 'Yellow Submarine', which became my first favorite song and remained so well into my grammar school years. At age nine, it became the first song not chosen for me by someone else that I would ever perform, as I accompanied my older brother and his freshly learned guitar chords on an overturned bucket, replicating the distinctive bass drum figures that follow each verse phrase.

I eventually parlayed that bucket into a career in music as a drummer and musicologist. I am currently Visiting Assistant Professor in Musicology at the University of California, Los Angeles, where I have taught courses on topics ranging from nineteenth-century orchestral music to the music of the Beatles. My research focuses on music and the politics of culture in late-nineteenth-century America, and I have also published articles on the music of Maurice Ravel, Felix Mendelssohn, and Alice Cooper.

Walter Everett, University of Michigan, USA

I've been a Beatles fanatic since February, 1964, and since then have striven to hear more and more in their music – hard to believe it's become a paying gig! *Revolver* was not a very important album for me until the spring of 1972, when I undertook the dubbing of all 223 Beatles songs known to me on my new reel-to-reel deck, in the track sequence originally released in Europe. Then with the reinsertion of Lennon's three great songs that had been stolen for an earlier American release the magic came through, and *Revolver*'s been one of my two favorite Beatles LPs, often *the* favorite, ever since.

I am now Associate Professor of Music at the University of Michigan, where I teach music theory. I have written *The Beatles as Musicians*, a two-volume book that covers all of the group's musical activity from their earliest group efforts in 1957 to the group's demise in 1970 in more than 800 pages of text based on all known sources including hundreds of rehearsals and other outtakes. Some of my other projects include editing or co-editing three other books of essays on rock-music topics, and publishing scholarly essays on music by the Grateful Dead, Paul Simon, and Billy Joel, as well as Mozart, Schubert, and the Beatles. I have presented scholarly papers at conferences and university-sponsored gatherings throughout North America and Europe.

Sarah Hudson Kaufman, University of British Columbia, Canada

My friends and I began listening to the Beatles when we were fourteen years old on hand-me-down recorded tapes. As soon as the compact disc became affordable, we began to convert our collections. I specifically enjoyed the artwork on the *Revolver* album and bought it for my co-author for her fifteenth birthday. Thus my first Beatles purchase!

Currently, I practice as an obstetrical nurse in Vancouver, Canada, having received a Bachelor of Applied Science in Nursing from the University of British Columbia. Growing up, I studied classical piano, musical theatre, and enjoyed listening to Beatles music. While I still enjoy the latter, I have expanded to researching their history and studio practices.

Jim LeBlanc, Cornell University, USA

From my first listening of *Revolver* in August, 1966, I recall only my reaction to 'Tomorrow Never Knows' – a mixture of 'Cool!' and 'What the hell is this?!' A few years later, I found out.

I hold a PhD in French Literature from Cornell University in Ithaca, New York, and am currently a catalogue librarian at the Cornell University Library. I have written on Louis-Ferdinand Céline, James Joyce, and Alberto Moravia, as well as on cataloguing.

Kari McDonald, University of British Columbia, Canada

Revolver was my first Beatles album, given by a friend fascinated with the psyche-delic cover (my esteemed co-author). As a second-generation Beatles fan, introduced to the band with a disorderly mixture of badly recorded singles, *Revolver* was my first exposure to a coherently organized concept album. It was love at first listen!

My passion for all types of music continued. While living in British Columbia, Canada, I received my Associate of the Royal Conservatory of Toronto (ARCT) Diploma in Piano Performance; a Bachelor of Music in Music History and Literature from the University of Victoria; and a Masters in Music Theory from the University of British Columbia. I currently teach music theory, history, and piano in Vancouver, and plan on pursuing studies in Popular Music. A special 'Thank You' is necessary to Rommel Montes, who first noticed the striking simi-larity between the Beatles and the Chemical Brothers discussed in our chapter.

Shaugn O'Donnell, Tulane University, USA

As a second-generation Beatles fan, I'm sure I heard *Revolver* as early as its release in '66 when I was two years old, but I discovered it for myself a decade later. I remember spending that summer in rural Pennsylvania where I would ven-ture off alone into the deep woods to 'listen to the colour of my dreams'.

I am currently an Assistant Professor at Tulane University in New Orleans where I teach music theory and electronic music. I have written on topics ranging from chromaticism in eighteenth-century symphonies to the space metaphor in the music of the Grateful Dead. A guitarist before joining the academic commu-nity, I still try to keep my Stratocaster warm.

Russell Reising, University of Toledo, USA

I first heard *Revolver* when I was thirteen, probably in mid-August of 1966, depending on when my local store got it in. 'Taxman' and 'Love You To' simply stunned me, swooping me up into some new kind of world that, for better or worse, I've inhabited ever since. I recall sitting, cross-legged on the floor, playing the George Harrison tracks (the American *Revolver*, of course, was short of a few Lennon cuts!) over and over. My son, James, had a similar reaction when he first heard 'Eleanor Rigby'. He was walking through the room as I was doing 'research' for this volume and, at the first notes of the cut, absolutely stopped in his tracks, sat down, and listened in rapt attention. When the song finished, he just muttered 'Wow, what was *that*!' 'Eleanor Rigby' still never fails to arrest his attention.

As a literature professor, I have spent much of my professional career teaching and writing about American literature and culture. Many of my articles and books have examined American literary culture from a political perspective, with a special focus on the ways in which political pressures during and since the Cold War have impacted the academic study of American literature. Over the past several years I have shifted gears somewhat and returned to some of my roots, devoting most of my research time to Japanese literature, popular music and Anglo-American psychedelic culture.

Ronald Schleifer, University of Oklahoma, USA

I first encountered *Revolver* as an album in my freshman year of college in 1967. Of course, I had heard many of the songs on the radio, but down the hall in my dorm Michael Murphy would play the album over and over again, his door standing open so that the music became part of the life on our dormitory floor when we studied, talked about other things, and even just listened to its songs. 'Eleanor Rigby' haunted those days: the sounds on our floor is one of the things – among those other things of the new world of college – I most remember about college and being away from home. At home we rarely listened to records: it was only playing pool at my friend Ricky's house that music became part of our games. But at college I found music, along with reading, movies, and talking late into the night became part of the rhythms of life. It was that year, I think, that I decided to study English, which allowed me to work at all the different things I cared for: literature, psychology, history, music, linguistics – that other music! – even science. It's as if the remarkable transformation of pop music accomplished in good part by *Revolver* patterned (or at least repeated) the transformation of life for those of us growing up in the 1960s.

Now, I am George Lynn Cross Professor of English and Adjunct Professor of Medicine at the University of Oklahoma. In the last few years, I have been working on the relationship between postmodernism and what I have been calling (even in my Beatles essay) 'post-Enlightenment' cultural formations in the arts and sciences. Besides this essay, and one on Cole Porter that came out a few years ago, I examine early-twentieth-century music in relation to literature, history, and science in a recent book entitled *Modernism and Time: The Logic of Abundance in Literature, Science, and Culture 1880–1930* and what might be called the musical power of language in a recent essay entitled 'The Poetics of Tourette Syndrome: Language, Neurobiology, and Poetry'.

Cyrus Schleifer, University of Iowa, USA

I bumped into *Revolver* rather by chance when I was thirteen or fourteen. When I was hanging out with one of my buddies, he asked if he could borrow my Bob Marley tape. Of course, I said 'sure', but knowing this friend I knew it was in my best interest to procure something of his if I ever wanted my tape back. So we went over to his house and I was leafing through his collection of albums and I came across *Revolver*. I asked him if I could borrow that one as well as the *White Album*. Needless to say, I never saw my tape again but in the same vein I managed to begin my Beatles collection at a young age with two slightly used CDs. Now that I've listened again and again to the Beatles I realize how lucky I was to begin my collection with *Revolver*.

As for now, I am attending the University of Iowa studying music and oboe performance with Professor Mark Weiger. One of my favorite recent experiences was hearing 'Blackbird' scored for oboe and small string orchestra.

Ger Tillekens, Netherlands

On my first encounter with *Revolver*, I must have been approaching the age of seventeen. In those days my friends and I used to listen to our new pop records, gathering around the turntable in our favourite place. We used to stand there, leaning against the wall and commenting on the music. Hearing this new Beatles album, however, we all just shut up and sat down to listen to the songs, realizing to our surprise that this was rock music to sit down and really listen to. I just did that and I never gave it a further thought.

I went on studying sociology and some years later I took on working as a sociologist of education and youth at the University of Groningen, the Netherlands. Only over thirty years after *Revolver*'s release, when I decided to write a socio-musicological study on the early Beatles songs, I got some idea how this urge to sit down and to contemplate the songs was effectuated by the music itself.

Stephen Valdez, University of Georgia, USA

My first exposure to *Revolver* was as a pre-teenager back in the late 1960s when I listened to the Beatles' albums and tried to learn the melodies and chord progressions on my guitar. One of the first songs I learned, because of the simplicity of the chord shapes and the infrequency of changes, was 'Eleanor Rigby'. It was during this time that I realized that I loved teaching others about music and set my goal to major in music at the university. Little realizing that I would have to fight my way through Bach, Beethoven, Brahms, and Bartok – the other Bs of music history – before I could focus my studies on the Beatles, I became familiar with western art music styles. Had it not been for my informal lessons with John, Paul, George, and Ringo, I would quite possibly never have gotten through music theory and ear training as an undergraduate and be able to appreciate the great treasures of music that the world has to offer.

A native New Mexican, I received a Bachelor in Music Education (1977) and a Master of Music in Music History (1984) from New Mexico State University. I earned my Doctor of Musical Arts degree in Music History (1992) from the University of Oregon, submitting as my dissertation *The Development of the Electric Guitar Solo in Rock Music, 1954–1971*. Currently Assistant Professor of Music History at the University of Georgia, I teach a variety of music history courses, including the music of the baroque period, a graduate seminar on the music of the Beatles, and the history of rock. I recently published a second, revised edition of my textbook *A History of Rock Music* (2001) with Kendall-Hunt Publishers. My national and international conference presentations include papers on the music of the Beatles and the Doors, and the guitar techniques of Keith Richards and Robert Johnson.

Naphtali Wagner, Hebrew University, Israel

I was born in Jerusalem in 1949. I grew up during the 1960s on a classical menu of music that relied mainly on the four Bs: Bach, Beethoven, Brahms, and Beatles. When *Revolver* was being sold around the world, I was seventeen years old. Because I couldn't afford the album, I bought it together with a friend, and every week we would switch off (until in the end it remained with me). At first I was drawn mainly to the 'strange' songs in the album, such as 'Taxman' and 'She Said She Said', but I soon learned to appreciate the more lyrical songs, too, such as 'Here, There and Everywhere' and 'For No One'.

During my years of research and teaching at the Hebrew University of Jerusalem, I dealt mainly with theory and analysis of western tonal music of the eighteenth and nineteenth centuries. Only when I discovered that the twentieth century was nearing its end without my having set foot in it as a researcher did I decide to include the love of my youth among my academic pursuits, and I wrote an analytical book about the Beatles (Wagner, 1999).

Jacqueline Warwick, UCLA, USA

I got to know the Beatles through my older sisters, who had all the records and bought me my own *Magical Mystery Tour* for my eighth birthday. When they left home, I would sit in their bedroom and listen to their records so I could still feel connected to them – this was undoubtedly as important a part of my musical education as any of my piano lessons or choir rehearsals. *Revolver* was an album that seemed to grow up with me; 'Yellow Submarine' was my childhood favourite, and ten years later 'Tomorrow Never Knows' was the track I listened to constantly.

I am now a doctoral candidate in musicology at UCLA, where I was the founding editor of *ECHO: a music-centered journal* (www.humnet.ucla.edu/echo). My dissertation is about the 1960s girl groups, and I also work on French art song from the fin de siècle and South Asian music in the diaspora.

Sheila Whiteley, University of Salford, UK

I first heard *Revolver* in September 1966. Having recently 'dropped out' of the swinging London scene, I was living in a seventeenth-century farmhouse in Thorington, Suffolk, making music and paying a 'pepper corn' rent of 6p a year. The experience was mesmeric. Suffolk is known for its skies – the enormous, cotton wool variety known as cumulus – and 'Tomorrow Never Knows' said it all. Small wonder, my daughter Bryony was born in June of the following year, the so-called 'Summer of Love'.

I was made Chair of Popular Music in July, 2000 and am Associate Dean (Academic Enterprise) in the Faculty of Arts, Media, and Social Sciences at the University of Salford, Greater Manchester, England. My principal research interests lie in the relationship between popular music and issues of identity, subjectivity, and gender, and in popular music and hallucinogenic drugs. My books include *The Space Between the Notes* (Routledge, 1992), *Women and Popular Music* (Routledge, 2000), and, as editor, *Sexing the Groove* (Routledge, 1998).

My chapter 'Love is all and love is everyone' is dedicated to my grandson, Daniel.

Part I
'Where do they all come from'?

Revolver's influences

Chapter 1

Detroit and Memphis: the soul of *Revolver*

Walter Everett

As magnificent as the Beatles' career was – as high as were the peaks they climbed – many great plans and dreams went unrealized throughout their years together. In January 1969, the group considered various possibilities for a large open-air concert, all scuttled with the last-minute compromise of a rooftop performance above their Apple headquarters. Early in 1968, the group announced philanthropic goals intending to support any and all fledgling artists who were to ask for their help; all applications went unanswered. In early 1967, a budget was drawn up to shoot a separate film for each song on the upcoming *Sgt Pepper's* album; only one, accompanying 'A Day in the Life,' was completed. Continuing back yet one more year to the early days of 1966, we find plans that could have taken the Beatles' musical career in a surprising direction that was never followed. Reliable reports have the Beatles initiating discussions from December 1965 through March 1966 aimed at recording some or all of their follow-up LP to *Rubber Soul* at either Detroit's Motown studio, Memphis's Stax studio, or New York's Atlantic studio, and at having new compositions supplied by resident composers of those enterprises, altogether famed as the preeminent producers of black-based soul music in the mid-1960s. During this four-month period, a number of American and British periodicals ran versions of the following press release entitled 'The "Detroit Sound" Achieves New World Wide Fame,' written and circulated by Motown's press agent, Al Abrams, on 15 December 1965:

> The top songwriting team of Holland-Dozier-Holland, which has written and produced the Six Million Selling Records for THE SUPREMES, recently received a transatlantic phone call from George Martin, the recording director for the Beatles. Martin, who operates out of the London Offices of EMI Records (parent company of America's Capitol Records), asked Holland-Dozier-Holland if they would, upon personal request of the Beatles, write the next two songs for the Beatles' recording session if Holland-Dozier-Holland 'could find the time.' The songwriting trio eagerly responded to the Beatles' request.[1]

Singer-lyricist Eddie Holland, lyricist-composer Lamont Dozier, and composer-engineer Brian Holland, aided by vocal arranger Maurice King and Motown's house band, the Funk Brothers, wrote and produced the twenty-five biggest hits for the Supremes and the Four Tops (twelve of which reached #1 on *Billboard*'s

Hot 100) in 1964–1967. The Beatles would have recorded the new H-D-H songs at Motown's studio at 2648 West Grand Boulevard, Detroit (now a thriving museum), presumably under the direction of the composer-producers and perhaps with George Martin's collaboration.

For whatever undocumented reason, this plan fell through. The Beatles' manager, Brian Epstein, then began talks with Stax and its parent company, Atlantic Records, towards similar arrangements for American recordings of the next LP and single. Musicologist Rob Bowman has written the following regarding this venture:

> When Brian Epstein came to [Memphis] in March 1966 to inquire about the possibility of the Beatles recording their next album at Stax, it was nearly too much to bear. ... According to Estelle [Axton, co-founder of Stax Records], Epstein initially contacted Atlantic, which then notified Stax . ... Before all hell broke out, Estelle had told several of the Stax songwriters that they needed to get material together as the Beatles were intending to cover some contemporary rhythm and blues. ... Johnny Keyes and Ronnie Gordon wrote 'Out of Control,' which eventually was recorded by L. H. and the Memphis Souls. [Guitarist-Producer Steve] Cropper was hopeful that the Beatles would want to use him as an engineer and that perhaps some of the Stax session musicians would be asked to contribute a lick or two. ... According to Steve, from what he was told, Epstein concluded that there was not enough security in Memphis and consequently decided the Beatles should record at Atlantic in New York. Cropper still hoped to be involved. 'By the time Epstein got back,' recalls Steve, 'he called me and said, "Well, I guess we're gonna have to do it on the next project because they've already got almost all the album recorded." '[2]

Stax Studios, on McLemore Avenue in Memphis, produced a more authentic rhythm-and-blues groove on sister labels Stax and Volt than did the pop-styled Motown group; the Beatles particularly admired Stax artists Wilson Pickett and Otis Redding and their backing group the MGs, featuring horns above rhythm players Steve Cropper, bassist Donald 'Duck' Dunn, and drummer Al Jackson.

Recording the early-1966 LP and single in Detroit or Memphis would have made sense for many reasons: (1) the Beatles' previous album, *Rubber Soul*, highlighted an interest in the soul music produced by Motown and Atlantic/Stax, the most popular black-produced music in the US, and owed its title to that genre; (2) the sonic qualities of Motown's recordings, particularly showing off James Jamerson's bass lines that were direct-injected into the mixing board for added clarity, outdid what could be done with EMI's equipment, which lagged by several years the technical lead held by studios from Los Angeles to New York; Motown used eight-track machines by 1965, three years before the Beatles had a taste of this; (3) George Martin had gained his release from EMI's A&R team in August 1965, opting instead to work as an independent producer who would be free to record the Beatles anywhere they wished; (4) the choice of studio and production team had everything to do with the atmosphere, available musicians, and arrangement techniques for a given set of recordings (as proven by the Rolling Stones' June 1964 and May 1965 sessions in Chicago's Chess studios, and their other work over the course of three periods in 1965–1966 at RCA in Hollywood); and (5) by the end of 1965, the Holland-Dozier-Holland team were the hottest composer-producers in the entire business; Motown led all record labels for total American single record sales in 1965 according to *Billboard* – ahead of Capitol, which sold Beatles product.

The *Cashbox* Top Ten of 1965 included the Supremes' 'Back in My Arms Again' [the #1 record of the year], the Four Tops' 'I Can't Help Myself' [#4], and the Supremes' 'Come See About Me' [#8], all Holland-Dozier-Holland creations; there was not a single Beatles record on the list.[3] So the Beatles would have followed one album that had been largely dedicated to the sounds of contemporaneous American soul music, *Rubber Soul*, with another that was as authentic a part of that scene as it would have been possible for them to produce. Although the Motown- and Stax/Atlantic-Beatles deals went unrealized, *Revolver* shows a strong continuing dependence on American R&B. In this chapter, I will summarize the history through 1965 of the Beatles' interest in American black artistry and will then probe the importance of that literature for the composition and recording of songs for *Revolver*.[4]

Atlantic Records emerged from the 1950s as the top label for black rock 'n' roll, having pushed ahead of older 'race' labels such as Columbia's subsidiary Okeh, Chess/Checker and Vee-Jay in Chicago, King in Cincinnati, and other indie labels in Philadelphia, New Orleans, Los Angeles, and New York. The Atlantic/Atco family grew to distribute the Dimension, Stax, Volt, Allwood, Dial, and Fame labels by early 1966, most significantly giving the New York base satellite operations in Memphis and Muscle Shoals, Alabama. But this group was not nearly as successful in 1964–1966 as was the Motown/Tamla/Gordy family, which rivalled Atlantic's and then Red Bird's Lieber-Stoller productions, and also the New York/Los Angeles work of Phil Spector and Shadow Morton, for measured slickness of arrangement and ostensible drama of performance. Motown expanded in 1964 through the earthier Soul label, and also used the V.I.P. imprint for pop releases, Workshop for jazz, and Mel-O-Dy for its few country-and-western offerings. Motown emerged in England as the dominant force in American black music. Following their first tour of Britain, the Supremes were voted by English teens in January 1965 as the third-best vocal group in the world, behind the Beatles and the Stones.[5] Motown's early British releases had been leased to the Oriole, Fontana, and Stateside labels; in February 1965, EMI began distributing the Tamla-Motown label in the UK, giving new identity to 'Stop! In the Name of Love', the first of many examples of the 'Tamla-Motown' sound through 1985. The Tamla-Motown Revue, which played Britain in March-April and again in October 1965, further solidified the use of this label in identifying America's most popular black music. For the Beatles, rightly and wrongly, 'Tamla-Motown' became synonymous with modern rhythm and blues.

Table 1.1 lists those black artists and their songs known to have been covered by the Quarry Men and the Beatles in live performances, and sometimes in EMI recordings and BBC-Radio broadcasts, roughly in order of when the artists were first covered. Many other songs introduced by these performers were also done by the Beatles but do not appear here in cases where the Beatles clearly based their arrangements on previous cover versions, such as one by Lonnie Donegan, Elvis Presley, or Jerry Lee Lewis. Among R&B numbers covered on the Beatles' EMI releases, one might trace a progression from a slick New York emphasis ('Chains,' 'Boys,' and 'Baby It's You' all appearing on *Please Please Me* alongside the raw 'Twist and Shout'), to a Detroit fixation (Motown's 'Please Mr. Postman,' 'You've Really Got a Hold on Me,' and 'Money,' plus Detroiter Robert Bateman's obscure 'Devil in His Heart,' all heard on *With the Beatles*), through much grittier examples from New Orleans, Chicago, and Cincinnati in 1964 recordings ('Long Tall Sally,' 'Slow Down,' 'Rock and Roll Music,' 'Kansas City,' and 'Leave My Kitten Alone,' the last of which was unfortunately omitted from *Beatles for Sale)*. The Beatles' last publicly performed R&B covers were the coarse 'Rock and Roll Music' and 'Long Tall Sally,' both shouted on the 1966 tours.[6]

Table 1.1   R&B artists and their songs known to have been covered by the Beatles

Leadbelly: 'Alabammy Bound'
Sonny Terry & Brownie McGhee: 'John Henry,' 'Long Gone,' 'Diggin' My Potatoes'
Jesse Fuller: 'Take This Hammer'
Fats Domino: '(When) The Saints Go Marching In,' 'Ain't That a Shame,' 'I'm in Love Again,' 'Coquette,' 'I'll Always Be in Love with You,' 'I'm Gonna Be a Wheel Someday,' 'Red Sails in the Sunset,' 'I Know'
Lionel Hampton: 'Hey! Ba-Ba-Re-Bop'
Lloyd Price: 'Lawdy Miss Clawdy,' 'Mailman Blues'
Ray Charles: 'A Fool for You,' 'I Got a Woman,' 'Hallelujah! I Love Her So,' 'Don't Let the Sun Catch You Crying,' 'What'd I Say,' 'Sticks and Stones,' 'Hit the Road, Jack'
Chuck Berry: 'Maybelline,' 'Thirty Days,' 'You Can't Catch Me,' 'Brown-Eyed Handsome Man,' 'Too Much Monkey Business,' 'Roll Over Beethoven,' 'Rock and Roll Music,' 'Sweet Little Sixteen,' 'Reelin' and Rockin',' 'Johnny B. Goode,' 'Vacation Time,' 'Carol,' 'Almost Grown,' 'Little Queenie,' 'Memphis,' 'I Got to Find My Baby,' 'I'm Talking About You'
Little Richard: 'Tutti-Frutti,' 'Long Tall Sally,' 'Slippin' and Slidin',' 'Ready Teddy,' 'Shake a Hand,' 'Lucille,' 'Send Me Some Lovin',' 'Jenny Jenny,' 'Miss Ann,' 'Can't Believe You Wanna Leave,' 'Good Golly Miss Molly,' 'Ooh! My Soul,' 'Kansas City/Hey-Hey-Hey-Hey'
Larry Williams: 'Short Fat Fannie,' 'Bony Maronie,' 'Dizzy Miss Lizzie,' 'Slow Down,' 'Bad Boy,' 'Peaches and Cream'

Table 1.1 *concluded*

The Coasters: 'Youngblood,' 'Searchin',' 'Yakety Yak,' 'Three Cool Cats,' 'Sweet Georgia Brown,' 'I'm a Hog for You,' 'Besame Mucho,' 'Thumbin' a Ride'

Bobby Freeman: 'Do You Wanna Dance,' 'You Don't Understand Me'

The Olympics: 'Well ... (Baby Please Don't Go),' '(Baby) Hully Gully,' 'Shimmy Like Kate'

The Platters: 'September Song,' 'September in the Rain'

Bo Diddley: 'Crackin' Up,' 'Road Runner'

The Isley Brothers: 'Shout,' 'Twist and Shout'

Barrett Strong: 'Money (That's What I Want)'

Fats Waller: 'Your Feet's Too Big'

The Jodimars: 'Clarabella'

Little Willie John: 'Leave My Kitten Alone'

Davy Jones: 'Mighty Man'

The Drifters: 'Save the Last Dance for Me,' 'When My Little Girl is Smiling'

The Shirelles: 'Will You Love Me Tomorrow,' 'Boys,' 'Mama Said,'

'Baby It's You,' 'Love is a Swingin' Thing'

Ben E. King: 'Stand By Me'

Bobby Parker: 'Watch Your Step'

Bobby Lewis: 'One Track Mind'

Lee Dorsey: 'Ya Ya'

The Marvelettes: 'Please Mr. Postman'

James Ray: 'If You Gotta Make a Fool of Somebody'

Joey Dee & the Starliters: 'Peppermint Twist,' 'Hey Little Twist'

Arthur Alexander: 'You Better Move On,' 'A Shot of Rhythm and Blues,' 'Where Have You Been All My Life,' 'Soldier of Love (Lay Down Your Arms),' 'Anna (Go to Him)'

Richie Barrett: 'Some Other Guy'

Little Eva &/or the Chains: 'Locomotion,' 'Chains,' 'Keep Your Hands Off My Baby'

Sam Cooke: 'Bring It on Home to Me'

Lenny Welch: 'A Taste of Honey'

The Donays: '(There's a) Devil in His Heart'

The Miracles: 'You've Really Got a Hold on Me'

In the Beatles' earliest years together, R&B artists took a backseat to Elvis Presley, Carl Perkins, Gene Vincent, the Everly Brothers, and perhaps most of all Buddy Holly in directing their budding compositional interests. But by 1961 and beyond, George Harrison was adding raucous and then sophisticated blues lines to his Gretsch playing, and more importantly John Lennon was adopting the soulful melodic vocal ornamentation of Ben E. King, Arthur Alexander, and the related 'uptown' soul music that was to include the first Motown hits. Other than a solitary C&W vehicle adopted by Ringo in 1965 ('Act Naturally'), the final cover songs were chosen in January 1963, by which time the Lennon-McCartney writing team began to hit its stride, no longer requiring material written by and for others. But one Beatle or another has admitted to basing one of his own compositions on a riff or lyric from a previous R&B number: the bass line from 'I Saw Her Standing There' having been based on Chuck Berry's 'I'm Talking About You,' the I-^{b}VII chorus-ending tag of 'I Wanna Be Your Man' coming from Benny Spellman's 'Fortune Teller,' the bass line for 'Drive My Car' taken from Otis Redding's 'Respect,' the bridge lyrics for 'Michelle' originating in Nina Simone's version of 'I Put a Spell on You,' and lyrics from 'Come Together' borrowed from Berry's 'No Particular Place to Go.'[7] A contemporaneous review nailed the backing vocals of 'Day Tripper' as having origins in Lee Dorsey's 'Ride Your Pony.' And then, one needs no admissions from the composers to hear the chord progressions of Arthur Alexander's 'Anna (Go to Him)' in 'Not a Second Time,' the rhythms of Marvin Gaye's 'Hitch Hike' in 'You Can't Do That,' the vocal arrangement of 'Please Mr. Postman' in the introduction to 'Help!,' the organ part of Booker T. & the MGs 'Soul Dressing' as a sure model for Billy Preston's playing in 'I Want You (She's So Heavy),' the meter and harmonic changes of Carla Thomas's 'How Do You Quit (Someone You Love)' as the basis of Paul McCartney's and Elvis Costello's 'You Want Her Too,' or, for that matter, just about any aspect of the Chiffons' 'He's So Fine' in 'My Sweet Lord.'[8] The Beatles' growing compositional reliance upon blues is obvious in a stylistic shift from all of the 1963 A-sides to all those of 1964. In interviews from early 1964 through late 1965, the Beatles singled out Mary Wells, Marvin Gaye, Smokey Robinson & the Miracles, the Supremes, Otis Redding, James Brown, Nina Simone, and Chuck Jackson among their favorite singers (citations also included white performers Bob Dylan, Brian Wilson and the Beach Boys, the Lovin' Spoonful, and the Byrds).[9] Stronger support is evidenced by their having black American artists appear among their opening acts: Motown's Mary Wells closed the first half for the Beatles' October-November 1964 UK tour, Motown's Brenda Holloway toured the US with the Beatles in August 1965, Atlantic's Esther Phillips lip-synched on the November 1965 television special, 'The Music of Lennon-McCartney,' and Phil Spector's artists, the Ronettes, joined the Beatles for their August 1966 US tour. McCartney recalls how some artists were chosen for the 'Music of Lennon-McCartney' show:

> Before the show, [Director] Johnny Hamp had asked us if we had any real favourites of the Lennon/McCartney cover versions out at the time. Esther Phillips was my big favourite. She'd changed our 'And I Love Her' to 'And I Love Him' and did a great version of it. The sort of people we were listening to then were on Stax and Motown, black American, mainly. George used to have a great collection of Stax records on his jukebox. I liked Marvin Gaye, Smokey Robinson, people like that. The Miracles were a big influence on us, where Little Richard had been earlier. Now, for us, Motown artists were taking the place of Richard. We loved the black artists so much; and it was the greatest accolade to have somebody with one of those real voices, as we saw it, sing our own songs.[10]

Table 1.2 (in the Appendix at the end of this chapter) lists the 353 singles studied for the writing of this chapter that were performed by black artists and were hits between January 1963 (the end of the Beatles' period of cover-song borrowings) and early-June 1966 (the end of the recording of *Revolver*), in order of popularity for each month of original chart entry. Entries in bold face were released on Motown- or Atlantic-family labels, suggesting the dominance of those rosters of vocal artists, composers, producers, backing musicians, engineers, and distributors over their peers. Many of these titles have been mentioned by the Beatles over the past thirty-some years as sources of inspiration, and a number of references are to be made to these songs below in their role in shaping *Revolver*. While this album is rightly appreciated as the beginning of the Beatles' groundbreaking psychedelic period, it is hoped that the comments below will help place the album as a firm companion to *Rubber Soul* as a dual investment by all four Beatles in the R&B groove.

The black forebears of *Revolver*

The Beatles began *Revolver* in their usual London EMI studios in April 1966, following their first three-month break from scheduled group activities in six years, owing to an inability to decide upon the script for a film that was to have been shot during these months. The first two tracks brought to the studio were 'Tomorrow Never Knows' and then 'Got To Get You Into My Life'. Of the latter, Lennon says, 'We were influenced by our Tamla Motown bit on this' (Miles, 1978, p. 88), and McCartney remembers, 'That's mine. ... One of the first times we used soul trumpets' (Goodman, 1984, p. 107). Perhaps the album's most obvious tip of the hat to black American sources, this track has attracted several comparisons to R&B models. Terence O'Grady (1975, pp. 344–345): 'The four beat repeated note bass pattern with equal emphasis on all four beats demonstrated here is heard on many of the Supremes' hits (e.g., "Baby Love" and "Where Did Our Love Go?", 1964)'; Tim Riley (1988, p. 198): 'The vigorous horns, pulsating bass, knockabout drumming, and, above all, the untamed Wilson Pickett vocalisms in the refrain echo the charged brilliance of the Motown and Atlantic labels' finest pop rhythm and blues.' The reader might be more surprised to find that we'll also find strong, unacknowledged black influences upon Lennon's initial offering for the album, 'Tomorrow Never Knows', but the group's having begun the sessions with two soul-based numbers makes sense, in hindsight, in light of the abandoned Detroit/Memphis plans.

It is hard to guess if there might have been a specific 'Tamla-Motown' (read 'soul') basis for 'Got To Get You Into My Life'. The title is reminiscent of Solomon Burke's Atlantic hit, 'Got to Get You Off [of] My Mind' (March, 1965), the strong bass line and brass interjections of which are similar to those of McCartney's number, but Burke's song is a slower shuffle, [dotted] quarter note =

108, as opposed to McCartney's quarter = 136. In fact, 136 beats per minute is also exactly the same tempo taken in Harrison's three *Revolver* songs, all a notch faster than the normal dance-based quarter = 128, a favored tempo the Beatles would have heard most recently in soul numbers 'Baby I Need Your Lovin',' 'Out of Sight,' 'Back in My Arms Again,' 'I Can't Help Myself (Sugar Pie, Honey Bunch),' 'Papa's Got a Brand New Bag,' 'It's the Same Old Song,' 'Nothing but Heartaches,' 'Ride Your Pony,' 'Danger Heartbreak Dead Ahead,' 'Rescue Me,' 'Going to a Go-Go,' as well as in older examples. Whereas the Beatles may have strong roots in soul music, they rock a bit harder – but then note the Supremes' 'My World is Empty without You,' where the quarter = 176 whereas *Revolver* peaks at 168 in 'Doctor Robert'!

Still looking for a possible single model for 'Got to Get You,' we are drawn to its 'soul trumpets.' The horn section actually comprises three trumpeters and two tenor saxophonists, who worked out their own head arrangement in the studio.[11] Opening horn mottos occur in three well-known examples by others: Martha Reeves and the Vandellas' 'Dancing in the Street' (charting in August 1964), Wilson Pickett's 'In the Midnight Hour' (June 1965), and Stevie Wonder's 'Uptight (Everything's Alright)' (December 1965).[12] All three are transcribed in Figure 1.1. Of the three, Pickett's Stax-built example (perhaps featuring the Mar-Key horns: Wayne Jackson on first trumpet, 'Bowlegs' Miller on second, Andrew Love on tenor sax, and Floyd Newman on bari sax) was the most influential globally – its cascading tones of the minor-pentatonic scale (that is, the natural minor scale without second or sixth scale degrees) doubled in major triads was repeated in Eddie Floyd's 'Knock on Wood' (1966) and Creedence Clearwater Revival's 'Proud Mary' (1969), but more generally had a great impact on the guitar voicings of Cream, Led Zeppelin, and the resulting British blues-rock approach to harmony. But it was the two examples by the Vandellas and Stevie Wonder, both produced at Motown by Mickey Stevenson, with the timing of Wonder's early-1966 hit most propitious, that seem to be directly related to the horn writing in 'Got To Get You Into My Life,' the intro to which is transcribed in Figure 1.2. Note the bass pedal

Figure 1.1a   Horn motto opening 'Dancing in the Street' (William 'Mickey' Stevenson/Marvin Gaye/Ivy Jo Hunter), prod. Stevenson; horns arranged by trombonist Paul Riser

Figure 1.1b   Horn motto opening 'In the Midnight Hour' (Wilson Pickett/Steve Cropper), prod. Jim Stewart and Jerry Wexler

Figure 1.1c   Horn motto opening 'Uptight (Everything's Alright)' (Henry Cosby/Sylvia Moy/Stevie Wonder), prod. Mickey Stevenson

Figure 1.2   Horn motto opening 'Got to Get You Into My Life' (Paul McCartney)

of first and fifth scale degrees in both 'Uptight' and in 'Got To Get You' sustaining below the trumpets' assertion of minor-pentatonic neighbors in the subtonic ♭VII chord.[13] (In 'Got To Get You,' the F, A, and C comprising ♭VII are, respectively, lower neighbors to tonic members G, B, and D, the ♭VII chord being derived from the minor-pentatonic scale, here G - B♭ - C - D - F - G. Essentially, it's a bluesy F-natural, rather than the expected and polite major-mode F♯, that serves as lower neighbor to G). The horns of 'Got to Get You' bring the vocal 'beep beeps' of

'Drive My Car' (*Rubber Soul*) home to their proper timbre. The motto is revoiced in the coda, but is not heard in the song proper. Here, the horns have three functions: (1) reinforcing the neighboring ^{b}VII chord (F-A-C) in the two opening phrases of each verse, (2) sustaining the mediant harmony over a chromatic descent in the third phrase of each verse, the two tenor saxes doubling the bass, and (3) punctuating the ending of each refrain with minor-pentatonic fills over the cadential IV, V, and I chords, the final appearance of which alternates horns with electric guitar [edited out of most of the song] to support an improvising vocalist in a manner established in Solomon Burke's 'Everybody Needs Somebody to Love' (July 1964). The chromatic descent has double the harmonic rhythm of one possible model heard in verse of the Supremes' 'Stop! In the Name of Love' (February 1965), and quadruple the harmonic rhythm of Len Barry's '1 2 3' (September 1965) and the Supremes' 'I Hear a Symphony' (October 1965). (The tempo of the chromatic descent in 'Stop!' is maintained, conversely, in the bridge of Lennon's 'And Your Bird Can Sing.') While McCartney's vocal, based on an opening ascending arpeggiation of the major tonic triad, may not seem to have roots in R&B prior to its blue-note refrain, it is related to approaches taken in Doris Troy's 'Just One Look' (June 1963, six years before the Beatles signed her to an Apple contract) and, even more closely, the Ronettes' G-major song, 'Born to Be Together' (February 1965), which also features the minor-pentatonic F-major neighbor to tonic. But whereas any of these black-American numbers may have had an effect on 'Got To Get You Into My Life,' I believe 'Uptight,' by the only Motown artist of the mid-1960s with whom McCartney would ever record, might have been the central inspiration.

But what of 'Tomorrow Never Knows'? What could such an acid-drenched tape-effects-and-backwards-guitar setting of ideas from the *Tibetan Book of the Dead* have to do with soul music, at least before H-D-H used an oscillator in the Supremes' 1967 hit 'Reflections' and before Norman Whitfield took the Temptations to 'Cloud Nine' and their 'Psychedelic Shack' in 1968–1969? For starters, the song's only harmonic component is a tonic pedal that underlies motions from I to its Mixolydian lower-neighbor subtonic ^{b}VII chord. (This is the function by which the C-major harmony is embellished by B^b, D, and F, which act, respectively, as modal lower neighbors to the C-E-G members of the tonic triad, all taking place over a sustaining tonic, C.) Not only does this feature link the first two songs recorded for *Revolver*, but we also hear a vocal arpeggiation of the major tonic triad as the basis of both opening melodies. Lennon's tune seems like a slowed-down version of that heard in the eponymous 'Bo Diddley' (1955), whereas the lack of harmonic change reminds one of the I^7 chord maintained throughout Jr. Walker & the All Stars' 'Shotgun' (February 1965). And actually, the tape effects might offer another clue for us all: once 'Tomorrow Never Knows' establishes its hypnotic beat, the first sound we hear is a seagull-like effect; the only pop-song antecedents of such an opening are all black-produced: the Tymes' 'So Much in Love' (June 1963), Stevie Wonder's 'Castles in the Sand' (February 1964), and the Shangri-Las'

'Remember (Walkin' in the Sand)' (August 1964).[14] The unusual, unprepared piano part played in right-hand octaves in the track's final moments also has black roots, recalling more than anything else the fade-out of Chuck Berry's last Top-20 hit of the 1960s, 'You Never Can Tell' (August 1964). But Ringo's hard-hitting drumming, quarter = 128, is perhaps the song's strongest Motown link; he sounds here like Benny Benjamin banging the toms on 'Fingertips,' 'My Guy,' 'Dancing in the Street,' 'My Girl,' 'Nowhere to Run,' 'It's Growing,' 'I Can't Help Myself,' 'Tracks of My Tears,' 'Don't Look Back,' 'Uptight,' 'Back Street,' 'My World Is Empty without You,' 'Shake Me, Wake Me,' 'This Old Heart of Mine,' and 'You're the One.'[15] While Lennon asks us to 'relax and float downstream,' Ringo is doing a vigorous swim – or is it the jerk?

There are small, almost hidden ways in which *Revolver* reminds one of lesser-known black hits. A singular model can be heard for the change in 'She Said She Said' from a verse in 4/4 to a bridge in 3/4; this first occurs in the Marvelettes' 'He's a Good Guy (Yes He Is)' (February 1964), which like 'She Said' moves from 4/4 to 3/4 for a childhood flashback, as the bridge takes up the tune of 'Did You Ever See a Lassie.' Another pair of anomalies: the never-again-heard introduction that graces 'Here, There and Everywhere' is a rare attribute of soul numbers, but this idea was exploited in the beginning of Lenny Welch's 'Since I Fell For You' (October 1963). The Beatles had used Welch's 'A Taste of Honey' not only as the basis of their own cover version of that song, but also as a source of the opening guitar chord of 'Do You Want to Know a Secret.' The opening expansion of tonic in 'Here, There and Everywhere,' with its I - II - III - IV 'progression,' is functionally equivalent to the bluesy I - II - III - II vamp heard in Barbara Mason's 'Yes I'm Ready' (May 1965) and the Mad Lads' 'Don't Have to Shop Around' (October 1965). The surprising move in 'I Want to Tell You' from tonic to a major II$^{\#}$ chord (followed by V, but not seemingly leading to it as its own dominant) is reminiscent of a similar move in Sam & Dave's first hit for Stax, 'You Don't Know Like I Know' (January 1966); compare 0:22 in 'I Want to Tell You' with 1:31 in 'You Don't Know.'

While such one-to-one relationships exist, the Beatles' debt to Motown is much more sweeping; it exists in McCartney's fascination with James Jamerson's active and amplified electric bass lines (sharing register with Mike Terry's ubiquitous solo baritone sax), which began to influence Beatles music when McCartney adopted the Rickenbacker bass during the making of *Rubber Soul*. On *Revolver*, active lines like those on 'Taxman' (particularly in the bridge) and 'And Your Bird Can Sing' owe their existence to Jamerson's example (compare, for example, 'It's the Same Old Song'). Likewise, Harrison's fascination with vocal syncopation, at a peak in 'I Need You' (*Help*), 'If I Needed Someone' (*Rubber Soul*), 'Taxman,' and 'I Want To Tell You,' might have been encouraged by 'Dancing in the Street' and many other Motown creations.

Soul traits will be traced in two other *Revolver* songs: 'Good Day Sunshine' and 'Taxman.' McCartney has said that the first has origins in his hearing of the Lovin' Spoonful's 'Daydream,' but the shuffling beat, honky-tonk piano, applied dominants, and the lazy-day attitude seem to be the primary witnesses to this source.[16] The piano in 'Daydream,' in fact, is buried so far behind the bass and guitars, that the only real precedent for Paul's dominant bass-heavy piano in 'Good Day' comes from Fats Domino, whereas the barrelhouse electric-piano solo really reminds one far more of the Dixiebelles' '(Down at) Papa Joe's' (September 1963) or Marvin Gaye and Kim Weston's 'What Good Am I without You' (October 1964, another Mickey Stevenson production for Motown). The strong changes of meter of 'Good Day Sunshine' might remind one first of the many Bacharach-David songs made popular by Dionne Warwick, but note Marvin Gaye's almost unpredictable though repeated 3/4 + 3/4 + 2/4 changes in the verses of 'Pretty Little Baby' (July 1965), exactly the same repeated meter of the 'Good Day Sunshine' chorus. We know McCartney loved Gaye's work so thoroughly in 1964–1965 that we can't accept this as pure coincidence! I suppose the complex web of full overdubbed and overlapping imitative vocals in 'Sunshine,' particularly in its coda, would be linked most often by others to the Beach Boys (the Beatles singled out 'California Girls' for praise in August 1965), but there are plenty of possible black models: note the extended overlapping of 'pain' / 'pain' / 'pain' / 'pain,' or 'stronger' / 'stronger' / 'stronger' / 'stronger,' etc. in the refrain of Marvin Gaye's 'Ain't That Peculiar' (October 1965), and similar imitation in the Jaynetts' 'Sally Go Round the Roses' (August 1963), the Dixie Cups' 'People Say' (July 1964) and their 'Little Bell' (December 1964).[17] The last-named number has a totally unprepared 'truck-driver's' modulation from B$^\flat$ to C like that from B to C in the 'Sunshine' fade; another rare example of this in the black literature, moving from F to F$^\sharp$, occurs as if by splice in the Marvelettes' 'Danger Heartbreak Dead Ahead' (August 1965).[18] Further, and more significantly, it seems that McCartney may have based the chromatic line of his piano part and its underlying harmony on the backing vocals of Barbara Lewis's 'Baby I'm Yours' (June 1965); compare these aspects of Figures 1.3a and 1.3b. So there exists an intricate web of R&B/soul techniques in the fabric of 'Good Day Sunshine.'

Laying its cards right out on the table, the dauntless 'Taxman' has the most strongly minor-pentatonic vocals of any on the album (rivalled perhaps by 'Doctor Robert'), a sure sign of the blues. And we are swinging with Stax blues here – note the slight delay of every second beat in drums, bass, and Harrison's

Figure 1.3a   'Baby I'm Yours' (Van McCoy), opening

Figure 1.3b   **'Good Day Sunshine' (Paul McCartney), opening of verse**

backbeat rhythm guitar. This behind-the-beat rhythm is celebrated as the creation of Atlantic producer Jerry Wexler, in Memphis with MGs drummer Al Jackson, bassist Donald 'Duck' Dunn, and guitarist Steve Cropper for the May 1965 recording of Wilson Pickett's 'In the Midnight Hour':

> It was during the May session that the Stax rhythmic conception of a minutely delayed beat two and four was developed, inspired by Wexler's dancing of the then-new northern fad, the Jerk. This rhythm can be heard on all subsequent 1960s up-tempo Stax recordings, including [Sam & Dave's] 'Hold On! I'm a Comin'' [April 1966], [Otis Redding's] 'Respect' [September 1965], [Eddie Floyd's] 'Knock on Wood' [September 1966], and [Sam & Dave's] 'Soul Man' [September 1967].[19]

So while Harrison poses as the threatening 'Taxman,' his underlying persona is the hypercool Staxman. The backbeat guitar chord is a sure soul hallmark, holding down the rhythm in such 1965 numbers as the Temptations' 'My Girl' and 'Don't Look Back,' Marvin Gaye's 'I'll Be Doggone,' the Four Tops' 'Ask the Lonely,' Stevie Wonder's 'Uptight,' the Ronettes' 'Born to Be Together,' and James Brown's 'Papa's Got a Brand New Bag' and 'I Got You (I Feel Good).' To the guitar, the Beatles add backbeat tambourine, notable in such 1965 Motown productions as the Velvelettes' 'He Was Really Sayin' Something,' Martha & the Vandellas' 'Nowhere to Run,' the Marvelettes' 'I'll Keep Holding On,' the Supremes' 'Back in My Arms Again,' the Four Tops' 'I Can't Help Myself' and 'Something About You,' and the Miracles' 'Tracks of My Tears.' The *delayed* accented backbeat, however, is a Memphis creation, pure Steve Cropper, and 'Taxman' follows in the lineage of Booker T. & the MGs' 'Green Onions' and 'Boot-Leg' and Rufus Thomas's 'Jump Back.'

But it's the content of Harrison's backbeat chord that is most interesting. Through the verse, Harrison plays a D^7 for tonic function on backbeats. (This superfunky tonic with minor seventh, serving through much of the verse, could be progeny of Sam and Dave's 'Hold On! I'm a Comin'.') But in some measures (as at 0:12–0:13 and subsequent places in all verses) George articulates the first beat as well. Here and on the immediately following and sustaining second beat, he plays what is usually known as the 'Purple Haze' chord, immortalized in Jimi Hendrix's August 1967 release of that name. But Harrison was a year ahead. This chord is spelled D-F#-(A)-C-F, essentially including both the lowered and raised thirds of the tonic triad, along with minor seventh. Usually called the #9 chord and usually functioning on the dominant, this sonority has a great blues heritage, occurring for example at several structural points in Gershwin's 'Rhapsody in Blue.'[20] The chord is suggested in the cadential dominant of 'Got to Get You Into My Life,' where the D-major chord supports a trumpet melody including F-naturals. This mimics the turnaround $V^{\#9}$ heard in the entire texture of Martha & the Vandellas' 'Dancing in the Street' (there B-D#-A-D). But articulated by an unusual hand position on guitar alone, as is done by Harrison and Hendrix, this chord is previously heard only in Dave Hamilton's jazz-oriented guitar part in Mary Wells' 'Two Wrongs Don't Make a Right' (there F-A-E♭-A♭, written by Berry Gordy, Jr. and Smokey Robinson). While not complete examples of the #9 chord, the closely related mixture of minor and major thirds in a I^7 context is much more out front in Willie Woods's guitar contributions to Jr. Walker & the All Stars' 'Shotgun' (February 1965) and '(I'm a) Road Runner' (April 1966), also heard in Lee Dorsey's 'Ride Your Pony' (July 1965). Here, the guitar's first (highest) string sustains the fifth of the chord while the second string is bent to raise the flatted third to the major third. Add McCartney's hot bass line, and we've got a full mixture of Motown, Stax, and James Brown.

It's this sort of 'full mixture' that makes a larger point. Even considering the suggestive references in 'Got to Get You Into My Life,' no *Revolver* song identifiably steals the whole of a single earlier Motown or Stax creation. Rather, it's the blending of characteristics drawn from a variety of sources – the Beatles' usual modus operandi – that leads to this new music. Harrison, who was simultaneously bringing north-Indian music to the Beatles' attention and who would later introduce the group to the Moog synthesizer and to the music of the Band, seems to have brought the Stax backbeat to bear in *Revolver*. Starr has apparently amplified and sped up Benny Benjamin's Motown work, creating rock drumming out of rock 'n' roll in the process. McCartney seems to have been most interested in the composition and production work of Motown's Mickey Stevenson and in the bass playing of James Jamerson. And it didn't take more than a simple Bo Diddley tune to move Lennon. The eventual potpourri results from a relaxed working environment that allowed composers who knew exactly what they wanted from their Beatles sidemen to also accept their suggestions of different ideas.

I hope the above examples of the Beatles' borrowing of a wide range of soul-music characteristics has shown the group's dependence upon that type of music for the creation of their own in *Revolver*. But what is important to recognize is that had the Beatles recorded *Revolver* in Detroit or Memphis or New York, it would have been an R&B LP – sort of a Beatles Traffic album – rather than a true Beatles record. For the genius of McCartney, Lennon, Harrison, and Starr lies in their ability to take a pinch of this and a dash of that, mixing traits from all sorts of styles to come up with their own original product. For all the soul in *Revolver*, R&B is not the album's single most defining characteristic.

In 1979, one of the first American musicologists to address the Beatles' work, Terence O'Grady, showed how *Rubber Soul* as a mature work was veering away from the social dance tradition so central in popular music, a direction that was to allow the Beatles to write *Sgt Pepper* for a listening and thinking, rather than a simply gyrating, audience. But here, we have seen how dance – one of the major supportive functions served by R&B – is still a big player in *Revolver*. Furthermore, it seems ironic both that the Beatles derived so many materials from a singles-based industry to continue their quest for making artistic statements in full-length albums, and that the technical limitations of their studio equipment led to such revolutionary recording techniques. Perhaps had the Beatles worked with Holland-Dozier-Holland in Detroit or Wexler-Cropper in Memphis, their own eclectic-woven and revolutionary soul would have been submerged in a purer, more derivative state. As it was, instead of being overwhelmed by a single style, John, Paul, George, and Ringo were able to draw from the soul and nurture the mind as well.

Notes

1. A carbon of the original typewritten press release is located among the Alan E. Abrams papers in the Bentley Historical Library, Ann Arbor, Michigan, call no. 9943Aa2, Box 1. Abrams (who had worked with Motown Records founder Berry Gordy, Jr. in various capacities as early as 1959) was press agent for Motown in 1964–1966 and then worked as a public-relations consultant for Stax Records through 1968, notably covering the death of Otis Redding. The Abrams collection includes scrapbooks of news clippings, correspondence, press releases, photos, and several drafts dated January 1970 of one chapter of a never-published memoir with many heretofore unrevealed personal recollections, including the shocking story that singer Tammi Terrell's numerous head surgeries and ultimate death were the result of an attack with a hammer by one-time boyfriend David Ruffin of the Temptations.

    The Abrams text cited above was the basis for many news reports, as seen in the Detroit *Free Press* (22 December 1965, p. 13B), London's *Melody Maker* (1 January 1966, p. 5), and *BMI: The Many Worlds of Music* (March 1966, p. 14). A subsequent release found in the same collection, dated 21 December 1965, and entitled 'Brian Holland appointed V-P of Motown Record Corporation,' repeats the story of the Beatles' request and also mentions the fact that the Beatles featured [one line from] the Four Tops' record 'It's the Same Old Song' in the Christmas 1965 record made for their fan club.

2. Bowman 1977, pp. 96–97. A news article in the 31 March 1966, edition of the Memphis *Press-Scimitar* says 'the Beatles were scheduled to arrive at Stax on April 9 and were slated to stay two weeks recording one LP and one single' (Bowman 1977, p. 97 n). Across the water, it was reported that 'the boys may fly to Memphis on April 11 to record their new single' ('Beatle News', 1966, p. 29). A two-week stay in a foreign city would have created highly exacerbating logistical problems; perhaps it was Motown's fan-rousing publicity that had killed that deal.

3. See the Alan E. Abrams press release, 'Motown Now Number One in US Single Record Sales,'

dated 3 January 1966, housed among the Abrams papers at the Bentley Historical Library. (This text also contains the third and final announcement pertaining to the Beatles' request of Holland-Dozier-Holland.) The Supremes took H-D-H songs to #1 in the pop charts in five consecutive releases in 1964–1965, an achievement topped only by Whitney Houston's seven in a row in 1985–1988. Forty-two Motown singles hit the *Billboard* Hot 100 in 1965 (George 1985, pp. 138–139); in 1966, 75 per cent of Motown's releases hit the pop charts, as opposed to an industry-wide average of 10 per cent (Walker 1985, p. 11).

4. It is practically as well as socially difficult to discriminate among the designations 'rhythm and blues,' 'soul,' and 'black.' In nearly every case, records are so categorized when the lead singer is of African-American descent, regardless of musical style; thus, while Johnny Mathis and Dionne Warwick may be heard more correctly as pop singers, they are for many purposes counted among R&B artists because of their skin color. *Billboard* published a black-oriented chart separate from their 'Hot 100' pop chart in 1958 through November 1963 under the rubric 'Hot R&B Sides' and in January 1965 to August 1969 as 'Hot Rhythm & Blues Singles,' without a separate black-singles chart during the intervening months including all of 1964. *Billboard* used the designation 'Soul' in the chart title from 1969 to 1973.

5. As reported in the Detroit *Free Press*, 13 January 1965 (an unnumbered page found in the Abrams collection clippings, Box 2).

6. For more information on the Beatles' early covers of R&B literature, see Price 1997. Berry Gordy, Jr. (1994, pp. 203–205) relates the story of how he relented to accept a discounted publisher's royalty rate offered by Brian Epstein for the Beatles' uses of 'Money,' 'You've Really Got a Hold on Me,' and 'Please Mr. Postman,' only to subsequently find that the Beatles had planned to release their recordings of these songs at full price if need be.

7. For details, see Everett 2001 and 1999.

8. Heading into the alto sax solo in 'This Song' (1976), George Harrison ironically spoofs his legal troubles over plagiarism in 'My Sweet Lord' while pointing to obvious models by suggesting in an Eric Idle voice that he might be accused of stealing from the Four Tops' 'I Can't Help Myself (Sugar Pie, Honey Bunch)' or Fontella Bass's 'Rescue Me' in the very song being recorded.

9. Among other documentation of the Beatles' musical preferences, see Lewisohn 1992, p. 142, and Winn 2001, p. 20. One widely published press release by Al Abrams originates in the Beatles' 6 September 1964, press conference connected with a pair of Detroit concerts; asked what they liked about Detroit, 'The Beatles' unanimous reply was "TAMLA-MOTOWN RECORDS, and their artists," evidence of the Beatles' knowledge of the Motown label months before its appearance in the UK. The press release is dated 10 September and is found in Box 1 of the Abrams papers; the conference is not known to have been tape-recorded.

10. Beatles 2000, p. 198.

11. Trumpeters are Eddie Thornton, Ian Hamer, and Les Condon; Peter Coe and Alan Branscombe played sax. Condon says of their overdub session, 'The arrangement? Well, they didn't have a thing written down. We just listened to what they'd done and got an idea of what they wanted. Then we went ahead from there and gradually built up an arrangement. We tried a few things, and Paul McCartney – he's really the prime mover who gets everyone at it – and recording manager George Martin decided between them what would be used.

    'But most of it went right the first time. Ian and I jotted down some voicings but everybody chipped in and credit for the arrangement must be evenly divided. I suggested something for the trumpets for an ending, and we dubbed that on. They didn't think it was quite strong enough, so we dubbed it on with the three trumpets again. You'll really be hearing six trumpets in that coda' ('Beatles Plus Jazzmen' 1966, p. 1). Coe's similar recollections are seen in Lewisohn 1988, p. 79.

12. Wonder's follow-up single to 'Uptight,' 'Nothing's Too Good for My Baby' (Moy/Cosby/Stevenson) (April 1966), transposes virtually the same horn arrangement as that used in 'Uptight' down a minor third.

13. Earlier, non-horn appearances of $\flat$VII neighbors above an opening tonic pedal are found in the

Drifters' 'On Broadway' (March 1963), the Marvelettes' 'I'll Keep Holding On' (May 1965, another Mickey Stevenson composition), and the Miracles' 'Going to a Go-Go' (December 1965). Similarities must also be noted between this situation in 'Got To Get You' and the famous opening chord of 'A Hard Day's Night,' all F-major neighbors to the G-major tonic, plus an anticipation of the first scale degree over D in the bass. A much more recent example is produced when McCartney maintains a tonic pedal in the A-major verse of Harrison's 'If I Needed Someone' (*Rubber Soul*) while guitars and vocals pull down to the neighboring G-major triad and then rise back to tonic, perhaps the single greatest portent of *Revolver* in the previous LP. Also related is the embellishment of this 'counterpoint' by moving to IV before the subtonic returns to I; this 'double-plagal progression,' $\flat$VII - IV - I, is the basis of verses in Martha Reeves & the Vandellas' 'Nowhere to Run' (February 1965), Edwin Starr's 'Backstreet' (December 1965), and many others, before being adopted by the Beatles, notably here in *Revolver*'s 'She Said She Said.'

14. 'Remember (Walkin' in the Sand)' has been linked to the bridge of Lennon's posthumous hit, 'Free as a Bird'; see Everett 1999, p. 57n12.
15. Ringo's hard-rock drumming is out front in 'Tomorrow Never Knows' and 'Dr. Robert,' but has been submerged in the mix in many *Revolver* songs due to the bouncing-down of the basic tracks, often necessitating extra dubs of tambourine, maracas, handclaps, and cymbals to reaccentuate the heavy R&B backbeats originally articulated, in percussion, by Ringo alone.
16. See Everett, 1999, p. 328n106, for further discussion on this point.
17. Harrison mentions 'California Girls' in a Minneapolis press conference of 21 August 1965 (Winn 2001, p. 20).
18. The 'truck driver's modulation' is any unprepared and nonreturning motion from one tonic area to another that lies a half-step or whole-step above. I have defined the usual variety, most often heard on New York indie pop labels, with more specificity in Everett 1997, p. 151n18.
19. Bowman, 1977, pp. 61–62; see also Gillett 1974, pp. 194–196, which cites Don Covay's 'See Saw' (November 1965) as a further Stax example of the delayed backbeat.
20. This sonority is given more detailed discussion in Everett 1994, pp. 130–131.

Appendix

Table 1.2   R&B hits from the beatles' final R&B covers to the final recording of *revolver*

Artist	Title	Label	*Billboard* Peak, R&B/Pop Charts
December 1962:			
Mary Wells	**Two Lovers**	**Motown**	**#1/#7**
The Miracles	**You've Really Got a Hold on Me**	**Tamla**	**#1/#8**
Brook Benton	Hotel Happiness	Mercury	#2/#3
Johnny Thunder	Loop De Loop	Diamond	#6/#4
Dee Dee Sharp	Ride!	Cameo	#7/#5
Dionne Warwick	Don't Make Me Over	Scepter	#5/#21
The Rebels	Wild Weekend	Swan	#28/#8
LaVern Baker	**See See Rider**	**Atlantic**	**#9/#34**
The Marvelettes	**Strange I Know**	**Tamla**	**#10/#49**

Artist	Title	Label	*Billboard* Peak, R&B/Pop Charts
The Crystals	He's Sure the Boy I Love	Philles	#11/#18
Barbara Lynn	You're Gonna Need Me	Jamie	#13/#65
The Contours	**Shake Sherry**	**Gordy**	**#21/#43**
Booker T. & the MGs	**Jelly Bread**	**Stax**	**—/#82**
The Supremes	**Let Me Go the Right Way**	**Motown**	**#26/#90**
January 1963:			
Bobby Bland	That's the Way Love Is	Duke	#1/#33
Sam Cooke	Send Me Some Lovin'	RCA	#2/#13
Bobby Bland	Call on Me	Duke	#6/#22
Jan Bradley	Mama Didn't Lie	Chess	#8/#14
Johnny Mathis	What Will Mary Say	Columbia	#21/#9
Marvin Gaye	**Hitch Hike**	**Tamla**	**#12/#30**
Jimmy McGriff	All About My Girl	Sue	#12/#50
February 1963:			
Ruby & the Romantics	Our Day Will Come	Kapp	#1/#1
The Chiffons	He's So Fine	Laurie	#1/#1
The Orlons	South Street	Cameo	#4/#3
Mary Wells	**Laughing Boy**	**Motown**	**#6/#15**
Ray Charles	Don't Set Me Free	ABC-Paramount	#9/#20
Gene Chandler	Rainbow	Vee-Jay	#11/#47
Chuck Jackson	Tell Him I'm Not Home	Wand	#12/#42
Chubby Checker	Twenty Miles	Parkway	#15/#20
Little Eva	**Let's Turkey Trot**	**Dimension**	**#16/#20**
Chubby Checker	Let's Limbo Some More	Parkway	#16/#20
Rufus Thomas	**The Dog**	**Stax**	**#22/#87**
Bob B. Soxx & the Blue Jeans	Why Do Lovers Break Each Other's Heart?	Philles	—/#38
Sam Cooke	Baby, Baby, Baby	RCA	—/#66
March 1963:			
Jimmy Soul	If You Wanna Be Happy	SPQR	#1/#1
Jackie Wilson	Baby Workout	Brunswick	#1/#5
The Cookies	**Don't Say Nothin' Bad About My Baby**	**Dimension**	**#3/#7**
The Shirelles	Foolish Little Girl	Scepter	#9/#4
Brook Benton	I Got What I Wanted	Mercury	#4/#28
The Drifters	**On Broadway**	**Atlantic**	**#7/#9**
Dee Dee Sharp	Do the Bird	Cameo	#8/#10
Jimmy Holiday	How Can I Forget	Everest	#8/#57

Artist	Title	Label	*Billboard* Peak, R&B/Pop Charts
Baby Washington	That's How Heartaches are Made	Sue	#10/#40
Otis Redding	**These Arms of Mine**	**Volt**	**#20/#85**
The Miracles	**A Love She Can Count On**	**Tamla**	**#21/#31**
The Marvelettes	**Locking Up My Heart**	**Tamla**	**#25/#44**
Dionne Warwick	This Empty Place	Scepter	#26/#84
The Exciters	He's Got the Power	United Artists	—/#57
Mary Wells	**Two Wrongs Don't Make a Right**	**Motown**	**—/#100**

April 1963:

Artist	Title	Label	*Billboard* Peak, R&B/Pop Charts
Sam Cooke	Another Saturday Night	RCA	#1/#10
Solomon Burke	**If You Need Me**	**Atlantic**	**#2/#37**
Theola Kilgore	The Love of My Man	Serock	#3/#21
The Crystals	Da Doo Ron Ron	Philles	#5/#3
James Brown	Prisoner of Love	King	#6/#18
Martha & the Vandellas	**Come and Get These Memories**	**Gordy**	**#6/#29**
Ray Charles	Take These Chains from My Heart	ABC-Paramount	#7/#8
Etta James	Pushover	Argo	#7/#25
Darlene Love	The Boy I'm Gonna Marry	Philles	—/#39

May 1963:

Artist	Title	Label	*Billboard* Peak, R&B/Pop Charts
Barbara Lewis	**Hello Stranger**	**Atlantic**	**#1/#3**
Marvin Gaye	**Pride and Joy**	**Tamla**	**#2/#10**
Nat King Cole	Those Lazy Hazy Crazy Days of Summer	Capitol	#11/#6
Mary Wells	**Your Old Standby**	**Motown**	**#8/#40**
Ruby & the Romantics	My Summer Love	Kapp	—/#16
Chubby Checker	Birdland	Parkway	#18/#12
The Marvelettes	**Forever**	**Gordy**	**#24/#78**
Johnny Mathis	Every Step of the Way	Columbia	—/#30
Big Dee Irwin	**Swinging on a Star**	**Dimension**	**—/#38**

June 1963:

Artist	Title	Label	*Billboard* Peak, R&B/Pop Charts
The Essex	Easier Said Than Done	Roulette	#1/#1
Little Stevie Wonder	**Fingertips, Part 2**	**Tamla**	**#1/#1**
The Tymes	So Much In Love	Parkway	#4/#1
Inez and Charlie Foxx	Mockingbird	Symbol	#2/#7
Doris Troy	**Just One Look**	**Atlantic**	**#3/#10**
The Chiffons	One Fine Day	Laurie	#6/#5
Brook Benton	My True Confession	Mercury	#7/#22
The Orlons	Not Me	Cameo	#8/#12

Artist	Title	Label	*Billboard* Peak, R&B/Pop Charts
Ray Charles	No One	ABC-Paramount	#9/#21
Ray Charles	Without Love (There is Nothing)	ABC-Paramount	#15/#29
Ben E. King	**I (Who Have Nothing)**	**Atco**	**#16/#29**
The Shirelles	Don't Say Goodnight and Mean Goodbye	Scepter	—/#26
Bob B. Soxx & the Blue Jeans	Not Too Young to Get Married	Philles	—/#63

July 1963:

Major Lance	The Monkey Time	Okeh	#2/#8
Sam Cooke	Frankie and Johnny	RCA	#4/#14
Freddie Scott	Hey Girl	Colpix	#10/#10
The King Pins	It Won't Be This Way (Always)	Federal	#13/#89
Jackie Wilson	Shake! Shake! Shake!	Brunswick	#21/#33
Kim Weston	**Love Me All the Way**	**Tamla**	**#24/#88**
Chubby Checker	Twist It Up	Parkway	—/#25
Darlene Love	Wait 'Til My Bobby Gets Home	Philles	—/#26
Carla Thomas	**What a Fool I've Been**	**Atlantic**	**#28/#93**
Solomon Burke	**Can't Nobody Love You**	**Atlantic**	**—/#66**
The Cookies	**Will Power**	**Dimension**	**—/#72**
The Supremes	**A Breath Taking Guy**	**Motown**	**—/#75**
Booker T. & the MGs	**Chinese Checkers**	**Stax**	**—/#78**
Chuck Jackson	Tears of Joy	Wand	—/#85

August 1963:

Martha & the Vandellas	**Heat Wave**	**Gordy**	**#1/#4**
Garnet Mimms	Cry Baby	United Artists	#1/#4
Little Johnny Taylor	Part Time Love	Galaxy	#1/#19
The Ronettes	Be My Baby	Philles	#4/#2
The Jaynetts	Sally Go Round the Roses	Tuff	#4/#2
The Miracles	**Mickey's Monkey**	**Tamla**	**#3/#8**
The Crystals	Then He Kissed Me	Philles	#8/#6
The Tymes	Wonderful! Wonderful!	Parkway	#23/#7
The Essex	A Walkin' Miracle	Roulette	#11/#12
Nat King Cole	That Sunday, That Summer	Capitol	#19/#12
Patti Labelle	Down the Aisle	Newtown	#14/#37
Ruby & the Romantics	Hey There Lonely Boy	Kapp	—/#27

Artist	Title	Label	*Billboard* Peak, R&B/Pop Charts
The Marvelettes	**My Daddy Knows Best**	**Tamla**	**—/#67**
Dionne Warwick	Make the Music Play	Scepter	—/#81
September 1963:			
The Impressions	It's All Right	ABC-Paramount	#1/#4
Ray Charles	Busted	ABC-Paramount	#3/#4
The Dixiebelles	(Down At) Papa Joe's	Sound Stage	—/#9
Mary Wells	**You Lost the Sweetest Boy**	**Motown**	**#10/#22**
Betty Harris	Cry to Me	Jubilee	#10/#23
Brook Benton	Two Tickets to Paradise	Mercury	#15/#32
The Orlons	Crossfire!	Cameo	#25/#19
The Drifters	**I'll Take You Home**	**Atlantic**	**#24/#25**
Fats Domino	Red Sails in the Sunset	ABC-Paramount	#24/#35
October 1963:			
Lenny Welch	Since I Fell for You	Cadence	—/#4
Rufus Thomas	**Walking the Dog**	**Stax**	**#5/#10**
Sam Cooke	Little Red Rooster	RCA	#7/#11
Mary Wells	**What's Easy for Two is Hard for One**	**Motown**	**#8/#29**
Lloyd Price	Misty	Double L	#11/#21
Major Lance	Hey Little Girl	Okeh	#12/#13
Chubby Checker	Loddy Lo	Parkway	—/#12
Marvin Gaye	**Can I Get a Witness**	**Tamla**	**#15/#22**
Dee Dee Sharp	Wild!	Cameo	#25/#33
Otis Redding	**That's What My Heart Needs**	**Volt**	**#27/—**
Little Stevie Wonder	**Workout, Stevie, Workout**	**Tamla**	**—/#33**
Darlene Love	A Fine Fine Boy	Philles	—/#53
November 1963:			
Solomon Burke	**You're Good for Me**	**Atlantic**	**#8/#49**
Martha & the Vandellas	**Quicksand**	**Gordy**	**—/#8**
Shirley Ellis	The Nitty Gritty	Congress	—/#8
Sammy Davis, Jr.	The Shelter of Your Arms	Reprise	—/#17
The Supremes	**When the Lovelight Starts Shining in His Eyes**	**Motown**	**—/#23**
Garnett Mimms	For Your Precious Love	United Artists	—/#26
Garnett Mimms	Baby Don't You Weep	United Artists	—/#30
Jerry Butler	I Need to Belong	Vee-Jay	—/#31

Artist	Title	Label	*Billboard* Peak, R&B/Pop Charts
The Cookies	**Girls Grow Up Faster than Boys**	**Dimension**	—/#33
The Miracles	**I Gotta Dance to Keep from Crying**	**Tamla**	—/#35
The Marvelettes	**As Long As I Know He's Mine**	**Tamla**	—/#47
Otis Redding	**Pain in My Heart**	**Volt**	—/#61
Chuck Jackson	Any Other Way	Wand	—/#81
December 1963:			
Dionne Warwick	Anyone Who Had a Heart	Scepter	—/#8
The Tams	What Kind of Fool	ABC-Paramount	—/#9
Chubby Checker	Hooka Tooka	Parkway	—/#17
The Tymes	Somewhere	Parkway	—/#19
Ray Charles	That Lucky Old Sun	ABC-Paramount	—/#20
The Ronettes	Baby, I Love You	Philles	—/#24
Bob & Earl	Harlem Shuffle	Marc	—/#44
January 1964:			
Major Lance	Um, Um, Um, Um, Um, Um	Okeh	—/#5
Sam Cooke	Good News	RCA	—/#11
The Impressions	Talking About My Baby	ABC-Paramount	—/#12
The Dixiebelles	Southtown, U.S.A.	Sound Stage	—/#15
James Brown	Oh Baby Don't You Weep	King	—/#23
The Sapphires	Who Do You Love	Swan	—/#25
February 1964:			
Louis Armstrong	Hello, Dolly	Kapp	—/#1
Betty Everett	The Shoop Shoop Song	Vee-Jay	—/#6
Tommy Tucker	Hi-Heel Sneakers	Checker	—/#11
The Temptations	**The Way You Do the Things You Do**	**Gordy**	—/#11
Martha & the Vandellas	**Live Wire**	**Gordy**	—/#42
Rufus Thomas	**Can Your Monkey Do the Dog**	**Stax**	—/#48
Little Stevie Wonder	**Castles in the Sand**	**Tamla**	—/#52
The Marvelettes	**He's a Good Guy**	**Tamla**	—/#55
Eddie Holland	**Leaving Here**	**Motown**	—/#76
The Crystals	Little Boy	Philles	—/#92
James Brown	Please Please Please	King	—/#95

Artist	Title	Label	*Billboard* Peak, R&B/Pop Charts
Booker T. & the MGs	**Mo' Onions**	**Stax**	—/#97
March 1964:			
Danny Williams	White on White	United Artists	—/#9
Marvin Gaye	**You're a Wonderful One**	**Tamla**	—/#15
Irma Thomas	Wish Someone Would Care	Imperial	—/#17
Major Lance	The Matador	Okeh	—/#20
Bobby Bland	Ain't Nothing You Can Do	Duke	—/#20
Chuck Berry	Nadine	Chess	—/#23
Chubby Checker	Hey, Bobba Needle	Parkway	—/#23
Lenny Welch	Ebb Tide	Cadence	—/#25
The Miracles	**The Man in You**	**Tamla**	—/#59
The Coasters	**T'Ain't Nothin' to Me**	**Atlantic**	—/#64
Otis Redding	**Come to Me**	**Volt**	—/#69
Chuck Jackson	Hand It Over	Wand	—/#92
The Supremes	**Run, Run, Run**	**Motown**	—/#93
April 1964:			
Mary Wells	**My Guy**	**Motown**	—/#1
Dionne Warwick	Walk on By	Scepter	—/#6
The Impressions	I'm So Proud	ABC-Paramount	—/#14
Nat King Cole	I Don't Want to Be Hurt Anymore	Capitol	—/#22
Solomon Burke	**Goodbye Baby**	**Atlantic**	—/#33
The Ronettes	Breakin' Up	Philles	—/#39
The Contours	**Can You Do It**	**Gordy**	—/#41
Martha & the Vandellas	**In My Lonely Room**	**Gordy**	—/#44
May 1964:			
The Dixie Cups	Chapel of Love	Red Bird	—/#1
Millie Small	My Boy Lollipop	Smash	—/#2
Chuck Berry	No Particular Place to Go	Chess	—/#10
Brenda Holloway	**Every Little Bit Hurts**	**Tamla**	—/#13
Marvin Gaye & Mary Wells	**What's the Matter with You Baby**	**Motown**	—/#17
Marvin Gaye & Mary Wells	**Once Upon a Time**	**Motown**	—/#19
The Temptations	**I'll Be in Trouble**	**Gordy**	—/#33
Chuck Jackson	Beg Me	Wand	—/#45
Eddie Holland	**Just Ain't Enough Love**	**Motown**	—/#54
Rufus Thomas	**Somebody Stole My Dog**	**Stax**	—/#86

Artist	Title	Label	*Billboard* Peak, R&B/Pop Charts
Otis Redding	**Security**	**Volt**	**—/#97**
Barbara & the Browns	**Big Party**	**Stax**	**—/#97**
June 1964:			
The Drifters	**Under the Boardwalk**	**Atlantic**	**—/#4**
The Jelly Beans	I Wanna Love Him So Bad	Red Bird	—/#9
The Impressions	Keep on Pushing	ABC-Paramount	—/#10
Sam Cooke	Good Times	RCA	—/#11
Nancy Wilson	How Glad I Am	Capitol	—/#11
Marvin Gaye	**Try It Baby**	**Tamla**	**—/#15**
Jimmy Hughes	**Steal Away**	**Fame**	**—/#17**
The Miracles	**I Like It Like That**	**Tamla**	**—/#27**
Stevie Wonder	**Hey Harmonica Man**	**Tamla**	**—/#29**
The Ronettes	Do I Love You?	Philles	—/#34
Barbara Lynn	Oh! Baby	Jamie	—/#69
Rufus & Carla	**That's Really Some Good**	**Stax**	**—/#92**
Rufus & Carla	**Night Time is the Right Time**	**Stax**	**—/#94**
July 1964:			
The Supremes	**Where Did Our Love Go**	**Motown**	**—/#1**
Bobby Freeman	C'mon and Swim	Autumn	—/#5
The Dixie Cups	People Say	Red Bird	—/#12
The Marvelettes	**You're My Remedy**	**Tamla**	**—/#48**
Solomon Burke	**Everybody Needs Somebody to Love**	**Atlantic**	**—/#58**
Garnett Mimms	A Quiet Place	United Artists	—/#78
The Showmen	It Will Stand	Imperial	—/#80
August 1964:			
Martha & the Vandellas	**Dancing in the Street**	**Gordy**	**—/#2**
The Shangri-Las	Remember (Walkin' in the Sand)	Red Bird	—/#5
The Four Tops	**Baby, I Need Your Loving**	**Motown**	**—/#11**
Jackie Ross	Selfish One	Chess	—/#11
Joe Hinton	Funny	Back Beat	—/#13
Chuck Berry	You Never Can Tell	Chess	—/#14
Little Anthony & the Imperials	I'm on the Outside	DCP	—/#15
James Brown	Out of Sight	Smash	—/#24
Major Lance	Rhythm	Okeh	—/#24
Willie Mitchell	20-75	Hi	—/#31

Artist	Title	Label	*Billboard* Peak, R&B/Pop Charts
Dionne Warwick	You'll Never Get to Heaven	Scepter	—/#34
Brian Holland	**Candy to Me**	**Motown**	**—/#58**
Carla Thomas	**I've Got No Time to Lose**	**Atlantic**	**—/#67**
Dionne Warwick	A House is Not a Home	Scepter	—/#71
Booker T. & the MGs	**Soul Dressing**	**Stax**	**—/#95**
The Crystals	All Grown Up	Philles	—/#98
September 1964:			
Betty Everett & Jerry Butler	Let It Be Me	Vee-Jay	—/#5
The Impressions	You Must Believe Me	ABC-Paramount	—/#15
The Temptations	**Girl (Why You Wanna Make Me Blue)**	**Gordy**	**—/#26**
Marvin Gaye	**Baby Don't You Do It**	**Tamla**	**—/#27**
Sam Cooke	Cousin of Mine	RCA	#40/#31
The Miracles	**That's What Love Is Made Of**	**Tamla**	**—/#35**
The Jelly Beans	Baby Be Mine	Red Bird	—/#51
October 1964:			
The Supremes	**Baby Love**	**Motown**	**—/#1**
The Shangri-Las	Leader of the Pack	Red Bird	—/#1
Dionne Warwick	Reach Out for Me	Scepter	—/#20
Maxine Brown	Oh No, Not My Baby	Wand	—/#24
The Dixie Cups	You Should Have Seen the Way	Red Bird	—/#39
The Velvelettes	**Needle in a Haystack**	**V.I.P.**	**—/#45**
Rufus Thomas	**Jump Back**	**Stax**	**—/#49**
Marvin Gaye & Kim Weston	**What Good Am I Without You**	**Tamla**	**—/#61**
Otis Redding	**Chained and Bound**	**Volt**	**—/#70**
The Shirelles	Maybe Tonight	Scepter	—/#88
Chuck Jackson	Somebody New	Wand	—/#93
November 1964:			
The Supremes	**Come See About Me**	**Motown**	**#3/#1**
Marvin Gaye	**How Sweet It Is (To Be Loved By You)**	**Tamla**	**#4/#6**
Little Anthony & the Imperials	Goin' Out of My Head	DCP	#22/#6
The Impressions	Amen	ABC-Paramount	#17/#7

Artist	Title	Label	*Billboard* Peak, R&B/Pop Charts
The Larks	The Jerk	Money	—/#7
The Marvelettes	**Too Many Fish in the Sea**	**Tamla**	**#15/#25**
The Drifters	**Saturday Night at the Movies**	**Atlantic**	**—/#18**
The Four Tops	**Without the One You Love**	**Motown**	**—/#43**
Chuck Jackson	Since I Don't Have You	Wand	—/#47
Solomon Burke	**The Price**	**Atlantic**	**—#57**
Carla Thomas	**A Woman's Love**	**Atlantic**	**—/#71**
December 1964:			
Joe Tex	**Hold What You've Got**	**Dial**	**#2/#5**
Shirley Ellis	The Name Game	Congress	#4/#3
Alvin Cash & the Crawlers	Twine Time	Mar-V-Lus	#4/#14
Ben E. King	**Seven Letters**	**Atco**	**#11/#45**
Major Lance	Sometimes I Wonder	Okeh	#13/#64
The Contours	**Can You Jerk Like Me**	**Gordy**	**#15/#47**
The Shangri-Las	Give Him a Great Big Kiss	Red Bird	—/#18
Martha & the Vandellas	**Wild One**	**Gordy**	**—/#34**
Chuck Berry	The Promised Land	Chess	—/#41
The Miracles	**Come On, Do the Jerk**	**Tamla**	**—/#50**
The Dixie Cups	Little Bell	Red Bird	—/#51
January 1965:			
The Temptations	**My Girl**	**Gordy**	**#1/#1**
Sam Cooke	Shake	RCA	#2/#7
Ad-Libs	The Boy from New York City	Blue Cat	#6/#8
Shirley Bassey	Goldfinger	United Artists	—/#8
Sam Cooke	A Change is Gonna Come	RCA	#9/#31
The Drifters	**At the Club**	**Atlantic**	**#10/#43**
The Manhattans	I Wanna Be (Your Everything)	Carnival	#12/#68
Mary Wells	**Use Your Head**	**Motown**	**#13/#34**
Walter Jackson	Suddenly I'm All Alone	Okeh	#13/#96
The Velvelettes	**He Was Really Sayin' Something**	**V.I.P.**	**#21/#64**
The Ronettes	Walking in the Rain	Philles	#28/#23
Otis Redding	**That's How Strong My Love Is**	**Volt**	**#18/#74**
February 1965:			
Jr Walker & the All Stars	**Shotgun**	**Soul**	**#1/#4**
The Supremes	**Stop! In the Name of Love**	**Motown**	**#2/#1**

Artist	Title	Label	*Billboard* Peak, R&B/Pop Charts
Little Anthony & the Imperials	Hurt So Bad	DCP	#3/#10
The Impressions	People Get Ready	ABC-Paramount	#3/#14
Martha & the Vandellas	**Nowhere to Run**	**Gordy**	**#5/#8**
Fontella Bass & Bobby McClure	Don't Mess Up a Good Thing	Checker	#5/#33
Billy Stewart	I Do Love You	Chess	#6/#26
The Four Tops	**Ask the Lonely**	**Motown**	**#9/#24**
Otis Redding	**Mr. Pitiful**	**Volt**	**#10/#41**
Joe Tex	**You Got What It Takes**	**Dial**	**#10/#51**
Willie Tee	**Teasin' You**	**Atlantic**	**#12/#97**
Joe Tex	**You Better Get It**	**Dial**	**#15/#46**
Dionne Warwick	Who Can I Turn To	Scepter	#36/#62
Carolyn Crawford	**My Smile is Just a Frown**	**Motown**	**#39/—**
Carla Thomas	**How Do You Quit**	**Atlantic**	**#39/—**
The Ronettes	Born to Be Together	Philles	—/#52
Ray Charles	Cry	ABC-Paramount	—/#58

March 1965:			
Marvin Gaye	**I'll Be Doggone**	**Tamla**	**#1/#8**
Solomon Burke	**Got to Get You Off My Mind**	**Atlantic**	**#1/#22**
Little Milton	We're Gonna Make It	Checker	#1/#25
The Miracles	**Ooh Baby Baby**	**Tamla**	**#4/#16**
Shirley Ellis	The Clapping Song	Congress	#16/#8
Tony Clarke	The Entertainer	Chess	#10/#31
Brenda Holloway	**When I'm Gone**	**Tamla**	**#12/#25**
Mary Wells	**Never Never Leave Me**	**Motown**	**#15/#54**
Dionne Warwick	You Can Have Him	Scepter	—/#75

April 1965:			
The Temptations	**It's Growing**	**Gordy**	**#3/#18**
Gene Chandler	Nothing Can Stop Me	Constellation	#3/#18
The Impressions	Woman's Got Soul	ABC-Paramount	#9/#29
Chuck Jackson	Something You Got	Wand	#10/#55
Jerryo	Boo-Ga-Loo	ABC-Paramount	#11/#47
Esther Phillips	**And I Love Him**	**Atlantic**	**#11/#54**
Joe Tex	**A Woman Can Change a Man**	**Dial**	**#12/#56**

Artist	Title	Label	*Billboard* Peak, R&B/Pop Charts
Sam Cooke	It's Got the Whole World Shakin'	RCA	#15/#41
The Dixie Cups	Iko Iko	Red Bird	#20/#20
Chuck Jackson	I Need You	Wand	#22/#75
Ray Charles	I Gotta Woman	ABC-Paramount	—/#79
May 1965:			
The Supremes	**Back in My Arms Again**	**Motown**	**#1/#1**
The Four Tops	**I Can't Help Myself**	**Motown**	**#1/#1**
Barbara Mason	Yes I'm Ready	Arctic	#2/#5
Otis Redding	**I've Been Loving You Too Long**	**Volt**	**#2/#21**
Solomon Burke	**Tonight's the Night**	**Atlantic**	**#2/#28**
Fred Hughes	Oo Wee Baby, I Love You	Vee-Jay	#3/#23
The Marvelows	I Do	ABC-Paramount	#7/#37
Maxine Brown	Something You Got	Wand	#10/#55
Booker T. & the MGs	**Boot-Leg**	**Stax**	**#10/#58**
Sam Hawkins	Hold On Baby	Blue Cat	#10/#133
The Marvelettes	**I'll Keep Holding On**	**Tamla**	**#11/#34**
James Phelps	Love is a Five-Letter Word	Argo	#12/#66
The Knight Brothers	Temptation 'Bout to Get Me	Checker	#12/#70
The Radiants	It Ain't No Big Thing	Chess	#14/#91
Walter Jackson	Welcome Home	Okeh	#15/#95
Sir Mack Rice	Mustang Sally	Blue Rock	#15/#108
The O'Jays	Lipstick Traces	Imperial	#28/#48
The Shangri-Las	Give Us Your Blessings	Red Bird	—/#29
The Ronettes	Is This What I Get for Loving You?	Philles	—/#75
The Ad-Libs	He Ain't No Angel	Blue Cat	—/#100
June 1965:			
Wilson Pickett	**In the Midnight Hour**	**Atlantic**	**#1/#21**
Billy Stewart	Sitting in the Park	Chess	#4/#24
Little Milton	Who's Cheating Who?	Checker	#4/#43
Barbara Lewis	**Baby I'm Yours**	**Atlantic**	**#5/#11**
Billy Butler	I Can't Work No Longer	Okeh	#6/#60
Mel Carter	Hold Me Thrill Me Kiss Me	Imperial	—/#8
Jr. Walker & the All Stars	**Do the Boomerang**	**Soul**	**#10/#36**
The Impressions	Meeting's Over Yonder	ABC-Paramount	#12/#48

Artist	Title	Label	*Billboard* Peak, R&B/Pop Charts
Little Anthony & the Imperials	Take Me Back	DCP	#15/#16
Carla Thomas	**Stop! Look What You're Doin'**	**Stax**	**#30/#92**
Brenda Holloway	**Operator**	**Tamla**	**#36/#78**
July 1965:			
James Brown	Papa's Got a Brand New Bag	King	#1/#8
The Four Tops	**It's the Same Old Song**	**Motown**	**#2/#5**
Ramsey Lewis Trio	The 'In' Crowd	Argo	#2/#5
The Miracles	**The Tracks of My Tears**	**Tamla**	**#2/#16**
The Temptations	**Since I Lost My Baby**	**Gordy**	**#4/#17**
The Supremes	**Nothing But Heartaches**	**Motown**	**#6/#11**
O. V. Wright	You're Gonna Make Me Cry	Back Beat	#6/#86
Lee Dorsey	Ride Your Pony	Amy	#7/#28
Jr. Walker & the All Stars	**Shake and Fingerpop**	**Soul**	**#7/#29**
Edwin Starr	Agent Double-O Soul	Ric-Tic	#8/#21
The Spinners	**I'll Always Love You**	**Motown**	**#8/#35**
G. L. Crockett	It's a Man Down There	4 Brothers	#10/#67
Baby Washington	Only Those in Love	Sue	#10/#73
Arthur Prysock	It's Too Late Baby, Too Late	Old Town	#11/#56
The Astors	**Candy**	**Stax**	**#12/#63**
Marvin Gaye	**Pretty Little Baby**	**Tamla**	**#16/#25**
Sam Cooke	Sugar Dumpling	RCA	#18/#32
Nina Simone	I Put a Spell on You	Philips	#23/—
August 1965:			
Joe Tex	**I Want to (Do Everything)**	**Dial**	**#1/#23**
Bobby Bland	These Hands (Small but Mighty)	Duke	#4/#63
The Dixie Drifter	Soul Heaven	Roulette	#8/#99
The Marvelettes	**Danger Heartbreak Dead Ahead**	**Tamla**	**#11/#61**
Barbara Mason	Sad Sad Girl	Arctic	#12/#27
The Contours	**First I Look at the Purse**	**Gordy**	**#12/#57**
Joe Simon	Let's Do It All Over	Vee-Jay	#13/—
Sam & Bill	For Your Love	JoDa	#14/#95
Chuck Jackson	If I Didn't Love You	Wand	#18/#46
Solomon Burke	**Someone is Watching**	**Atlantic**	**#24/#89**
Stevie Wonder	**Hi-Heeled Sneakers**	**Tamla**	**#30/#69**
September 1965:			
Fontella Bass	Rescue Me	Checker	#1/#4

Artist	Title	Label	*Billboard* Peak, R&B/Pop Charts
The Toys	A Lover's Concerto	DynoVoice	#4/#2
Len Barry	1-2-3	Decca	#11/#2
Otis Redding	**Respect**	**Volt**	**#4/#35**
Johnny Nash	Let's Move and Groove	JoDa	#4/#88
Jr. Walker & the All Stars	**Cleo's Back**	**Soul**	**#7/#43**
Fred Hughes	You Can't Take It Away	Vee-Jay	#12/#96
October 1965:			
The Supremes	**I Hear a Symphony**	**Motown**	**#2/#1**
Marvin Gaye	**Ain't That Peculiar**	**Tamla**	**#1/#8**
The Miracles	**My Girl Has Gone**	**Tamla**	**#3/#14**
The Temptations	**My Baby**	**Gordy**	**#4/#13**
Kim Weston	**Take Me in Your Arms**	**Gordy**	**#4/#50**
Jimmy McCracklin	Think	Imperial	#7/#95
Barbara Lewis	**Make Me Your Baby**	**Atlantic**	**#9/#11**
The Mad Lads	**Don't Have to Shop Around**	**Volt**	**#11/#93**
The Ikettes	I'm So Thankful	Modern	#12/#74
Leon Haywood	She's with Her Other Lover	Imperial	#13/#92
Roy 'C'	Shotgun Wedding	Black Hawk	#14/—
Martha & the Vandellas	**Love (Makes Me do Foolish Things)**	**Gordy**	**#22/#70**
Dionne Warwick	Looking with My Eyes	Scepter	#38/#64
November 1965:			
James Brown	I Got You (I Feel Good)	King	#1/#3
Gene Chandler	Rainbow '65 Part 1	Constellation	#2/#69
Jackie Lee	The Duck	Mirwood	#4/#14
Wilson Pickett	**Don't Fight It**	**Atlantic**	**#4/#53**
The C.O.D.'s	Michael	Kellmac	#5/#41
The Packers	Hole in the Wall	Pure Soul	#5/#43
Don Covay	**Seesaw**	**Atlantic**	**#5/#44**
Ramsey Lewis Trio	Hang on Sloopy	Cadet	#6/#11
The Shangri-Las	I Can Never Go Home Anymore	Red Bird	—/#6
The Four Tops	**Something About You**	**Motown**	**#9/#19**
The Impressions	You've Been Cheatin'	ABC-Paramount	#12/#33
Bobby Powell	C. C. Rider	Whit	#12/#76
Little Richard	I Don't Know What You've Got	Vee-Jay	#12/#92
Ted Taylor	Stay Away from My Baby	Okeh	#14/#99
The Temptations	**Don't Look Back**	**Gordy**	**#15/#83**
Brook Benton	Mother Nature, Father Time	RCA	#26/#53

Artist	Title	Label	*Billboard* Peak, R&B/Pop Charts
December 1965:			
Stevie Wonder	**Uptight (Everything's Alright)**	**Tamla**	**#1/#3**
Joe Tex	**A Sweet Woman Like You**	**Dial**	**#1/#29**
The Miracles	**Going to a Go-Go**	**Tamla**	**#2/#11**
Ray Charles	Crying Time	ABC-Paramount	#5/#6
Otis Redding	**I Can't Turn You Loose**	**Volt**	**#11/—**
Fontella Bass	Recovery	Checker	#13/#37
Otis Redding	**Just One More Day**	**Volt**	**#15/#85**
The Toys	Attack	DynoVoice	—/#18
Edwin Starr	Back Street	Ric-Tic	#33/#95
Dionne Warwick	Are You There (With Another Girl)	Scepter	#35/#39
January 1966:			
Slim Harpo	Baby Scratch My Back	Excello	#1/#16
The Marvelettes	**Don't Mess With Bill**	**Tamla**	**#3/#7**
Deon Jackson	Love Makes the World Go Round	Carla	#3/#11
Lee Dorsey	Get Out of My Life, Woman	Amy	#5/#44
The Supremes	**My World is Empty without You**	**Motown**	**#10/#5**
Sam & Dave	**You Don't Know Like I Know**	**Stax**	**#7/#90**
Bobby Bland	I'm Too Far Gone	Duke	#8/#62
Jimmy McCracklin	My Answer	Imperial	#11/#92
Jr Walker & the All Stars	**Cleo's Mood**	**Soul**	**#14/#50**
Johnny & the Expressions	Something I Want to Tell You	Josie	#14/#79
Tammi Terrell	**I Can't Believe You Love Me**	**Motown**	**#27/#72**
Len Barry	Like a Baby	Decca	—/#27
Ramsey Lewis	A Hard Day's Night	Cadet	#29/#29
The Monitors	**Say You**	**V.I.P.**	**#36/—**
February 1966:			
Wilson Pickett	**634-5789 (Soulsville, U.S.A.)**	**Atlantic**	**#1/#13**
The Temptations	**Get Ready**	**Gordy**	**#1/#29**
Martha & the Vandellas	**My Baby Loves Me**	**Gordy**	**#3/#22**
Marvin Gaye	**One More Heartache**	**Tamla**	**#4/#29**
The Elgins	**Darling Baby**	**V.I.P.**	**#4/#72**
The Four Tops	**Shake Me, Wake Me**	**Motown**	**#5/#18**

Artist	Title	Label	*Billboard* Peak R&B/Pop Charts
The Isley Brothers	**This Old Heart of Mine**	**Tamla**	**#6/#12**
Mary Wells	**Dear Lover**	**Motown**	**#6/#51**
Edwin Starr	Stop Her on Sight (S.O.S.)	Ric-Tic	#9/#48
The Mad Lads	**I Want Someone**	**Volt**	**#10/#74**
Mar-Keys	**Philly Dog**	**Stax**	**#19/#89**
James Brown	I'll Go Crazy	King	#38/#73
Sam Cooke	Feel It	RCA	—/#95
March 1966:			
The Poets	She Blew a Good Thing	Symbol	#2/#45
Joe Tex	**The Love You Save**	**Dial**	**#2/#56**
Otis Redding	**Satisfaction**	**Volt**	**#4/#31**
James Brown	Ain't That a Groove	King	#6/#42
Bobby Moore's Rhythm Aces	Searching for My Love	Checker	#7/#27
Ray Charles	Together Again	ABC-Paramount	#10/#19
Mitty Collier	Sharing You	Chess	#10/#97
Kim Weston	**Helpless**	**Gordy**	**#13/#56**
Garnett Mimms	I'll Take Good Care of You	United Artists	#15/#30
Johnnie Taylor	**I Had a Dream**	**Stax**	**#19/—**
Len Barry	Somewhere	Decca	—/#26
April 1966:			
Percy Sledge	**When a Man Loves a Woman**	**Atlantic**	**#1/#1**
James Brown	It's a Man's Man's Man's Man's World	King	#1/#8
Sam & Dave	**Hold On! I'm a Comin'**	**Stax**	**#1/#21**
Robert Parker	Barefootin'	Nola	#2/#7
The Capitols	Cool Jerk	Karen	#2/#7
Stevie Wonder	**Nothing's Too Good for My Baby**	**Tamla**	**#4/#20**
Jr. Walker & the All Stars	**(I'm a) Road Runner**	**Soul**	**#4/#20**
Ko Ko Taylor	Wang Dang Doodle	Chess	#4/#58
Dionne Warwick	Message to Michael	Scepter	#5/#8
The Platters	I Love You 1,000 Times	Musicor	#6/#31
The Supremes	**Love is Like an Itching in My Heart**	**Motown**	**#7/#9**
James Carr	You've Got My Mind Messed Up	Goldwax	#7/#63
The Holidays	I'll Love You Forever	Golden World	#7/#63
Carla Thomas	**Let Me Be Good to You**	**Stax**	**#11/#62**

Artist	Title	Label	*Billboard* Peak R&B/Pop Charts
The Marvelettes	You're the One	Tamla	#20/#48
The Monitors	Greetings (This is Uncle Sam)	V.I.P.	#21/#100
Isley Brothers	Take Some Time Out for Love	Tamla	—/#66
May 1966:			
The Temptations	Ain't Too Proud to Beg	Gordy	#1/#13
Ray Charles	Let's Go Get Stoned	ABC	#1/#31
Jimmy Hughes	Neighbor, Neighbor	Fame	#4/#65
Joe Tex	S.Y.S.L.J.F.M.	Dial	#9/#39
The Chiffons	Sweet Talkin' Guy	Laurie	—/#10
The Four Tops	Loving You Is Sweeter than Ever	Motown	#12/#45
Wilson Pickett	99 1/2 (Won't Do)	Atlantic	#13/#53
Marvin Gaye	Take This Heart of Mine	Tamla	#16/#44
The Spinners	Truly Yours	Motown	#16/#111
The Contours	Just a Little Misunderstanding	Gordy	#18/#85
Ruby Johnson	I'll Run Your Hurt Away	Volt	#31/—
Ike & Tina Turner	River Deep–Mountain High	Philles	—/#88
Early June 1966:			
Bobby Bland	Good Time Charlie	Duke	#6/#75
Otis Redding	My Lover's Prayer	Volt	#10/#61

Chapter 2

I'm Eleanor Rigby:
female identity and *Revolver*

Jacqueline Warwick

Revolver was the first record I ever lost in the wars of love. A starry-eyed seventeen-year-old, I lent it to my first boyfriend, and felt proud and excited at the prospect of introducing him to this album. I remember it was a bitter winter day in Toronto as I walked to his house – so cold that my Indian silver hoops sent icy volts through my ears, and I held the record against my chest so I could avoid the fashion *faux pas* of doing up my jacket. A few months later, we broke up so that he could devote more time to playing guitar for other starry-eyed seventeen-year-old girls. I never got the record back.

I wish I could report that I never made that mistake again, but of course there were many more records lost, many perfectly good bands tainted by unfortunate associations. But I never did replace my copy of *Revolver*. So today as I sit in Los Angeles listening to it, it's a CD that I've borrowed from my current boyfriend (and one, I might add, that I have every intention of returning). It's as though at some level I wanted the injustice of not having *Revolver* in my record collection to serve as a lesson to me. Or maybe it's that even now, thousands of miles away, more than a decade and several heartbreaks later, I still somehow expect him to drop by, give me back the record, and tell me how sorry he is about everything.

I share this anecdote to explain *Revolver*'s importance to my adolescence in the late 1980s, and its continued significance in my life. Since 1966, countless teenagers and adults have found the record crucial to their strategies of self-fashioning, learning from these songs to venerate Asian religious philosophies, admire lifestyles involved with LSD, and daydream about a community of kindred spirits travelling to a better world in a yellow submarine. For many listeners at the time of its release, *Revolver* marked a watershed moment, a paradigm shift that put the lie to conventional values. The persona crafted through *Revolver* is a man open to exotic adventure, worldly and sensitive, opposed to institutional authority and possessed of an aloof loneliness that draws him to like-minded outsiders; in short, the consummate hip counter-culture hero. Small wonder that most of the boys I knew growing up embraced *Revolver* as their musical bible.

But what do female listeners make of *Revolver*? Should they will themselves to be like Paul McCartney's ethereal spirit guide in 'Here, There and Everywhere', emulate the sensual earth goddess who grounds George Harrison in 'Love You To', become cold and materialistic like the subjects of 'For No One' and 'And Your Bird Can Sing', or else resign themselves to Eleanor Rigby's lonely fate?

Revolver is hardly the only music that centres around masculinist experience yet still manages to be meaningful to women fans, and I don't want to assert dictatorially that listeners identify only with songs that speak from their own gendered positions. In a discussion of Led Zeppelin's music, Susan Fast argues 'that women engage with this music in the same way as their male counterparts and that both men and women engage with it in a variety of ways with respect to gender and sexuality' (1999, p. 257). Norma Coates has examined her attraction to the Rolling Stones' misogynist songs; she suggests that the band's appeal to female fans is not necessarily based on the 'manly beauty of Mick, Keith, or even Bill or Charlie [but rather in] the sound of the Stones ... the way the music hits the body' (1997, p. 50). Certainly, *Revolver* has been compelling to female listeners, and women are as capable as men of experiencing delight in a satisfying chord progression, a thrilling vocal timbre, or an energizing drum fill. Nevertheless I am concerned with issues of representation – which seem particularly important in the case of such an influential musical text – and so I want to shed some light on the kinds of female identity depicted in the songs of *Revolver*, and to consider some of the ways in which women negotiate them.

To begin with, female fans are accustomed to navigating a 'youth culture' that is often actually 'boy culture'; whether or not they consciously recognize it, the onus is invariably on girls to find ways of making cultural institutions fit them. Terms such as 'child', 'youth' and 'teenager', while nominally gender-neutral, have always been assumed to be male, and female experiences of youth must be distinguished as such with gender-specific pronouns. Entertainments created for children usually assume male experience as the norm, so that little girls watching a film like Disney's *Bambi* must perform a cross-gender identification in order to sympathise with the fawn and his forest friends; as adults, they learn to enjoy action movies as well as the 'chick flicks' that make their boyfriends squirm. From early on, females become adept at this kind of flexible identification with role models, and I would argue that learning to identify across gender boundaries makes women more agile at self-invention than men. Perhaps accepting boy culture as youth culture and inventing ways to find themselves in it empowers girls, because it requires them to learn the language of boys as well as their own, making them – in a sense – bi-cultural.

Music is a particularly valuable site for making these kinds of translations and negotiations, because its ephemeral form does not tie it to a single meaning, but rather it takes on new meanings as it circulates. Simon Frith writes:

> Because of its qualities of abstractness (which 'serious' aestheticians have always stressed) music is an individualizing form. We absorb songs into our own lives and rhythms into our own bodies; they have a looseness of reference that makes them immediately accessible. Pop songs are open to appropriation for personal use in a way that other popular cultural forms ... are not. (1987, p. 139)

Thus, a female fan listening to *Revolver* can pick and choose among the stances of: enigmatic philosophizing in 'Tomorrow Never Knows'; incisive fury in 'Taxman'; confident exultation in 'Good Day Sunshine'; fond sentimentality in 'Yellow Submarine'; and complacent languor in 'I'm Only Sleeping'. The male subject position in these songs can be read as gender-neutral and available to a whole host of listeners.[1] But in the case of songs that insist on heterosexual relationships described from a male viewpoint, and those that revolve around female characters, this process of identification is less fluid.

Of course, the woman in one of the songs from *Revolver* underwent a sex change before the final version of the piece was recorded: 'She Said She Said' is famously based on a conversation between John Lennon and Peter Fonda, pin-up boy of the California counterculture (Brown and Gaines, 1983, p. 171; Dowlding, 1989, p. 140, and elsewhere). Tripping on acid with the Byrds (whose sound the Beatles reference here through guitar style) in the hills above Los Angeles, the Beatle and Easy Rider talked about a near-death experience in Fonda's childhood. Lennon was appalled by the macabre discussion and his efforts to shut Fonda up served as the basis for a song that skilfully conveys frustration and discomfort. Walter Everett has examined compositional sketches with the lyrics 'he said "I know what it's like to be dead"', and notes that the final version involved 'a change of pronoun from "he" to a more mainstream boy/girl "she"' (p. 62)'. This raises a question that interests me: why would a conversation about death be more acceptable to the mainstream if between a boy and a girl?

I can begin to unravel this riddle by examining the character of Fonda/'She' as depicted here. The woman whom listeners came to know through the song claims to possess a mystical knowledge of death and sorrow, and dismisses Lennon's objections as ignorant ('you don't understand what I said'). Lennon refuses to be taken in by her pretentious anecdotes, and draws on his own lived experience to refute her. In a harmonic move to the dominant, he abruptly changes metre to a lilting triple time as he retreats to boyhood memory; here, he fills in the ascending fifth of the opening vocal gesture we associate with her ('She said') with careful stepwise motion ('When I was a boy'). Still she comes back, stubbornly clinging to her point, to her leap of a fifth, and to her duple metre, and at the end of the song she is heard repeating herself endlessly as the song fades out and we leave her. The looping phrase 'she said/I know what it's like to be dead' overlaps itself over a directionless tonic seventh chord, growing gradually fainter as though Lennon and the listener are walking away.

'She', then, can be understood as tenacious but unconvincing, a foil for the more easygoing and down-to-earth Lennon who controls the telling of the story. But she can also be powerful, sexy, and possibly attractive to female listeners because of the hold she has over him; in this reading, the recurring 'she said' phrase that structures the song shows the extent to which she has got under Lennon's skin, and his fascination with her. In either case, the fact that this troubling character is female might best be understood as an effort to project undesirable traits as far away from Lennon's masculine position as possible. I want to align this strategy with Judith Butler's theory of the 'abject' in transgressive sexual practices:

> The 'abject' designates that which has been expelled from the body ... literally rendered 'Other'. This appears as an expulsion of alien elements, but the alien is effectively established through this expulsion. The construction of the 'not-me' as the abject establishes the boundaries of the body which are also the first contours of the subject. (1990, p. 133)

In the context of 'She Said She Said', the effect of mapping qualities of arrogance and affected posturing onto an abject female character is to differentiate her as much as possible from Lennon, reinforce his own boundaries, and shore up his vulnerable masculinity. Note that Lennon counters the woman's creepy tale by invoking the homosocial universe of his boyhood days at school, when 'everything was right'. This opposition would be less compelling had the character retained Peter Fonda's gender, and the song would have been a complicated presentation of different kinds of masculinity, rather than a conventional binary of male vs. female, he said/she said.

If this song presents heterosexual relations negatively, depicting a woman who will not stop talking and a man who doesn't want to listen (but has difficulty tearing himself away), then it is balanced within the larger context of *Revolver* by 'I Want To Tell You', which replies with a more hopeful take on communication. Here the dialogue is between 'you' and 'I', as it is in so many pop songs about relationships. These pronouns leave the genders of both characters open to subjective interpretation,[2] but it is nevertheless reasonable to understand 'I Want To Tell You' as George Harrison's effort to get through to a woman. The song mirrors 'She Said She Said' in many ways; both songs are about conversation, and both end with a repeating sung phrase over a tonic seventh chord that gradually fades away. Here, though, the man sings about his own struggles to express himself, and indicates that he is patient enough to allow intimacy to develop slowly. Furthermore, the song is respectful of the woman he addresses, implying that she is worthy of hearing his most complex and private thoughts, and hoping that she will understand.

Structurally, both songs adhere to a conventional verse/chorus form, opening with a prominent guitar riff, and both are sung in a fairly relaxed vocal style, comfortably in mid-range. The unsettled feeling of 'She Said She Said' owes a great deal to the grating timbre of Harrison's lead guitar, while McCartney's piano in 'I Want To Tell You' conveys a similar frustration with jarring F naturals against E major chords, hammered insistently 'when you're near'. An important difference between the songs involves the harmonic trajectory of each. 'She Said She Said' operates over a descending motion from the tonic B♭ (with added seventh) through the major subtonic A♭ to the subdominant E♭, with an attention-grabbing move to the dominant F to indicate an opposing idea. By contrast, chord progressions in 'I

Want To Tell You' travel optimistically upward from A through the supertonic B (with seventh) to the dominant E and then home to A, before contrasting sections over B chords when the singer muses on his own shortcomings and insecurities ('if I seem to act unkind' and then 'sometimes I wish I knew you well'). With its musical illustration of a complex male subject who struggles to reach out, but hesitates to make himself vulnerable, 'I Want to Tell You' is courteous and flattering to a woman imagining herself in the role of the addressee. The song implies that hers is a character of sufficient depth to merit his efforts, and mitigates against the bitterness of 'She Said She Said'.

A less empowering contrast to the woman in 'She Said She Said' might be the woman described in 'Here There and Everywhere'. Harrison approaches the woman in 'I Want To Tell You' with awkward trepidation, but in 'Here There and Everywhere', McCartney's cooing vocals describe a love he is already sure of. In her contribution to this volume, Sheila Whiteley questions whether a celebration of woman as 'earth mother ... provider, forgiver, and healer' is any less repressive than images that intend to denigrate femininity. A veritable throwback to Victorian ideals, this 'angel in the house' provides comfort, devotion and spiritual guidance without, seemingly, ever turning her attention away from the male subject of the song ('someone is speaking, but she doesn't know he's there').

Of course this type of image is pervasive, as Whiteley notes, and has often issued from a woman's standpoint, even in 'I'll Be Your Mirror', released the year after *Revolver* by Andy Warhol's protégée Nico with The Velvet Underground (all intimates of Doctor Robert's circle). Nico's collaborations with The Velvet Underground are generally jaded and cynical – in fact, the female figure in the mordant 'All Tomorrow's Parties', also from the album *The Velvet Underground and Nico*, is not unlike the *poseur* in 'She Said She Said'. But 'I'll Be Your Mirror' is a sweet song through which Nico begs to be 'the light on your door to show that you're home'. Perhaps, after all, a world-weary woman can find some pleasure in invoking ideals of females as vessels of tranquillity and light. Similarly, McCartney's vocals on 'Here, There and Everywhere' may be soothing and reassuring to a listener of any gender, as though he is singing a lullaby. His voice is high, breathy and soft, and he has cast aside the rough timbres he adopts in more aggressive songs like 'I'm Looking Through You'; it seems that he has come to the listener with his guard down, allowing himself to be vulnerable and creating a safe and comforting intimacy.

This beatific contentment and trustfulness may be what country artist Emmylou Harris was responding to in her 1975 version of 'Here, There and Everywhere' from *Elite Hotel*. In this recording, Harris's lyrics change only the pronouns to describe a numinous male figure who dotes on her as she does on him, and thus she serenely positions herself as the cherished recipient of adoration. This rendition of the song is considerably slower than the Beatles', and the relaxed tempo allows Harris to indulge herself and her listeners in the shimmering sounds of acoustic guitar arpeggios, sighing pedal steel, and a warm wash of strings. It is a welcome solace in an album loaded with self-recrimination in cover versions of 'Feelin' Single – Seein' Double' and 'Sin City'.

Before she released this paean to love, Harris was already known for her version of 'For No One' from her solo debut *Pieces of the Sky* (1975). The significant alterations she makes to this song do not involve lyrics; rather, she reinvents the harmonic language, alters the instrumentation to give it a country sound, and changes the piece considerably while leaving the words and basic melody intact. New chord progressions, different instruments, and above all, the sound of a female voice uttering McCartney's words combine to make her interpretation of the piece a meaningful reply to the original. The pitiless account of the end of a romance becomes, in her treatment, an expression of sympathy.

Ian MacDonald notes that the structure of 'For No One' '... precisely reproduces [its] hero's obsessive examination of his predicament: exhausting every possibility, yet hesitating (over a suspension at the end of each chorus) before going round again to make sure all the options have been covered' (1994, p. 164). The Beatles' version of the song evokes a preoccupied figure numbly going through the motions of an ordinary day, but unable to shake the image of his former beloved moving on without so much as a backward glance. The steady tempo relents only on the brink of harmonic moves to a new tonal area, only to return each time to the beginning, as though pacing restlessly around a confining room. McCartney itemizes the minutiae of this forlorn existence in an expressionless voice, and the French horn – an instrument whose almost human tone often evokes pathos in other settings – coldly executes a technically flawless solo that provides no relief.

The chilly atmosphere of the song is established from the beginning; indeed, there is no introductory phrase to prepare the listener, as the voice enters immediately with observations on an F# monotone ('Your day breaks, your mind aches'). McCartney's piano and clavichord tracks enact a stepwise descending bass line that evokes the elegant precision of eighteenth-century instrumental works like Bach's Air on the G String. It is also reminiscent of Baroque laments such as Dido's dying aria in Purcell's *Dido and Aeneas*, where a descending bass line repeats endlessly, providing the ground for expressions of grief that never achieve transcendence because they are fettered by the cyclical harmonic pattern. In 'For No One', these brittle harmonic movements provide the backdrop to a story told with almost clinical detachment, of a cold-hearted woman who has left her man behind with no trace of regret. Twice, the song moves to the dominant F#, implying an effort to move on to a new kind of sound, and then lapses back to the tonic B and repeats the cycle, until it ends, unsatisfyingly, on the dominant, with a 4-3 suspension over this unresolved harmony left hanging in the air like someone's last words as they leave the room.

Here, the use of 'you' in the lyrics pins the listener uncomfortably in the position of the abandoned lover, compulsively rehearsing everything that went wrong, and also creates distance between the narrator and the actors in the story. This might be understood as a strategy by the narrator to disengage himself from what are in fact his own difficult circumstances, and to summon some objectivity in order to deaden his pain; in any case there is no expectation that 'you' can respond to the person singing the song. While 'you' usually implies 'I', and thus a dialogue between us, this song provides no way for its characters to speak, no insight into why the woman behaved as she did.

Emmylou Harris's revision of the song, by contrast, suggests an intimacy between the singer and 'you', the listener, and gently breaks through the icy formality of McCartney's piece. Gone is the clavichord whose strings resonate mechanically and at such distance from the fingers of the person manipulating them; instead the piano is surrounded by guitars, mandolin and other instruments that are held close to the body and whose strings are touched by hands. Harris's aching voice treats the lyrics with an expressivity that seems heartfelt, creating an impression that she is addressing a man still mourning a lost love, while she hopes and waits for him to recover. Crucially, the harmonic language is different; the lament-style bass pattern is replaced by chord progressions that move from tonic F through mediant A minor, submediant D minor, and seventh chords on subdominant B♭ and major subtonic E♭ before returning home to F. The final cadence of the song, instead of dangling agonizingly like the original, resolves gently while Harris hums a stepwise descent to the tonic, providing closure and release from the frustrating cycle. While Harris's version of the song does not attempt to redeem the callous female who 'no longer needs you', it does proffer a woman who is kind and promises an end to grieving.

Tim Riley argues that cover versions provide listeners with a new way of singing along with a favourite song. Discussing Wilson Pickett's rendition of 'Hey Jude', he writes that 'it wouldn't be out of line to say that Pickett's popularity with this song, a million-plus copies sold that same year, came out of an audience's urge to participate in that irresistible refrain. In fact, the point of Pickett's recording may indeed be simply to reference the original' (2000, p. 21). Pickett's 'Hey Jude' can thus be read as an example of a soul singer paying tribute to musicians whose admiration for soul and other styles of African American music was readily apparent.[3] He translates the song into the vocabulary of southern soul, with organ, horns, and his own bittersweet voice, which is characterized by a timbral quality that McCartney himself conjures in songs like 'Oh Darling'. McCartney, Pickett and Harris begin as fans, listeners who imagine themselves in what they hear; they each in turn take music into their own lives, rhythms, and experience, demonstrating Simon Frith's theory (cited above), and re-contextualizing sounds to make them signify in a new way. These interpretations can both appeal to listeners outside the audience of an original version or style, and also can surprise regular listeners with a new experience of something familiar. Harris's cover version of 'For No One' suggests the possibility of relief from the unrelenting pain described in the original song, and also offers listeners a different kind of female character to relate to their own lives.

The bleakest depiction of femininity on *Revolver* is, of course, Eleanor Rigby, whose story makes even Father Mackenzie's existence enviable by comparison – he, at least, is still alive at the end of the song. The story of the lonely spinster's demise adheres to one of the great narratives of the European tradition; countless operas and works of literature require a woman's death to bring the drama to its climax, redeem other characters and provide closure. In the Beatles' song, however, her death is irrelevant, and 'no one [is] saved'. Indeed, the purpose of the song is to draw attention to the lives of disconnected and lonely people, and it is predicated on the belief that institutions like the church are empty, and cannot provide meaning or value to human existence. Solitary women like Rigby might at one time have had full and satisfying lives governed by their faith and the reassuring knowledge that they played important roles in a religious community, but by 1966, Father Mackenzie's sermons go unheard and no one attends Rigby's funeral.

While a woman listening to *Revolver* can negotiate many of the gendered subject positions it presents in order to make them fit her, 'Eleanor Rigby' seems insurmountably unappealing. Yet the song has been interpreted by a woman, who transforms the song into an affirmative response to the Beatles' rigid view of hopelessness. McCartney's unflinching gaze at Rigby's wretched existence, and his pitiless opening phrase 'Look at all the lonely people', was turned on its head in 1969 when Aretha Franklin declared '*I'm* Eleanor Rigby'. Given her intimate and vital relationship to the church, it seems surprising that Franklin would be attracted to this song. As a preacher's daughter and gospel singer, she might reasonably have taken offence at the description of useless existences devoid of human interaction. And indeed, Franklin's version of the song brings all the weight of the gospel tradition to bear as she contradicts the Beatles' pessimistic social commentary.

Throughout her career, Franklin has repeatedly made a point of interpreting men's songs and subverting male positions, most recently in her 1998 performance at the Grammy Awards, where she sang 'Nessun Dorma', the heroic tenor aria from Puccini's *Turandot*, as a last-minute replacement for Luciano Pavarotti. Her famous 1967 interpretation of Otis Redding's 'Respect' responds tartly to Redding's misogynist complaint, demanding consideration for black women like herself as well as for him. Her version of Simon and Garfunkel's pretty 'Bridge Over Troubled Water' takes the song to transcendent heights as a powerful gospel anthem, and her cover of Robbie Robertson's 'The Weight' carves out a space for independent women on The Road.

Franklin's version of 'Eleanor Rigby' transforms the song in many ways, not least at the level of lyrics. She omits important lines and adds phrases. Note the absence of the phrase 'look at all the lonely people', which recurs throughout the original song, encouraging the listener to identify with the position of the watcher rather than the lonely people gazed upon. Franklin eschews this patronizing distancing, and insists not once, but twice, that *she* is Eleanor Rigby – reinforcing

VERSE
I'm Eleanor Rigby
I pick up the rice in the church
where weddings have been
Yeah
I'm Eleanor Rigby
I'm wearing the face that I keep
In a jar by the door
Lord knows who is it for?
Well:

CHORUS
All the lonely people
Where do they all come from?
All the lonely people
Where do they all belong?

VERSE
Father Mackenzie
Writing the words of a sermon
That no one will hear
No one comes near
Look at him working
Darning his socks in the night
When there's nobody there
What does he care?

CHORUS

BREAK
Eleanor!
Eleanor Rigby!
Eleanor!
Eleanor Rigby!

VERSE
Eleanor Rigby
Died in the church
And was buried along with her name
Nobody came
Father Mackenzie
Wiping the dirt from his hands
As he walks from the grave
Saying:
CHORUS

her identity, the sassy backing vocalists shout her name during the drum break. The spiky, jagged sounds of the string octet are replaced by Franklin's distinctive piano-playing in a soulful ensemble of guitar, bass, drums and organ. Crucially, backing female vocalists demonstrate that Rigby is far from alone, and Franklin's own inimitable voice is the sound of a robust and confident woman, not a dour and friendless spinster. Throughout, Franklin bends and stretches the even phrasing set forth in Paul McCartney's singing and reinforced by the precise string octet; the liberties she takes are an audible manifestation of her reconfiguration of Eleanor Rigby's experience. Father Mackenzie, too, fares better in Franklin's version of the story – she ascribes some agency and awareness to him, as he walks from Rigby's grave pondering 'all the lonely people'.[4]

Shifting from her stance of identification with Eleanor Rigby, Franklin sings of Rigby's death and funeral in the third person, as in the Beatles' version. Thus, she enacts the roles of both observer and observed, and shifts between them as circumstances dictate; for the duration of this song, at least, she is at once the solitary churchwoman and also the survivor who tells us her story. This is an enactment of the 'splitting in two' that John Berger considers fundamental to female experience:

> A woman must continually watch herself. She is almost continually accompanied by her own image of herself … From earliest childhood she has been taught and persuaded to survey herself continually. And so she comes to consider the *surveyor* and the *surveyed* within her as two constituent yet always distinct elements of her identity as a woman. (1972, p. 46)

Franklin/Rigby presents herself as an agent in her own story, but also narrates her own death and then keeps right on singing. Her note E on the word 'died' is the highest sung pitch in the song, and exceeds the upper boundary of the D minor scale in a move not indicated in the Beatles' original. This pitch creates an exciting dissonance with the underlying harmony, and her gospel inflection and deliciously rough timbre make this the climax of the song; Rigby's death becomes a transfiguration. What is more, the dead woman is not silenced. While the song heard on *Revolver* finishes with a merciless descending arpeggio on the tonic minor (E minor in their version), Franklin ends by fading out over bluesy alternations between tonic D minor and subdominant G while she trades call and response with her backup singers and instrumentalists.

Franklin manages, then, to have her cake and eat it too. By foregrounding the kind of divided identity typical of women's experience, she turns her death into a rhapsodic experience, attends her own funeral, and can still watch the lonely people (even counting herself among their number). Franklin's recording of 'Eleanor Rigby' doesn't so much deny the story set forth by the Beatles as comment on it, intersecting with the original song but also departing from it. Her recording is a documentation of the ways in which women interact with rock – sometimes rebelling against the images put forth about us, sometimes ceding to them, we continually negotiate and re-imagine our relationships to the records we care about so much.

So in a way, even writing an article about a favourite record might turn out to be another kind of metaphorical singing along. If a cover version can be understood as a fan's effort to interact with a song and dialogue with the original version, then perhaps an article about an album I love is my way of trying to carve out some space for myself in *Revolver*. I have spent countless hours listening obsessively to it, singing with vocal and instrumental lines, taking apart songs to find out how they worked, trying to get inside the record and see the world from in there – I consider this time well spent. Even the least appealing roles presented on the record have been instructive, offering stances to try on in my attempts to develop a complex but coherent self to present to the world. This may account for the reason that women's cover versions of songs from *Revolver* are so revelatory to me; hearing them is like participating in other women's efforts to work through the challenges the record presents. And knowing that this kind of give and take is possible helps me to believe that there really might be a yellow submarine that we can all live in together.

Notes

1. Indeed, Ann Shillinglaw identifies possibilities for queer readings of the Beatles in an article focusing largely on their film *A Hard Day's Night.* She points out that the spectacle of the moptops running *away* from screaming girls (among other moments) could be liberating for gay viewers (1999, p. 130).
2. Careful use of second-person address is a liberating strategy often used in songs that do not wish to be limited to a rigid understanding of gender relationships. For example, many of Dusty Springfield's love songs are built on 'me/you' dialogues, both before and after her coming out in 1970.
3. The Beatles were so enthusiastic about the sound of southern soul that in 1966 they investigated the possibility of recording at the Stax Studios in Memphis; these sessions would have been tracks for the album that became *Revolver*. The venture was abandoned because Stax's security proved inadequate for the Beatles, but Rob Bowman invites us to 'imagine the horns on a track such as "Got to Get You Into My Life" or "Good Day Sunshine" being played by Wayne Jackson and Andrew Love' of the Memphis Horns (1977, p. 97).
4. Franklin was undoubtedly familiar with Ray Charles's 1968 recording of 'Eleanor Rigby.' Charles does not reconfigure the character of Rigby as radically as does Franklin, but he alters Mackenzie considerably, with spoken lines such as '[Father Mackenzie] said to me: "All the lonely people …"'

Chapter 3

Sailing to the sun: *Revolver*'s influence on Pink Floyd

Shaugn O'Donnell

Introduction

The complex musical relationship between the Beatles and Pink Floyd spans more than three decades. When Paul McCartney returned to the Cavern Club in December 1999, Pink Floyd guitarist David Gilmour performed by his side.[1] The same month, original Pink Floyd bassist Roger Waters justified the importance of Pink Floyd's body of work specifically by its connection to the Beatles' work (Simmons, 1999, p. 95). In prior decades, Gilmour played on McCartney's 'We Got Married' (*Flowers in the Dirt*, 1989), 'No More Lonely Nights' (*Give My Regards to Broad Street*, 1984), and as part of the 'Rockestra' on *Back to the Egg* (1979).[2] While Gilmour cultivated a performing relationship with McCartney, Waters developed an indirect and more cerebral association with John Lennon. Lennon's influence on Waters extended beyond the sounding music to his aesthetic principles, as evidenced by Waters's comments in a 1988 *Penthouse* regarding 'the sense of artistic decency that' he dubbed 'the Lennon Instinct' (White, 1990, p. 507). He previously demonstrated his enduring interest in Lennon's music by recording an arrangement of 'Across the Universe' for a 1985 BBC-TV tribute to the late Beatle.[3]

A decade earlier, Paul and Linda McCartney took part in the series of interviews used as source material for the dialogue heard on *Dark Side of the Moon* (1973). Their cautious responses did not make it onto the album (Fitch, 1999, p. 194), but engineer Alan Parsons – who began his career with the Beatles in 1969 – recorded them. When Parsons still worked with the Beatles, former Beatles engineer and George Martin protégé Norman Smith produced Pink Floyd's early work from 1967–1970. The Beatles' imprint existed even at the first glow of Pink Floyd's success. In the *New Musical Express* questionnaire 'Life Lines', a rite of passage for burgeoning pop artists, Waters, drummer Nick Mason, and keyboardist Rick Wright all listed the Beatles as their favourite band or group (1967, p. 10). Wright also noted that Lennon was his favourite singer, while Mason mentioned that Lennon and McCartney were his favourite composers.

For most knowledgeable fans, the story begins during the spring of 1967 when the two bands were recording in adjacent facilities at EMI Studios on Abbey Road in St John's Wood. The Beatles were working on *Sgt Pepper's Lonely Hearts Club*

Band in Studio 2, while Pink Floyd were working on their debut album *The Piper at the Gates of Dawn* in Studio 3. Therefore, critics often argue that *Sgt Pepper* had a tremendous influence on Pink Floyd, and this is obviously the case; *Sgt Pepper* had a huge impact on virtually all rock music. However, the seed was planted even earlier, back in 1966 with the release of *Revolver*, when the Beatles were at their zenith and the Pink Floyd sound was a bold new idea.

Historical context

The initial reaction to Pink Floyd's music was that it was radically, even dangerously, different to most pop, particularly the Beatles. A commentator for the Canadian Broadcasting Company stated some common fears during the lead-in to an early 1967 interview: 'Is this then the music destined to replace the Beatles? Are the melodic harmonies, poetic lyrics, and soulful rhythms of today to be swept into the archives totally undermined by a psychotic sweep of sound and vision such as this displayed by the Pink Floyd?'[4] Maybe that was just the reaction of the uninitiated critics; perhaps people in the inner circle heard it differently. The following comments by EMI engineer and Beatles veteran Peter Bown suggest that was not the case. This was his reaction upon walking into EMI Studio 3 and hearing Pink Floyd for the first time: 'I opened the door and nearly shit myself. By Christ, it was loud! I thought "how the fuck are we going to get this on tape?" I certainly never heard anything quite like it, and I don't think I ever did again. It was very exciting' (Jones, 1999, p. 29).[5] Coincidentally, they were rehearsing 'Interstellar Overdrive' (*The Piper at the Gates of Dawn*, 1967), the same composition used as background music behind the CBC commentary cited above. Evidently, Pink Floyd's performance techniques bore little resemblance to any musical experience outside the London underground scene.

On the other hand, such a complete sonic divorce from the Beatles seems improbable since Pink Floyd, first forming in 1965, were young enough to have the Beatles as a direct influence. Moreover, as suggested in the introduction, they specifically measured musical creativity and success by standards set by the Beatles. Two blatant musical quotations illustrate the close connection early Pink Floyd felt to the Beatles. The first, shown in Figure 3.1, is a reference to 'Lucy in the sky' in Waters's song 'Let There Be More Light' from Pink Floyd's second album, *A Saucerful of Secrets* (1968).[6] Several musical gestures reinforce the obvious textual reference in this example. Rhythmically, note the steady eighths starting on the downbeat for 'Lucy in the' and the longer held 'sky'. Regarding pitch, despite the different keys, note the descending semitone of the lead vocal on 'Sky' – <G, F-sharp> for the Beatles and <E, E-flat> for Pink Floyd – and that the entrance of the upper harmony in the Pink Floyd excerpt coincides precisely with the quote. Additionally, Pink Floyd incorporate the gesture of the Beatles' 'Ah' into their held 'sky' with the long whole note and the subsequent elision back

'Lucy in the Sky with Diamonds' (*Sgt Pepper's Lonely Hearts Club Band*, 1967), 1:00–1:08

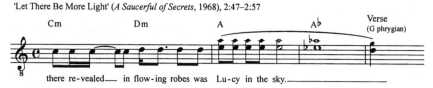

'Let There Be More Light' (*A Saucerful of Secrets*, 1968), 2:47–2:57

Figure 3.1   'Lucy in the sky'

into the modal verse. Finally, the prominent perfect fourth <E4, A4> that completes the Beatles' 'Ah' is precisely the same one that Pink Floyd use for the quotation.

The second quote, shown in Figure 3.2, is from Pink Floyd's third single, Syd Barrett's song 'Apples and Oranges' (1967). In this pair of excerpts the rhythm for the quoted text is identical and the pitches virtually so. In 'Sgt Pepper's Lonely Hearts Club Band' the Beatles embellish G4 with a lower neighbor F-natural, while Pink Floyd embellish it with an F-sharp. The principal differences between

'Sgt Pepper's Lonely Hearts Club Band' (*Sgt Pepper's Lonely Hearts Club Band*, 1967), 1:40

'Apples and Oranges' (single, 1967), 2:18

Figure 3.2   'Thought you might like to know'

the two are the supporting harmonies and the G-sharp plus descending glissando that Barrett sings on 'know', but this inflected G only seems to intensify the quote. The quoted text in this example is less immediately identifiable than the previous 'Lucy in the sky' example, but Pink Floyd bring 'Thought you might like to know' into relief by its context. First, Barrett sings this excerpt an octave higher than all the other comparable verse passages. More subtly, this verse immediately follows the middle instrumental portion of the song that concludes with a held D chord and three familiar thumps on the drums that signal the return to the verse. The D chord and the quarter note <2, 3, 4> on the drums are borrowed from the anacrusis or extended upbeat to the 'Lucy in the Sky with Diamonds' chorus. The framing of this quotation by the 'Lucy' thumps on one side and by the glissando and silence on the other, as well as the shift in vocal register, make it much richer than a simple borrowing of text.

The above examples confirm *Sgt Pepper*'s influence on Pink Floyd, but it is important to keep in mind that these songs were among the second efforts of the band. They had already released two singles and an album, all of which were more successful than the works in the preceding examples. *Sgt Pepper* had been out for five months before Pink Floyd recorded 'Apples and Oranges', and about another three before work began on 'Let There Be More Light'. A comparison of their first single, 'Arnold Layne' (1967), and 'Lucy in the Sky with Diamonds' reveals more deeply rooted musical similarities. Figure 3.3 illustrates the descending fourths that underlie the verses in both songs. It is a rather common musical gesture, but in this case, the shared pitches – particularly the chromatic passing tone F-natural – make the resemblance significant. The harmonic content of the two songs is also quite similar as shown in Figure 3.4. The example

'Lucy in the Sky with Diamonds' (*Sgt Pepper's Lonely Hearts Club Band*, 1967), 0:06–0:13

'Arnold Layne' (single, 1967), 0:05–0:14

Figure 3.3   Descending fourths supporting 'Lucy' and 'Arnold'

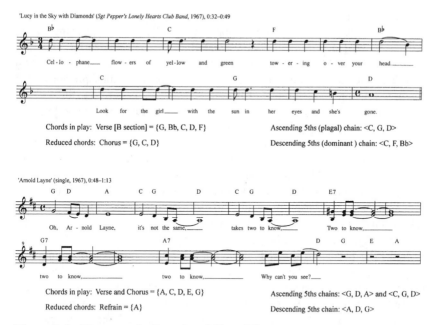

Figure 3.4   Harmony in 'Lucy' and 'Arnold'

shows the second section of the verse in 'Lucy in the Sky with Diamonds' and the chorus of 'Arnold Layne.' Considering the harmonic content in its entirety as a system or unordered collection (listed as 'chords in play' at the bottom of the excerpts), one finds major triads built on each member of the pentatonic scale. This is extremely common in rock music, but with their contemporaries insisting on dramatic differences between the two bands, it is worth pointing out that they are working with similar materials. It is also worth noting that, despite other foreground differences, chains of perfect fifths form a common feature in their harmonic language.[7] Furthermore, the two songs each have another formal section that is even simpler in harmonic construction, using a subset of the chords previously in play. The chorus of 'Lucy in the Sky with Diamonds' reduces the set to a simple, but effective, I-IV-V, while the refrain of 'Arnold Layne' reduces the content to a single primal harmony to facilitate Pink Floyd's characteristic free improvisation.[8] The figure does not show these comparable sections, but instead it lists the reduced chords in play at the bottom of each excerpt.

The above comparison may seem like it further substantiates the influence of *Sgt Pepper* on Pink Floyd, but in fact, it does the opposite; it weakens the connection. EMI released 'Arnold Layne' almost three months before *Sgt Pepper*, and Pink Floyd recorded it on 27 February at Sound Techniques Studio (Hodges and Priston, 1999, p. 36). That is one day before the Beatles even began working on 'Lucy in the Sky with Diamonds' at EMI (Lewisohn, 2000a, p. 247). As virtually simultaneous recordings, the similar song structures point to prior common influences rather than direct impact. Certainly, there were many mutual influences, ranging from Bo Diddley and Bob Dylan in the early 1960s to a steady supply of LSD in 1965. However, at this point in the careers of these musicians the most significant shared influence was the Beatles' previous work. The Beatles were in the middle of the introspective process of redefining themselves and Pink Floyd were longtime fans, as demonstrated by their 'Life Lines' answers. Barrett, who did not mention the Beatles in his answers, was perhaps the biggest fan. Storm Thorgerson, co-founder of the design company Hipgnosis, recalled Barrett's reaction to hearing 'Love Me Do' (*Please Please Me*, 1963): 'He grabbed my shoulder and said: "Storm, man, this is it!" The effect was as immediate as that' (Watkinson and Anderson, 1991, p. 26). Storm also recounted that Barrett frequently 'played Beatles songs, asking enthusiastically "Have you heard this?" and strumming and singing "Please Please Me" (*With the Beatles*, 1963)' (Thorgerson, 1997, p. 15).

Figure 3.5 presents a timeline of the critical twenty months leading up to the August 1967 release of Pink Floyd's debut album. The Beatles' work during this period – compressed between their final UK tour and Brian Epstein's death – was arguably the pinnacle of their career. Significantly, it was the same period that saw Pink Floyd establish themselves as the house band of the London underground, release their first singles and debut album, and already see the beginning of Barrett's mental disintegration.[9] The timeline presents a very broad history; detailed information is readily available elsewhere for both bands.[10] The first row keeps track of time, while the second presents significant Beatles items, and the third does the same for Pink Floyd. Between the first two rows 'B' and 'PF' icons

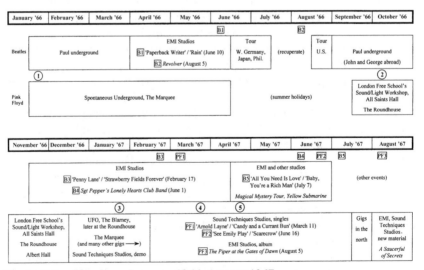

Figure 3.5   Timeline, January 1966–August 1967

mark release dates to clarify their chronology. The five markers between rows two and three signify crucial points of intersection between the two bands.

Marker 1 represents McCartney's involvement with the founding of the Indica bookshop, run by Barry Miles, Peter Asher, and John Dunbar (Green, 1988, pp. 74–80). A hotbed of *avant-garde* interests in multiple media, the Indica embroiled McCartney in the London underground, the same underground that was giving birth to Pink Floyd. While he was dabbling with experimental composition and filmmaking, Pink Floyd was performing for the Spontaneous Underground events at the Marquee. At the time, Pink Floyd were playing a mix of chestnuts like Bo Diddley's 'Road Runner' (1960) and the Kingsmen's 'Louie Louie' (1963), interspersed with extended instrumental passages featuring layers of feedback and noise. This style was a precursor to their characteristic ternary form in which relatively traditional song patterns surround freer electronic middle sections. No documentation suggests that McCartney specifically attended any of the Spontaneous Underground events, but his circle and Pink Floyd's certainly intersected. For example, Pink Floyd also played the University of Essex during this period, sharing the bill with long-time Beatles cohort Marianne Faithfull (Povey and Russell, 1997, p. 35). That performance happened to be Pink Floyd's first use of moving images, their first true mixed-media event. Despite a lack of hard evidence, it is likely that with such similar interests and circles, McCartney would have been aware of Pink Floyd as early as the making of *Revolver*.

Marker 2 is an offshoot of the first, with Miles and John 'Hoppy' Hopkins launching the paper *International Times* or *IT*. McCartney again chimed in with support, and this is the same publication about which American promoter Chet Helms commented: 'There seemed to be little distinction between UFO and the Pink Floyd, and *IT* magazine for that matter. It was all the same circle of people who hung out together and smoked dope together' (Schaffner, 1991, p. 50). The marker specifically represents the *IT* launch party held at the Roundhouse on 15 October. This is the first documented case of McCartney being at a Pink Floyd performance. The earliest known set list for Pink Floyd dates from the previous evening and shows that by this time Pink Floyd replaced most of their covers with original material.[11] McCartney definitely experienced Pink Floyd in their full psychedelic multimedia glory. A subsequent review mentions that Pink Floyd got 'a rave from Paul' (Povey and Russell, 1997, p. 36).[12]

Marker 3 takes place during the height of Pink Floyd's tenure as UFO's house band. Many writers place various Beatles in various states of chemical enhancement at various times at UFO, but it is a slippery era and hard to document precisely. It is likely that at one time or another, all the Beatles experienced Pink Floyd during this period. Established musicians regularly attended these events, as illustrated by the following Pete Townshend quote:

> When the Floyd played it was very exciting. Their sound [fit] that period with echo on all the instruments. I once got Eric Clapton to come down because I thought what Syd was doing was very interesting. We both enjoyed him, although you could never quite hear what he was up to because he used two or three different echo units in a row. He used to have them coming out of different amps which formed a kind of sound field – a textural wash of sound that wasn't always melodically or harmonically correct but always very interesting and satisfying. (Watkinson and Anderson, 1991, p. 45)

The marker during this period specifically represents the Granada TV special on the underground titled 'It's So Far Out It's Straight Down'.[13] Pink Floyd were recorded at UFO as the movement's band and McCartney did an interview essentially acting as the movement's spokesperson.

Marker 4 represents the numerous anecdotes about the two bands crossing paths at EMI studios. The story most frequently reported has Pink Floyd dropping in during the 'Lovely Rita' session on 21 March. Ironically, Lennon was absent after he accidentally dosed himself during that infamous session.[14] Other stories involve McCartney and/or the others stopping by to encourage Pink Floyd and put in a good word for their former engineer Norm Smith. The fifth and final marker in Figure 3.5 represents the 14-Hour Technicolour Dream held at Alexandra Palace on 29 April. It was similar to many of the other events Pink Floyd played, but on an enormous scale. There are numerous accounts of the event available, but the timeline includes it as the only documented Pink Floyd performance with Lennon in attendance. Peter Whitehead captured him on film at the event.

The two threads in the timeline are never far apart thanks to Indica, *IT*, and UFO, but even a cursory glance suggests that Pink Floyd events accelerate dramatically after marker 2. By marker 3 they were the premier house band of the London underground, and by marker 4 they were recording next door to the Beatles at EMI. Even more than the obvious connection at EMI, the shift in gears between the first two markers captures the imagination. Around marker 1 Pink Floyd were playing covers – reportedly unique versions, but covers nonetheless – at private events, yet by marker 2 they were playing mostly originals at paying gigs. In June 1966, future managers Peter Jenner and Andrew King told them: 'You lads could be bigger than the Beatles.' The band, considering a breakup and still more concerned with architecture (Waters and Mason) and painting (Barrett), offered this lukewarm response: 'we'll see you when we get back from our hols' (Schaffner, 1991, pp. 12–13). What changed their minds during that summer holiday? *Revolver*, released during the lull in the timeline, may have been the catalyst for this dramatic transformation.

Revolver and Pink Floyd

Walt Everett phrases it most succinctly: '*Revolver* was fundamentally unlike any rock album that had preceded it' (1999, p. 31). The album blazes trails through virtually every musical parameter, but this chapter examines the areas that had lasting impact on the music of Pink Floyd: meter, harmonic organization, timbre, and poetry. *Revolver*'s influence is so pervasive that the following discussion only surveys some of the most prominent examples in the Pink Floyd catalog. For each parameter, an early period example establishes a close link to *Revolver*, and a later period example demonstrates that the influence was lasting.

Meter is one of *Revolver*'s many areas of innovation. Everett points out that 'after "Love You To", "She Said She Said" is only the second example of contrasting meter in a Beatles song' (1999, p. 66). These songs are examples of two different kinds of metric shifts, both of which appear in Pink Floyd's music. The latter song, 'She Said She Said', uses meter to differentiate formal sections and emphasize the text with a motion to triple meter in the bridge ('when I was a boy'). An early Pink Floyd example of this kind of form-defining metric shift is 'Matilda Mother' (*The Piper at the Gates of Dawn*, 1967) with its shift from 4/4 to 6/8 for the coda (2:26 through the end). In 'Money' (*Dark Side of the Moon*, 1973), a middle-period instance, the twelve-bar blues-inspired verses move in a surprisingly smooth 7/4 (3 + 4) for eight bars, but the four-bar turnaround features a metric shift that coincides with the change in harmony.[15] Figure 3.6 shows the relevant passage; it includes bar 8 to illustrate the prevailing 7/4. The metric changes define the form as they punctuate each verse. A larger ternary form encompassing these blues verses arises from another metric shift as the central guitar solo moves to 4/4. The triplets at 3:02 announce this meter change, and the return to the irregular meter does not occur until 5:04.[16] A much later example is 'Mother' (*The Wall*, 1979), with its tense asymmetrical verses sung by Waters, primarily 8s grouped as 3 + 5 (the same partition as in 'Good Day Sunshine'), and its warm reassuring choruses in 6/8 sung by Gilmour.

The first song Everett mentions, 'Love You To', exhibits metric elasticity. The periodic bars of triple meter interspersed throughout the governing quadruple meter do not define any formal division or even disrupt the flow of time; they merely meet the demands of the content. An early Pink Floyd example of this occurs in 'Bike' (*The Piper at the Gates of Dawn*, 1967); Figure 3.7 shows the final verse.[17] The seemingly haphazard metric shifts simply support the text, and earlier verses have different patterns to match their different texts. However, that does not imply that the music is subservient to the lyrics; they are in a symbiotic relationship. A couple of later instances occur on *Wish You Were Here* (1975). Figure 3.8 shows the isolated bar of 3/4 within a prevailing 4/4, similar to 'Love You To', in 'Welcome to the Machine'.[18] 'Have a Cigar' also includes an occa-

'Money' (*Dark Side of the Moon*, 1973), 1:04–1:16

Figure 3.6   Metric punctuation

'Bike' (*The Piper at the Gates of Dawn*, 1967), 1:30–1:46

Figure 3.7   Early metric elasticity

sional 3/4 riff within the primary 4/4, for example at 0:48 in the introduction.[19] *Revolver*'s moments of ambiguous meter – particularly evident in the introductions to 'Love You To' and 'I Want To Tell You' – also influence Pink Floyd. The willingness to suspend meter entirely extends the flexibility described above, and relates to the suspension of harmonic motion discussed below.

Typical rock idioms, such as pentatonicism, fifth cycles, and extensive use of flat-VII, are prominent in the music of both bands, but the moments of harmonic inactivity on *Revolver* contribute more to Pink Floyd's style. The verses of 'Taxman', with their single harmony and repetitive bass riff, introduce the potential of static harmonic within a song framework.[20] Pink Floyd's 'Corporal Clegg' (*A Saucerful of Secrets*, 1968) seems related, with its blocks of sharp-9 chords and its similar acerbic tone. 'Eleanor Rigby' restricts harmonic motion even further, as Everett points out: 'the tonic Em and a neighboring C are its only chords' (1999, p. 53). Everett's description of 'Eleanor Rigby' applies equally well to 'Welcome to the Machine', the only exception being the two bars shown in Figure 3.8. The wandering introduction of 'Love You To' hints at the possibilities of freedom from harmonic progression, but 'Tomorrow Never Knows', embodying all of the above, is the principal model for the Pink Floyd sound.[21] Lennon's exploration of inner space has virtually no harmonic motion, a strong and extremely repetitive rhythmic ostinato, and a very heavy text. Without the usual form-defining elements, even the text consists solely of poetic verses; timbre and embellishments shape the large ternary form: introduction, verses (A), electronic exploration (B), verses (A), coda. That structure is also the blueprint for the bulk of Pink Floyd's music. The most obvious example is 'Interstellar Overdrive' with its six-bar chromatic head occurring four times at the opening (0:07–0:51) and twice at the end (8:40–9:05),

'Welcome to the Machine' (*Wish You Were Here*, 1975), 1:18–1:22

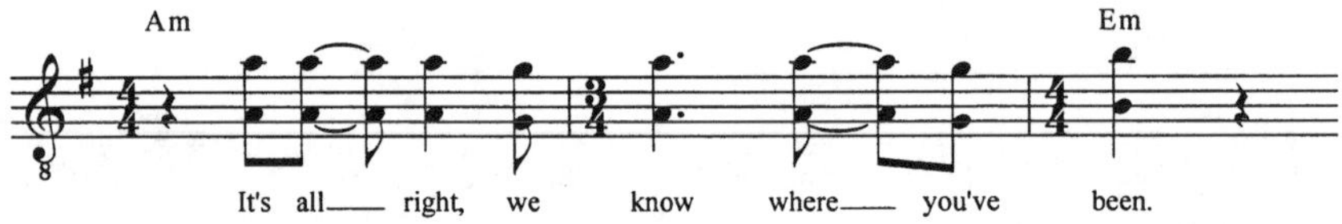

Figure 3.8   Later metric elasticity

and a rupture in the space-time (pitch-rhythm) continuum between those poles. Even Pink Floyd's version of pop songs, such as 'Arnold Layne', feature a central breakdown of harmonic progression and some wandering improvisation. The static A-major harmony, discussed back in Figure 3.4, leads from reiterations of Arnold's name to Wright's typical organ solo for a block of harmonic inactivity that amounts to approximately twenty percent of the song.

The middle section of 'Matilda Mother' also bears a particularly strong resemblance to 'Tomorrow Never Knows'. Everett notes the 'odd accent on the second half of every third beat and a constant cymbal sheen' in 'Tomorrow Never Knows' (1999, p. 36). Figure 3.9 shows the guitar accompaniment in 'Matilda Mother' from 1:24–1:55. It very closely reproduces the 'Tomorrow Never Knows' drum part, with the lower F-sharps playing the role of the bass drum and the upper tones standing in for the snare. The heavily manipulated vocal 'ch-pow' that accents the upper notes emphasizes the syncopation on the 'second half of every third beat' as well as the 'cymbal sheen'. Over this ostinato, Wright's organ solo, with its augmented seconds and turns, is loosely similar to both the backward guitar solo and the tape loops in 'Tomorrow Never Knows'.[22] There is an overall sense that this Pink Floyd passage is an impression of the Beatles' song. That is, it sounds like what might result from a band trying to play 'Tomorrow Never Knows' live.

'Matilda Mother' (*The Piper at the Gates of Dawn*, 1967), 1:24–1:55

Figure 3.9 Ch-pow!

Similar musical structures occur throughout the Pink Floyd catalog. 'Careful With That Axe, Eugene' (single, 1968) and 'One of These Days' (*Meddle*, 1971) exemplify harmonic inactivity as texture and dynamics replace harmony entirely in creating their forms.[23] The 'Atom Heart Mother Suite' (*Atom Heart Mother*, 1970) features very slow harmonic motion, but the technique culminates in 'Shine On You Crazy Diamond' (*Wish You Were Here*, 1975), which unfolds at a glacial pace. 'Echoes' (*Meddle*, 1971) and later 'Dogs' (*Animals*, 1977) include notable exploratory centers and therefore conform to the ternary structure of 'Tomorrow Never Knows'. These are just a few of the many examples that illustrate that the formal and harmonic innovations of *Revolver* resonate in Pink Floyd's music for years after its release.

Everett describes *Revolver* as 'an often mystifying blend of more new sounds from guitar and unusual instruments, sound effects, and non-Western materials, all engineered with creative wizardry' (1999, p. 33). Essentially, *Revolver* set a new standard for rock timbres and Pink Floyd leapt to embrace it. At the most basic level, the two bands share important sonic similarities generated by record-ing in the same physical spaces, with the same equipment, and with many of the same engineers at EMI. For example, this shared environment produced similar miking techniques, pervasive use of ADT (EMI's automatic double tracking), and similar stereo mixdowns. At the next level, the timbral influence of *Revolver* com-prises two broad categories: instrumentation and special effects.

The creative use of winds and strings on the album has minimal impact on Pink Floyd, probably owing to early budgetary constraints. Barrett's use of a Salvation Army band in 'Jugband Blues' (*A Saucerful of Secrets*, 1968) is a noteworthy exception. Alan Civil's recollection of being 'asked to "busk" along' on 'For No One' is not entirely unlike accounts of the 'Jugband Blues' session that describe the brass band being told 'to play "what they wanted".'[24] However, unlike Civil's poignant horn solo, the 'Jugband Blues' results are reminiscent of 'Yellow Submarine', particularly the 'organized' arrangement at 1:06–1:38, though they are reshaped in Barrett's fragmented polytonal image, particularly at 1:54–2:22. The album *Atom Heart Mother* (1970) makes more traditional use of brass on 'Summer '68' and during the title suite. 'Summer '68', with its prominent trum-pet part at 1:42–2:02 and the expanded brass section at 3:28–3:48, is closer in character to 'Got To Get You Into My Life'.[25] The arrangements in the 'Atom Heart Mother Suite' are vaguely similar to *Revolver*, but only in a generic way.[26] The main brass theme features arpeggios and neighbor tones that resonate with the 'For No One' solo, but these are typical horn gestures. The suite also features a solo cello with a prominent E-minor theme in a high register somewhat remi-niscent of 'Eleanor Rigby'. However, rather than incorporating aspects of art music into a rock context, the suite is more of an attempt at the converse, there-by making it aesthetically far removed from the Beatles.

Pink Floyd's most successful use of winds occurs later with Dick Parry's sax-ophone work on *Dark Side of the Moon* (1973) and *Wish You Were Here* (1975), though the direct link to *Revolver* is lost by then. 'The Trial' (*The Wall*, 1979) is their most ambitious orchestral effort with a fifty-five-piece arrangement by Michael Kamen. It is, however, probably closer to Gilbert and Sullivan than the Beatles (Schaffner, 1991, pp. 230–231). As keyboards improved after the breakup of the Beatles, Pink Floyd often synthesized traditional sounds rather than use acoustic players. Wright's horn and string effects on 'Shine On You Crazy Diamond' (*Wish You Were Here*, 1975) are good examples. The Beatles' experi-ments with the Mellotron brought a similar component to their music, though with their budget and George Martin's talents, orchestral players were usually more effective.[27]

While orchestral instruments exert only a minimal influence on Pink Floyd, special effects have an enormous impact. All three types of effects on *Revolver* – the everyday chatter of the introduction to 'Taxman', the humorous narrative set-ting for 'Yellow Submarine', and the abstract sounds in 'Tomorrow Never Knows' – become integral parts of Pink Floyd's music. Virtually the entire Pink

Floyd catalog employs such effects, so the following discussion presents a small sampling. Several authors point to the significance of George Harrison's artificial count-off before 'Taxman'.[28] Like 'Yellow Submarine' it incorporates mundane sounds (spoken words and ambient noises), but its placement makes it important. Not only does it critically comment on the approaching endeavor, it acts as a frame or doorway, a boundary between reality and the mystical world of *Revolver*. This seemingly trivial moment (after all, the music did not even start yet) reverberates the full length of Pink Floyd's career. An outgrowth of their underground origins, where the boundaries between audience and performer were blurred, *musique concrète* was a logical extension for their sound. Concrete frames are one of the principal building blocks of Pink Floyd's musical structures. Their first album, *The Piper at the Gates of Dawn* (1967), uses megaphone dialogue and random Morse code to frame the opening in the introduction to 'Astronomy Domine'. The sound collage coda of 'Bike' frames the end, as the coda of 'Tomorrow Never Knows' does for *Revolver*. Later works, such as *Dark Side of the Moon* (1973) and *The Wall* (1979), feature concrete frames both internally and externally. The heartbeat and sound collage 'Speak to Me' opens *Dark Side of the Moon*, while the heartbeat completes the cycle as it accompanies the spoken: 'There is no dark side of the moon really, matter of fact, it's all dark.'[29] In *The Wall* the external frame is minimal, just the spoken '… we came in' at the beginning and the matching 'isn't this where … ' at the end, but it is enough to portray the cyclical nature of the album, not unlike 'the end of the beginning' that concludes *Revolver*. Within the Pink Floyd albums, explosions, clocks, cash registers, military sounds, and spoken dialog frame the individual songs. These later examples inhabit a world apart from the Beatles and *Revolver*, but they descend directly from the earlier frames of the Barrett era.

Concrete sounds can also further a narrative as they do in 'Yellow Submarine'. The swishing water, clanking chains, and the spoken dialog set the scene for the text. 'Corporal Clegg' (*A Saucerful of Secrets*, 1968) creates a similar atmosphere through spoken dialog, though a kazoo replaces the submarine band. Pink Floyd even borrow the mocking tone of Lennon's vocal imitations in the last verse.[30] Ambient sounds – wind, animals, bells, footsteps, etc. – occur in similar roles throughout the Pink Floyd catalog. Very often these sounds are more than ambient noise; they become part of collages that represent climactic moments within the narrative. In 'Jugband Blues' (*A Saucerful of Secrets*, 1968) Barrett uses a collage to represent his eviction from the band, a process initiated before going into the studio. The collage combines the freely improvising Salvation Army band and vintage Pink Floyd psychedelia before it climaxes and ceases to exist. After a moment of silence, Barrett returns alone, accompanied only by his acoustic guitar.

The most famous example, with the possible exception of 'Speak to Me', is the sound collage at the end of 'Bring the Boys Back Home' (0:53–1:24) from *The Wall* (1979). This collage signifies the point at which the main character, Pink, transforms from a downtrodden and vulnerable musical artist to a neo-fascist rock demigod. Sounds and scenes from the past and present cascade through the character's mind, culminating in the rhetorical question: 'Is there anybody out there?' Whether metaphorical, as in 'Jugband Blues', or literal, as in 'Bring the Boys Back Home', these internal collages serve as dramatic intensifiers. Despite its great aesthetic distance from these examples, the whimsical narrative of 'Yellow Submarine' breaks the necessary ground.

Like the found sounds of *musique concrète*, the abstract sounds of signal modification form another cornerstone of Pink Floyd's music. The tape speed effects so definitive of *Revolver* make their way into Pink Floyd's repertoire. The sped-up piano of 'Good Day Sunshine' occurs in a few Pink Floyd songs, most notably in 'See Emily Play' (single, 1967) and 'Bike' (*The Piper at the Gates of Dawn*, 1967). Vocal speed effects occur throughout *Revolver* and reach an extreme in Pink Floyd's 'Several Species of Small Furry Animals Gathered Together in a Cave and Grooving with a Pict' (*Ummagumma*, 1969).[31] In this case, the technique is the same, though again the aesthetic intent is quite different. The Beatles also modify sounds with Leslie speakers on *Revolver*. 'I Want To Tell You' and 'Got To Get You Into My Life' use them for the guitars, and this effect turns up on Gilmour's guitar throughout much of *Dark Side of the Moon* (1973). Vocals through them occur during 'Eleanor Rigby' and 'Tomorrow Never Knows', and later Pink Floyd's 'Echoes' (*Meddle*, 1970).[32]

Backward tape effects are less common than the above sounds in Pink Floyd's work. However, when Tim Riley describes the backward guitar lines of 'I'm Only Sleeping' as 'surreal' and 'hallucinatory', he might as well be describing the bulk of Barrett's guitar work (1988, p. 185). Barrett did use backwards guitar, most prominently on his solo song 'Dominoes' (*Barrett*, 1970), but an amazing feature of his playing is that on many occasions it does not sound much different than a more traditional guitarist recorded in reverse. Barrett's unorthodox playing style, with its emphasis on slide, volume swells, feedback, echo, not to mention his rhythmically loose phrasing, is already surreal and hallucinatory without reversing the tape.[33] Developing his technique at underground events while *Revolver* was on the charts and in his ears, the results sound as though Barrett learned to play by doing his best to generate the backward sounds of *Revolver* in live (forward) performance.[34]

An elaborate discussion of the poetic influence of *Revolver* on Pink Floyd is beyond the scope of this chapter, maybe any chapter, but a few brief comments are necessary. Riley suggests that 'starker realities intrude on *Revolver*: embracing life also means accepting death.' He goes on to describe its 'overall tone' as 'bleak', and its 'world' as 'ominous' (1988, pp. 181–185). It sounds very similar to the world of Roger Waters, once described as the 'gloomiest man in rock' by *Q* magazine (MacDonald, 1997, p. 145). *Revolver*'s themes of money, politics, time, communication, loneliness, and death are the same concerns explored on *Dark Side of the Moon* (1973). Both albums conclude with grand litanies to altered states of consciousness, though the final destinations are rather different locations on the continuum of insanity and transcendence. The parallels between these two albums merit their own chapter.

A few additional text relations are worth noting. The eastern influence that is noticeably absent regarding instrumentation does exist regarding text, particularly in 'Chapter 24' (*The Piper at the Gates of Dawn*, 1967) and the verses of 'Set the Controls for the Heart of the Sun' (*A Saucerful of Secrets*, 1968). The title refrain of the latter song virtually charts out Pink Floyd's course to emulate the Beatles, who had already 'sailed up to the sun' in 'Yellow Submarine'. The nostalgia for the simplicity of childhood in 'She Said She Said' recurs most obviously in 'Comfortably Numb' (*The Wall*, 1979), but also earlier in 'Remember a Day' (*A Saucerful of Secrets*, 1968). Then there is the truly childlike in 'Yellow Submarine' that conjures up the fairy songs of Syd Barrett, such as 'Matilda Mother', 'The Gnome', and 'Scarecrow' (*The Piper at the Gates of Dawn*, 1967). Even beyond those are the Barrett songs where he *is* a child at play. The descriptive colours 'Sky of blue and sea of green, In our yellow submarine' become 'Lime and limpid green, a second scene, a fight between the blue you once knew' in 'Astronomy Domine'. The coincidental resonance of that example is quite different from the very literal 'Sgt Pepper's Lonely Hearts Club Band' quote shown back in Figure 3.2, but there are also all the shades between. An intriguing instance occurs in 'Flaming' (*The Piper at the Gates of Dawn*, 1967), shown in Figure 3.10. Barrett replaces Lennon's scornful attitude in 'And Your Bird Can Sing' with a more playful tone. Unlike Lennon, he does not appear to care about his subject's lack of awareness; he is content with his own awareness. While Lennon is taunting, Barrett is flaunting!

'And Your Bird Can Sing' (*Revolver*, 1967), 0:27–0:35 & 1:25–1:33

'Flaming' (*The Piper at the Gates of Dawn*, 1967), 0:24–0:32 & 0:44–0:52

Figure 3.10 'You can't see/hear me'

Conclusion

Revolver is the musical universe that spawned Pink Floyd. The innovations of meter, harmonic organization, timbre, and poetry that make *Revolver* a landmark recording are precisely the characteristics that define the Pink Floyd sound. *Sgt Pepper* makes use of many of the same techniques, and critics often consider it a more significant influence on Pink Floyd owing to the recording studio connection, but the band had already begun to develop its voice by then. Miles, after witnessing the Beatles and Pink Floyd crossing paths at EMI in 1967, stated:

> It was like the Beatles passing on the mantle – at least some of it – and acknowledging the existence of a new generation of music. In my discussions with him, McCartney had always been convinced that there would be a new synthesis of electronic music and studio techniques and rock 'n' roll. He didn't see the Beatles as being quite the vehicle for that. But the Pink Floyd, he thought, were the very stuff that we'd been talking about. (Schaffner, 1991, pp. 68–69)

To be worthy of such praise, the Pink Floyd sound had to be alive already. Compare the June 1966 cover band that was on the verge of breaking up with the original band that ruled the London underground just six months later; only *Revolver* has that kind of transformative power. The album that made *Sgt Pepper* even conceivable, is the same one that gave birth to Pink Floyd.

Notes

1. The Cavern gig took place on 14 December 1999. In addition to McCartney and Gilmour, the band included Deep Purple drummer Ian Paice, Pirates guitarist Mick Green, session keyboardist Pete Wingfield, and Chris Hall on accordion, all of whom worked on McCartney's album *Run Devil Run* (1999).
2. *Back to the Egg* features Gilmour on 'Rockestra Theme' and 'So Glad to See You Here'.
3. The tribute 'A Journey in the Life' aired on 5 December 1985. The performance also featured guitarist Andy Fairweather-Low, a member of Waters's Bleeding Heart Band from 1986–1990, who subsequently toured Japan with George Harrison.

   Digression #1: The association of McCartney with Gilmour and Lennon with Waters accentuates the similar dissolution of the two bands. Each group suffered an acrimonious rupture between guitarist and bassist, or grossly generalizing, between the talented romantic melodicists and the brilliant cynical wordsmiths. Gilmour illustrates how close the analogy hits to home when he protests: 'I hate it when you get these situations, like in the Beatles, where people say Paul did the melodies and John did the words. John could be just as melodic as Paul, and Paul could write some brilliant lyrics when he was in the right frame of mind' (MacDonald and Walker, 1991, p. 13). However, the pairing of these musicians is not rigid. Gilmour, for example, wrote his song 'Murder' (*About Face*, 1984) in reaction to Lennon's assassination. A more convincing generalization might be that each quartet was greater than the sum of its parts as evidenced by subsequent interesting, but generally weaker, solo output. Gilmour even used the Beatles as an analogy to concede that point about Pink Floyd in a 1988 interview (Schaffner, 1988, p. 76).
4. A precise date for this CBC interview is unavailable. However, as the commentator mentions

Pink Floyd performing at the Albert Hall (December 1966), but not yet debuting on record (March 1967), the interview probably took place during the first two months of 1967. It was rebroadcast as part of *The Pink Floyd Story Part I: The Early Years*, Capital Radio, London on 17 December 1976 (Hodges and Priston, 1999, p. 27).

5. Unfortunately, Cliff Jones's book *Another Brick in the Wall* is not an entirely reliable source. While there is no evidence against the veracity of this particular Bown quote, the author is guilty of a number of factual errors (mistaken dates, mislabeled photos, etc.) and a great deal of conjecture (rumors and dubious interpretations). See page 29 for an example of the former and page 9 for examples of the latter.

6. 'Lucy in the Sky with Diamonds' resonates in many Pink Floyd songs, but most of them, such as the closely related 'Point Me at the Sky' (single, 1968), are beyond the scope of this chapter.

7. Guy Capuzzo (2001) explores a wide repertoire of rock songs for systematic use of similar cyclical progressions in his paper 'Rotation as a Model for Rock Chord Progressions'.

8. Sheila Whiteley (2000a) interprets 'Lucy' as romanticized femininity, and the musical similarities between the two songs become increasingly amusing as one considers this interpretation in the context of the cross-dressing 'Arnold'.

9. Most of the Pink Floyd literature documents Barrett's rise and fall; see the references for more information, particularly Schaffner (1991) and Watkinson and Anderson (1991).

10. Lewisohn (2000) is the best source currently in print for Beatles details. There are similar works – though less complete – examining Pink Floyd, particularly Povey and Russell (1997) and Hodges and Priston (1999).

11. Miles (1980) reproduces Syd's song sheet for the London Free School gig on 14 October 1966. The set list reads: 'Pink, Let's Roll Another, Gimme a Break, Piggy Back, Stoned Alone, I Can Tell, The Gnome, Interstellar Overdrive, [interval] Lucy Leave, Stethascope [sic], Flapdoodle Dealing, Snowing, Matilda Mother, Pow.R. Toc.H., Astronomy Domine'.

12. An *IT* review of a performance at the London Free School (29 November 1966) mentions Paul McCartney's 'rave'. Miles (1980) reproduces a portion of the review and identifies the author as Norman Evans.

13. The special, directed by John Sheppard, aired on 7 February 1967. See Lewisohn (2000a, p. 241), Povey and Russell (1997, pp. 37–38), and Hodges and Priston (1999, pp. 30–33).

14. For Lennon's trip see Lewisohn (2000a, pp. 249–250), or Martin and Hornsby (1979, pp. 206–207). Most Pink Floyd sources include some Beatles EMI anecdotes, see references.

15. Surprisingly, the bars of eight and six sound more irregular than the sevens in this context. After the previously steady 7/4, it sounds as though bar 9 steals a beat from bar 10 to create this disruptive syncopation.

16. The shift to common time gives Gilmour's solo a sense of urgency after the extended bars of seven. Another form-defining metric shift occurs in the coda as it returns to 4/4. The grand conclusion of *Dark Side of the Moon*, the segue 'Brain Damage' into 'Eclipse', also features a change in meter from quadruple to triple that strengthens its effectiveness.

17. Digression #2: The extremely chromatic vocal line shown in Figure 3.7 is characteristic of Barrett's Pink Floyd. The chorus of 'Bike' transposes and expands the line further. Similar chromatic lines occur in the Beatles' music, though more commonly in inner or bass parts. On *Revolver,* notable inner chromatic lines occur in the chorus of 'Eleanor Rigby' and the bridge of 'I Want To Tell You', while chromatic bass lines support the bridge of 'And Your Bird Can Sing' and the verse of 'Got To Get You Into My Life'. However, such lines occur in much earlier Beatles music too, such as the bridge of 'It Won't Be Long' (*With the Beatles*, 1963) and the coda of 'Tell Me Why' (*A Hard Day's Night*, 1964) (Everett, 1999, p. 18). A less common and more significant example on *Revolver* is the bridge of 'I'm Only Sleeping' in which a chromatic line fleetingly surfaces in the lead vocal. This example is much closer to Barrett's chromaticism, though Lennon does not take it to the Barrett extreme until his later 'What's the New Mary Jane' (*Anthology III*, 1996).

18. When this passage returns at 4:12, the supporting harmony is A major. The change in quality

reflects the contrast between the minor-mode reality of the 'pipeline' and the major-mode 'dream' of stardom. This conflict between reality and dreams certainly resonates with the themes of *Revolver*.

19. Both of these songs also include form-defining metric shifts. 'Welcome to the Machine' moves to 6/4 for the long middle instrumental (2:38–3:54) and bars of 5/4 accompany the 'gravy train' refrain in 'Have a Cigar'.

20. The bass riff – with its octave leap, hammer-on, and flat-7 – is almost a compilation of Waters's most common gestures.

21. Everett specifically relates 'Tomorrow Never Knows' harmonically to Pink Floyd's 'Pow R. Toc H.' (*The Piper at the Gates of Dawn*, 1967) (1999, p. 324, n. 35).

22. As Andy Mabbett points out, Wright's solo is an excellent 'example of what Peter Jenner christened "one of his Turkish Delight riffs", referring to its similarity' to a contemporaneous advertisement (1995, p. 6). The core of this sound is the fifth mode of the harmonic minor scale, sometimes referred to as major phrygian, though Wright does embellish it in this solo.

23. John Cotner (1999) examines the role of texture and timbre in the formal design of 'Careful With That Axe, Eugene'.

24. Everett quotes Civil's description of events at the 'For No One' session (1999, p. 54). He also relates the 'self-negation' of 'Jugband Blues' to 'Strawberry Fields Forever' (p. 95). Most Pink Floyd sources cite the infamous 'Jugband Blues' session, but this quote comes from Mason, Gilmour, and Thorgerson (1992, p. 21).

25. 'Summer '68', particularly the untexted vocalizations, also suggests the influence of the Beach Boys, whose impact on the Beatles is well documented.

26. Composer Ron Geesin wrote, orchestrated, and arranged the additional instruments used in the 'Atom Heart Mother Suite'.

27. Pink Floyd occasionally dabbled with the Mellotron during the late '60s, but despite its continuing popularity with other bands in the early '70s, they became more enamored of EMS' VCS3. The VCS3 is probably best known for generating the electronic instrumental 'On the Run' (*Dark Side of the Moon*, 1973).

28. See Everett (1999, p. 34) and Riley (1988, p. 182).

29. Jerry Driscoll, the doorman at EMI during these sessions, provided the voice and text for this conclusion, as well as a few of the other memorable comments on the album (Fitch, 1999, p. 91).

30. Incidentally, Pink Floyd performed 'Yellow Submarine' at least once as they 'joined in the grand finale: a tongue-in-cheek rendition' of the song at a 12 December 1966 benefit at the Albert Hall (Povey and Russell, 1997, p. 36).

31. The Beatles alter vocal speeds in 'I'm Only Sleeping', 'Here, There and Everywhere', 'Yellow Submarine', 'She Said She Said', and 'For No One' (Everett, 1999, pp. 49–65).

32. The sonic 'ping' that begins 'Echoes' is also the result of a Leslied piano. The text and vocal line of 'Echoes' is very similar to 'Across the Universe' (*Let It Be*, 1970) and therefore the effects probably derive from that source rather than *Revolver*.

33. The primary component in Barrett's sound was the Binson Echorec, though unusual slides like his Zippo lighter and ball bearings certainly contributed to his unique style.

34. Digression #3: Gilmour's early work with the band, as a self-conscious stand-in for Barrett, is similar to Barrett's in style. His own voice begins to surface around 1970, on *Atom Heart Mother*, and he firmly establishes himself by *Dark Side of the Moon* (1973). Pink Floyd's film *Live at Pompeii* (1972) vividly documents Gilmour's transition. One hears the last vestiges of Barrett in 'A Saucerful of Secrets', witnesses the emerging guitar hero in 'Echoes', and gets the first glimpse of the mature Gilmour recording tracks for *Dark Side of the Moon*.

Part II

'It is shining'

Revolver's musicality

Chapter 4

Revolver as a pivotal art work: structure, harmony, and vocal harmonization

Stephen Valdez

In 1965 and 1966, rock music was undergoing significant changes, turning away from the typical teen-oriented love song to a more refined commentary of the time. Many popular musicians were at the forefront of this change: Bob Dylan, the Byrds, and the Grateful Dead were all leaders in their styles. Practically everyone looked to the Beatles as leaders of this trend, and, whether they wanted to be or not, they were leaders. The music of the Beatles had been growing and changing like a living entity since their first release in 1962. The growth was gradual: non-rock instruments were introduced into rock music, song structures gradually changed the shape of popular song, and lyrics grew in sophistication to become descriptive poems set to music.

Revolver is the pivotal album of the Beatles' career, and, consequently, it is the pivotal album, or one of them, in the history of rock music. Although they played their last concert at the end of August 1966, the recording sessions for *Revolver*, beginning in April 1966, demonstrate that the Beatles were concerned with creating studio art works rather than the dance-oriented pop songs that could readily be reproduced live. Many of the sounds on *Revolver* could not have been reproduced in their concerts, yet in many ways the Beatles retained a measure of their early musical style in the songs that appear on the album. *Revolver* evenly balances conservative, traditional rock musical practice with progressive, experimental techniques. All musical elements – sound, structure, time, melody, and harmony – are treated both traditionally and experimentally at some point on the album, and this is what makes *Revolver* such a fascinating work of art and why the album has stood so well for almost forty years. We immediately recognize the overall sound of the Beatles, the unique tone colors of their voices, and the artistic quality of their work. While every musical element is interesting to work with, in this study I will concentrate on the elements of structure and harmony in order to present an understanding of some of the parts that make up the whole.

Structure

All of the songs on *Revolver* are either strophic song forms, with alternating verses and choruses, or standard (AABA) song forms, consisting of a verse (A) and contrasting bridge (B). The strophic form is common to folk music styles, including the blues that is the primary basis of rock music. Of course, standard song form, a more contrived song structure common in American popular music (particularly ballads), also influenced the development of rock. The legacy of standard song form – especially the compositions of popular songwriters like George Gershwin, Jerome Kern, Cole Porter, among others – generally dictates a balanced structure in which the length of the A section is equal to the length of the B section. This frequently resulted, during the 'golden age of American popular song' (roughly 1925 through 1950), in a song structure in which each section consisted of eight measures, yielding a thirty-two-measure form.[1]

Examples of strophic song form on *Revolver* are 'Eleanor Rigby', 'Love You To', 'Yellow Submarine', 'Good Day Sunshine', 'For No One', 'Got To Get You Into My Life' and 'Tomorrow Never Knows'. Of these, the songs 'Love You To', 'Yellow Submarine' and 'Good Day Sunshine' alternate verses with a recurring chorus, although the last song begins with the chorus while the first two both begin with the verse; 'Tomorrow Never Knows' consists of a series of verses with no recurring choruses. These three songs represent the traditional aspect of strophic form on the album.

The other three strophic songs incorporate aspects of experimentation. 'Eleanor Rigby' begins with an introduction that recurs as an interlude between the second chorus and the third verse, and then appears again as a countermelody against the final chorus. McCartney's 'For No One' presents the strophic song form in another experimental way. Upon the return of the verse after the first chorus, symphonic hornist Alan Civil performs a solo, which later turns out to be a countermelody to the final verse. The chorus is repeated followed by two statements of the verse and a final presentation of the chorus ends the song. The harmony at the end of the chorus is constructed as a turnaround, that is, it harmonically sets up a return of the verse progression. However, with the song ending on the turnaround, we are presented with a feeling of unfinished business not only harmonically but structurally as well. The unfinished character of the harmony and the structure leaves the listener expecting more. Harmonically, the 4-3 suspension F-sharp chord demands a resolution to the tonic chord, but the harmony is left unresolved. The open-ended feeling of the bridge suggests a return of the verse, which harmonically closes on the tonic, but the song denies us this closure as well. These musical representations of non-resolution heighten the understanding of McCartney's lyrics: the music tells us that there are unresolved matters in the relationship, at least in the narrator's point of view.

'Got To Get You Into My Life' presents a strophic structure and recurring refrain cleverly constructed so as to blur the distinction between strophic and standard forms. Sixteen measures long, the verse consists of two eight-measure periods. The first period alternates the tonic G chord with the subtonic F chord; to the ear, this harmony is clearly unfinished, ending as it does on the weak subtonic, so it cannot be considered a complete verse. The second period begins on the mediant B minor chord supported by a bass line that descends chromatically from B to A-flat. This phrase is repeated, followed by a third phrase that harmonically closes the verse with a subdominant gesture (C, E minor7, and A minor7) to the dominant (D7) to tonic (G) cadence. At this point the listener has a feeling of closure; the verse is complete.

The verse is repeated but this time leads to the refrain. Six measures long, the refrain consists of the title phrase sung as a hook for two measures followed by an instrumental fill played by the horn and rhythm sections. The brevity of the refrain creates a striking imbalance against the sixteen-measure verse. Too short to be considered a chorus, it is also too short to be considered a bridge. Yet the way in which McCartney uses the refrain implies the AABA structure of standard song form: verse one, verse two, refrain, verse 3, refrain, refrain, coda. This structure of the song, in conjunction with the harmonic progression, shows a strophic form, but the clever application of the refrain causes one to wonder whether it is a standard song form – the distinction is effectively blurred.

The other seven songs on the album are examples of standard song form. The songs that exhibit conservative or traditional traits of standard song form are 'Here, There, and Everywhere', 'She Said She Said', 'And Your Bird Can Sing' and 'I Want To Tell You'. However, even in these songs we encounter various degrees of imbalance: 'She Said She Said' features ten-measure verses against an eleven-measure bridge, 'I Want To Tell You' has eleven-measure verses countered by an eight-measure bridge, and 'Here, There, and Everywhere' presents eight-measure verses with a four-measure bridge. Only 'And Your Bird Can Sing' follows the traditional standard song structure of thirty-two measures, with verse and bridge sections balanced at eight measures each. This asymmetry of sections is of course not new to the Beatles or to popular music; there are many previous examples, both by the Beatles and their predecessors, in which the bridge is shorter or longer than the verse. My point is that these songs, imbalanced as they are, still represent the more traditional aspects of standard song form on *Revolver*. Other songs on the album are more radically imbalanced between sections, for instance 'Doctor Robert' in which eighteen-measure verses are countered by a ten-measure bridge.

The most progressive examples of song form on *Revolver* occur in the songs 'Taxman' and 'I'm Only Sleeping'. Hybrids of both strophic and standard forms, these songs have the clearly defined verses and choruses of the strophic, yet they also have the bridge sections characteristic of standard form. Both songs are represented in the form:

[verse/chorus] [verse/chorus] bridge [verse/chorus]
    A   A   B   A

so that, if the verse and chorus are considered together as a unit, the form resembles the AABA structure of standard song form. Yet, because of the clear delineation between the verse and the chorus, the songs depart from the traditional standard song form.

Hybrid strophic/standard song forms were not the norm in the mid-1960s, although the Beatles and others had certainly experimented with them earlier. Already in their debut album *Please Please Me* (1963), the song 'I Saw Her Standing There' is a standard song form in which the verse section presents a recurring chorus-like segment that contains the hook of the song and sounds essentially like a chorus, though it is not a chorus. After *Revolver*, hybrid strophic/standard song forms appear more frequently in the Beatles' corpus, for example 'With a Little Help From My Friends' on *Sgt Pepper* (1967). By the 1970s, most rock groups had adopted this structure, and today practically every rock and pop song on commercial radio and recordings take this form.

Many songs in standard form repeat both the bridge and the final verse, resulting in an overall form of AABABA. This brief repetition is present in most of the standard songs on *Revolver*. Again the Beatles take some liberties with this basic format: Harrison, in 'Taxman', presents the bridge only once in the song but repeats the verse and chorus segments twice after the bridge, resulting in an overall form of AABAA. In 'Doctor Robert', Lennon repeats the bridge and goes immediately into the coda of the song, creating an overall form of AABAB (coda). However, since the coda is derived from the guitar riff and lyrics of the first part of the verse, it sounds as if the form of the song follows the conventional AABABA structure; not until the coda begins to fade do we realize that the song form proper ended with the bridge.

The introductions and/or codas of some songs also contribute to the successful presentation of structure. Most of the songs on *Revolver* feature a brief two- or four-measure introduction, for example 'Taxman' and 'Doctor Robert', in which the basic accompanimental riff sets the stage for the rest of the song. Many songs have a coda derived from either verse or chorus material. Some songs, like 'For No One', have neither introductions nor codas. Others feature an innovative use of introductory material, such as 'Eleanor Rigby''s use of its introduction as both interlude and countermelody. One such interesting introduction appears in Harrison's song 'Love You To'.

The unique 'Love You To' represents Harrison's first real excursion into North Indian music. Having been introduced to the sound of the sitar by Byrd guitarist David Crosby, Harrison had first used the instrument in the accompaniment of 'Norwegian Wood' on *Rubber Soul* (1965). However, the use of the sitar on 'Norwegian Wood' was more in the way of a western instrument, in that it was used to double Lennon's vocal melody. With 'Love You To' Harrison makes a whole-hearted attempt to reproduce the Indian style of music which he had been studying since June 1966 with Ravi Shankar (Everett, 1999, p. 40). He stated that '["Love You To"] was the first song where I consciously tried to use the sitar and tabla on the basic track' (Harrison, 1980, p. 102). This is the only song on *Revolver* in which none of the other three Beatles takes part, either as vocalists or instrumentalists.

Based on Indian practice, the introduction of 'Love You To' begins with two upward strokes of the plectrum on the svaramandal, from high to low pitches. This is followed by a brief, free-metered section, called *alap*, in which the sitar outlines the *raga*, or mode, of the piece. This improvised melody gradually rises and falls in pitch and increases the rhythmic intensity before ending on the tonic note, or sa in the Indian system. At this point the tabla enters to establish the *tala*, or rhythm, while a tamboura establishes the key by droning the *sa* and *pa*, the tonic and dominant pitches, of the *raga*. This introduction effectively sets up the Indian mood of the song.

The creativity that the Beatles employ in regard to song structure demonstrates the pivotal nature of these songs, and thus the pivotal nature of *Revolver* as a whole. Most of the Beatles' earlier songs remained true to traditional strophic and standard forms. The structural experimentation on *Revolver* led to further experimentation on a larger scale, including the conceptual structures of *Sgt Pepper's Lonely Hearts Club Band* and the second side of *Abbey Road*. Occurring contemporaneously with works by Bob Dylan, Frank Zappa, Mick Jagger and Keith Richards, and Brian Wilson, the Beatles' conceptions of structure changed forever from the simple strophic and standard pop formats to more original structures defined by the design of the lyrics.

Harmony

Two aspects of harmony on *Revolver* should be considered: the overall chord progressions of the songs and the manner in which the lead and supporting vocals are harmonized above the chord progressions. As with structural concerns, the songs of *Revolver* provide examples of traditional and experimental harmony. Although the chord progressions are not thoroughly traditional, often employing seventh chords in non-dominant functions, many progressions function traditionally relative to the blues foundation of rock. This discussion explores the Beatles' approach to harmony, illustrating both traditional and experimental aspects of harmony.

Many songs on *Revolver* are written in basic diatonic harmony. Their classic children's song, 'Yellow Submarine', is a well-known example of the Beatles' more traditional harmonic writing. Everything about the song presents an idea of simplicity: the words are immediately intelligible, the rhythms easy to sing, and the melody, with its small range, easy to remember. Perhaps the most traditional harmonic progression on the album, the diatonic progression of the verse in G major also depicts simplicity:

```
I V7 IV I    vi        ii     V
G D  C  G  E minor  A minor  D7
```

The opening phrase of the verse presents a traditional harmonic departure from tonic to dominant (G to D7) immediately followed by a soft plagal return from subdominant to tonic (C to G) – two different traditional harmonic motions melded together in an opening gesture. The remaining half of the verse progression flows easily to the half cadence, the dominant D7 approached by the relative minor of the key (E minor) and the minor supertonic (A minor) – a very traditional progression leading to the chorus.

In Harrison's song 'I Want To Tell You', the harmonic progression of the verse is also traditional, a three-chord structure in A major:

```
I  V7/V  V7  I
A  B7    E7  A
```

However, as basic as the chord progression is in this song, the application of dissonances in the accompaniment brings out an experimental character of this song. The presence of the tritone F-natural/B in the piano part on the E7 chord intentionally upsets the traditional aspect of the harmony:

Figure 4.1   'I Want To Tell You', verse 1, m. 6, accompaniment

The harmonic progression of the bridge is interesting in that the chord progression is the result of a chromatically descending inner voice. The bridge progression remains essentially in A major, although the emphasis on B (major, minor, and diminished chords) presents a briefly contrasting harmony, a common feature of the bridge:

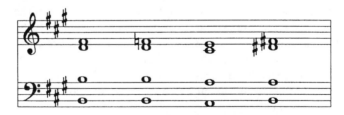

Figure 4.2   'I Want To Tell You', bridge, mm. 1–4, harmony

While the fundamental harmony of 'I Want To Tell You' is traditional, the chromatic motion of the inner lines, particularly in the bridge, moves the song closer to an experimental application of harmony.

Another song by Harrison, the album opener 'Taxman', presents a relatively traditional approach to harmony as well. The song is based on a repetitive guitar riff on a D7 chord; the harmony of the verse and refrain appears to be a simple progression in the D Mixolydian mode; however, the lowered third scale degree (F natural), used as the seventh of the subdominant G7 chord, acts as a blue cross relation with the F-sharp of the key:

I7   VII   IV7   I7
D7   C   G7   D7

The harmony of the bridge shifts between the tonic D7 and the subtonic C7, contributing to the modal, rather than tonal, harmonic tendencies of 'Taxman'.

Harmonies and melodies on *Revolver* frequently exploit modal tendencies. Modality can be said to have existed in rock music since its inception because of the strong influence of the blues on the music. Blues harmony and melody are modal rather than tonal through the use of the blue, or slightly lowered, third and seventh scale degrees. Since the earliest rock 'n' roll developed from the blues, and the Beatles were influenced by those early forms, it stands to reason that blues modality is present in their compositions. In addition, the folk music of Great Britain and the US with which the Beatles were also familiar (and by which they were influenced) is often modal as well. And, of course, their experimentation with Indian music led them to explore eastern modalities. The Beatles had earlier used non-blues modality, for example in Lennon's 'Norwegian Wood'; in this song the verse is written in E Mixolydian while the bridge is written in E Dorian. They experimented with non-blues modality even further on *Revolver*.

'Tomorrow Never Knows' is another such modal piece, not quite a western mode but not quite an eastern mode either. The foundation of the song is a bass guitar riff that emphasizes a pedal C with a brief, syncopated B-flat on the upbeat of beat three:

Figure 4.3   'Tomorrow Never Knows', introduction, m. 3, bass riff

The bass riff is strongly supported by the drum rhythm. In addition to the C riff, the tamboura, the first instrument heard on the track, drones the pitch C throughout the piece and the organ fills in block chords on C7 and B-flat. 'Tomorrow Never Knows' is based on the C mixolydian mode (a C major scale with a B-flat rather than a B natural) with the solo melody, sung by Lennon, outlining a C7 chord (C-E-G-B-flat). Oddly, this same tonic to subtonic motion when used in

'Taxman' is perceived as a western modality because of the vocal harmonization that works with the chord progression. The lack of other pitches from the mode in 'Tomorrow Never Knows' emphasizes the mysterious quality of the sound, while the stark, almost chant-like melody is a perfect vehicle for the philosophically serious content of the lyrics.

'Eleanor Rigby' also experiments with mode, though more of an English folk-like approach to modality than an eastern approach. The harmony of the song proper is essentially in E minor following the C major introduction; the chorus, while still based on an E minor mode, features a chromatically descending inner part played by the first viola, resulting in the chromatic harmony E minor-E minor7-C6-E minor. The melody of the verse fluctuates between E Dorian (with the use of C-sharp) and E aeolian (with a C natural).[2]

In Harrison's song 'Love You To', the modal basis of the raga is the Indian *kafi that* in C, which corresponds to the western C Dorian mode. Dorian melodies and harmonies frequently occur in rock music, due in part to the ease in which the Dorian mode fits the hand and the guitar fretboard. Furthermore, the mode closely approximates the blues mode, with lowered third and lowered seventh scale degrees, but a natural sixth degree. At any rate, the harmonic and melodic structure of 'Love You To' is clearly based on Indian modal practice: the tamboura drones sa and pa (tonic and dominant notes of the mode), the tabla sets forth a sixteen-beat tala (rhythm), the introductory improvisation in the alap follows Indian melodic practice, and as Harrison stated, he was trying to express himself in Hindu terms. This is a new turn for the Beatles and for rock music in general; the culmination of Hindu-based rock appears in the so-called 'raga rock' of the late 1960s. Practitioners of raga rock, besides the Beatles, include the Byrds, the Rolling Stones, the Buffalo Springfield, the Paul Butterfield Blues Band, and the Yardbirds.[3]

In McCartney's 'Good Day Sunshine' we have a song that clearly straddles the Beatles' old and new styles. The harmony, which on a local level makes tonal sense, is ambiguous when seen in the light of the actual key in which the song was written. The chorus clearly tonicizes B major:

```
I      V       IV
B  F-sharp  E
```

However, the verse is written in A major and follows the progression A-F-sharp7-B7-E7, incorporating a secondary dominant of the secondary dominant as a sub-dominant substitution:

```
I   V7/V7/V7   V7/V   V7
A   F-sharp7    B7    E7
```

This results in a progression that is tonally ambiguous: it is unclear if the harmony is in A major or B major.

'Doctor Robert' features another variety of ambiguous harmony. On the surface, the song seems to be traditional, but hidden eccentricities demonstrate how experimental the Beatles were becoming. The harmony of 'Doctor Robert' is in A major and stresses the tonic with a flattened seventh from the country-like introduction through the first nine measures of the verse. The last half of the verse tonicizes the supertonic B with the use of major submediant (F-sharp7) as a secondary dominant. The further stress on B major in the bridge, which shifts from B major to E major over a pedal B in the bass and guitar parts, also seems to point to a tonic on B major. However, suddenly the harmony shifts to an A7 chord as the introductory riff reappears to bring about a return to the verse. The harmonic ambiguity of 'Doctor Robert' has been suggested to be an aural depiction of mind expansion; the song is notoriously known as one of Lennon's drug songs with various explanations for its origins given. As Walter Everett points out, 'such irregular tonal contrasts will be exercised more often in the psychedelic songs of 1967' (Everett, 1999, p. 46).

One of the most experimental endeavors on *Revolver* is Lennon's 'I'm Only Sleeping'. The recording quality evokes the hazy, sleep-like quality associated with hallucinogens, a fitting atmospheric effect for one of Lennon's first drug songs. Shifting between E-flat minor and G-flat major, the harmony gives the song a dark tone color that fits the dream-oriented ambiance. An interesting experimental touch is presented with a guitar solo that is recorded backwards, also contributing to the dream-like effect of the song.

On the hook phrase – 'I'm only sleeping' – the three voices (Lennon, McCartney, and Harrison) harmonize 'sleeping' on a tonic triad. The voicing of the vocal harmony – B-flat, E-flat, and G-flat, lowest to highest pitch – adds to the modal sonority and is reminiscent of the English Renaissance technique of vocal polyphony known as faburden.[4] This harmony, however, is supported very softly by the bass guitar on a C-flat, turning the actual chord into a C-flat major 7 chord, the subdominant of the relative G-flat, thereby anticipating the tonic harmony a full measure before the accompanying instruments reach the chord:

Figure 4.4   'I'm Only Sleeping', refrain, m. 5

The comparatively low volume of the bass tone against the force of the vocal harmony creates a harmonic ambiguity that is nearly negated in favor of the minor tonic triad.

The songs on *Revolver* present the listener with a variety of chord progressions. Like the song structures on the album, the chord progressions explore a spectrum from traditional, rock-based harmonies to experimental chord structures that in 1966 were generally atypical in rock. The Beatles' experiments with harmony on *Revolver* are not without precedence; similar experimental harmonies are found in songs from the album and single releases leading up to *Revolver*. These chord progressions clearly influenced the harmonic language of many songs that followed. However, on *Revolver* there is an aesthetic balance between traditional and progressive chord progressions that emphasizes the pivotal quality of the album.

Vocal harmonization

One of the most individual characteristics of the Beatles' recordings was the manner in which they harmonized their melody lines. Their vocal harmonizations, series of parallel dyads and triads, work with and against the basic harmonic structure supplied by the accompanying instruments. The result is an interesting fabric of consonant chord harmonies mixed with dissonant passing and neighbor harmonies over triadic and seventh-chord accompaniments.

The Beatles developed their style of harmonized singing from a number of influences. The full three-part harmonization of such Beatles songs as 'Here, There, and Everywhere', for example, is influenced by the harmonizing styles of Soul and Motown vocal groups such as Smokey Robinson and the Miracles (the Beatles had covered the Miracles' 'You've Really Got A Hold On Me' on *With the Beatles*) and especially the girl groups like the Shirelles ('Baby It's You') and the Marvelettes ('Please Mr Postman'). Another source of the Beatles' vocal harmonization was the dual-harmony style of the Everly Brothers ('Wake Up, Little Susie' and 'All I Have To Do Is Dream'), particularly influential on the singing styles of Lennon and McCartney, and the solo call/harmonized response style of Buddy Holly and the Crickets ('Oh Boy'), sometimes reversed by the Beatles to be a harmonized call and solo response.

From their earliest singles to their final albums, the Beatles' style of vocal harmonizing was unique – for example, the parallel open fifths that predominate in 'Love Me Do' or the parallel chord voicings that open 'Eleanor Rigby' – and it is this trait that so strongly influenced contemporary and later performers. In the instances of songs featuring full three-part harmony, Lennon, McCartney, and Harrison tend to sing in block chords, typically root position chords but also chord voicings as dictated by voice leading. This style of vocal harmonization is derived mostly from the cover songs that the Beatles recorded, but, in part, their harmonizations are derived from the chords played on their accompanying instruments. Because they principally used guitars to accompany themselves, the resulting harmonies the Beatles sing are often based on the tunings of those instruments – fourths, fifths, and thirds. The dual harmonizations of Lennon and

McCartney (sometimes Lennon or McCartney and Harrison) in imitation of the Everly Brothers are also often based on the tunings of their guitars as well as the parallel thirds and sixths common in the Everlys' songs.

From their earliest recordings, the Beatles' use of vocal harmony often defined the structure of their songs. The Beatles use vocal harmonization in three important structural ways: (1) to reinforce or emphasize the hook or to emphasize the climactic point of a song, (2) to contrast or differentiate the various song sections (such as the verse from the chorus or the verse from the bridge), and (3) to underscore the importance of certain lyrics or help describe the lyrics and relate the narrative. Sometimes vocal harmony is used throughout a song in conjunction with changes in vocalizing techniques, such as changing from harmonized words to harmonized 'oohs' and 'aahs'. A fourth use of vocal harmonization could be said to exist in a very few instances throughout the Beatles' career in which harmonization is completely absent in favor of a solo melody supported by instruments: Harrison's 'Don't Bother Me', McCartney's 'Yesterday', and Lennon's 'Any Time At All' are notable examples of Beatles songs that do not use harmonized vocals. As with other musical elements on *Revolver*, the use of vocal harmonies is sometimes traditional and sometimes experimental.

The more traditionally harmonized songs are 'Eleanor Rigby', 'Here, There, and Everywhere', 'Yellow Submarine', 'She Said She Said', 'Good Day Sunshine', and 'I Want To Tell You'. In a more experimental vein are 'Taxman', 'I'm Only Sleeping', 'Love You To', 'And Your Bird Can Sing', and 'Doctor Robert'. The songs 'For No One', 'Got To Get You Into My Life', and 'Tomorrow Never Knows' do not use harmony vocals.

Just as its standard song form is traditional, the vocal harmony of McCartney's 'Here, There, and Everywhere' is likewise traditional. The harmonic progression is an ascending diatonic harmony in the verse:

```
I      ii         iii     IV
G   A minor   B minor   C
```

and an even more traditional G minor progression in the bridge:

```
V7/III   III        i          iv        V7
 F7     B-flat   G minor   C minor   D7
```

The vocal harmony is a three-part harmonization overdubbed onto McCartney's lead vocal in the verses; the bridge is sung as a solo melody with instrumental accompaniment. The use of harmonization in the verse contrasted with the lack of vocal harmony in the bridge defines the structure of the song.

The vocal harmony in the verses consists of simple root position triads that follow the basic diatonic harmony. The only change in this chord structure occurs with a ii/vi chord (F-sharp minor) in measures 5 and 6 and the vi chord (E minor) of measure 7 where, because of voice-leading, the chord structure becomes inverted:

Figure 4.5   'Here, There, and Everywhere', verse 1, mm. 3–8, vocal harmony

An interesting touch to the vocal harmony occurs in measures 5 and 6 of the final verse where a bit of counterpoint has been added to the main melody. A counter-melody sung by Lennon is overdubbed onto McCartney's melody and the accompanying triadic vocal harmonization. The oblique motion of Lennon's descending line creates passing consonances and dissonances (unison, major second, major third, perfect fourth) with McCartney's static melody:

Figure 4.6   'Here, There, and Everywhere', final verse, m. 5, lead and harmony vocal

In all, the harmony vocals in 'Here, There, and Everywhere' represent a look back to where the Beatles had been, reminiscent especially of the harmonization used in the Beatles' first number one hit single, 'Please Please Me', in 1963.

The vocal harmony in 'Eleanor Rigby' can also be considered traditional in that the harmonized vocals differentiate the introduction from the verse/chorus unit. The three-part harmonized introduction recurs as an interlude after the second chorus and the top-line melody of the introduction is presented as a harmonized counterpoint to the final chorus. This harmony – from lowest to highest, Harrison, Lennon, McCartney – begins on a second inversion of a C major triad and ascends and descends diatonically in parallel motion until the final syllable of the word 'lonely'. At this point, Harrison drops out of the harmony leaving a duet in thirds between Lennon and McCartney:

Figure 4.7   'Eleanor Rigby', introduction, mm. 1–3, lead and harmony vocals

The descending harmonized melody leads into the stark solo melody of the verse and contributes dramatically to the song's lyrical themes of loneliness and alienation.

The use of harmonized vocals on the introduction/interlude not only sets this section apart from the verse and chorus, the harmonization also emphasizes the underlying theme of McCartney's lyrics. The song is not just about a lonely old woman and her lonely pastor; rather, it is about all the lonely people in the world. George Martin's stark, Bernard Herrmann-inspired string accompaniment and the harmonic shift from C major to E minor in the introduction emphasizes the angst that comes with loneliness. As Tim Riley states, the 'opening "ahs" are not soothing, they're aching' (Riley, 1988, p. 184). This theme is further emphasized in the final chorus in which the upper line of the introduction (McCartney's part) is overdubbed on top of McCartney's solo melody:

Figure 4.8 **'Eleanor Rigby', final chorus, mm. 1–8**

Vocal harmonization is used in 'She Said She Said' to help relate the narrative of the song. Solo melody indicates the narrator ('She said') while harmonized vocals are used to indicate that character's statements ('I know what it's like ... '). The harmony, sung by Harrison beneath Lennon's melody, is performed primarily in parallel thirds. The only non-tertian vocal harmony in the song occurs in measure 5 of the verses, when Harrison sings a perfect fourth below Lennon on the words 'be sad' (verse 1), 'I'm mad' (verse 2) and 'to leave' (verses 3 and 4). Non-tertian intervals also appear in measures 7–8 and 10–11 of the bridge on the opening syllable (perfect fifth) and the final syllable (perfect fourth) of the phrase 'Everything's alright':

Figure 4.9 'She Said She Said', bridge, mm. 7–8

The coda of the song fades with a unison echo performance between Lennon and Harrison, almost, but not quite, suggesting a resolution to the song's drama of battling personas.

The use of vocal harmony in 'Good Day Sunshine' is also traditional: it is used in the chorus, which sets the chorus apart from the solo vocal line of the verse, and since the chorus is also the hook of the song, the vocal harmony also emphasizes the hook:

Figure 4.10 'Good Day Sunshine', chorus, mm. 3–6

The emphasis of the hook by means of vocal harmonization in 'Good Day Sunshine' is especially brought out in the pseudocounterpoint of the coda as the song fades out.

Unlike the harmonic ambiguity of the song, the vocal harmony in 'Doctor Robert' appears to be more traditional in style. The first verse is sung by Lennon as a solo melody with accompaniment. From the start of the second verse through the rest of the song, McCartney harmonizes Lennon's melody. For the first part of the verse (measures 1–7), McCartney sings diatonically a third above Lennon over the tonic seventh chord. With the ambiguous tonal shift toward the supertonic in the last half of the verse (measures 10–18), the interval of the vocal harmony widens to emphasize perfect fourths and fifths on sustained notes:

Figure 4.11 'Doctor Robert', verse 2, mm. 10–13

The use of perfect intervals at this point heightens the tension of the song after the more smoothly presented parallel thirds.

The bridge, which harmonically settles on B major, also features total harmonization between the vocal parts. Here, Lennon and McCartney sing ascending and descending contrapuntal lines against sustained chords in the harmonium and pedal notes (B) in the bass guitar and lead guitar. On the first phrase, the vocal harmony begins on a third and widens to a tenth at the end of the phrase:

Figure 4.12   'Doctor Robert', bridge, mm. 1–4

The second phrase repeats this figure but concludes on a third, leading back to a repetition of the opening guitar riff on the tonic A7 and a return of the verse harmonized in thirds. Although vocal harmony is used throughout 'Doctor Robert' from the second verse on, the form of the song is defined by the way in which the Beatles utilize vocal harmony: homorhythmically with flowing parallel thirds in the first part of the verse, homorhythmically with increased tension introduced through the use of perfect fourths and fifths in the second part of the verse, and contrapuntally against the sustained chords of the accompaniment in the bridge.

In Lennon's song 'And Your Bird Can Sing', vocal harmonization is used primarily to emphasize the hook of the song. The title is first harmonized in measure 3 of the first verse as McCartney sings a perfect fourth above Lennon's lead melody for two beats before converging on parallel thirds:

Figure 4.13   'And Your Bird Can Sing', verse 1, mm. 3–4

The song suddenly reverts to a solo melody for the next phrase on the supertonic (F-sharp minor), and McCartney returns with a major third above on the last syllable of the verse, emphasizing the statement 'you don't get me'.

The sporadic use of harmony vocal on the hook is not as traditional as with earlier songs, which brings out an experimental aspect of *Revolver*. Yet the lack of harmonized vocals in the bridge, contrasting with the slight harmonization of the verse, is a more traditional and structural use of vocals. This traditional feeling is further accentuated with the three-part harmonization of the last verse, on the phrase 'You tell me that you've heard every sound there is ... ' The phrase is harmonized by McCartney and Harrison, respectively an octave and a sixth higher than Lennon. The harmony lines gradually descend diatonically until the three singers form root position triads:

Figure 4.14   'And Your Bird Can Sing', verse 4, mm. 1–4

With this traditional use of vocal harmony, we have perhaps 'heard every sound there is', though considering the sparse harmonization of the earlier verses, Lennon implies that we have not heard everything the Beatles have to say, a perfect statement for the blending of traditional and experimental characteristics that permeate *Revolver*.

More experimental in application of vocal harmony is the opener of the album, Harrison's 'Taxman'. Used sparingly at the outset of the song, vocal harmony gradually increases as the song progresses. The first two verses are sung solo to the accompaniment of the D7 riff; in the refrains the hook of the song, 'yeah, I'm the Taxman', is harmonized by McCartney a third above Harrison's lead vocal, with additional dissonant seconds, ending on a perfect fourth:

Figure 4.15 'Taxman', refrain, mm. 2–4

Vocal harmony is used more extensively in the bridge. In this section, performed as call and response, Lennon and McCartney sing a harmonized call that states the situation ('If you drive a car') which is followed by Harrison's response over their sustained harmony, which indicates the resulting action ('I'll tax the street') from the Taxman. Presented as two sets of antecedent and consequent phrases based on the D7 and C7 chords, both phrases begin with a perfect fourth that converges to a major third. The antecedent phrase sustains a major third above Harrison's descending melody while the consequent phrase sustains a perfect fourth above Harrison's descending line, ending with a root position tonic triad on the word 'Taxman':

Figure 4.16 'Taxman', bridge, mm. 4–11

The use of vocal harmony is increased in the subsequent verses: as call and response in perfect fifths ('Ah ah, Mr Wilson') in verse three and as call and response on a perfect fifth ('Taxman') in verse four. This last harmonization in fifths is also used in the coda.

An experimental use of vocal harmony also characterizes both the verse and the refrain of Lennon's 'I'm Only Sleeping'. In the verse, the vocal harmony occurs as call and response in which McCartney and Harrison sing in descending parallel thirds, reinforcing the idea of the text, but melodically in opposition to Lennon's ascending phrase:

Float up— stream————————(Float up—stream)———

Figure 4.17   'I'm Only Sleeping', verse 1, mm. 8–9

But, in the refrain, which contains the song's hook, Harrison and McCartney sing wordless vocalizations in thirds and fourths against Lennon's rising and falling, sing-songlike melody. The harmony vocals end in fourths on a harmonic cross-relation to Lennon's melody, creating an uncomfortable dissonance that contributes to the dream-like quality:

Figure 4.18   'I'm Only Sleeping', refrain, mm. 3–4

On the hook phrase – 'I'm only sleeping' – the three voices harmonize 'sleeping' on a tonic triad, as discussed above.

The truncated bridge is double-tracked by Lennon when he sings the melody in unison until he reaches the phrase 'going by my window'. At this point, he harmonizes his melody in seconds that suddenly open to an augmented fifth before settling on a perfect fifth and finally descending in parallel thirds that lead to the solo line 'taking my time':

Figure 4.19   'I'm Only Sleeping', bridge (Lennon double-tracked)

This brief dissonance is just enough to pique the narrator's attention, to perhaps make John look and see what of interest is going on elsewhere in the world. The sudden reversion to the solo vocal, however, indicates the singer's original torpor – he will check on how the world is functioning in his own good time.

The use of vocal harmony in 'Love You To' is not like that of other songs; harmony is not used to differentiate the verse from the chorus or to emphasize a hook, nor is it used to help relate the narrative. Instead, the harmony vocal functions descriptively and atmospherically, to help evoke the sense of Indian musical practice. Vocal harmony is used briefly at the end of each verse before moving to the chorus. The Beatles double-track Harrison's voice throughout the song, a practice that was becoming more common with the group. While Harrison most often doubles his voice at the unison, his double-tracking also provides a vocal harmonization at the end of the verse where one voice track sustains the sa (tonic) and the other track decorates the tone with a descending melody in imitation of Indian vocal practice:

Figure 4.20   'Love You To', verse 1, mm. 7–8

The practice of the Beatles, and especially of Harrison, of double-tracking their own harmony points to future recording sessions in which the group will become less dependent on each other to complete their album tracks. The ultimate in double-tracking one's own harmony comes in Harrison's 'choir' with producer Phil Spector – as the 'George O'Hara-Smith Singers' – of the hit single 'My Sweet Lord' from his first solo album *All Things Must Pass* (1970).

The songs 'For No One', 'Got To Get You Into My Life', and 'Tomorrow Never Knows' are all recorded without any vocal harmony, yet in each song, the lack of vocal harmony contributes to the total understanding of that song. McCartney's solo melody in 'For No One' is a stark statement of finding oneself suddenly alone after the demise of a relationship, a different feeling from the aching loneliness presented in 'Eleanor Rigby'. McCartney's soul-influenced 'Got To Get You Into My Life' is more effective as a solo-vocal arrangement, modeled after performances by soul singers like James Brown, Wilson Pickett, and Otis Redding, in which the horn section, rather than backup singers, is used to supply the harmonized call and response. And Lennon's masterpiece, 'Tomorrow Never Knows', is so over-layered with sounds that harmonized vocals would either detract from the overall texture of the song or be lost in the mix.[5]

Conclusion

'You tell me that you've heard every sound there is ... ' Lennon sings in the final verse of 'And Your Bird Can Sing', and this is exactly what the Beatles have successfully achieved with *Revolver*. More importantly, we find on *Revolver* an integration of conservative and progressive musical elements. This balance of conservative and traditional is especially notable in regard to song structure, harmonic structure, and vocal harmonization. These three elements work together with and counter to each other, achieving a subtle aesthetic expression that permeates *Revolver*.

In traditional songwriting, the choruses of strophic forms and the bridges of standard forms are composed so as to provide contrast to the verse both harmonically and melodically. The contrasting sections often briefly tonicize a different key, traditionally going to the subdominant and returning to the tonic for the final verse. On *Revolver*, the Beatles sometimes tonicize new keys in the bridge, a traditional approach to form; however, they often move to obscure keys: to B major from A major in 'Doctor Robert', from E-flat minor to C-flat major in 'I'm Only Sleeping', and retaining the tonic D7 to subtonic C7 movement of the verse in the bridge of 'Taxman'. The structure of these songs is essentially traditional, but the corresponding harmony is progressive.

The application of vocal harmony often functions in a traditional manner on *Revolver*, used structurally to contrast sections. However, the manner in which the Beatles harmonize their vocals provides a progressive contrast to the structural usage, for example the triadic inversions of the vocal harmony over the fundamental bass as heard in the introduction of 'Eleanor Rigby' and the bridge of 'I'm Only Sleeping'. Besides harmonizing with parallel thirds and block root position triads in the manner of their influences, the Beatles also make use of vocal harmonizations that exploit the open, modal sound of parallel fourths and fifths. In these ways, the music on *Revolver* is constantly in flux, constantly revolving from the traditional to the progressive and back again.

There is always something new to hear on *Revolver*; no matter how many times one has heard the album, a new turn of a melodic phrase or a new combination of instrumental sounds, a different perception of a chord progression or a harmonized vocal passage, or a new feel for a syncopation all may lend a new appreciation for the artistic genius that permeates the album. *Sgt Pepper*, *Magical Mystery Tour*, *The Beatles*, *Let It Be*, and *Abbey Road* all follow suit and continue the Beatles' penchant for blending the traditional with the progressive. And certainly *Rubber Soul*, *Help!*, *Beatles for Sale*, and *A Hard Day's Night*, which precede *Revolver*, all have elements of experimentation that lead to the progressive quality of *Revolver*. However, it is the unique and balanced blend of the conservative and the progressive, of the traditional and the experimental on *Revolver* that places the album at an important juncture in both the Beatles' career and the history of rock music.

Notes

1. See Forte (1995), *The American Popular Ballad of the Golden Era 1924-1950*, Princeton, NJ: Princeton University Press.
2. It is interesting to note that according to the Baroque Doctrine of Affections, the key of E minor is considered to be suitable for music that is 'pensive and grieving,' by the German theorist Johann Georg Mattheson (1739). According to Plato, the Dorian mode (though not the same intervallic pattern as the Medieval Dorian mode), while considered suitable for warriors, was also recognized as being suitable for helping one 'accept and cope with setbacks'. Both of these descriptions seem to fit both characters Eleanor Rigby and Father Mackenzie. See James (1995), *Music of the Spheres*, New York: Copernicus, p. 57. Were the Beatles aware of these philosophies? It is doubtful, though they seem to feel the affect instinctively.
3. This should perhaps be interpreted as 'groups that played around with sitar sounds and modes' rather than an independent rock substyle.
4. Faburden is the technique of improvising harmony around a given pitch or melody. In Renaissance practice, the melody would be the middle voice and the harmony was improvised a third below and a fourth above it. The Beatles' technique is not true faburden technique, as the main melody (sung by John) is the lowest pitch and George and Paul harmonize a fourth and a sixth, respectively, above John. However, the sound of the parallel fourths and sixths adds a distinctive modal flavor to the hook of 'I'm Only Sleeping' and, even more noticeably, to the introduction of 'Eleanor Rigby'. This style of harmonization was not in 1966, nor is it today, typical of rock music. See Randel (1986), 'Faburden' in *The New Harvard Dictionary of Music*, Cambridge, MA: The Belknap Press of Harvard University Press, p. 297.
5. It could be said, however, that Lennon's double-tracked voice, fed through a Leslie speaker of a Hammond organ, on 'Tomorrow Never Knows' is a sort of harmony vocal. Lennon had originally wanted the sound of 'a thousand Tibetan monks chanting' as the background to this song, but had to settle for George Martin's solution of using the Leslie speaker. See MacDonald (1994), pp. 152–153, Dowlding (1989) p. 146, Everett (1999), p. 36, and others.

Chapter 5

Tonal family resemblance in *Revolver*

Naphtali Wagner

The Beatles' albums are ultimately anthologies of songs and not coherent musical works. Even in a Baroque suite or a Romantic song cycle the units are more coherent. This, however, does not mean that the album is meaningless as a unit. Each of the Beatles' albums can be regarded as a representation of a particular phase in the group's musical biography, and *Revolver* represents an especially critical phase.

Someone with a special interest in sound and recording will find in *Revolver* a decisive stage in the Beatles' transition from a stage band to a studio band; someone interested in the textual aspect of the songs will find in it the early phase of the Beatles' psychedelic poetry; but a person who is particularly interested in the tonal factor (melodic-harmonic-contrapuntal) faces a real methodological difficulty: how can we find the similarities that link the songs and give an ostensibly heterogeneous album a uniform hue? It is not hard to find tonal elements that are repeated numerous times in the album (e.g., various modal and harmonic tendencies), but these elements can be found throughout the Beatles' repertoire, not just in this album.[1] Hence, instead of looking for a broad common denominator among the songs in the album that distinguishes it from the other albums, we should settle for a weaker affinity in the form of 'family resemblance' among the songs in the album. If song A shares property X with song B, and song B shares property Y with song C, then even if song A has nothing in common with song C, all three songs are related through family resemblance.[2]

Family resemblance is the key to solving the riddle of *Revolver*: How can we reconcile the homogeneous impression that it gives the listener with its stylistic heterogeneity? The differences in the compositional approaches of Harrison, Lennon, and McCartney, which would reach their peak in *The Beatles* (the White Album), and which are already distinctly visible in *Revolver*. Previously the three had not gone in such different directions. Now Harrison turns to the east and records his first Indian song; Lennon becomes less tonal and develops a heightened sensitivity to sound and texture in an effort to achieve a psychedelic affect; whereas McCartney expands his melodic and harmonic means of expression. In the present chapter I attempt to show that beyond these obvious external differences there is a great deal of reciprocal influence, manifested by structural similarity between the songs composed by the different members of the group. The shared structural elements, in both the narrow and broad dimensions, thus produce a family resemblance that gives the album some tonal homogeneity in addition to its extreme stylistic diversity.

I begin with three pairs of songs by different composers that reflect a similar tonal plan (Figures 5.1, 5.3, and 5.4). Lennon's 'And Your Bird Can Sing' (Figure 5.1a) and McCartney's 'Got To Get You Into My Life' (Figure 5.1b) differ from each other in character but share many structural properties:

- In both songs there is a tonic/mediant relationship between successive sections (see the movement from I to III, from section A to section B, in Figures 5.1a and 5.1b).[3]
- The intro and section A of each song are static and are connected to the tonic by a pedal point or by a repeating bass figure.
- In both songs section A (including the intro) does not diverge from a diatonic scale framework. In 'Bird' the melody is pentatonic and the harmony is diatonic; 'Get You' is dominated by the Mixolydian mode.
- In both songs, section B begins with a chromatic expansion of the diatonic mediant. In 'Get You' the expansion occurs in the bass (B–A#–A–G#–G), whereas in 'Bird' it occurs in the inner voice (G#–Fx–F#–E#–E).

Both of these expansions conclude with a chromatic retreat (a disalteration of the E# to E-natural in 'Bird' and of the G# to G-natural in 'Get You'), and the section ends with the original scale: a half-close in 'Bird' and a perfect cadence in 'Get You'.

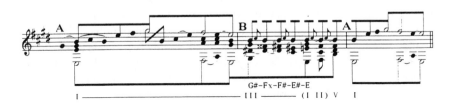

Figure 5.1a   'And Your Bird Can Sing'

Figure 5.1b   'Got To Get You Into My Life'

In both songs the shift to the mediant entails a textual reversal: in Lennon's song the reversal is linked to a potential change in the situation of the person being addressed, which may affect her relationship with the speaker: from superiority and arrogance in the present, which precludes reciprocity, to the possibility of a fall and distress in the future, which brings with it a chance for connection. The speaker conveys the message that when her stunning success subsides she will be able to turn to him: 'I'll be round.' In McCartney's song the same tonal shift is accompanied by a dramatic reversal from an unfocused search – 'I didn't know what I would find there' – to a sudden focus: 'Then I suddenly see you …'

The tonic-mediant relationship is also present in 'Here, There and Everywhere' (Figure 5.2),[4] although the mediant is flatted (bIII). The relationship appears first

Figure 5.2   'Here, There And Everywhere'

in the intro, which foreshadows the harmonic relationship between the beginning of A and the beginning of B. As in 'Get You', here, too, we find that section B, which begins with III, is based on an auxiliary cadence vis-à-vis the tonic.

Another tonal relationship – tonic/supertonic – between two successive sections links McCartney's 'For No One' (Figure 5.3a) and Harrison's 'I Want To Tell You' (Figure 5.3b):

Figure 5.3a   'For No One'

Figure 5.3b   'I Want To Tell You'

The I-II relationship is given more support in McCartney's song than in Harrison's: McCartney uses an interesting parallel between the arpeggiated ascents in section A (F#–B–D#) and in section B (G#–C#–E). Furthermore, he establishes the tonicization of the supertonic before going on to the dominant. Harrison, however, prepares the movement toward the supertonic as early as section A by means of the progression I–II#. Even in the parallel chords in the vocals A–Bm we can see some anticipation of the progression from one section to the next. Harrison, in contrast, does not establish the II in section B with a strong tonicization, but moves from II to I by a stealthy chromatic movement in the inner voices. Essentially, he uses II as a neighboring chord of I, without touching the dominant to any significant extent. Nevertheless, Harrison creates an interesting textual parallel between the two sections. In the tonic section (A) there is a split between the thoughts running through his head and his inability to express them in words:

I want to tell you
My head is filled with things to say.
When you're here
All those words, they seem to slip away

In the supertonic section (B), in contrast, there is a psychophysical split between the self and the mind, manifested in the contrast between the outward behavior and the person engaging in this behavior:

But if I seem to act unkind
It's only me, it's not my mind
That is confusing things.

The confusion between things that appear similar but are different in their essence is manifested in the three different chord appearances of the II in section B: once as a minor chord, once as a major chord, and once as a diminished chord.

Interestingly, the two songs deal differently with communication problems between lovers (or former lovers). In 'Tell You' the words race around copiously in the speaker's mind but cannot find an outlet when the person he is speaking to is around (the vocal arrangement that thickens the texture illustrates the idea of the excess of thoughts).

In contrast, in 'For No One' the words don't stop flowing, but they lose their meaning:

You find that all the words of kindness linger on
When she no longer needs you

The phrase 'my mind' appears in both songs, reflecting a general tendency in *Revolver* to perform a musical-textual dive into the recesses of the mind.

A major second between successive sections is also found in another pair of songs: Lennon's 'Doctor Robert' (Figure 5.4a) and McCartney's 'Good Day Sunshine' (Figure 5.4b). In this case, however, the two are opposites: in 'Sunshine' the movement is from B major to A major, whereas in 'Robert' it is from A to B. In both songs there is transitive modulatory movement in section A toward section B, but only in Harrison's song is there also retransitive movement from section B to section A. This key relationship appears in *Revolver* for the first time but will reappear in additional songs, including McCartney's 'Penny Lane' and Lennon's 'I Am The Walrus.' Oscillation between scales also exists in 'I'm

Figure 5.4a   'Doctor Robert'

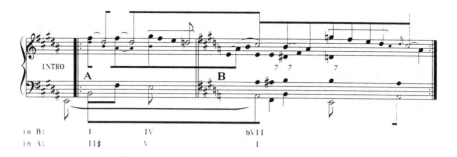

Figure 5.4b   'Good Day Sunshine'

Only Sleeping,' but there it is between nearby tonal centers (E minor and G major); such oscillation is common in the Beatles' overall repertoire but rare in *Revolver*.

Another weak association with 'I'm Only Sleeping' is manifested in the major second between the beginnings of the main sections in the song. The section that begins with the words 'When I wake up early in the morning' starts on the chord E♭m, whereas the section beginning with 'Keeping an eye on the world' starts on D♭m (which is interpreted as IV in the progression IV–V–I in the tonicization of A♭ minor).

So far we have found examples of all three possible pairs of the three composers: McCartney and Lennon, Harrison and McCartney, and Lennon and Harrison. Each of these examples shows a different shared tonal relationship that contributes to shaping the overall structure of the song. Are there similarities among all three? To find out, let us turn from the broad dimension of structural relationships between sections to the narrow dimension of a comparison of diminutions. In Figure 5.5 we find a series of parallel fragments that are all transposed to C major.

The common denominator among all the fragments is the arpeggiated ascent G–C–E or its inversion, E–C–G. But there are also many other parallels:

● In 'I Want To Tell You' and 'And Your Bird Can Sing' the arpeggiation is on the title of the song.

Figure 5.5   A series of parallel fragments all transposed to C major

- In 'I Want to Tell You' and 'Good Day Sunshine' the diminution concludes on a descending third (G–C–E–C). In 'For No One' the descent continues to another arpeggiated note, thus giving the arpeggiation an inverted answer (G–C–E, E–C–G).
- This inversion (E–C–G) is also found at the start of 'Doctor Robert' and 'Tomorrow Never Knows,' which have still another common denominator: each has an ascending fourth added with a Mixolydian aroma (G–Bb–C).
- The reduction of the melody to tonic arpeggio material links 'Tomorrow' with a song that appears to have little in common with it: 'For No One'.

The last pair in the list above deserves more attention. Walter Everett raises the question of whether the horn solo in 'For No One' is there because of the arpeggiated nature of the melody or due to the nostalgic character of the song (Everett, 1999, p. 54). As I see it, both the reduction to tonic notes and the resultant function of the horn are connected to the atmosphere of alienation radiated by the text: not only is the speaker a victim of alienation; he himself also transmits a certain degree of alienation. When he wakes up it is his mind that aches rather than his heart. The song oscillates between the second person and the third person. The frequent use of the second person in place of the first person ('Your day breaks, your mind aches') produces more of a sense of distance than of empathy. The limited selection of notes in the melody of the verse corresponds to the natural selection of notes of brass instruments and thus really demands the inclusion of such an instrument. Unlike string instruments, for example, brass instruments are not good at 'emotional' expression, and therefore they are consistent with the distant character of the verse. The use of the French horn is justified, because the trumpet (as in 'Penny Lane') might have made the song fanfare-ish, too lively, and not foreign enough.[5]

Similarly, Lennon's text, which is based on the Tibetan Book of the Dead (a guide to Nirvana) as understood through Leary and Alpert's *The Psychedelic Experience* (a guide to spiritual elevation by means of LSD), projects a sense of distance and separation (see Macdonald 1994, pp. 150–151). Thus two very different songs that seem to be extremely alienated from each other are shown to be similar, as they use a similar compositional means – melodic arpeggiation of the tonic together with a Mixolydian element.

McCartney's 'Here, There and Everywhere' (Figure 5.2) also begins with melodic arpeggios, but here the music is devoid of any connotation of alienation. The arpeggios on the I and the ♭III in the intro open a tonal space that is gradually filled in as the song progresses. At first the melody still retains an arpeggiated nature, with a neighboring note on top (G–B–D–A–G). As in 'For No One', the bass sets out on a scalar march from I toward IV, but in the opposite direction (Figure 5.2, beginning of section A). Another example of an arpeggiated beginning of a melody can be found in McCartney's 'Got To Get You Into My Life' (see Figure 5.1b, beginning of section A). For Walter Everett, this, combined with the use of ♭VII, evokes an association with 'For No One', which is also by McCartney (Everett 1999, p. 327, n. 95).

Another melodic pattern found in several songs is an ornamented scalar melodic descent with an oriental contour, usually with an initial accent and above a static bass, as we can see in Figures 5.6a–e, which all have a transposition to C but with different key signatures, depending on the mode.[6] The most sophisticated manifestation of the pattern is found in Harrison's 'Love You To' (Figure 5.6b) on the words 'You don't get time to hang a sign on me.' But the contour also appears in his less Indian songs in the album. In the trills at the end of 'I Want To Tell You' it appears on the words 'I've got time' (Figure 5.6d). The ornamented melisma draws in the word 'time' as a sort of counterpoint to the riff that origi-

Figure 5.6a–c   Transpositions to C with different key signatures

d) I Want To Tell You

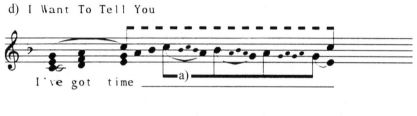

e) She Said She Said

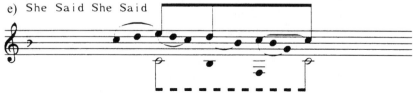

Figure 5.6d–e   Transpositions to C with different key signatures

nates in the intro. The riff represents rhythmic, metronomic 'western time,' whereas the melisma conveys a sense of 'eastern time', which is arrhythmic and has no borders. A similar case of instrumental improvisation on a riff can be found in 'Taxman' (Figure 5.6c; the riff patterns of the two songs can be seen in Figure 5.7).

This curved contour is not unique to Harrison. In McCartney's 'Eleanor Rigby' (Figure 5.6a), an almost identical counter-pattern organizes the vocal line that bears the text 'picks up the rice in the church where a wedding has been.' The resemblance to Harrison's 'Love You To' is also manifested in the similar modal properties of the two songs: in both cases the $\hat{3}$ and the $\hat{7}$ are flatted. Harrison's selection of the *kafi gat* from the Hindustani *raga* system puts the song closer to the Dorian mode of McCartney's melody (Reck, 1985, p. 102).[7] Lennon, too, uses this contoured pattern in 'She Said She Said' (Figure 5.6e) on the words 'And she's making me feel like I've never been born.' Whereas in Harrison's song the contour is distinctly melismatic, in Lennon's and McCartney's it appears in a syllabic melody.

The singles 'Paperback Writer' by McCartney and 'Rain' by Lennon, recorded in April 1966 around the same time as songs in the album, should also be included in the creative phase of *Revolver*. These two songs could easily have been recorded on *Revolver* and contributed to its family resemblance. The riffs of 'Paperback Writer' and 'Rain' are similar in structure to Harrison's riffs in 'Taxman' and 'I Want to Tell You,' which are mentioned above. Figure 5.7 illustrates the similarity among these four songs in terms of the riff structure (they all appear with a transposition of G major):

- The riffs are based on the same selection of notes: G ($\hat{1}$), C ($\hat{4}$), D ($\hat{5}$), and F-natural ($\hat{7b}$). In each of them the chord G_4^7 is spread.
- All four begin with an ascending skip of an octave (in 'Paperback' the octave is spread in an arpeggio).

- All four include movement from G to F-natural in the upper register. In 'Tell You' the movement continues on to E and the riff ends with E–C–G. This prepares the initial arpeggiation of the melody (see Figure 5.5a).
- In all four an angular melodic curve (zigzag) is obtained.
- Each of the riffs has a unique, distinctive rhythmic profile.

Another similarity between the single 'Rain' (Lennon) and two songs from the album – Lennon's 'She Said She Said' and McCartney's 'Yellow Submarine' – is shown in Figure 5.8. The figure demonstrates shared structural properties at the beginning of each of the three songs. 'Rain' shares the melodic skeleton of the entire opening phrase (G–A–G–E) with 'She Said' and shares the melodic skeleton of the beginning of the phrase (E–F–G–C) with 'Yellow Submarine'; thus we again see family resemblance in action. The two singles 'Rain' and 'Paperback

Figure 5.7a–d   Transpositions to G major

Writer' also fit in with *Revolver* in terms of other musical components, such as color and texture, but these are beyond the scope of the present discussion.

Revolver thus reflects an extreme diffusion of ideas among the members of the group. On the one hand, the individual traits of each of them as a composer are sharpened in *Revolver* and become more and more distinct. On the other hand, they still work as a team of creative minds and absorb a lot of influences from each other, and these influences take the form of short- and long-term tonal structures. Each of them adapts these influences and translates them into his own personal compositional style, after which they are returned to the studio to the common melting pot. The structural family resemblance that emerges in the final products of the process discloses the reciprocal influences and contributes to our sense that the inclusion of the songs in one album is not coincidental.

Figure 5.8a-c   **'She Said She Said', 'Rain' and 'Yellow Submarine'**

Notes

1. Many of the identifying marks in the Beatles' songs are not limited to a particular creative phase in their careers and can be found throughout the repertoire. These include typical flatted degrees, harmonic regressions, disalterations, oscillations between competing tonal centers, characteristic uses of blues elements, and melodic pentatonicism that expands to diatonicism. As a result, I decided to arrange my book about the Beatles' music by topic and not chronologically by album (Wagner 1999).

2. Ludwig Wittgenstein used the term *family resemblance* to denote the various similarities among all the phenomena to which a particular word applies, in the absence of a single property shared by them all: 'we see a complicated network of similarities overlapping and criss-crossing: sometimes overall similarities, sometimes similarities of detail' (see Wittgenstein, 1963, paragraphs 65, 66, and 67).
3. Walter Everett explains the appearance of the mediant as having to do with the prolongation of the VII/II (Everett, 1999, pp. 47–48).
4. Unlike Walter Everett's position, the graph in Figure 5.2 does not show a descending fundamental line but sticks to the $\hat{5}$ throughout the song (cf. Everett 1999, p. 61).
5. Ian Macdonald (1994, p. 164) draws an analogy between McCartney's composing of 'For No One' and the calculated moves of a chess player, attributing a sense of detachment to the composer as he wrote the song.
6. The frequent use of the drone in *Revolver* appears to be related to the Beatles' exposure to Indian music, but McCartney states that they had used a drone even earlier (Anthology, 2000).
7. The Beatles may have been receptive to Indian music because they found modal elements in it that were already part of their style and had a blues, pentatonic, folk, or Elizabethan origin.

Chapter 6

A flood of flat-sevenths
Ger Tillekens

1. A closer look at just one chord

Revolver is the first Beatles' album showing the combined marks of the group's experimental period. The compositions exploit the sound and feel of classical and Indian instruments, the mood of nostalgic and drowsy, psychedelic lyrics and the impact of subtle studio sound effects. In the harmonies we also find a real flood of flat-sevenths. The *Revolver* recording project, taking place between 1 April 1966, and 31 October 1966, all in all includes sixteen songs: to the fourteen tracks on the album we have to add the songs of the double A single 'Paperback Writer' and 'Rain'. In no less than seven out of those sixteen songs, almost half of them, the flat-seventh one way or another makes its presence heard. Four of those songs are written by Lennon, two by Harrison and, remarkably, only one by McCartney. The flat-seventh chord, or subtonic, is taken as one of the marks of the Beatles' experimental period (Eerola, 1998), by some even as one of the group's real musical innovations (O'Grady, 1979b; 1983). On *Revolver* this chord appears in close connection to the Beatles' use of quartal harmonies. Does this have something to do with the album's atmosphere? Answering this question, we here will take a closer look at this particular chord. Looking at the harmonic technicalities of the *Revolver* compositions we will show how the Beatles successfully put the flat-seventh chord to full use in that album: harmonically to underpin their surprising melodies, and semantically to stress the meaning of their lyrics.

2. An overload of chords

Now we have grown used to them, but at the time of their release the songs on *Revolver* evoked many startled comments. For a moment even McCartney himself had his doubts: '... I was in Germany on tour just before *Revolver* came out. I started listening to the album and I got really down because I thought the whole thing was out of tune. Everyone had to reassure me that it was all okay' (Garbarini, 1980). Even to McCartney the songs of the album, or at least some of them, seemed out of key. It was not the first time this remark was made of the Beatles' songs. Other people had said the same thing before of the group's early songs. From the start of their career the Beatles filled their songs with daring harmonic experiments and that to some people did make their songs go wrong. To classical trained critics, the songs sounded harsh and sometimes even downright out of key. Blues-oriented critics complained that the Beatles did not apply the right blue notes. Others, however, liked the songs for that very same reason. To their ears the compositions of the Beatles, though harmonically adventurous, were also remarkably melodious.

In their own way both the critical and the affirmative responses to the Beatles' songs were right. The musical style of the Beatles was so new and unusual, that one had to get used to it. To enjoy their songs one's ear first had to learn the musical grammar, to adapt to the underlying musical structure of the harmonies. What was so special about the Beatles' harmonies? The sheer number of chords the Beatles performed in their compositions, offers a first clue for an answer to that question. Compared with the standards of earlier popular music the Beatles' songs show far too many chords. Most simple harmonies are built upon the three basic chords: the tonic (I), the subtonic (IV) and the dominant (V).

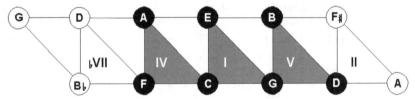

Figure 6.1   Tone material of the three basic chords

The tone material of these three chords defines seven to eight notes unequivocally, starting from the root of the tonic (Figure 6.1). Not by accident, these notes coincide with the diatonic scale. Of course, we can add chords like the subtonic (♭VII) – the flat-seventh – one fourth below the root of the subdominant, or the supertonic (II) – one fifth above the root of the dominant. This, however, imports ambiguous tones in the tone material. In the key of C, for instance, the supertonic (II) adds an A – at first sight the same tone that also regularly belongs to the subdominant (IV). However, though both tones share their names, they are not exactly the same. They differ by slightly more than one tenth of a full tonal distance – to be more exact a microtonal distance of 21.5 cent. Other chords add similar 'enharmonic' tones with even greater distances. On hearing these tones on well-tempered instruments a listener has to reinterpret them unconsciously, or else a composition threatens to sound out of key (Helmholtz, 1862). That's why, in the system of western diatonic music, the tonal key is so important. It also explains why composers usually tend to keep to a small supply of chords.

The Beatles' songbook, however, is quite another story. To play a Beatles' song the right way, chances are a guitarist has to master far more than three chords. Listen for example to *Revolver*'s fifth track, McCartney's composition 'Here, There, and Everywhere'.[1] The song's harmonies count up to no less than ten chords: G (I), G minor (i), A minor (ii), B♭ (♭III), B (III), C (IV), C minor (iv), D (V), E minor (vi) and F♯ minor (vii). To account for all these chords from a classical perspective, we have to assume that some parts of the song modulate or shift to other keys. The home key of G major, no doubt, dominates the intro, the verse and the coda. For the middle of the verse section, however, we have to resort to the key of the relative minor (E minor) and for the bridge section even to the keys of the parallel minor (G minor) and its relative major (Bb).

3. Diagonal substitutions

So, to analyse and explain the harmonic structure of 'Here, There, And Everywhere' we have to write down four different keys. Seen from this perspective, the alternating sections of the song confront the listener with no less than eleven subsequent modulations, tonal oscillations or key shifts within the song's short duration of 2:26 minutes. In its harmonic complexity 'Here, There, And Everywhere' is no exception in the Beatles' songbook (Riley, 1988, p. 55). On average the songs of their complete work have a stock of about eight to nine chords with a maximum of twenty-one for 'You Never Give Me Your Money'. Blurring major and minor modes or importing new enharmonic tones, such numbers of chords endanger the key and, moreover, unexpected chords tend to be perceived as syntactical disturbances of the musical grammar (Mulder, 2000). To denote the Beatles' extended chord material, some musicologists even speak of an 'exploding functional harmony' (Johansson, 1999). In short, there is reason enough for someone to get lost in the harmonic maze of the songs. For the naïve and willing listener the harmonies, however, also possess some naturalness preventing this from happening. Clearly, the Beatles' songs have some self-explanatory power, helping the listener to adapt to their intricate harmonic twists. If we want to explain the Beatles' songs in a musicological way, however, we are still confronted by severe problems.

Because of their harmonic peculiarities, the Beatles' songs have been called a-tonal or non-tonal. Others have said that the Beatles did retreat to premodern tonal systems, pointing at the way chords are combined in Renaissance music according to the principle of common tones.[2] In a similar way their songs have been qualified as modal – i.e., built upon a tonic with one or more related co-tonics – mostly a combination of major and minor modes. This use of co-tonics facilitates addressing additional chords and notes. That way the Beatles' style can be seen as a return to premodern music (Mellers, 1969; 1973), or as an extension of an earlier trend in popular music (Van der Merwe, 1989). However, the Beatles' chords are not always connected by common tones, and, though the group was not averse to modulations and an intermingling of minor and major modes, most of the time their songs tend to keep to one solid tone centre.

Instead of going back in time, the Beatles rather took a step forward (Peyser, 1969). Adding up all the chords used in their songbook and relating them to a common key, some kind of system emerges (Figure 6.2). All possible chords are

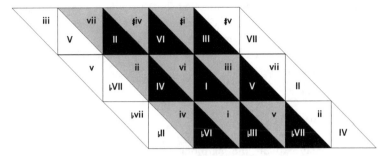

Figure 6.2   The tone grid of diagonal substitution

related to each other in a fixed grid, keeping to a fixed tone centre (Tillekens, 1998). Along the diagonal lines, chords are treated as substitutes for the subtonic, tonic and dominant. So in 'Here, There, and Everywhere' the tonic G (I) sometimes is replaced by E minor (vi), sometimes by G minor (i) or again sometimes by B♭ (♭III). The subdominant C (IV) is swapped for C minor (iv), A minor (vi) or F♯ minor (vii). The B chord (III) in turn functions as a stand-in for the dominant D (V). In that way the principle of diagonal substitution accounts for all of the song's chords.

The Beatles developed and explored this system from the start of their career – not guided by theory, of course, but by a felt need to express themselves musically. Piecing chords together seemed their way of composing. Or, as Ian MacDonald (1994, p. 10) says: 'In short, they had no preconceptions about the next chord, an openness which they consciously exploited ... .' With each new song and record their experiments became more adventurous. At first they sought some support in standard chord sequences like the chain of fifths (II – V – I) and the turn-around (I – vi – IV – V). Later on, in their songs any chord seemed fit to follow any other (Widders-Ellis and Gress, 1994), at least if the sequences could be smoothed by some good leading notes. To that end the Beatles took to exploiting the possibilities of the microtonal differences of the tones in their system more fully. They could take their pick. For their compositions the Beatles had an extended tonal array at their disposal, as the diagonal tone grid comprises twenty-four different tones.

On a modern, well-tempered instrument we find only half this amount and each tone of the chromatic scale seems to appears twice in the tone grid. Each pair of tones, however, differs significantly by microtonal distances. The grid itself, however, will help the listener in interpreting which tone is which. If a listener, be it unconsciously, knows the place of the accompanying chord within the grid, the tones are defined accordingly. When the tones are part of a melody line or a sung harmony, they must be sung pure. This, in turn, helps the listener to position the chord within the grid. That is one of the reasons that the sung harmonies of the Beatles, built upon the chords they played on their guitars (Valdez, 2001), were

Figure 6.3   Tonal differences in the melody line of 'Help!'

so important. Their song lines glued the chords together by using many of these microtonal differences as leading notes. In the third and fourth measure of 'Help!' the Beatles, for instance, sing a D that belongs to the G chord. In the fifth measure the same note is sung, this time accompanied by the E seventh (Figure 6.3). Though seemingly the same, both notes differ by nearly a quarter of a tonal distance, which the Beatles knew to catch perfectly (Kramarz, 1983, p. 137). This mark of many Beatles' songs also explains why their compositions seem to integrate harmony and melody. The system of diagonal substitution thus accounts for most of the Beatles' chord and song characteristics. Some chords, however, ask for another explanation.

4. Variants of the flat-seventh

About 66 out of the 187 canonical Beatles' songs incorporate the flat-seventh chord. That is over one-third of the complete corpus. The flat-seventh has its own place within the system of diagonal substitution. With the flat-submediant (bVI) and the flat-mediant (bIII) the subtonic forms a trio of substitutions for the subdominant, the tonic and the dominant respectively. The roots of these chords are the flat-thirds of the roots of the basic chords. Because of their resemblance to similar chords in the Classical Style, these chords sometimes are called Neapolitan chords.[3] However, the use of these chords in popular music probably has other origins as their roots coincide with the so-called blue notes. In the idioms of parlour music, blues and folk, these blue notes made an early entrance as accidental notes, sometimes accentuated in the melody lines, sometimes also added to the chord settings.

The blue notes are an integral part of the blues idiom. Here they appear in three

variants: as the fourth of the subdominant's root, as the minor third of the dominant's root, and as a perfect seventh to the tonic's root. With their microtonal differences, each variant seems to accentuate a separate meaning. The first one –
sounding 3.9 cent lower than the well-tempered tone of the same name on a keyboard – transmits a feeling of distance and loss; the second one – reaching up to
17.6 cent higher than its well-tempered relative – expresses a deep-felt, private
and urging emotion. And, the perfect seventh – by no less than 31.2 cent lower
than its keyboard equivalent – gives a chord a feeling of completeness by its consonant qualities, and thereby suggests a sense of healing.

A guitar is an excellent instrument to play, or at least to hint at, these blue notes.
By bending the strings with their left-hand fingers on the neck of their instruments, guitarists can accentuate these different meanings. As an accidental note
the blue note can be added to every chord. Applied to the tonic, however, its
semantic power seems at its strongest. That's the way the Beatles use it, for
instance, in 'I Wanna Be Your Man' where the verse centres on just this only
chord, adorned with flat-sevenths. Listen, for instance, to the first line of the
song's lyrics: 'I wanna be your lover, baby, I wanna be your man.' Here the flat-
seventh is emphasized in the melody line on both occurrences of the verb 'be' and
the first syllable of 'baby'. Just like in many blues songs, the seemingly sober harmony gets its thrill out of a subtle variation in 'longing', 'distance', and 'healing'.

Accidental blue notes never have disappeared from the idiom of popular music,
but in time they also developed into full-blown chords. In pre-war popular music,
the Neapolitan chords were approached by introducing a chain of fifths starting
from the tonic and modulating to the root of the flat-third (I – IV – ♭VII – ♭III)
(Forte, 1995). Later on, in blues and folk music we find more ad lib insertions.
The growing popularity of the guitar furthered the use of these chords by facili-
tating the use of so-called chord streams, stepwise root movement of chords.
Guitarists adapted the style of ragtime and jazz to their instrument by picking a
barré chord and sliding the whole hand one or more frets up or down on the neck
of the guitar. The intro of Elvis Presley's 'Hard Headed Woman' offers a good
example (Van der Merwe, 1989, pp. 265–266). Chord streams and incidental, isolated Neapolitan chords first made their entrance in popular music especially in
the intro and the coda of songs. Later on, in the Brill Building and British appro-
priation of rock 'n' roll, the harmonizing of the blue notes almost came to be a
standard (Kramarz, 1983, p. 51 ff.).

All these elements reappear in the early Beatles' songs. Stepwise diatonic or
chromatic chord progressions, for instance, can be found in songs as early as 'P.S.
I Love You', 'Ask Me Why' and 'Do You Want to Know A Secret'. Likewise on
Revolver the refrain of Lennon's 'I'm Only Sleeping' is built upon such a chord
stream (Figure 6.4). Isolated, as incidental chords, Neapolitan chords show up in
'I Saw Her Standing There'. All this was not new within the musical idiom of
popular music. The songs of Buddy Holly and Carl Perkins, for instance, predate
those of the Beatles in their use of the flat-sixth (♭VI). Learning from these exam-

Please don't wake me. No, don't shake me. — Leave

G♭		**a♭**			

e♭:   ♭III   iv

— me where I — am.   I'm on – ly — sleeping.

b♭		**a♭**			

e♭:   v   iv

Figure 6.4   A chord stream in the refrain of 'I'm Only Sleeping'

ples and importing all the tricks and treats of rock 'n' roll and rhythm and blues, the Beatles fitted them into their own overarching style. The same goes for the flat-seventh, to which the Beatles were acquainted by their cover song 'A Taste of Honey'. For their own songs they applied it in the intro of 'Thank You Girl'. The same chord also provides the powerful opening – like an exclamation mark – of 'A Hard Day's Night', the verse of 'I'll Be Back' and, as we have seen before, the adventurous intro of 'Help!' (Figure 6.3), which opens with the daring sequence: ii – ♭VII – V – I.

On the album *Help!* and next on *Revolver* this trend in using the flat-seventh chord is extended and even more daringly applied. 'Doctor Robert', also written by Lennon, for instance, opens with a four-measure vamp on the A chord, which is further sustained for no less than eight measures in the verse. This gives the listener the impression that this chord is the tonic. After six bars of accompaniment by the F♯ chord, the harmony reaches its tonic in the last measure of the verse by a sequence of E – F♯ – B. This last sequence only can be interpreted as IV – V – I, thus forcing the listener to interpret the A chord in retrospect as the flat-seventh. That way the flat-seventh helps to give the opening lyrics their feel of an urging insistence, making it an uncensored utterance of deep-felt feelings. In the refrain – 'Well, well, well, I'm feeling fine' – this tonal drift at last keeps to its definite tonic, turning the anxiety of the verse into a sudden calmness and thereby suggesting the soothing effects of Doctor Robert's drugs (Wagner, 2001, p. 95).

Harmonizing the blue notes deprives them of their ambiguity. That's one of the reasons why many of the blue notes of the Beatles and other British groups did sound wrong, or at least not flexible enough, to the ears of blues fanatics. This also goes for the chord forms, at least for the flat-sixth and the flat-third. These chords only appear as the minor thirds of the subdominant and the tonic respectively. The flat-seventh, however, also can represent another chord in the tonal grid, i.e., the fourth of the subdominant. This chord lies farther away from the tonic and so it stresses the feeling of distance and loss. This is also the preferred treatment of this chord in the idiom of folk music. In the Beatles' song repertoire this use of the flat-seventh, for instance, shows up in their ballad 'Things We Said

Today', where the four-bar chord sequence I – I – IV – ♭VII underlines the lyrics: 'Someday when I'm lonely, wishing you weren't so far away.'

Sometimes as in 'All My Loving', where the flat-seventh behaves like a connecting chord between the ii and V chords, the chord is more folk-oriented – accentuating the separation from a distant lover. In other instances the blues interpretation of strongly felt feelings dominates, like in 'We Can Work It Out', where the opening verse starts with an alternating I – ♭VII sequence. To discriminate both, almost identical chords, we shall here call the first one the folk variant and the second one the blues variant. Giving them other names, however, will not always make it easier to discriminate both variants. In the songs of the Beatles the flat-seventh often will shift back and forth between its folk and blues variants.

In his analysis of the Beatles' songs Walter Everett (1999) points toward one of their favourite chord progressions, the 'Hey-Jude' progression (♭VII – IV – I) we can hear for instance in 'You Never Give Me Your Money' and, of course in the jamming phrase ('na, na, na ...') of 'Hey Jude'. Everett calls this sequence a 'double plagal cadence', thereby suggesting that the chord equivocally is our folk variant. But in reality in 'Hey Jude' it is not – at least not always – the folk variant we hear. The first time we hear the chord in this sequence it is the blues variant, with its root on the flat-third of the dominant. The second time the sequence comes around it is the folk variant. Here the Beatles make good use of the ambiguous character of this chord. In the verse of 'For No One' McCartney turns the sequence just the other way around. Now it becomes: IV – ♭VII – I, which makes the flat-seventh into a kind of pseudo-dominant. Again, however, the chord is used ambiguously. The last two chords of this progression accompany the lyrics: 'When she no longer needs you.' Here we hear a subtle shift from the experience of distance of the folk variant to the deep-felt feeling of the blues variant of the flat-seventh. Clearly, its ambiguity is what makes the chord so interesting (Figure 6.5).

As 'For No One' shows, the ambiguous character of the flat-seventh is being

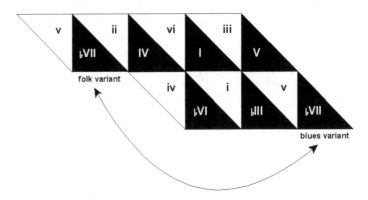

Figure 6.5   Shifts of the flat-seventh between the folk and blues variants

cleverly exploited on *Revolver*. This intermingling of both flat-sevenths and their meanings can also be heard on the album's first track, Harrison's 'Taxman'. The song's verse is built out of three parts, of which the third and last one opens with the flat-seventh. The chord is kept on for two bars, followed by one bar for the subdominant and next by two bars for the tonic: bVII – bVII – IV – I – I. Apart from its unusual five-measures length, this part of the song conforms to the blues-form. Again, both variants of the flat-seventh show up. In the first bar, accompanying the lines 'Cause I'm the taxman' we hear a blues flat-seventh. Next, in the second bar and underlining the phrase 'Yeah, I'm the …', the folk variant appears, creating the impression that the dreaded taxman is nearing from a distance, moving from the background to the foreground.

5. Quartal harmonies

The Beatles developed and explored the principle of diagonal substitution in their early songs. After their experimental period, they returned more fully to this system, as can be shown by the interplay of chords traditionally ascribed to the keys of A major, A minor, and C major in the 'Abbey Road Medley'. Many tracks on *Revolver*, however, show a predilection for so-called quartal harmonies, i.e., harmonies in which the key leans toward the roots of the subdominant or even the subtonic. These quartal harmonies play with horizontal movements through the harmonic grid, leaning downward to the subdominant and the subtonic – in this case our folk variant.[4]

Just like the blue notes, quartal harmonies by themselves are not special for the Beatles' songs. The blues preference for the subdominant above the dominant can be interpreted as an inclination toward quartal harmonies. The same goes for the preference in rock 'n' roll and rhythm and blues for the plagal cadence (IV – I). Maybe this preference can even be held responsible for the introduction of the flat-seventh chord itself (Wagner, 2001, p. 94). Many good rock 'n' roll songs, moreover, like to blur the key, at least in the intro taking it as far as possible into the verse. These songs just start with harmonic ostinatos of two alternating chords a fifth apart, postponing the third chord which will decide the exact key as long as possible. As their covers show, the Beatles learned this special rock 'n' roll effect from Chuck Berry's 'Roll Over Beethoven', Little Richard's performance of 'Kansas City' and Buddy Holly's 'Words Of Love'. Their first official song 'Love Me Do' and later on 'I Should Have Known Better' prove that the Beatles had learned this game quite as well.

As we have seen, the subtonic adds a surplus of meaning to the lyrics of popular songs. The same goes for the three basic chords. The lyrics of popular songs generally regard conversations (Tillekens, 2001). As a rule the dominant stresses the voicing of a public statement toward someone else. The subdominant underlines a retreat into thinking things over in the back of one's mind, an inner monologue. In between, the tonic accentuates the grounding of a decision. So, a long alternation of just two basic chords at the start of a song not only creates uncertainty about it being a sequence of I – V or IV – I. It also leaves it up to the listener to decide if the singer is voicing his inner thoughts or bringing them out into the open. By the way, this same chord movement also is responsible for creating the two-chord walking rhythm of many rock 'n' roll songs. In 'Love Me Do', for instance, it strengthens the impression of someone walking to his lover, voicing his thoughts in an inner monologue and preparing to voice his commitment to her in the open. When at last we do hear the dominant, this chord underscores that the singer at last has resolved his doubts and is ready to do so.

Quartal harmonies accentuate that the singer is biding his time – daydreaming, still being busy thinking things over and postponing final decisions – and thus offer a powerful means of accentuating the meaning of the song lyrics. They can be effectuated by different harmonic tricks. A subtler variant lies in the use of suspended chords, like those applied by Harrison in his 'I Want To Tell You'. Here the guitar ostinatos vary on two instances of the tonic, A7 and A7sus4, in which musicologist Alan Pollack (1995, #101), by the way, also discovers traces of an embedded 'Hey Jude' progression. Quartal inclinations also show up in one of the Beatles' more adventurous modulations, of which 'She Said She Said', recorded in the key of B♭, again offers a good example (Figure 6.6):

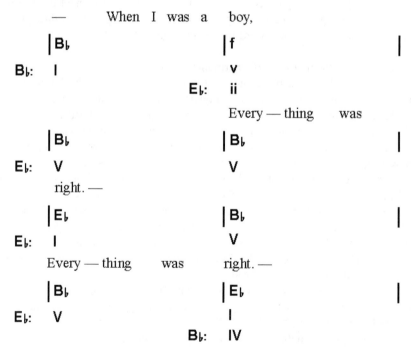

Figure 6.6   Downward modulation in the bridge of 'She Said She Said'

In 'She Said She Said', we find a clear modulation to E♭ – the root of the sub-dominant (IV) – in the bridge, pivoting on the F minor chord (v). At the time this modulation was not new to the Beatles' songbook. They had performed this feat before in the middle eight of 'From Me To You', and that moment was a real musical discovery (Kramarz, 1983, pp. 51–53). 'From Me To You' is written in the key of C and so the minor dominant is G minor. In respect to this song McCartney himself voiced it this way in an interview with Mark Lewisohn (1988, p. 10):

> ... that middle eight was a very big departure for us. Say you're in C then go to A minor, fairly ordinary, C, change it to G. And then F, pretty ordinary, but then it goes [sings] 'I got arms' and that's a G minor. Going to G minor and a C takes you to a whole new world. It was exciting.

The new world McCartney is referring to here implies not only an expansion of the chord material for the composer, but also an extension of the semantic scope of the writer of the song lyrics. Turning the subdominant into the tonic can be used to signify a retreat into the inner self. Once they had discovered it, the Beatles used this harmonic manoeuvre more often. They repeated it in the middle-eight of 'I Want To Hold Your Hand' and as we have seen in 'She Said She Said'. Here it is aptly applied to signify a retreat into a memory of lost innocence, when Lennon sings: 'When I was a boy, everything was right.' It doesn't stop there, as the bridge of 'I'm Only Sleeping' again takes this move one step further, by using the flat-seventh itself as a pivot chord to modulate and even doing it twice (Figure 6.7).[5]

With this modulation the bridge directly jumps into a deeper introspection. In the song Lennon is expressing the feeling of being half-awake, half-sleeping. Again the modulation is used for a further retreat into the inner world of reflective thought. Lennon tries to explain his mental state, assuming there is an outsider who's threatening to wake him fully. In the bridge he defines the semi-awareness of waking up to himself: 'Keeping an eye on the world going by my window / Taking my time ...' The use of the flat-seventh, with its subtle variations, as a pivot chord instead of the minor dominant, softens the transition between the song sections.

6. Indian inspirations

The overflow of flat-sevenths can have implications that are seemingly difficult for those unfamiliar with the intricacies of musicology. One of those is the preference of transcribers for Mixolydian or other outlandish modes and scales. The reference to Greek musical scales of old is not as difficult as it may seem at first sight. Most of the time the qualification Mixolydian, for instance, just means that the seventh step of the major scale is replaced by the flat-seventh. In that case using the key of the subdominant for the end of transcription facilitates the notation of songs on sheet music. The qualification Mixolydian again offers an indi-

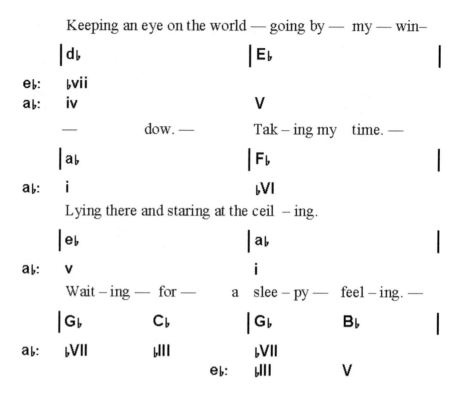

**Figure 6.7   Downward and upward modulations in the bridge of 'I'm
Only Sleeping'**

cation for the use of quartal harmonies in a song. Many of the songs mentioned
above, like 'Love Me Do', fall into this category. Not all songs qualified as
Mixolydian always are pure examples of this scale. Mostly this scale is applied to
account for the ample use of the flat-seventh as an accidental tone. Just like the
key of 'Love Me Do' fluctuates between G and C, the tone centre of 'She Said
She Said' moves around the keys of Bb and Eb. 'She Said She Said', however, can
be qualified as pure Mixolydian major, as the song's harmonies forgo the use of
the dominant and show a preference for the subtonic instead.

An inclination to the Dorian mode can be found in 'Love You To'. In this mode
the third, sixth and seventh steps of the major scale are all flattened, thus addressing all three blue notes. Most Beatles' songs are not so shy to keep to only one
scale. Combinations of Mixolydian, Dorian and more common major modes, for
instance, can be found on both *Revolver*'s 'Taxman', which skips the use of the
dominant, and 'Tomorrow Never Knows', a Lennon composition deserving special attention, because it shows a specific use of the flat-seventh.

The key of 'Tomorrow Never Knows' is a Mixolydian C, which is equivalent to F major. The second half of virtually every verse is built out of eight measures of an alternating ♭VII – I sequence, which all in all is repeated seven times (Figure 6.8). Again the lyrics express a retreat into a distanced, deep inner feeling, the first time saying: 'It is not dying.' In this case it is not even a flat-seventh chord itself that is directly addressed. There is only, as Pollack (1995, #103) calls it, an 'implied vacillation' toward the flat-seventh. Many songs that were recorded during the *Revolver* recording project possess this drone-like – we could almost say 'revolving' – quality. The effect can result out of a slowing down of the two-chord walking rhythm of an alternating tonic and the subdominant, as we hear in 'Paperback Writer'. It can be strengthened by treating the subdominant as a suspended chord, as we hear in the coda – right after the modulation – of 'I'm Only Sleeping', as well as in the refrain of 'Rain'. A more powerful effect results from leaving the subdominant out and implying it by alterations of the tonic, as Harrison's guitar ostinatos do in 'I Want To Tell You'.

The use of these harmonic feats turns the original walking rhythm of rock 'n' roll into a more quiet rocking feeling. The negligence of the dominant takes away any sense of fulfilment and determined action. Keeping to the tonic itself and just

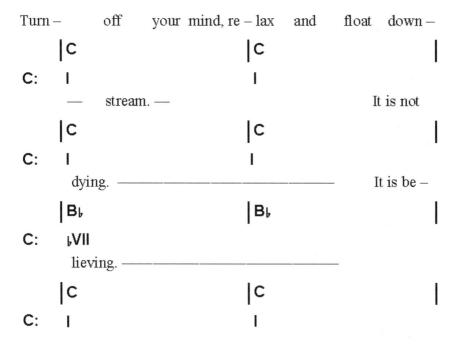

Figure 6.8   A vacillating drone in the verse of 'Tomorrow Never Knows'

hinting at the subdominant strengthens this effect, and, by inserting the flat-seventh instead, the walking rhythm even becomes quieter still.[6] With subtle microtonal transitions, the flat-seventh is addressed in both its meanings – placing the violence of private, uncensored inner feelings themselves at a distance. This calms down the pace of revolving thoughts, leading to a feeling of detachment. Here we find a seeming paradox: the flat-seventh, though in a musicological sense a syntactical disturbance, gives the song and the phrasing of the lyrics a soothing quality, quieting the inner voice even further. It almost stops the flow of time, inherent in any music, by creating an oscillating, standing wave of deep feelings and distancing. Of course, the song effectuating this effect to the full is Harrison's 'Love You To', which brings us to quite another question.

Both 'Tomorrow Never Knows' and 'Love You To' make ample use of the sitar. This seems to imply that the growing influence of classical Indian music promoted the use of flat-sevenths in the Beatles' songs. At that time, there certainly was something hanging in the air. Classical Indian influences already had made themselves felt in the streams of jazz, folk and classical music from the mid-1950s on. McCartney confirms this influence in regard to the drone we hear in 'Tomorrow Never Knows' (Miles, 1997, pp. 290–291):

> This was because of our interest in Indian music. We would be sitting around and at the end of an Indian album we'd go, 'Did anyone realise they didn't change chords?' It would be like 'Shit, it was all in E! Wow, man, that is pretty far out.' So we began to sponge up a few of these nice ideas.

Here McCartney is suggesting the Indian sounds of the song all came from outside influences. And, indeed, there are some strong resemblances between the musical idiom applied in many of *Revolver*'s songs and the classical Indian style. Apart from all the intricacies of the Indian *raga* as a tonal framework for composition and improvisation, Indian scales are true scales. They are built around a tonic and a perfect fifth or fourth. These tones are used to set up a drone. The other tones of the scale are variable. The tunes make subtle variations and ornamentations, often with microtonal distances. In combination with the tonic, the flat-seventh proves to be a good chord to imitate an Indian sound, at least to western ears, as both variants of this chord offer some of the same microtonal distances that are familiar to the idiom of Indian music. So, being part and parcel of the Beatles' compositional techniques, the flat-seventh itself may have accustomed them to the sound of Indian music. This, at least, seems to go for other British groups who imported Indian sounds into their songs at about the same time.

George Harrison came across the sitar during the takes for the film *Help!* in London. It would, however, not be until 12 October 1965 before the first fruits of his study of the instrument would be used in recording 'Norwegian Wood'. In the meantime other British groups, also known for their use of the flat-seventh, had begun experimenting with Indian sounds. Here the inspiration worked the other way around. It seems to be their use of the flat-seventh that accustomed and sensitised them to Indian music. As soon as they heard the sounds of Indian chants or sitars, they felt the correspondence with their own kind of music. That is how the Kinks, who had shown a predilection for the flat-seventh chord before (Fitzgerald, 2000, p. 69), for instance, came to the idea of imitating a sitar in their song 'See My Friends'. The group got the idea during a short stay in Bombay on the way back from their Australian tour.

The same goes for the Yardbirds, who preceded the Kinks by a few months, when they added some Indian flavour to their song 'Hearts Full Of Soul' because, as they said themselves, the riff on an earlier demo already seemed to suggest the use of a sitar (Harrison, 2001). Neither song used a sitar as an instrument. By a fraction the Yardbirds missed the chance to be the first rock group to do this. Jeff Beck did an expert imitation of a sitar on his guitar after the hired studio musician failed to get the song lines right on his sitar. So for these groups, and probably the Beatles as well, it was something already present in their own musical idiom which seemed to ask for some Indian additions. If so, maybe the secret in the fascination of the Beatles for Indian music also lies in their adoption of the flat-seventh and a renewed perception of its ambiguity.

7. Stopping the flow of time

Quartal harmonies, strengthened by the use of suspended chords and flat-sevenths, dominate many of the *Revolver* songs. The use of flat-seventh (♭VII) and the minor fifth (v) in this way meant a deviation, for the preferred method of diagonal substitution and songs like these are a subcategory in the Beatles' canon. As we have seen, the flat-seventh chord was there all along before *Revolver*. This album, however, shows their most creative use of it. The use of the inherent ambiguity of the subtonic softens the walking and dancing character of early rock music and also points the way to the adoption of Indian sounds and music. This inclination to quartal harmonies and the flat-seventh may rest on their power to suggest a peace of mind, an end to longing and a recourse to a nostalgic past. Maybe that is why McCartney initially had the impression of the album being out of tune. Clearly, he hadn't yet incorporated the extreme use of the flat-seventh, as he himself only wrote one song with this particular chord, 'For No One', which at that time was rather ordinary for a Beatles' song. Perhaps, in his personal life at that moment McCartney felt less need than the others of stopping the flow of time. He must have had some feel for it, however. McCartney answered Lennon's 'I'm Only Sleeping' by writing 'Good Day Sunshine'. This song has the same horizontal movements, but inverted, directed toward the dominant and the supertonic as the pure fifth of the dominant. Consequently the song's atmosphere is more open, lending a more outward-bound feeling to the lyrics. Soon he would prove his abilities, when the Beatles gave a new interpretation of nostalgia with

'Penny Lane' and 'Strawberry Fields'. In the latter song Lennon again plays with quartal harmonies (Thompson, 2001); in the former, McCartney, showing that he had acquired a taste for the new sound of the group, performs a direct pivot modulation in the transition of verse to refrain towards the key of the flat-seventh.

Notes

1. The presented chord sequences are checked against the transcriptions of Tetsuya Fujita, Yuji Hagino, Hajime Kubo and Goro Sato (Beatles, 1989) and Alan W. Pollack's 'Notes on ... Series' (Pollack, 1989–2001).
2. For this mark of Renaissance music see Bettens, 1998. Some Beatles' bootleg records, so-called Beatlegs, even present the group as 'The Renaissance Minstrels'.
3. In what must be the first academic PhD on the Beatles, Steven Porter (1979a, p. 72) builds his case for the influence of European western music on the style of the Beatles on their use of just these Neapolitan chords. At the end of his study he, however, has to admit that the Beatles use these chords in their own manner.
4. This same movement, by the way, is called 'vertical' in respect to medieval polyphony and early music (cfr. Schulter, 1998).
5. Just like their cover song 'A Taste Of Honey', both 'Love You To' and 'I'm Only Sleeping' are written in a minor key. Therefore, strictly speaking, the $\flat$vii must be notated as the vii, because in the minor mode the flat-seventh is native to key. Here, however, we will keep to the conventions presented in the tone grid.
6. At about the same time, the Beatles slowed down the rhythmic patterns of their songs, thereby creating, as Len McCarthy (2001) argues, a new rhythmic paradigm for pop and rock music.

Part III

'And our friends were all aboard'

Revolver's players

Chapter 7

'Tomorrow never knows': the contribution of George Martin and his production team to the Beatles' new sound

Kari McDonald and Sarah Hudson Kaufman

In 1991, two fourteen-year-old girls were rummaging through their parents' dusty box of untitled tapes in a suburb of Vancouver, Canada. We began listening to what we thought was the greatest new sound – even though it was obviously a fifth-or-sixth generation recording originating from a scratchy, old record. We then passed around seventh-generation recordings until most of the fourteen-year-old girls in our junior high school were enthralled by this 'new sound'. As our copy had no label, we did not realize that many a fourteen-year-old had previously enjoyed it throughout the past thirty years. Unbeknownst to us, we had discovered the Beatles.

Almost ten years later, the same two girls prepared to go overseas to present a paper at the Beatles 2000 conference. Our topic focused on the 'Fifth Beatle', establishing that the Beatles' producer, Sir George Martin, fulfils that role.[1] The research leading to that paper was revealing in many ways. Martin's role evolved throughout the Beatles' career. He began as simply an arranger and authority figure – someone that could educate them in the art of studio production. As the Beatles' sound progressed he began orchestrating and realizing their often vague ideas. Common belief is that his direct influence on their music coincides with the 1967 recording sessions for *Sgt Pepper's Lonely Hearts Club Band*.[2] Throughout the course of further research, we discovered that not only did this influence begin one album earlier, during the *Revolver* sessions, but also that Martin was not alone in his contributions. Furthermore, these contributions were both musical and technical, as the Beatles were on their way to becoming a studio band. The technical innovations revolutionized the Beatles' sound as well as permanently transforming studio practices for bands and solo artists to come.

The first section of this chapter establishes the significant roles of George Martin and his engineers, Ken Townsend and Geoff Emerick, including several inventions made during the *Revolver* recording sessions. The second section focuses on Martin and his relationship with the primary songwriters, Paul McCartney and John Lennon, with particular emphasis on the specific roles he undertakes with each collaborator. A third section describes changes in both the role of the producer and in studio practices. Finally, we discuss how the innovations introduced previously carry through to today's pop industry.

Introducing 'the team'

George Martin brought to the group a background in classical music that the Beatles lacked. In 1947, after three years of music college, he began at the Guildhall Music School of London. There he studied a variety of musical subjects, including orchestration, harmony, composition, piano, and oboe. In 1950 he began at EMI, and by 1955 he was the head of their Parlophone division. There he produced comedy and spoken word albums and dabbled in jazz with the likes of Cleo Laine. Martin signed the Beatles to his label in 1962 and released their first single shortly thereafter. Their second single, 'Please Please Me', reached number one nationally on 11 January 1963.

When they signed with Martin, approximately fifteen years their senior, the Beatles were ignorant of the complexities surrounding composition and recording. Throughout their early recording sessions, the group began learning various techniques by observing Martin. Although he involved the band, Martin then held the authority. Acting as a father figure, or teacher, he dictated which singles were to be recorded and released, which Beatle was to sing, and even attempted to choose a leader for the group. Like any good mentor, he eventually guided the group in its own direction regardless of his initial inclinations.

As mentioned by Russell Reising in the introductory comments to this volume, *Revolver* is an album of 'firsts'. We could add that, from the production side of things, it was the first album in which Martin's role evolved from simply teaching to collaborating equally with the other members of the band;[3] the first album produced by Martin's new production company, AIR;[4] and the first album engineered by Geoff Emerick. Emerick, a young engineer without any pre-conceived limitations, acted as Martin's 'sidekick', devising new ways of miking and recording (Lewisohn, 2000a, p. 70). Unlike Emerick, Ken Townsend had joined Abbey Road in 1954 and had intermittently worked with Martin and the Beatles since their 1962 audition. He was responsible for the many new studio inventions pioneered during these recording sessions, although he was a maintenance engineer – one of the 'backroom boy[s]' (Laurence, 1978, p. 58) – who was rarely credited with working directly with the Beatles.[5] Townsend, Emerick, and Martin were key to the groundbreaking sound displayed on *Revolver*.

Townsend's most influential discovery was that of Artificial Double Tracking (ADT) after a Beatles session in 1966.[6] The Beatles had been double tracking their voices to create a fuller sound since 'A Taste of Honey' in 1963. This consists of 'the superimposition of one or more parts onto an already existing recording ...' (Everett, 1999, p. 316). There were several inefficiencies to this process.

It monopolized two of the four tracks available, as well as being extremely time-consuming.[7] ADT was the solution to these problems – it was quicker and required the use of only one track. Ken Townsend recalls:

> I got the idea of double tracking the vocals in order to cut down the amount of time we spent double-tracking. Using various pieces of equipment I was able to create a system whereby we could record two sets of voices at once and then space the second voice at any required time interval either side of the original. (Southall, 1982, p. 81)

It is beyond the scope of this chapter to provide a complete technical definition for ADT; however Julien (1999) provides a detailed technical description of the process.[8] For the less technically-inclined, Mark Lewisohn describes ADT best by equating it with photography:

> In photography, the placement of a negative directly over another does not alter the image. The two become one. But move one slightly, and the image widens. ADT does this with tape. One voice laid perfectly on top of another produces one image. But move the second voice by just a few milli-seconds, and two separate images emerge. (Lewisohn, 2000a, p. 70)

ADT became a characteristic Beatle sound, used on virtually every *Revolver* track. Post-*Revolver* examples include McCartney's guitar solo in 'Good Morning Good Morning'; Lennon's vocals in 'I Am the Walrus'; the saxophones in 'Savoy Truffle'; Ringo Starr's vocals in 'Octopus' Garden'; and Eric Clapton's guitar solo on 'While My Guitar Gently Weeps'.[9] On this particular track, Clapton felt that his solo was not 'Beatley enough,' and it was thus treated with ADT to give it the required sound (Everett, 1999, p. 202). ADT, sometimes known as *automatic* double tracking, has since become a staple of any good recording studio. It has also evolved into various other effects, such as chorus, phasing, flanging, and digital delay, used both live and in the studio.[10]

Another of Townsend's inventions was discovered during the recording of 'Paperback Writer' on 14 April 1966.[11] In order to enhance the sound of the Rickenbacker bass played by McCartney, he used 'a loudspeaker as a microphone' (Lewisohn, 2000a, p. 74). By creating a 'harmony' of electronic currents, fuzz or distortion resulted. This type of experimentation was not considered appropriate at the time, and Townsend's superiors admonished him as he could have severely damaged the equipment by overload. They were, however, able to cut the final record using the new ATOC (Automatic Transient Overload Control) to stop the stylus from jumping (Lewisohn, 2000a, p. 74). Townsend continued these sorts of inventions throughout the Beatles' career, including a DIT (Direct Injection) box, which allows for a bass or guitar to be plugged directly into the recording console. Townsend believes that the Beatles were the first to use this during the *Sgt Pepper* sessions.

Geoff Emerick was also experimenting with creating new sounds through the use of microphones. He describes his philosophy best in his essay 'Recording Techniques', where he compares the role of an engineer to a photographer:

> ... microphones can be thought of as camera lenses. They can be bright or dull, and can have a wide sensitive pick-up area like a wide-angle lens, or a narrow sensitive area like a telephoto lens. Like the photographer, the recording engineer will use whichever is most appropriate for the job at hand.
>
> Tone, or equalization, is added to the mikes to enhance the sound, and I often think of this in terms of colour: treble brings out the greens, high treble brings out the blues and silvers, and the bass can be described in shades of browns and golds. As a recording engineer, therefore, you are painting a picture with sound. (Emerick, 1988, p. 256)

For example, he almost lost his job as engineer at Abbey Road studios for trying to capture a new vocal sound by putting a microphone into a bowl of water and singing into the bowl (Martin and Pearson, 1994a, p. 78). More significant were his innovative ways of miking the various instruments used on *Revolver* tracks, such as 'Tomorrow Never Knows', 'Eleanor Rigby', and 'Got To Get You Into My Life'.

Emerick was responsible for developing the Beatles' signature drum sound heard beginning with *Revolver* and later on *Sgt Pepper*, instigated by Starr's request to enhance his sound on recording (Sharp, 1998, p. 19). He did this by putting a large sweater inside the bass drum, moving the mike closer, and then limiting and compressing the resulting sound.[12] Emerick used a similar technique on both 'Eleanor Rigby' and 'Got To Get You Into My Life', where he once again moved the microphones as close as he could. The mikes almost touched the fret-board on the string instruments during the former song, and were inside the bells of the brass instruments during the latter, instead of being six feet away as was done previously. Emerick continued this miking method in tracks such as 'Good Morning Good Morning', where the brass was once again recorded with microphones inside the bells. The Grateful Dead took the practice of separately miking each instrument to the stage that same year (Scully and Dalton, 1996, p. 36).

These innovations were not Emerick's only contributions that affected how the Beatles worked in the studio. During the recording of *Revolver* he worked closely with Martin and cultivated a unique relationship with him, which in itself influenced the Beatles' studio practice. Martin had not previously had a relationship with other engineers that allowed them to work virtually independent of one another. According to Martin, Emerick has 'the best pair of ears in the business' (Martin, 1988, p. 267):

> Geoff Emerick and I, for example, work very well as a team, because we work together so much, and respect what each other does. We keep our separate areas of responsibility quite definite. Our long collaboration has led to a deep understanding, so that I know in advance what he is going to do and he knows in advance what I want. (Martin and Hornsby, 1979, p. 249)

We have already established what some of Emerick's 'areas of responsibility' are in the preceding paragraphs. It is also necessary to discuss those of the producer, George Martin.

Due to Martin's formal music training, his contributions had always superseded those of a traditional producer. As on many of the Beatles' early albums, he continued to play various keyboard instruments throughout the *Revolver* recordings.[13] For instance, he played the opening organ sequence in 'Got To Get You Into My Life', and the honky-tonk piano heard throughout 'Good Day Sunshine' and ending 'Tomorrow Never Knows'. As well, instead of calling in outside arrangers, Martin had always arranged the Beatles' vocal harmonies and instrumentation himself, along with composing his own playing contributions.

Martin had developed an expertise in the use of sound effects making comedy records, such as those by Peter Sellers and Spike Jones, during his early Parlophone years. He incorporated this knowledge into the making of 'Yellow Submarine'. Mark Lewisohn comments in his chronicle *The Beatles Recording Sessions*: '... it is a very interesting recording, crammed full of sound effects, party noises, whoops, chants and general silliness' (Lewisohn, 2000a, p. 80). Everyone was involved: studio staff, friends, the Beatles and Martin – a true 'team' effort. For instance, to make the 'whooshing noises' they filled an old metal bathtub with water and dragged chains through it; they clinked glasses; blew bubbles in a bucket; Lennon cried commands from the adjacent echo chamber as well putting his voice through a Vox guitar amplifier; and everyone joined in to create the rowdy choruses. Other sound effects such as shaking coal in a box to simulate marching feet were not used in the final cut (Lewisohn, 2000a, p. 81). The brass band heard at the end of the second verse was an 'uncredited 78rpm snippet', cut and pasted in by Martin (MacDonald, 1994, p. 183). The engineers also used varispeed to speed up the vocals and slow down the instruments (Everett, 1999, pp. 56–57). Martin and the Beatles continued to use sound effects in later songs. Taped effects were used in songs such as 'Sgt Pepper's Lonely Hearts Club Band' and its reprise, and 'Good Morning Good Morning'. In 'You Know My Name (Look up the Number)', the Beatles once again produced their own sounds in a similar fashion to 'Yellow Submarine'.

George Martin as realizer and orchestrator

While Martin, Townsend, Emerick, and the Beatles continued to work as a team, Martin took on unique roles when working with both Lennon and McCartney. As they pushed their compositional limits, they made Martin an integral part of the group instead of simply their producer. For Lennon, Martin realized his ideas, whereas with McCartney, he continued to evolve as an orchestrator. When working with George Harrison, however, his role was less defined. Although Martin gives Harrison credit for his innovative sounds, such as his use of various Indian instruments, less time was spent perfecting Harrison's songs (Hertsgaard, 1995, p. 172; Norman, 1981a, p. 275). Emerick recalls: 'One really got the impression that George was being given a certain amount of time to do his tracks whereas the others could spend as long as they wanted. One felt under more pressure when doing one of George's songs' (Lewisohn, 2000a, p. 81). As such, the ensuing section will focus on Martin's contributions to Lennon's and McCartney's songs from *Revolver*.

Martin came upon the role of realizer with 'Tomorrow Never Knows'. This was the first song recorded during the *Revolver* sessions and, consequently, set the tone for the entire album. John Lennon had a vivid imagination, and it was often Martin's responsibility to fulfill musically the visual pictures Lennon was unable to articulate. Martin remembers: 'He'd make whooshing noises and try to describe what only he could hear in his head, saying he wanted a song "to sound like an orange"' (Lewisohn, 2000a, p. 99).[14] For 'Tomorrow Never Knows', Lennon instructed him to create a sound like 'the Dalai Lama singing from the highest mountain top' (Lewisohn, 2000a, p. 72). Martin remembers Lennon wanting to 'make real the voice he heard in his head when he was reading [*The Psychedelic Experience*]' (Martin and Pearson, 1994a, p. 79).[15] Under Martin's guidance, the Beatles and the production team brought these vague ideas to life by using voice altering methods, backwards guitar, tape loops, and other new recording techniques.

Many people working throughout the *Revolver* sessions, including Martin, describe Lennon's need to constantly alter his voice: 'He was always saying to [Martin]: "Do something with my voice! You know, put something on it. Smother it with tomato ketchup or something. Make it different." … [A]s long as it wasn't his natural voice coming through, he was reasonably happy' (Coleman, 1995, p. 384).[16] Martin did this for Lennon in 'Tomorrow Never Knows' by diverting Lennon's voice through the rotating Leslie speaker of a Hammond organ. When recorded by a microphone positioned on the outcoming end of the speaker this creates a swirling affect. The result was such a success that Emerick recalls the Beatles wanting to apply this technique as often and with as many instruments as possible (Lewisohn, 2000a, p. 72).[17] Jerry Garcia from the Grateful Dead had a similar need to mask his voice. He used devices such as a phaser (related to ADT), as well as stacking several of his vocal tracks in harmony to disguise the main voice (Scully and Dalton, 1996, pp. 156, 191). Bands or artists such as Steely Dan, Tom Petty, Megadeth, Wonderland, and Duran Duran continued to experiment with the Leslie speaker. In the late 1960s, the Univox Uni-Vibe was invented in an unsuccessful attempt to simulate this sound. However, artists such as Jimi Hendrix began to use it for its own unique sound (Gore, 1999, p. 108).

The cacophony of sound surrounding this Leslie-enhanced vocal as well as the 'psychedelic interlude' at 0:56 were created from a series of tape loops. In art music, this trend carries the name 'Musique Concrète', and began as early as Pierre Schaeffer's 1948 composition, *Etude aux chemins de fer*. Schaeffer discovered the ability to 'lock-groove', which loops one groove on a record (Snyder, 2001). This led to looping tapes as technology advanced. He and other composers such as Edgar Varése and Karlheinz Stockhausen eventually manipulated these loops by using different speeds and turning them backwards.[18] McCartney had begun listening to Stockhausen shortly before the *Revolver* sessions, and was experimenting with tape loops at home using his Brennell machines. Prior to 'Tomorrow Never Knows', he was already dabbling with tape speed and direction, splicing, and re-recording sound after sound without erasing the original. McCartney brought these ideas to the studio in order to complement Lennon's composition, and it was the first time that Musique Concrète carried over to the pop industry. This tradition was carried on by Pink Floyd, the Grateful Dead, and Frank Zappa, among other artists (MacDonald, 1994, p. 199).

A very elaborate set-up was used for the recording of the tape loops, utilizing all of Abbey Road's amenities. Martin selected a total of sixteen loops, which were later narrowed down to the five best. The Beatles and various technicians played these live in studio, while Martin and Emerick controlled the main studio console. They manipulated these loops in various ways. One loop is probably McCartney's laughter sped up; another is of Harrison's sitar at varying speeds, even changing from fast to slow within a single loop.[19] The guitar solo directly following the aforementioned 'psychedelic interlude' was added later. The tape was actually McCartney's guitar solo from 'Taxman', chopped up, spliced, turned backwards, and slowed down (MacDonald, 1994, p. 169). As with the use of the Leslie speaker, the Beatles continued to experiment with and incorporate tape loops into their music. As shown in the above discussion, 'Tomorrow Never Knows' was a precursor of what was to come. For example, these new forms of electronic manipulation are also demonstrated in 'Rain' and 'I'm Only Sleeping', among others during the *Revolver* sessions, as well as many tracks on succeeding albums.[20] Jimi Hendrix, Frank Zappa, Spirit, and Steely Dan took influence from the Beatles in this way. As technology advanced, digital looping became the norm for newer bands such as the Chemical Brothers and Garbage.

Martin similarly manipulated tape speed and direction in the making of 'Rain'. Both the vocal and instrumental tracks were recorded very fast and later slowed to add a more mysterious effect. When attempting to enhance the play-out of the song, Martin 'took one of John's phrases he had sung and turned it round, realizing that musically it would fit – the line would fit the chords – and that it might sound intriguing. [He] pasted it on, and it sounded good' (Martin and Pearson, 1994a, p. 79). Various accounts differ as to how this technique was discovered; this is irrelevant as backwards guitar was already used during the making of 'Tomorrow Never Knows' (Everett, 1999, p. 44).

The same techniques were used on 'I'm Only Sleeping', but in a more complex fashion. The vocal track displays 'a circuitous process of speeding up and down which ended with the track a semitone below its original key of E minor' (MacDonald, 1994, p. 179). Harrison added two backwards guitar tracks placed atop one another. Because he already had the melody for his solo in mind, Martin wrote the notes out in retrograde so that the final result resembled Harrison's original melodic idea but with a unique sound. This sound has since been reproduced by bands such as the Jimi Hendrix Experience, Tomorrow, Spirit, Frank Zappa, and the Red Hot Chili Peppers (in their song 'Give it Away').

'Tomorrow Never Knows', 'Rain', and 'I'm Only Sleeping' were thus three pioneering tracks in 'electrosong'. Al Lee coined this somewhat inane, albeit appropriate, term in his 1968 article 'The Poetics of the Beatles', using it to describe the Beatles' 'new art form': 'They have stopped giving concerts because their new art form is impossible before live audiences; they alone have switched completely from song to electronic stereo song. Let me phrase it "electrosong"' (Lee, 1968, p. 102). Martin, the Beatles, and the production team continued to build on this new sound in order to realize Lennon's ideas. McCartney and Harrison incorporated some of the discoveries for use in their own compositions as well. These, however, were not the only consequential aspects of *Revolver*. Martin also continued to develop as an orchestrator by collaborating with McCartney.

McCartney communicated more about what he was trying to achieve with a particular song. Even when he was not sure of how to accomplish a specific sound, he would work together with Martin until they realized the desired effect. Little less than a year earlier Martin first suggested complementing McCartney's 'Yesterday' with a string arrangement. McCartney then took the initiative to familiarize himself with other orchestral instruments. He would often suggest the instrument or the type of sound he wanted. During recording, McCartney would dictate the wanted notes, Martin would transcribe, and various session musicians would play, a process exemplified by McCartney's songs 'For No One' and 'Eleanor Rigby'. The only other track on the album that uses orchestral instruments is 'Got To Get You Into My Life'. In this case, there was no transcription – the musicians worked directly with McCartney while Martin remained in charge of the session.[21]

'For No One', however, followed the pattern as described above, although sources suggest that it was Martin who initiated the use of a French horn for the solo sections of the ballad (MacDonald, 1994, p. 182; Everett, 1999, pp. 54–55). McCartney sat down with Martin to get his ideas on paper. Together, they conspired to have their guest player, Alan Civil of the London Philharmonia, thrown by including a note outside the normal range in order to fit with McCartney's musical idea. McCartney remembers:

> George was in for the crack, he liked that. He said, 'It'll work, it'll work.' On the session Alan Civil said, 'George?' and looked at us both. He said, 'George, you've written a D,' and George and I just looked at him and held our nerve and said, 'Yes?' And he gave us a crafty look and went, 'Okay' (Miles, 1997, p. 289).

Martin and McCartney continued to collaborate on their notations, and even later similarly befuddled piccolo trumpet player David Mason when recording 'Penny Lane'.

The use of strings as rhythm on 'Eleanor Rigby' was McCartney's idea, but Martin realized the final product with only the melody in mind. To complement the composer's concept, Martin took inspiration from a film currently in theatres – Truffaut's *Fahrenheit 451*, with a score composed by Bernard Herrmann. Herrmann was well known for the scores from several Alfred Hitchcock movies such as *Vertigo* and *Psycho*. His individual style included short, punctuated, rhythmic motifs normally scored for a string orchestra. This new type of string writing departed from the previously established style. In an article dealing with the connection between Martin and Herrmann, and artists who they subsequently influenced, John Richardson surmises:

> When George Martin arranged 'Eleanor Rigby' for strings, there weren't a great many models to choose from of how strings could be used in the repetitive context of popular music. Herrmann's use of strings offered a clear alternative to the more stereotyped, romantic uses that had previously prevailed both in film and popular music; it was, moreover, a usage that, because of films like *Psycho*, was fast becoming a part of the musical vernacular of the general public. (Richardson, 1998, p. 171)[22]

Perhaps unbeknownst to Martin, in taking influence from Herrmann he used many techniques previously established in art music to signify the emotional state of the main characters (Eleanor Rigby and Father Makenzie) and the progression of the story. Richardson lists several of these processes, including using repetition to create suspense and to distance the listener from the events. He also introduces a characteristic 'death drive'. In 'Eleanor Rigby' the death drive is typified by a Baroque-influenced, chromatically-descending, lament theme. In his paper, Richardson describes the descending lines found in the chorus as 'mirror[ing] the irrevocable descent of Rigby herself at the same time as they invoke the death drive' (Richardson, 1998, pp. 172–173). These types of themes were often found in Baroque tragic operas, such as the ground bass and aria 'When I am laid in earth' from Henry Purcell's opera *Dido and Aeneas* (Figure 7.1):

Dido and Aeneas: When I am laid in earth

Henry Purcell

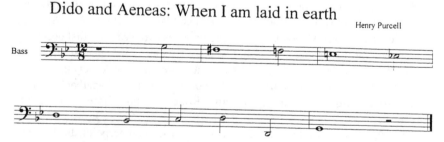

Figure 7.1a   Ground bass from *Dido and Aeneas*, 'When I am laid in earth', by Purcell, mm. 6–11[23]

Figure 7.1b   Descending chromatic line from 'Eleanor Rigby',
mm. 19–22[24]

Martin continued to provide orchestral arrangements for innumerable Beatles songs, for example: 'Within You Without You'; 'A Day in the Life'; 'Fool on the Hill'; 'I Am the Walrus'; 'Piggies'; 'Honey Pie'; and the smarmy 'Good Night'. Other artists also began using orchestral instruments. For example, David Bowie included several members from the London Philharmonia for his 1967 album *Deram*; the Who used a French horn in their 1969 'rock opera' *Tommy*; and in the same year, the Rolling Stones' 'You Can't Always Get What You Want' featured a French horn along with the London Bach Choir. Earth Wind and Fire began using symphonic instruments with their first album in 1971, and by their 1977 album *All'N'All* they were out-sizing the Beatles in their use of orchestral musicians. The Electric Light Orchestra was similar in this respect. The use of this instrumentation is so prevalent today that it is more difficult to find a band or artist that does not use it.

But Martin's instrumental work was only part of the story. His vocal arrangement also enhanced the sound of 'Eleanor Rigby'. Emerick describes this other 'Martin speciality': 'George's real expertise was and still is in vocal harmony work, there's no doubt about that. That is his forte, grooming and working out those great harmonies' (Lewisohn, 2000a, p. 83). In the song at hand, Martin suggested that McCartney combine two melodic lines: '... I had noticed that the phrase "Oh, look at all the lonely people," would work if it were sung against the end of the main tune. Counterpoint. So I suggested we did [sic] an overdub. They were knocked out with the result ...' (Martin and Pearson, 1994a, p. 136). In the more complex 'Lady Madonna', Martin again takes two ideas that first occur separately and integrates them. As well, two contrary ideas work against one another in 'She's Leaving Home', although they are introduced together. Other *Revolver* tracks also exemplify Martin's vocal arranging: 'Paperback Writer'; 'And Your Bird Can Sing'; 'Doctor Robert'; and 'Here, There, and Everywhere'.[25]

As with 'Eleanor Rigby', 'Paperback Writer' uses counterpoint. In this case, the material is not drawn from elsewhere in the song nor is it the combination of two contrary ideas. First, Martin closely overlaps several lines in the opening sequence, which recur throughout the song. The Beatles had not previously attempted this level of sophistication in counterpoint. Earlier uses of the technique were more similar to that which occurs later in the song. A second type of counterpoint is heard during the third verse where one voice slowly counters the faster melody with a rendition of 'Frère Jacques', reminiscent of the style heard in 'Help'. This repeats again during the fourth verse, with a second backing voice added as descant. The additive style demonstrated here, in the fourth verse, surfaces again in 'And Your Bird Can Sing'.

In the chorus from 'Doctor Robert', Martin simulates harmonic complexity. When listening, one imagines a three-or four-voice contrapuntal madrigal (O'Grady, 1975, p. 317). In reality, McCartney and Lennon each contribute only one line to a simply harmonized two-part refrain (Figure 7.2):

Doctor Robert

Lennon/McCartney

Figure 7.2   Chorus from 'Doctor Robert', mm. 19–25[26]

In the chorus, ADT may have been used to create the effect of more people singing. Martin's ingenious harmonic arrangement, however, creates the perception of many parts as opposed to only two voices.

Although recorded after all of the above, 'Here, There, and Everywhere' uses the simplest vocal texture in *Revolver*. According to Martin, he kept the accompanying voices uncomplicated, using mainly basic progressions in block chords – 'Very simple to do … but very effective' (Lewisohn, 2000a, p. 83). The opening progression uses an upper voice that slides downward chromatically to compliment the rising melody. This harmonizes I moving through iii to ♭III, before beginning the simplest aspect: a central progression that returns throughout the song. It consists of a two-measure motif of unadorned triads moving upward by step – from I to IV – repeated twice. This motif recurs in mm. 12–16 ('There, running my hands …'); mm. 24–28, which is repeated ('… ev'rywhere, knowing that love …'); and the closing mm. 44–47 ('To be there, and ev'rywhere …'). The only other harmonies used are a series of applied Vs that lead to the half-cadence at the end of each repeated verse.[27]

Throughout most of the *Revolver* sessions, Martin's arrangements grew more complex. This is a direction that continued in later albums. In this respect, 'Here, There, and Everywhere' was a step backward, most likely due to the fact that the Beatles' final tour was imminent. As a result the recording sessions for both this and 'She Said She Said' may have been rushed. Had time not been a factor, the complexity of 'Here, There, and Everywhere' may have reached that of *Abbey Road*'s 'Sun King' and 'Because' (incidentally, the only composition where Martin actually handed out scores as written by himself) (Porter, 1979a, pp. 402–404; Laurence, 1978, p. 56). The signature harmonies of the Beach Boys, Crosby Stills & Nash, and later Jefferson Airplane resemble and even surpass Martin's vocal arrangements. A perfect example is the Crosby Stills & Nash cover of McCartney's 'Blackbird,' found in their 1991 box set.

George Martin was essential in developing the sound heard on *Revolver*. In his new role of realizer he became a conduit, channelling Lennon's ideas into a coherent form. As an orchestrator not only did he articulate McCartney's musical conceptions, but he also instigated in the young songwriter a desire to further explore the use of art influences in his music. 'I suppose the indications were already there. "Eleanor Rigby" and "Tomorrow Never Knows", from *Revolver*, had been strong hints for those with ears to hear what was to come. They were forerunners of a complete change of style' (Martin and Hornsby, 1979, p. 199).

New trends in production aspects: a complete change of style

The above discussion demonstrates that the Beatles and their production team instigated a change of style not only for their own studio practices and music, but also for other bands and solo artists to follow. The various inventions developed by 'the team' during the *Revolver* sessions enabled the studio to become a creative medium, an instrument of sorts, for artists. Other characteristics of the Beatles' *Revolver* carried through to later bands, including the use of more complex vocal arrangements and orchestral instrumentation. A two-fold change in the role of the producer also followed: many artists chose to become their own producers and engineers, and the professionals continued the evolution that Martin began:

Professional producer Jimmy Bowen describes his vocation's role prior to *Revolver*: The record producer's role has changed. It used to be he was an A&R man. His main responsibilities were to find hit songs, properly cast them for the right artist, call in an arranger and book the musicians. It was a casting job, almost – a putting together of the music. (Denisoff, 1986, p. 165)

Having formal music background, Martin paved the way for combining these various roles. He not only produced music for the Beatles, but also was an active contributor as realizer, arranger, orchestrator, and even performer. Without Martin, the Beatles' sound would not have evolved as it did. This combination worked in reverse as well, as Lennon and especially McCartney joined Martin and his production team in refining, mixing, and editing their compositions. The reciprocal relationship that developed during the *Revolver* sessions eventually allowed these roles to merge, wherein artists became their own producers. This began as early as 1968 when Jimi Hendrix produced his album *Electric Ladyland*.

In earlier recording sessions, the Beatles followed strict studio guidelines, defining where, when, and how they were to record. Beginning with *Rubber Soul*, the Beatles began to break these rules by extending their hours in the studio. By *Revolver*, this was common practice. They were creating a true studio album – not only recording and mixing at Abbey Road, but also rehearsing, and even composing, their new songs inside Abbey Road. As aforementioned, time was also spent experimenting with new sounds and technology that could not be reproduced live. Bands such as Pink Floyd followed suit, demanding more studio time and resources to continue the Beatles' experiments in the use of the studio as an instrument (Southall, 1982, p. 126).[28] The sound manipulation innovations used on *Revolver*, such as new miking techniques, ADT, the use of the Leslie, and tape manipulation, made the studio essential.

The sound of *Revolver* has come full circle and can be heard today in the music of younger artists such as Oasis and the Chemical Brothers. These artists, like the two young girls introduced at the opening of this chapter, are a generation removed from Beatlemania. Today, artists use computer technology to simulate and further explore many of the above techniques. Oasis tries to capture sounds created by the Beatles during the *Revolver* period in their most recent album *Standing on the Shoulder of Giants*. The group is known for 'mercilessly aping the Beatles (as is their wont)' (Stewart, 2001), and this album is no different. The trajectory of the band's music resembles that of the Beatles, beginning with their first album, *Definitely Maybe*, followed by *(What's the Story) Morning Glory*. Both depict Beatlesque backing vocals and Liam Gallagher's Lennon-sounding lead. Like the Beatles' debut, these two albums are simpler in nature. *Standing on the Shoulder of Giants*, on the other hand, parallels *Revolver* in its shift of musical direction. Noel Gallagher, Oasis's songwriter, comments:

> It used to be that we never recorded anything that was *too* out there because we wanted to make sure we could reproduce onstage whatever we did in the studio. But that approach can limit the way you make a record. This time, we said, "Well, we can just take the damn computer on the road" (Molenda, 2000, p. 76).

The album was written over one year at Gallagher's sixteen-track home studio. With the help of an engineer, he prepared demos of each song using the foolproof mixing software Pro Tools. This treatment is most notable in 'Fuckin' in the

Bushes' and 'Who Feels Love'. The former uses the techniques discussed above without the melodic aspects. Most obvious are the digital loops, becoming more dense as the song progresses: both a man's and a woman's distorted speaking; the heavy drum beat; and several repeated guitar riffs. The more melodic 'Who Feels Love' is reminiscent of 'I'm Only Sleeping' in its use of backwards guitar. It is heard in both the opening and closing sequences, as well as complementing Liam Gallagher's haunting lead vocal (eerily similar to Lennon's in 'I'm Only Sleeping') and the Beatlesque harmonies mentioned above.

More blatant in their *Revolver* influence are the Chemical Brothers in 'Let Forever Be' and 'Setting Sun', ironically featuring Noel Gallagher as guest vocalist. The bass and drum loops in 'Let Forever Be' are heavily influenced by those heard on 'Taxman', elaborated upon the originals. As in Oasis' 'Who Feels Love', 'brothers' Tom Rowlands and Ed Simons use a collage of backward sounds throughout their song (i.e., guitar and keyboard), especially in the introduction and conclusion.[29] The two solos featured consecutively also utilize this technique – the first as backing, the second as a feature. It is 'Setting Sun', however, from the Chemical Brothers' 1997 album *Dig Your Own Hole*, that is truly akin to *Revolver*, in this case 'Tomorrow Never Knows'.

Figure 7.3 demonstrates just how similar 'Setting Sun' is to 'Tomorrow Never Knows'. The general construct of both songs are almost identical; variances are due to the differences in length – 'Tomorrow Never Knows' lasts three minutes whereas 'Setting Sun' extends to five and a half minutes.[30] As such there are added sounds in the longer track. 'Tomorrow Never Knows' presents two different vocals along with nine sound-types; 'Setting Sun' includes three contrasting vocals and over fourteen sound-types. The voices of Lennon and Gallagher are treated in like manners. As discussed earlier, Lennon's voice was treated with ADT during the first verse and with the Leslie speaker for the rest of the song. Gallagher, like Lennon, begins each verse with an ADT-like sound followed by a distorted sound similar to the Leslie. The third vocal in 'Setting Sun' does not occur in 'Tomorrow Never Knows'. It is most likely the repeated vocal line heard at 2:37 ('You're coming on strong') slowed to sound like an 'Ahh'.

The aforementioned sound-types of the two songs are linked in many ways. It is most straightforward to compare the songs by introducing each feature as it appears in Figure 7.3:

- The Chemical Brothers use a wah-like buzz to introduce 'Setting Sun' (SS). This strongly resembles the sitar which opens 'Tomorrow Never Knows' (TNK) – in each case it is the only time the sound is heard in this manner.
- Following the opening of SS, the buzz is mixed to the back of the track and is joined by the hypnotic drum loop. This is the greatest connection between the two songs, as the heavy drums are nearly identical to those of Ringo Starr in TNK. Like SS's buzz, McCartney's bass merges with the drums to form an ostinato lasting throughout the song.

'Tomorrow Never Knows'	'Setting Sun'
1. **0:00** – Sitar	1. **0:00** – Wah-like Buzz **0:11** – Building Chord
2. **0:04** – Drum & Bass Beat	2. **0:14** – Drum Beat joins Buzz
3. **0:08** – Seagull Sound	3. **0:43** – Seagull Sound (x2) **0:57** – 'Robotic' Sound (x2) **1:10** – Building Chord **1:11** – 'Ahhs', w/ backwards backing
4. **0:12** – ADT Lead Vocals (Continue until 0:57)	4. **1:25** – ADT-like Vocals, w/ backing oscillation **1:40** – Leslie-like Vocals w/ Wah-like Buzz underneath
5. **0:19** – Chord	5. **2:07** – Chord
6. **0:23** – Bird-like Sounds **0:31** – Seagull Sound	6. **2:08–2:15** – Rotating Seagull Sound (2 different pitch bases)
7. **0:35** – Chord **0:39** – String Loop **0:47** – String Loop **0:49** – Chord **0:54** – String Loop	7. **2:21** – Backward Sound Build-Up **2:23** – 'Ahhs', w/ backwards backing
8. N/A	8. **2:37–2:50** – Beat Stops, Repeated Vocal line & 'Robotic' Sound
9. **Solo: 0:57** – Loop Solo **1:05** – String Loop **Solo: 1:08** – Backward Guitar Solo	9. **Solo: 2:51** – Feedback Solo, with crescendo
10. **1:12** – Seagull Sound **1:16** – Chord **1:17–1:19** – Bird-like Sounds **1:21** – Chord **1:25** – Bird-like Sounds	10. **3:11** – Chord **3:12** – Beat Returns, Rotating Seagull Sound
11. **1:27** – Leslie Lead Vocal	11. **3:33** – ADT-like Vocal, w/ backing oscillation **3:48** – Leslie-like Vocal, w/ Wah-like Buzz Underneath
12. **1:31–2:50** – Various Repetitions of Above Loops	12. **4:14** – Chord **4:16** – Rotating Seagull Sound **4:30–4:44** – Held Guitar Notes **4:44** – Begin Breakdown of Drum Beat via Drum Loop Solo
13. **Change of Style: 2:43–end** – Honky Tonk Piano Enters **2:50–end** – Bird-Like Sounds Return	13. **Change of Style: 4:52–5:24** – Xylophone, Whistles, Tinkling, etc. **5:24–end** – Complete Breakdown

Figure 7.3 Chronological comparison of the Beatles' 'Tomorrow Never Knows' and the Chemical Brothers' 'Setting Sun'

- TNK and SS each use tape/digital loops representative of bird-like and seagull sounds.
- A sustained chord appears following the introduction of both lead vocals. In SS and in TNK this chord recurs often in connection with the above bird sounds.

- There is a solo section midway through TNK and SS. The TNK interlude begins with a 'loop solo' (the 'psychedelic interlude' discussed in the second section of this chapter) – an amalgamation of the existing loops. This is linked to the backward guitar solo by a string loop. In SS the hypnotic beat ceases for a twenty-second interval of feedback – where one signal decrescendos before splitting and building to another sustained chord.
- Both TNK and SS become more chaotic as they approach the closing. In TNK various repetitions of all previously introduced loops rotate. They are alternately mixed towards the back or front along with speed manipulation creating a build-up of sound. During this time, Lennon sings the last verse of the song through the Leslie speaker that ends by repeating the line: 'of the beginning'. To close SS, Gallagher also repeats the last line of the final verse in similar Leslie fashion ('I'll tell you that's just too bad'). In this case it precedes the chaos. The disorder heard in SS also contains previously heard loops mixed as above. As well, held guitar notes are introduced to link the breaking down of the drum beat via a hesitating drum loop solo.
- The endings of both songs begin with a complete change of style. In TNK, Martin plays rag-time on the honky-tonk piano along with a disintegration of the various loops until only the bird sound remains. The xylophone, whistles, chimes and other such sounds in SS also coincide with a collapse of the loop structure foreshadowing a complete breakdown.
- There are other sounds looped in SS that do not have a counterpart in TNK, and vice versa. These include the string loop in TNK as well as a building chord, a 'robotic' whine and a backward sound build-up in SS.

Being that the Chemical Brothers use samples on a regular basis, one wonders whether they sampled sounds from *Revolver* on 'Let Forever Be' and 'Setting Sun' (Rule, 1997, p. 33). On their interactive web-site Rowlands and Simons responded to just that question:[31]

> Ed [Simons]: We've never knowingly sampled the Beatles.
> Tom [Rowlands]: Yeah that is just an accident. The tracks are very different. We have never sampled the Beatles: Being influenced by a piece of music doesn't mean you have to steal it. (Rowlands and Simons, 2001)

This may be true. The resemblance, however, especially with 'Setting Sun', is undeniable.

The Beatles' early bursts of ingenuity were captured using only four-track technology. Later, continuing with albums such as *Sgt Pepper*, the band and their team continued to build on these innovations maximizing the limited technology available. Today, the most basic home recording studio is equipped with sixteen- or thirty-two-track recording consoles, personal computers and various mixing software so that it is possible for even demo tapes to sound professionally made. It is, therefore, ironic that new bands like Oasis and the Chemical Brothers continue to revert to sounds once generated (albeit via different methods using the technology of the era) more than thirty years ago as a base from which to begin their experimentation. Moreover this exploration often yields results sounding similar or related to the original on which they were based. It is incredible then to consider recordings of so long ago comparable in ingenuity and sound quality to recordings of today's standards and to imagine what could result from merely maximizing what is currently available, as once done by the Beatles.

Conclusion: the Beatles' 'family tree'

The repercussions of the *Revolver* innovations made by the Beatles, George Martin, Geoff Emerick, and Ken Townsend can be compared to a genogram ('family tree'). As already discussed in the chapter, many of these inventions or practices influenced other artists to further discover their own elements. Those techniques have further influenced the artists of today who work with computers to combine multiple techniques creating new and unique sounds. This can be illustrated by describing two possible branches of this tree: Martin's orchestral arrangements and the Beatles' extended use of the studio.

The first branch could depict Martin, who initiated the use of orchestral instruments in the Beatles' music beginning with 'Yesterday'. This practice was augmented in many songs during the *Revolver* sessions. He perfected it throughout the course of the Beatles' career. Meanwhile, bands such as the Who, the Rolling Stones, and Pink Floyd took influence from Martin's initial orchestrations. As aforementioned, it is more difficult to find a band or artist who does not complement their music with these sounds.

Another branch may be illustrated as follows. The Beatles began experimenting with new sounds while spending more time in the studio. One thing this led to was the live mix of tape loops in 'Tomorrow Never Knows'. As with orchestration, the Beatles continued to perfect this technique in subsequent albums. Their use extended to other artists such as Pink Floyd, who then demanded more studio time for experimentation and combined the use of techniques like tape looping with orchestration to create an entirely new sound. Eventually amalgamations like those made by Pink Floyd led to the various styles represented in today's music: DJs such as Paul Oakenfold and John Digweed; pop groups like Smashing Pumpkins and Oasis; as well as cross-genre groups including Garbage and the Chemical Brothers.

Little did we know, when we were two fourteen-year-old girls, that the music we discovered on the dusty old tapes was the root behind much of the music to which we were already listening. As adults our musical interests are selective. In writing this chapter we have discovered that the music to which we are drawn is oftentimes that which is most heavily influenced by the ideas discussed above. These affects may not be noticeable by the artists themselves but we now know that the roots of what we listen to today are most often found in the discoveries made by the Beatles, Geoff Emerick, Ken Townsend, and George Martin during the making of *Revolver*.

Notes

1. See 'Everything I Need to Know About Music I Learned from the Fifth Beatle: An Introspection into George Martin's Influence on the Beatles,' in Heinonen, Y., Whiteley, S. and Nurmesjärvi, T. and Koskimäki, J. (eds), *Beatlestudies 3*, University of Jyväskylä, 2001.
2. See, for example, Martin and Hornsby (1979); and this was even our belief as articulated in our previous paper.
3. For more information on George Martin's influence on other Beatles' albums, please refer to the authors' aforementioned article.
4. Unhappy working directly with Parlophone, in 1965 Martin began his own studio with three other producers: Associated Independent Recording (AIR).
5. He is listed as their engineer only three times in Lewisohn (2000a).
6. In Martin and Hornsby (1979), he recalls that this occurred in 1964, but subsequent references list 1966. This is more likely, as ADT was not used in recording until the *Revolver* session (Julien, 1999, pp. 361–362). Lewisohn does not mention the use of ADT until 6 April 1966 (the first day of the *Revolver* sessions) (Lewisohn, 2000a, p. 70).
7. The Beatles began recording on two-track machines, but by 1963 they were using four track machines. Their technology was behind American studio standards, and the Beatles did not obtain eight-track until after the making of *Sgt Pepper*.
8. Pay particular attention to Figure 1 on p. 358.
9. See Everett (1999) for these and other tracks treated with ADT.
10. See Julien (1999), pp. 361–363, with particular attention to Figure 5 on p. 363. The term 'flanging' was actually coined by Lennon, based on a private joke between him and Martin where the latter referred to ADT as 'a double-bifurcated sploshing flange' (Martin and Hornsby, 1979, p. 156). See also Lewisohn (2000a), p. 70; Southall (1982), p. 84; and other sources.
11. Although the single 'Paperback Writer' and its B-side 'Rain' were not included on the *Revolver* album, they were recorded during the same sessions (6 April – 22 June 1966) and utilize the same revolutionary techniques (Lewisohn, 2000a, p. 74).
12. Everett (1999) defines limiters and compressors as: 'electronic devices that would, respectively, either squeeze all constituent dynamic levels of a given recording in geometric ratios to add focus, or "clip" and thus eliminate extreme dynamic peaks so as to prevent distortion that would be caused by an overloaded signal' (p. 316).
13. For the most comprehensive account of Martin's performance contributions both before and after *Revolver*, see MacDonald (1994).
14. It is uncertain to which song Lennon is referring, although 'Lucy in the Sky With Diamonds' is most likely, as this was quoted during the *Sgt Pepper* sessions. As well, it is probably a reference to '… tangerine trees and marmalade skies'.
15. The lyrics from 'Tomorrow Never Knows' are in part taken from Timothy Leary's and Richard Alpert's *The Psychedelic Experience: A Manual Based on the 'Tibetan Book of the Dead'* (New Hyde Park, New York: University Books, 1964; republished in 1992 by Citadel Press and in 1995 by Carol Publishing Group).
16. See also Martin and Hornsby (1979); Martin and Pearson (1994a); Hertsgaard (1995); Lewisohn (2000a); and others.
17. Other songs in which vocals or instruments are run through the Leslie speaker include: 'Magical Mystery Tour' (guitar); 'Across the Universe' (tamboura, tom-tom and guitar); 'Old Brown

Shoe' (guitar); 'Yer Blues' (both lead guitars); 'Something' (rhythm guitar); 'Octopus' Garden' (guitar and backup vocals); and 'The End' (guitar) (Lewisohn, 2000a; MacDonald, 1994).

18. For more on 'Musique Concrète', Pierre Schaeffer, and other composers of the genre, see http://csunix1.lvc.edu/snyder/em/mc.html; Russcol, Herbert (1972), *The Liberation of Sound: an introduction to electronic music*, Englewood Cliffs, New Jersey: Prentice-Hall; Simms, Bryan R. (1996), *Music of the Twentieth Century: Style and Structure*, New York: Schirmer Books.

19. Both Everett and MacDonald provide detailed, albeit slightly conflicting, descriptions of the various loops (MacDonald, 1994, p. 169; Everett, 1999, pp. 37–38). Everett also provides time points for each loop and how often it occurs.

20. Speed manipulation can be heard on 'Penny Lane', 'Fool on the Hill', and 'Across the Universe', for instance, while more complex tape loop techniques were included in 'Strawberry Fields Forever'; 'Being For the Benefit of Mr Kite'; the unreleased 'Carnival Of Light'; 'Magical Mystery Tour'; 'I Am The Walrus'; 'Revolution 9'; and 'Sun King/Mean Mr Mustard'.

21. See Lewisohn (2000a) where Peter Coe, one of the brass players, reminisces on this session (p. 79).

22. For a more detailed description of the connection between Eleanor Rigby and the music from *Psycho*, see Richardson's paper.

23. Score found in Claude V. Palisca, ed. (1988), *Norton Anthology of Western Music, Vol. I*, 2nd edn, New York: W.W. Norton & Company.

24. Taken from Lennon and McCartney (1966) 'Eleanor Rigby', *Beatles Complete*, Warner Bros. Publications Inc.

25. In Porter (1979a), Martin responds to questions submitted by the author that he 'did all the arrangements for all the Beatles songs up to the LET IT BE album ...'. He clarifies that 'although their [vocal] harmonies were never written down they were the product of my arranging and the singers themselves'. It is likely that the more complex arrangements, especially those discussed in our chapter were those most influenced by Martin. See also Laurence (1978), p. 56.

26. Lyrics found in Lennon and McCartney (1966) 'Doctor Robert', *Beatles Complete*. Musical notation derived by the authors.

27. Lyrics found in Lennon and McCartney (1966) 'Here, There, And Everywhere', *Beatles Complete*.

28. Pink Floyd was heavily influenced by the Beatles in many respects. For more on this relationship, see Shaugn O'Donnell's chapter in this volume.

29. It is likely that Noel Gallagher was influenced by participating in this song which was released a year prior to *Standing on the Shoulder of Giants*.

30. It was common in the 1960s to keep a song under a prescribed time for radio play. No such limitations exist today.

31. http://www.astralwerks.com/chemical/ask/musicresponse.html

Chapter 8

The Beatles for everyone: rearranging base and superstructure in the rock ballad

Cy Schleifer

The Beatles, both as musicians and as pop icons, are one of the most influential and continually popular groups to ever find themselves on the world stage. Their songs defined an era and still manage to find a place in the hearts of younger audiences. Why have such longevity and importance grown out of the relatively simple musical structure created by these four heroes of rock and roll? One reason – besides the remarkable moment they encountered and helped define in Europe and America in the 1960s – is that they were able to create their own sense of the musical structure they inherited. In doing so they have restructured and rearranged the playing field of rock music.

To help show how the Beatles changed the face of music I intend to examine their deceptively simple and not overly popular song 'For No One' from *Revolver*. This song, written and recorded by Paul McCartney in one day, showcases how the Beatles take a simple traditional structure, in this case a ballad, and transform it into something uniquely their own. The ballad form has a long tradition in both folk and popular music. The popular ballad was developed in the twentieth-century work of Tin Pan Alley – Irving Berlin, George Gershwin, even Elvis Presley's 'Unchained Melody'. Additional examples I use in my discussion are the Beatles' 'Yesterday' and 'Yellow Submarine'. The ballad structure offers strict harmonic, musical, and lyrical forms, which McCartney rearranges in 'For No One' and in many songs that transformed subsequent rock music. 'For No One' presents a powerful example of the rearrangement of the harmonic form of the ballad by confusing and reconfiguring the relationship between 'basic' and 'ornamental' aspects of musical form. Specifically, I will show how McCartney's use of a plain 'walking bass line' in both the piano and the bass guitar, reminiscent of baroque counterpoint, confuses the relationship between bass and chord type found in the early rock 'n' roll music of the 1950s. In addition, I will show how the odd bridge of 'For No One' and George Martin's score rearrange and deepen the texture of rock music. Finally, I will show how the story implied in the ballad dissolves the rhyming and narrative structure of ballad. Many of these features of music, texture, and lyric have resurfaced, time and again, in the music of Paul Simon, Billy Joel, and many others who succeeded the Beatles.

The 'base' of the Beatles' music – the walking bass line I discuss – had been used previously in popular music, most notably perhaps, in the music of Motown. However, the bass was never emphasized as it was by the Beatles. Instead, it was intermingled with the chord progression, making it seem like a musical counterpoint rather than a 'basic' anchor of the traditional ballad form. Moreover, an examination of the bass (line) and (musical) superstructure of 'For No One' goes beyond showing the power of this harmonic element: it extends it to musical and conceptual terms beyond anything the Beatles encountered in popular rock music in the 1950s and 1960s. Paul's bass playing created a stylistic, formal, and thematic resource that has been infused into modern-day popular music.

The base of the bass

'For No One' is comprised of five different voices. The keyboard (piano and clavier), played by McCartney, provides the bass line in the opening chorus while articulating the chord changes throughout with the right hand. Dubbed over the keyboard, McCartney's bass guitar enters during the first bridge where it takes over, providing a grounding over which the piano, and later the French horn, can play. The bass guitar ornaments the bass line: it arpeggiates the 'base' with its

Figure 8.1   A short excerpt from 'For No One' bringing together its five voices

own superstructural formations that both coincide and counterpoint the melody in an elaborate transformation of the ballad form. The percussion, a drum kit, played by Ringo Starr, keeps simple time by strictly answering the bass line in the piano or the bass guitar by subdividing the beat. The French horn solo, added later by hornist Alan Civil, provides a solo line replacing the vocals during one of the choruses. Finally the vocals sung by McCartney form a uniquely Beatlesque thematic harmony which floats over the whole of the foundation. Figure 8.1 offers a short excerpt from 'For No One' that brings together its five voices.[1]

What makes 'For No One' a powerful transformation of traditional forms, and an equally powerful example of the Beatles' musical innovations, is the manner in which its bass intermingles with the chords themselves, confusing 'base' and superstructure, instead of simply anchoring the harmonic structure by emphasizing the tonic of each chord. Therefore, in approaching the transformed ballad form of 'For No One', I will focus on the relationship of the bass and the music. With the foundation of the bass, I will continue by examining the chord arrangements and instrumental score; and finally I will analyze the transformation of the ballad scheme of the lyrics which float, superstructurally, above the harmonics and musicality of the ballad itself. Because of this arrangement, the first two sections of this chapter will be most musically technical, following more or less abstract structures of sound and melody. The integration of abstractions of sound and melody with the sensible meanings and feelings of the song as a whole characterizes, as much as anything else, the achievement of the Beatles in popular music.

At the heart of 'For No One', McCartney uses a relatively simple bass line (Figure 8.2). During the chorus the bass starts on the tonic note, C, and descends down the scale five notes then jumps to a flat seven, B♭, for the turnaround. (A turnaround is a bar, a note, or a chord that leads the music back to whence it came. In this case the B♭ brings us back to the C or tonic.) Here is what the bass line looks like alone:

C- B- A- G- F- B♭- C

This bass line is played over eight bars (with a four-bar repeating pattern of the 'chorus'), after which 'For No One' presents what has traditionally been called a bridge, or the musical material that creates a transition between two themes.[2] Traditionally the ballad form in popular music is structured by two repetitions of

Figure 8.2   A transcript of the bass line in 'For No One' *(continued)*

Figure 8.2   A transcript of the bass line in 'For No One' *(concluded)*

the chorus followed by the bridge and then a third repetition of the chorus. 'Yellow Submarine' takes this form.[3] Both the chorus and the bridge are defined in terms of their musical and chordal lines. In 'For No One', however, the bass line 'walks' down the scale while the harmonic progression follows a completely different pattern. Against the falling bass line, the chords suggest a climbing motion, C major – E minor – A minor – C major – F major – and then B♭ major for the turnaround (Figure 8.3):

Figure 8.3   The chords in 'For No One' against a falling bass line

We can examine this relationship even more closely. Following the traditional form, the chorus – with its contrary movement – repeats itself twice before it moves to the bridge. The chords are all simple triads (three-note chords), yet they intertwine with the bass in an unusual but structured manner. The simplest of bass lines heard in the rock music of the 1950s – and, I should add, in a lot of pop music today (and, for the most part, in 'Yellow Submarine') – just re-emphasizes the root or the single tonic note of a chord. For instance, the bass notes C-F-G- would support the same harmonic progression. McCartney, however, used an easy variation of this idea for the bass line of 'For No One'. Instead of following the root of the chords, he alternates roots and fifths until he arrives at the turnaround. Thus McCartney replaces the unornamented bass line C – E – A – C – F – B♭ with C (the root) – B (the fifth) – A (the root) – G (the fifth), and then F (the root). This allows for a walking bass line, where the bass descends by step instead of searching for the root (Figure 8.4):

Figure 8.4   Transcript of bass and root triads

Such contrary motion is not simply ornamental: it allows the song to encompass in a harmonic cacophony, the positive or 'upward' motion of love and the negative or 'descending' motion of the end of love. Here, bass and chord do not speak in one voice, anchored by the 'base' of the bass: instead, they speak in contrary voices, up and down, for no one.

These complications are effected by chordal inversions – which is, in 'For No One', a remarkable, if simple, innovation for the ballad. By means of these inversions McCartney plays the descending bass line that rings with the ascending chords. Such simple changes were rarely encountered in rock music prior to the Beatles, although it is found in both jazz and classical music. In 'For No One' McCartney starts on I (C major) then moves to the iii (E minor), then to the vi (A minor). From there he returns to the I (C major); however, he manages to continue the ascension by using the third inversion of the I chord (that is, playing the C major triad starting on G and playing on top of that a C then a E). This is followed by second inversion of the IV chord (F major) and then finally the flat VII (Bb major) in the turn around. Figure 8.5 illustrates the inversions I am describing.

Figure 8.5   Inverted chords from score

This progression doesn't physically move upward in the song; rather, McCartney plays it all in the same register. Still, these chords musically move up the scale within that register. This ascension contrasts starkly with the descending bass line, but structurally and tonally they mesh harmoniously. The harmony and disharmony of bass and chords and the 'continuo' of 'For No One' offer a contradiction analogous to that of the ballad as a structure itself: 'no sign of love behind the tears / Cried for no one.' Tears cried for no one is a sign without referent (neither the beloved nor love itself is at the 'base' of these tears); the harmony and contrary motion of bass and chords go in two contradictory directions at once so that the base cannot easily be discerned within the bass. This integration of the details of the music and the thematics of song stands out prominently among a popular rock 'n' roll tradition in which music is usually simply a secondary vehicle for song.

Washing out the musical line: the bridge to nowhere

Above the combination of bass and chord in the continuo of 'For No One', McCartney sings a deceptively simple melody line, rising then falling for two bars each. To create the effect of a simple melody, McCartney once again returns to the basic chordal structure of the traditional ballad for stability and foundation. When the piano plays I (C major), the vocal part sings a fifth, G. Throughout the chorus, the melody follows the harmonic structures, singing triadic elements on each emphasized beat. McCartney's chorus melody moves continuously within the chord: he sings the fifth (G on top of C major), third (G on top of E minor), third (C on top of A minor), third (E on top of C major), fifth (C on top of F major), and a seventh resolving for the turnaround. (Figure 8.6)

This melody has the feel of a 'simple' melody since the musical line is clearly anchored in the bass and harmony. Such simplicity can be heard in 'Yellow Submarine', where the superstructure of melody plays out the base of chords. Here, McCartney complicates this traditional ballad formation somewhat with contrary movement up and down, but even Ringo is able to 'complicate somewhat' his goofy song. By beginning with a base of simplicity, McCartney was able to write some of the most remarkable songs of his time by complicating and enriching the simple forms of music and song. In doing so, he transformed the possibilities of rock music and helped determine the standards by which rock ballads are written today.

Figure 8.6   Melody on top of triads

More specifically, McCartney achieves this by complicating the simple connection between base and superstructure on the level of melody. That is, if the traditional ballad anchors chords in the bass line, then it also anchors the melody in
the chorus. In 'For No One', however, McCartney follows the simple chorus I
have been describing with a bridge that is both structurally and musically more
difficult. This deviates from the normal popular ballad format. The traditional pop
ballad has sixteen bars of chorus followed by an eight-bar bridge and finally recapitulates the eight-bar chorus at the ending. It can be noted that earlier Beatles'
ballads followed this form. Both 'Yesterday' and 'Yellow Submarine', for
instance, follow slight variations of this structure, still presenting the repeated
chorus, followed by a bridge, then the chorus, ending with the bridge and chorus.
In 'Yesterday' the chorus is just a bar shorter and it adds an additional recapitulation of the chorus/bridge.

McCartney thoroughly retools this form in 'For No One'. This song completely departs from the traditional ballad structure of the melody line and follows the
structure of an eight-bar chorus but adds a five-bar bridge (rather than the traditional eight-bar bridge), which it repeats three times. Its five-bar bridge stretches
the musicality of this piece. I have been calling it a bridge because the simple
opening melody line, tied as it is to the chord structure, builds to a 'transitional'
melody governed by the dominant fifth – here D minor and A seventh lead to G
major (the fifth to the chorus's C major) – which creates the effect, the musical
'feel', of a 'transition' back to the basic melody of the chorus, just as the V chord
in a traditional chord progression resolves to a I chord. However, the bridge of
'For No One' does not fulfill the promise of the resolution of the traditional
bridge. Most technically, the block triads of the chorus are not continued in the
bridge. Rather, McCartney breaks up the chords on the keyboard, replacing the
simultaneous soundings with their arpeggiations. (See Figure 8.7)

The chords covered in the bridge are the ii chord (D minor) and VIm^7 (A^7).
Where the traditional bridge offers a simple transition back to the chorus,
McCartney plays G major with a suspended fourth. This suspension grates
against the harmonies we expect in the popular music of this era, but we are
quickly settled as it is resolved to a V (G major). This produces two different
cadential moments: a transitional cadential moment where the final V (G major)
of the bridge seems to resolve to I (C major) at the beginning of the chorus; and
a half-cadence at the end of the bridge, where the VI seems to resolve to the V.
This harmonic ambiguity confuses the strict subordination of bridge (superstructure?) to chorus (base): in the first case, the bridge is subordinate by leading back
to the 'dominant' chorus (V to I), while in the second case the bridge *sounds* free-
standing and non-subordinate to its putative 'base' key of C.

In terms of scoring 'For No One', it is at the bridge where the bass guitar enters
to cover the bass. At first, as was typical in 'pop' music of the time, the bass covers the tonic of the chord in the first bar of the bridge. In the second bar, however, the bass starts to walk up the scale in a style more typical of jazz. In the third

Figure 8.7 Broken chords in the bridge of 'For No One'

bar the bass returns to cover the tonic, but it reverts to the walking bass feel for the fourth bar only to return to covering the tonic during the turnaround. (Figure 8.8). On top of this, McCartney sings a melody that can be described as a modified arpeggio. Here, unlike the chorus, McCartney chooses the less structured approach typical of pop music. Instead of singing a set group of notes he appears simply to sing what sounds good. Unlike the chorus, which is tightly tied to the chord progression, the melody here is ornamented with non-triadic tones that *sound* like improvisations and create the impression of a lack of structure.

This organization of the bridge, and especially its clear borrowings from the jazz style in its bass, is a mark of how powerfully innovative McCartney's bass is in *Revolver*. Now, a generation after this album, it is hard to believe how little jazz influenced popular music of the 1950s and early 1960s. Motown, of course, is a notable exception to this, but it is equally hard to believe how little Motown influenced popular standards before the Beatles. In important ways, much of a whole generation of popular music – the very structures of the popular ballad – exists in the context of the Beatles' innovations in music forms.

In fact, what is most striking about the 'formal' bridge of 'For No One' – perhaps its strongest innovation – is that it doesn't 'bridge' anything. McCartney *ends* the song with the bridge:

Figure 8.8   Whole bridge and bridge bass

And in her eyes you see nothing
No sign of love behind the tears
Cried for no one
A love that should have lasted years—

In addition, the song *ends* with McCartney singing II (D minor), a chord that normally signifies the turnaround. After the completion of the vocal line, the piano and horn resolve this chord with the fifth, G. Thus, the chords, like the structure itself, suggest something to follow when nothing does. This, in turn, enacts the musical structure and line, the theme of loss 'For No One' expresses.

This combination of musical line, structure, and theme appears nowhere else in the popular rock music of the Beatles' time and, for that matter, it rarely appears in popular music today. Another place we notice such a deviation from the set traditional structures of popular music is during the French horn solo during the second half of the second chorus. It is here that Alan Civil creates a horn line that is comparable to McCartney's vocals during the bridge. This is the only spot during the song where the concrete structure of the chorus intermingles with the freewheeling sound and style of the bridge. It is another place where the staid choral 'base' and freewheeling transitional-bridge superstructure confuse one another. McCartney also brings the horn back in during the last chorus with his voice on top, completing the combination of the two. Finally, this solo rearranges the chorus, supplementing voice with instrument, meaning with sound. It is as if, in the transformation of the meaning of ballad to the music of horn, the narrative of ballad dissolves itself into sound, another bridge to nowhere, a story for no one.

The lyrics of ballad: the structure of the superstructure

I've already touched upon the lyrics of 'For No One' – what I might call its theme – but here I would like to look more closely at the way in which it presents and disrupts the traditional elements of the lyrics of a ballad narrative. The governing structure – the 'base' – of the traditional ballad story line is the rhyme scheme. Lyrics are usually anchored in rhymes as firmly as a musical line is anchored in the chorus and a bass line anchors the chord progression. In 'For No One' this is not altogether the case. The freewheeling bridge, as we have seen, anchors itself in rhyme ('tears'/ 'years'). But the staid and strict chorus pursues rhymes that progressively break down into half-rhyme and no rhyme altogether, as if the order of rhyme is no longer congruent with the disorder of loss.

1. Your day breaks, your mind aches,
   You find that all her words of kindness linger on,
   When she no longer needs you.
   She wakes up, she makes up,
   She takes her time.
   And doesn't feel she has to hurry.
   She no longer needs you.

Bridge

   And in her eyes you see nothing
   No sign of love behind the tears
   Cried for no one
   A love that should have lasted years.
2. You want her, you need her

And yet you don't believe her when she says her love is dead
You think she needs you.
[*Horn solo*]

Bridge

3.   You stay home, she goes out
      She says that long ago she knew some-one
      But now he's gone, she doesn't need him.
      Your day breaks, your mind aches
      There will be times when all the things
      She said will fill your head
      You won't forget her.

Bridge

The chorus begins sustained by rhyme: 'breaks'/ 'aches'; 'wakes up'/ 'makes up';
and even the internal rhyme, 'takes'. The richness of the rhymes of the first stanza – not only their strict repetition of sounds, but even the crossing-over from
'aches' to '*makes* up' to the internal 'takes' – reinforces the strictness of the bass-
chord solidity and the chord-line congruence. The only thing to disturb the stability of the music – which otherwise rings almost as stably as the hymnal church
ballads – is the walking bass against the alignment of bass, chord, music, lyric I
have already discussed. The failure of the continuation of rhyme to the second
half of the stanza is hardly noticed against the repetition of the words 'she no
longer needs you'.

    The second time through, though, rhyme vanishes. It is replaced by opposition
('home'/ 'out'), and the larger sense of the stanza, 'she doesn't need him'/
'You think she needs you.' Even the pronouns reinforce the dissociation of meaning, the breakdown of the base of solid sense built upon repeated sounds. In the
third stanza this is complicated by the repetition of words ('Your day breaks, your
mind aches') where, as in the first stanza, the aches are for sounds that aren't
there, the pain of absence. In this repetition, the figure of 'day breaks' starts to
sound *literal*, with the day – the time of both the first and third stanzas – almost
literally breaking apart, falling apart. The stanza presents an emphasized half-
rhyme ('one'/ 'gone'), which itself emphasizes the absence of love and beloved
of the 'bridge', and it ends on a half-rhyme ('head'/ 'her') reminiscent of the half-
rhyme of stanza two ('doesn't *need* him'/ 'don't be*lieve* her'). It is as if by the
time 'For No One' gets to its final 'bridge' that connects nothing, the words
themselves – playing second and third persons, rhymes and half-rhymes, and tears
and love against one another – break down, uttered to no one and sounded for no
one.

Coda: rearranged ballad

'For No One' transforms the received rock music of the 1950s by upsetting set-tled relationships of base and superstructure in three different ways. In this song, McCartney is able to expand the possibilities of the bass from simply following root notes to using different parts of the chords to develop an independent and more ornamental line that repeats or augments the melody line of the song. Similarly, 'For No One' transforms the traditional 'bridge' of popular music. Not only is the bridge shortened, but it participates thematically in its structure: it is a bridge to nowhere, just as the lost love the song describes feels like it leaves you with nowhere to go. This is embodied by the song *ending* on the bridge, which itself ends without resolution to the tonic. Additionally, the introduction of a solo French horn sparks a new sound and tone quality that is unlike the popular rock music of the time.

In this discussion, I have followed a method by which musicians seem to be aware that music is built from the bass up. But in 'For No One', and indeed in the transformed ballads that the Beatles gave us from *Revolver* onward, such pro-gressive understanding of the 'building blocks' of music are often re-arranged (quite literally), confused, and used to different ends. In *Revolver* alone the ele-ments of song I have been tracing here are taken up, distended, removed, invert-ed, and played against each other. Such innovations are clearly representative of *Revolver* as a whole, which – among other things – accomplished a 'revolution' in musical forms. This revolution allowed the Beatles to rethink their songs on the level of lyric musicality by means of the complication of hierarchical structures in the development of the bass line, the re-formation of these structures in the relationship between chorus and bridge, and the inversion of these structures of the basic ballad structure in the relationship between voice and music with the horn and that between music and voice with the progressive loss of the ballad rhyme scheme. In accomplishing this revolution – repeated, in parts throughout *Revolver,* but never as completely as in 'For No One' – McCartney helped to reshape the popular rock ballad as fully as the studio recordings of the Beatles as a whole reshaped the styles of music available in the 1960s. We can notice simi-lar bass lines in Paul Simon's 'America' and Billy Joel's 'Piano Man'. The open-ing of the Rolling Stones song 'You Can't Always Get What You Want' begins with a children's choir and French horn. But perhaps the most far-reaching effect brought upon by this seemingly simple and plaintive song is the structural com-binations of music and song that, as I have shown, enlarged for us all the scope and effectiveness of the popular ballad.

Notes

1. It should be noted that I have transposed this and all other examples discussed in this chapter to C major for convenience. This piece is played on the album in the key of B major. All musical examples are derived from *The Beatles: Complete Scores* (1993).
2. While the transcription of 'For No One' in *The Beatles: Complete Scores* notes the chorus as a four-bar sequence repeated, it could have easily been scored as a more usual eight-bar cut time configuration. In this case the chorus would neatly fit the standard sixteen-bar ballad form.
3. In quoting Nicholas Schaffner's description of 'Yellow Submarine' Walter Everett hints at why this song may be the most conventional of ballads on *Revolver*: 'John and Paul coupled some incredibly disarming and idiotic lyrics about their improbable conveyance with an equally simple and ridiculous melody and proved the perfect vehicle for Ringo's goofy and toneless voice' (Everett, 1999, p. 65). The satiric thrust of 'Yellow Submarine' calls for a 'goofy' conventional form.

Chapter 9

Ringo round *Revolver*: rhythm, timbre, and tempo in rock drumming

Steven Baur

There were quite a few drummers around Liverpool and I used to go home and tell Paul about Ringo. I often saw him play with Rory Storm ... With Rory he was a very inventive drummer. He goes around the drums like crazy. He doesn't just hit them – he invents sounds.

– Mike McCartney

Q. What do you call someone who hangs out with musicians?
A. A drummer.

– Anonymous witticism

Being a drummer, I have heard this joke many times. I thought it was funny the first time I heard it, but it became substantially less funny to me after my first day of graduate school in a musicology program, when one of my professors reiterated the implication behind the joke – that drummers are not musicians. During the compulsory round of student self-introductions, we were each asked to identify our primary instrument. Upon hearing that I was a drummer, the professor proclaimed that drummers could not be musicologists, at least not good ones. For the rest of the year I identified myself as a 'percussionist' in an attempt to position myself closer to musician status as understood at this particular institution. The following year, I was appointed to serve as a teaching assistant for the same professor. Even though the course was on the music of J. S. Bach, he often found time in class to rail against rock music, which he routinely dismissed as simplistic, repetitive, barbaric rubbish.

While popular music has made remarkable inroads into academic publishing and university curricula over the last quarter-century, my field has come relatively late to the arena of popular music studies. With a few notable exceptions, musicologists have only recently been willing to consider popular styles of music, reserving their analytical methodologies for the larger-scale works of the European classical tradition. Yet in this relatively short time, music scholars have contributed much to the body of academic writing on popular music. Enriched with extensive analyses of specifically musical details, this work has greatly enhanced our understanding of the music of popular music and how it achieves its effects. Consistent with musicological work on more traditional repertories, however, most analytical writing on popular music privileges pitch over all other musical parameters, typically focusing on the melodic and harmonic content of a given song and the organization of the constituent pitches. While I value much of this work, I find that pitch-centric approaches to analyzing popular music can be problematic, particularly in the case of genres such as rock 'n' roll (and related genres) that depend to a great extent on rhythmic elements. Indeed, during its emergence in the 1950s and continuing into the 1960s, rock 'n' roll was commonly referred to as 'beat music' or quite simply 'the big beat', and fans and detractors alike identified the beat as the genre's most effectual component. Yet drums, percussion, and other instruments of indefinite pitch rarely garner much consideration in musicological studies on popular music.

The case of the Beatles is perhaps the most glaring example of this circumstance. To be sure, no band has received as much serious attention from music scholars, including volumes in book series typically reserved for classical composers, but most of this work focuses almost exclusively on the musical content specific to pitched instruments. While critics and scholars have canonized his bandmates, Ringo Starr remains one of the most reviled and least respected musicians of the twentieth century. Indeed, tales and anecdotes concerning Ringo's incompetence and technical limitations are legion. To this day, allegations that many of Ringo's drum tracks, marred by irreparable flaws, had to be overdubbed by other musicians, including Paul McCartney, persist in Beatles lore.[1] In the words of musicologist and Beatles scholar Wilfrid Mellers, Ringo's 'relative deficiency' emphasizes 'his dependence … on his colleagues' (1973, p. 144). I would counter that the reluctance of music scholars like Mellers to address adequately musical parameters other than pitch has contributed to an inordinate devaluation of the work performed by Ringo Starr and other drummers.

Fortunately, more recent work on the music of the Beatles, including book-length studies by Walter Everett, Ian MacDonald, Tim Riley, and Allen Moore, acknowledge the significance of the Beatles' drum and percussion tracks. I would like to build on this work and investigate in greater depth the subtle and complex manipulations of rhythm, timbre, and tempo that went into these tracks. Released in the mid-1960s, *Revolver* came at a moment during which significant developments in rock drumming performance and production were taking place on both sides of the Atlantic, and the album provides an extremely useful collection of texts for studying the percussive register in the music of the Beatles. The drum and percussion tracks on *Revolver* demonstrate new applications of the Beatles' unique approach to percussive timbre, present from their earliest recordings with Ringo, while pointing to developments in the Beatles' management of rhythm and tempo that would have significant ramifications for their post-*Revolver* sound.

Before turning to *Revolver*, it will be necessary to consider some general conventions of rock 'n' roll drumming that obtained during the late 1950s and early 1960s as the Beatles prepared to burst onto the international music scene. In most cases, the drummer dedicates most of his/her energies into holding down the beat, which usually consists of an agglomeration of several repetitive rhythmic patterns performed simultaneously on the various apparatuses of the drum kit. The beat defines (or helps to define) the metrical and rhythmic character of a song – that is, how the successive pulses are organized and how each pulse is subdivided. In an overwhelming majority of rock 'n' roll songs the underlying pulse is organized into quadruple groupings, or measures. Conventional rock drumbeats involve three basic elements. First is the backbeat – for some the primary identifying feature of rock 'n' roll music – consisting of accents on the second and fourth beats of each measure, most commonly played on the snare drum. The second component is the bass drum pattern, usually emphasizing the downbeat of each measure and often synchronizing accents or patterns in common with other instruments. Third, and perhaps most important, is the 'ride' pattern, which often defines the rhythmic feel of a song and is typically played on a ride cymbal or on hi-hat cymbals. Each pattern within a given beat is subject to variation or elaboration, allowing for an infinite number of beats deriving from the basic patterns. In addition to the beat, or beats, featured in a given song, the drummer typically embellishes with fills and accents, freely incorporating all components of the drum kit.

The earliest songs that feature a consistent backbeat almost invariably make use of either a 'swing' ride pattern or the closely related 'shuffle' ride pattern, both of which involve triple subdivisions of the quarter-note pulse. Most 1950s rock 'n' roll – including a vast majority of the recordings by Elvis Presley, Chuck Berry, Ruth Brown, Little Richard, Jerry Lee Lewis, Big Joe Turner, Bill Haley and the Comets, and others – features either a swing or shuffle ride pattern superimposed over the backbeat and bass drum pattern.[2] During the late 1950s and early 1960s, duple subdivisions of the quarter-note pulse became more common in rock 'n' roll drumming, replacing the triple subdivision characteristic of swing and shuffle patterns, and by the end of the 1960s the 'straight' (as opposed to 'swung' or 'shuffled') eighth-note ride pattern typified most rock drumbeats.[3]

The drum kit provides an enormous range of articulative variation under the direct control of the drummer, and numerous performative factors determine the tone, volume, duration, and timbre of the drums and cymbals, including: where the drummer strikes a drum or a cymbal (whether toward the center or toward the edge of the drum or cymbal); the force with which the drummer hits a drum or cymbal (affecting not only the volume, but the timbre and duration as well); what part of the stick is used (whether the beaded tip, the tapered 'shoulder', or the 'butt' end of the stick, which produce different sounds); pedal technique (particularly that of the hi-hat mechanism which opens and closes the hi-hat cymbals, or holds them together with varying degrees of tightness when played by stick); drum tuning (involving drum head tension and muffling, as well as the tautness of the snares stretched across the bottom snare drum head); and cymbal selection (with a wide variety of options depending on size, thickness, taper, bell size, and grade of metal).

The nature of the sound produced by cymbals varies to a greater extent depending on performative factors than does the sound of the drums themselves. This is particularly important with respect to the ride pattern, usually played either on closed hi-hat cymbals or on a ride cymbal. When a drummer rides on the hi-hats, the main factors that determine the resulting sound are the relative tightness or looseness with which the two cymbals are held together by the pedal mechanism, where and how hard the drummer hits the hi-hats, and with which part of the stick. Tightly closed hi-hats produce a short, crisp 'tih' sound, which becomes progressively less crisp the more loosely the hi-hats are held together, and thereby allowed to resonate and vibrate against each other more freely, creating a louder, dirtier, more 'sloshy' sound. Playing close to the center cup of the hi-hat produces a 'tinny' timbre and distinct, clearly articulated notes. As the playing moves closer to the edge of the hi-hats, the sound will either become thick and 'chunky' (if the hi-hats are tightly closed) or (if loosely held together) will produce a sustained, cresting overtone sheen, combined with the distorted 'shshsh' of the hi-hat cymbals clashing against each other – a combination that can render each note less distinct and rhythmic patterns less defined. Playing with the tip of the stick tends toward a 'tinny' timbre and produces clearly defined notes, while the wider shoulder of the stick produces a thick, chunky sound (if the hi-hats are tightly closed) or a distorted, cresting overtone-driven timbre (if they are loose).

The loud, distorted timbre of loose, edgy, heavily played hi-hats was rarely a feature of the more polite drumming style dominant on recordings from the 1950s and early 1960s. Accustomed to contending with the overwhelming din of screaming fans, Ringo was an extremely hard-hitting drummer for the early 1960s. This, among other performative factors, contributed to the idiosyncratic ride timbres that distinguish his early drum sound.[4] On almost every early Beatle hit – including 'Please Please Me', 'She Loves You', 'I Saw Her Standing There', 'I Want To Hold Your Hand', 'A Hard Day's Night', 'Can't Buy Me Love', and 'Eight Days a Week' – Ringo plays a heavy ride pattern on hi-hat cymbals held together with varying degrees of looseness. The shrill, pulsating hiss produced by the hi-hat cymbals vibrating against each other gives these recordings a live feel and approximates the excitement audible at the Beatles' live performances. Uncommon prior to the Beatles, the sound of loose, hard-hit hi-hats energizes each song with a kinetic intensity that is difficult to achieve in the studio, and this noisy, aggressive percussive timbre is crucial to the band's early sound.

Ride patterns are often performed on cymbals, freeing the hi-hat to be played by foot with the pedal mechanism (producing a 'chick' sound if shut and held closed or a 'splash' sound if allowed to ring). Like hi-hats, individual cymbals also produce a wide range of sounds depending on a number of factors. Ringo's familiar economical kit featured only two cymbals besides the hi-hats – a 'ride' cymbal and a 'crash' cymbal. Ride cymbals are typically used for performing sustained rhythmic patterns whereas crash cymbals are usually reserved for individual accents and often articulate points of structural significance in a given song. As with hi-hats, playing heavily and toward the edge of the cymbal will cause overtone swelling, often rendering the rhythmic pattern less distinct, whereas playing lighter and closer to the center produces less overtones and thinner, but more distinctly articulated notes. Playing with the tip of the stick creates a 'pingy' timbre with relatively little overtone swelling, while using the shoulder of the stick will produce a 'clangy' sound with increased overtone swelling, depending on the proximity to the edge of the cymbal. The drummer can also play on the centre cup of the cymbal which has its own distinctive bell-like timbre (as heard on 'I Feel Fine', during the choruses of 'In My Life', and later on 'Hey Jude' and 'I Want You').

Ringo favored deep ride cymbals prone to excessive overtone swelling, a sound often modified by cymbal rivets – flat-headed metal pieces that sit loosely in small holes drilled in the cymbal, producing a 'sizzling' sound as the rivet heads vibrate against the reverberating cymbal. (In fact, riveted cymbals are often referred to as 'sizzle' cymbals.) With Ringo's characteristic hard ride playing and his overtone-heavy ride cymbal, the ever-cresting overtone sheen is often so loud that it drowns out the sound of the sizzling rivets, and this peculiar overtone manipulation adds a distinct timbral layer to many early Beatles recordings. For instance, on 'The Night Before', Ringo builds and sustains a swelling, high-pitched overtone drone with a heavy ride cymbal pattern, played relatively close to the edge of the cymbal. The proximity to the cymbal edge and Ringo's heavy playing produce the obtrusive overtones, but because he plays with the tip of the stick, the straight eight-note ride pattern that drives the song is audible through the cresting cymbal sheen.

Ringo's nuanced timbral manipulations might have been imperceptible if not for George Martin's innovative recording techniques, featuring microphone placement closer to the respective instruments, rendering audible more of their timbral subtleties, as well as Martin's facility for bounced- and multi-track recording, which allowed for more elaborate sonic layering, including sophisticated percussion arrangements. By the time they began recording sessions for the *Help!* soundtrack in early 1965, Martin and the Beatles had established an efficient recording process by which they first perfected the rhythm parts before tracking vocals or instrumental leads, often freeing one or more of the other Beatles to play percussion instruments while recording the basic tracks, as did Martin himself on a number of songs. Greater attention to percussion than on earlier recordings is evident throughout the *Help!* album. Previous rock 'n' roll records, including those of the Beatles, commonly featured percussion instruments, but in most cases, pre-1965 percussion parts involve rhythmic patterns that remain constant throughout the song (often a tambourine doubling the backbeat or playing continuous quarter-, eighth-, or sixteenth-notes). Beginning with

Help!, almost every Beatle recording features multiple percussion parts, which – in close coordination with Ringo's drum tracks – vary throughout the song to serve a number of expressive ends. For instance, on the title track, Ringo's over-dubbed tambourine part, close-miked and placed up front in the mix, differentiates the chorus texture from that of the verse, rhythmically intensifying the accompaniment to Lennon's desperate plea. At the same time, Ringo switches from a tight hi-hat to a heavy crashing ride pattern to sustain a chaotic, ever-cresting overtone blare that places the anxious chorus on a turbulent timbral plane.[5]

Well before *Revolver*, then, the Beatles had demonstrated a unique approach to the percussive register. Prior to *Help!* this is most evident in the bold hi-hat and ride cymbal timbres sustained under Ringo's heavy hand.[6] On *Revolver*, Ringo began to develop a different approach to performing the ride pattern, and the over-driven ride timbres characteristic of the Beatles' early sound do not figure prominently on the album, with several conspicuous exceptions. On 'Tomorrow Never Knows', the first track recorded for the album, Ringo performs an eighth-note ride pattern on the ride cymbal. By playing heavily, toward the edge of the cymbal, and with the shoulder of the stick, Ringo blurs the rhythmic articulation under a sustained, swelling overtone drone loud enough to render the eighth-note pattern virtually inaudible. The ever-present, swirling overtones and the rhythmic obscurity of the ride pattern are essential to this pyschedelic soundscape. So too is the displaced backbeat. Ringo had originally opted for the conventional placement of the backbeat on the second and fourth beats of each measure, albeit with the novel use of a press roll to fatten the second half of the backbeat (The Beatles, *Anthology 2*, Disc 1, Track 17), but, upon McCartney's suggestion, Ringo altered the pattern and developed the mesmerizing beat upon which the song is built. It involves the expected snare drum accent on the second beat of the measure, but the latter half of the backbeat is shifted and performed as two sixteenth notes just before the fourth beat. Importantly, Ringo plays the two sixteenth notes on a low-tuned tom such that the backbeat alternates between snare drum and tom timbres. The effect is hypnotic, and the beat gives 'Tomorrow Never Knows' a primal feel that grounds Lennon's metaphysical musings.

Another instance of an overtone-heavy ride pattern on *Revolver* occurs in 'Taxman', the album's opening track. For much of the song, Ringo leaves out the ride pattern altogether, allowing other percussion instruments to fill out the rhythmic texture, and he constantly varies the drum and percussion tracks, endowing each section of the song with a slightly different percussive shading (see Figure 9.1). During the verses Ringo plays the rideless beat consisting only of a punchy bass drum pattern and the backbeat. This leaves room for the additional percussive layers, which move in and out of the aural texture such that all four verses have different percussive accompaniments. Ringo brings in an eighth-note ride pattern at each occurrence of the refrain ('Cause I'm the taxman ...'), thereby accompanying the lyric that identifies the unscrupulous subject of the song with the now familiar blustering ride cymbal, and he thickens the percussive texture for

Song Section	Percussion Parts Added to Snare and Bass Drum Patterns
Verse 1	No additional percussion
Refrain	Ride
Verse 2	Tambourine (embellishing backbeat)
Refrain	Ride, Tambourine (embellishing backbeat), Cowbell (quarter-notes)
Middle Eight	Tambourine (embellishing backbeat)
Verse (Guitar Solo)	Tambourine (sixteenth notes)
Refrain	Ride, Tambourine (sixteenth notes), Cowbell (quarter-notes)
Verse 3	Tambourine (embellishing backbeat), Cowbell (doubling backbeat)
Refrain	Ride, Tambourine (sixteenth notes), Cowbell (quarter-notes)
Verse 4	Tambourine (sixteenth notes)
Refrain	Ride, Tambourine (sixteenth notes), Cowbell (quarter-notes)

Figure 9.1   Percussion arrangement for 'Taxman'

subsequent occurrences of the refrain. The percussive register in 'Taxman' is also notable for the propulsive drum fills that Ringo uses to lead into each refrain (at 0:21, 0:44, 1:23, 1:46, and 2:10). No two fills are the same, yet they all reference each other with a similar rhythmic character and feel. Thus Ringo's drumming, like his overdubbed percussion tracks, creates a constantly changing, yet highly integrated percussive accompaniment.

Ringo's use of varied percussion parts for each section of 'Taxman' points to further developments in the Beatles' drum and percussion arrangements, which enable a number of subsequent songs to evolve dynamically in spite of harmonic and melodic repetition. This is perhaps best exemplified in the drum tracks for 'Let It Be'. Ringo sits out altogether during the first verse and chorus of the song. He enters at the second verse playing only 'chunky' hi-hat hits on the second and fourth beats of each measure, treated with an echo effect calibrated such that the decaying notes of the echo approximate sixteenth notes at the given tempo. Ringo comes in playing a full beat at the second chorus with an eighth-note ride pattern on tightly closed hi-hats, which he opens slightly on the second and fourth beats of each measure to enhance and fatten the backbeat (a technique he uses on numerous Beatles songs, including 'Oh Darling', 'Lovely Rita', 'I, Me, Mine', 'Sexy Sadie', 'Birthday', and 'I Dig a Pony', among others). Ringo intensifies the rhythmic accompaniment during the ensuing guitar solo by doubling up the hi-hat ride rhythm with a sixteenth-note pattern. For the subsequent chorus, Ringo shifts to an eighth-note ride cymbal pattern played on the bell of the cymbal, for a clear, overtone-free timbre, producing an almost church-like effect. At the last verse Ringo introduces a unique and wholly different beat, allowing maracas to take over the ride pattern and incorporating tom rolls woven around the backbeat, radically and unexpectedly changing the feel for the last return to the verse, dramatizing an otherwise routine maneuver.

Thus far I have emphasized timbre, but timbre is closely related to other aspects of performance. Beginning with the *Rubber Soul* album, the direct precursor to

Revolver, Ringo began evolving a fatter drum sound than heard on previous Beatles records. Extremely particular about his sound, Ringo spent hours at a time tuning his drums, and from 1965 on he favored loosely tuned, low-pitched drums. Around this time another timbral element begins to characterize Ringo's sound – his deep, slow-cresting crash cymbal, which can be heard prominently on several *Revolver* tracks. For instance, on the choruses of 'Good Day Sunshine', loud cymbal crashes color the sunny lyric with radiant, bursting cymbal crashes. Ringo's slack-tuned, thick-sounding drums and slow-developing cymbals are well suited for – and indeed tend to elicit – less hurried performances. Not coincidentally, the tempos of Beatles songs slow down substantially after 1965.[7] Prior to the Beatles, few drummers tuned their drums as loosely as did Ringo, largely because loose drumheads render the drums more difficult to play. The drum sticks don't respond as well to slack-tuned drumheads, which provide less rebound than do tighter heads, making rolls more difficult to perform. But Ringo was less interested in playing fast rolls than he was in making good records.

On 'She Said She Said' and 'Rain', also recorded during the *Revolver* sessions, Ringo's deep, slow-cresting crash cymbal and his fat drum sound come to the fore as he elaborates the beat in each song with plentiful drum fills, each concluding with the slow explosion of his deep crash cymbal.[8] In both cases, Ringo sits on the back end of the beat without, however, dragging the tempo. By laying back on the beat while simultaneously propelling each song with extensive and highly unpredictable syncopated drum fills, Ringo creates and sustains a kind of relaxed intensity that is crucial to the Beatles' later sound. In both cases, Ringo performs obtrusive drum fills that punctuate each line of the verse, a hallmark of his later style evident on a number of subsequent recordings, perhaps most notably on 'A Day In The Life'.

Aside from the ballad 'Here, There and Everywhere', the song on *Revolver* with the slowest tempo is 'I'm Only Sleeping'. Ringo performs an appropriately indolent beat, featuring a slow quarter-note ride cymbal pattern and a lazy backbeat played consistently on the back end of the pulse. Ringo's timbral character is well suited to the slow tempo – his slow-developing riveted ride cymbal (played on the edge so that the ride cymbal sounds very much like a crash cymbal, but struck softly in keeping with the mellow feel of the song) fills the space between quarter-notes with its prolonged sustain while the relaxed backbeat benefits from Ringo's slack-tuned snare drum, a sound he preferred to the then more common timbre of 'those fast jazz snares' (Clayson, 1991, p. 130). After *Revolver* the Beatles would explore much slower tempos. For many rock drummers slow tempos pose a serious problem. The slower the tempo, the more room there is between the notes for rhythmic imprecision and the more difficult it becomes to maintain a steady beat. Furthermore, many drummers find it difficult to play at a slow tempo and still maintain the desired level of intensity, and attempts to heighten the dynamic level often result in rushed tempos. Ringo, on the other hand, had an impeccable sense of time, and, regardless of the tempo, was capable of achieving whatever dynamic level the song demanded. We can contrast the slow, relaxed feel of 'I'm Only Sleeping' with the slow but intense drive of 'Helter Skelter'. In the latter tune, Ringo again plays steadily on the back end of the beat. He plays a hard ride pattern on a crash cymbal, each stroke producing a heavy, crashing swell, a sound that requires more time for its articulation than the conventional 'ping-y' ride cymbal timbre. Although he sits back on the beat, Ringo creates and sustains the tension crucial to the song, not only through timbral manipulation, but also by virtue of his abundant syncopated fills (looking back to 'She Said She Said' and 'Rain'), which he weaves in and out of his obtrusive, yet laid back beat, providing a highly effective foundation for this chaotic soundscape. The hard-rocking, fill-laden style of 'She Said She Said', 'Rain', and 'Helter Skelter' contrasts sharply with Ringo's nuanced percussion arrangement on 'For No One'. Here, Ringo – the only Beatle who appears on the recording aside from McCartney – successively layers percussion tracks with the subtlety and finesse of an orchestral percussionist, including delicate press rolls on the snare drum, judicious hi-hat shadings, and inventive tambourine rhythms, all performed with exacting precision.

In most accounts, Ringo has been characterized as an average drummer with severe technical limitations. I would counter that such a characterization demonstrates a very narrow understanding of what constitutes good drumming technique – one that takes into account only speed and intricacy without acknowledging timbre and tempo management as vital aspects of drumming performance practice. Many drummers may be able to duplicate *what* Ringo plays, but few can replicate *how* Ringo plays. While it remains an ambiguous notion, the 'feel' of a song is central to its efficacy, regardless of the quality of the composition, and Ringo's expert manipulations of rhythm, timbre, and tempo gave him and his band an incomparable, inimitable feel. As George Martin has stated, 'Ringo has a tremendous feel for a song and he always helped us hit the right tempo the first time. He was rock solid. This made the recording of all the Beatle songs so much easier' (Lewisohn, 1988, p. 95).[9] According to Mark Lewisohn, the most thorough chronicler of the Beatles' recording sessions, 'It is true that on only a handful of occasions during all of the several hundred session tapes and thousands of recording hours can Ringo be heard to have made a mistake or wavered in his beat. His work was remarkably consistent and excellent, from 1962 right through 1970' (1988, p. 95). If Ringo had not been such a consistent, solid player, or if he had committed as many mistakes in the studio as his bandmates did, it is unlikely that the Beatles could have accomplished as much in the studio as they did over the span of their recording career. Furthermore, Ringo rarely garners any credit for contributing drum and percussion parts that are, to my mind, essential to the given composition, whether it be the sumptuous drum fills that comment on every line of 'A Day In The Life', the galloping snare drum that is part of the 'hook' of 'Get Back', the swirling, rhythmically obscure ride cymbal pattern and displaced backbeat that give 'Tomorrow Never Knows' its singular feel, or the highly unconventional, swelling hi-hat triplets and rolling tom patterns that provide the creeping, slithery feel that animates the sinister character introduced in 'Come Together', to name just a few. As the story is often told, Ringo Starr is the luckiest man in the world to have hooked up with songwriters as talented as Lennon and McCartney, whose coat-tails he rode to stardom. I would argue that Lennon and McCartney were equally lucky to have such a fine musician as Ringo Starr to play drums and percussion on their songs. The songs simply would not have been as good without Ringo.

Notes

Earlier versions of this chapter were presented at the Beatles 2000 conference, 17 June 2000, in Jyväskylä, Finland and at the 11th biannual conference of the International Association for the Study of Popular Music, 10 July 2001, in Turku, Finland. I wish to thank the many attendees of both conferences who shared with me their thoughts on Ringo, rock drumming, and the Beatles.

1.   The most persistent allegations stem from New York session drummer Bernard Purdie's claim that he overdubbed Ringo's drum tracks on twenty-one early Beatles recordings. American session musicians were hired to enhance some tracks on the Beatles' early recordings with Tony Sheridan, which featured Pete Best on drums, and it is possible that Purdie did overdub Best's drum tracks on these recordings; however, no evidence (records concerning the hire and payment of Purdie, any form of documentation from any studio regarding session booking and scheduling, any recordings revealing overdubs by outside musicians to enhance or replace Ringo's drum tracks) or corroborating testimony (from any of the Beatles, George Martin or any other producer, engineer, or studio staff, Brian Epstein or other Beatle associates, or anyone else) has yet emerged in support of Purdie's allegations. The Beatles' recording sessions and the resulting tapes have been extensively chronicled and analyzed, and it would seem unlikely that all such evidence concerning twenty-one Beatles recordings could escape detection. Furthermore, the Beatles' numerous live recordings and videos demonstrate that Ringo was a very able drummer, capable of duplicating the quality of the playing on the studio recordings. Max Weinberg presses an evasive Purdie on his claims (1984, pp. 68–70). Being one of the most in-demand American session drummers during the 1960s and 1970s with thousands of songs to his credit, Purdie by his own admission often did not know on whose record he was playing at a given session. His claims may be a matter of genuine confusion and may stem from the likely case that he did overdub Pete Best's tracks from the Beatles' Tony Sheridan sessions. Purdie's insistence becomes more understandable when considering the fact that he worked in the recording industry at a time when studio musicians, African-Americans in particular, routinely saw their work and the resulting financial rewards credited to others.

   McCartney played drums on 'Back in the USSR' and 'Dear Prudence' during Ringo's brief 'strike' during the recording of the so-called White Album. Frustrated by the many hours spent waiting for his consistently tardy bandmates and by McCartney's patronizing studio manner and insistence on recording and re-recording numerous takes of each song, Ringo temporarily quit the band. McCartney also played drums on 'The Ballad of John and Yoko' while Ringo was away filming *The Magic Christian*. Harrison was also away from London for the recording of Lennon's autobiographical tune, performed entirely by McCartney and Lennon. None of these occasions involved replacing or 'fixing' previously recorded drum tracks, and in each instance McCartney plays very much in the style of Ringo Starr.

   There are only two instances involving overdubs of Ringo's parts by another drummer. London session drummer Alan White was brought in when the Beatles re-recorded 'Love Me Do' on 11 September 1962, after it was decided that the original recording from a week earlier with new-comer Ringo on drums – his first-ever studio session – was unsatisfactory. Ringo played tambourine on the later recording, doubling White's backbeat. The Beatles originally released the version featuring Ringo on drums. During the same session, the Beatles recorded 'P.S. I Love You' with White on percussion and Ringo on maracas (Lewisohn, 1988, pp. 18–20). On the other occasion, an unidentified drummer was brought in to Abbey Road on 10 March 1964 to work on 'Can't Buy Me Love', released ten days later, while the Beatles were busy filming *A Hard Day's Night* (Lewisohn, 1992, p. 150). (Ringo was particularly busy that day, filming his famous solo scene.) The nature of the work performed at this session remains unclear. In any event, there is nothing remarkable about the resultant drum tracks, which are among the least interesting on a Beatles recording.

2. The triple subdivision of the pulse characteristic of both the swing and shuffle pattern is exemplified particularly well on several tracks from *Revolver*. For instance, 'Good Day Sunshine' features a clearly articulated triple subdivision of the quarter-note superimposed over a forceful quarter-note pulse. The song opens with three measures of stark quarter-notes in the bass (doubled by the piano). Ringo enters in the fourth measure with a full measure of eighth-note triplets, clearly demarcating the triple subdivision of the pulse. During the verses, Ringo plays an unwavering quarter-note ride pattern on the hi-hat while the bass drum pattern sustains the underlying 'shuffley' triplet feel. Other *Revolver* tracks that employ triple subdivisions of the pulse include 'Got To Get You Into My Life', 'Yellow Submarine', 'I'm Only Sleeping', and 'I Want To Tell You'.

3. In fact, on several late-1950s recordings by Elvis Presley and Chuck Berry, we can hear ambivalence between triple and duple subdivisions of the quarter-note. For instance, on Presley's 'Treat Me Nice' (1957) and 'Jailhouse Rock' (1957), drummer D. J. Fontana plays a hi-hat ride pattern that falls somewhere between the two – not quite a shuffle, but not quite straight eighth notes either. On 'Johnny B. Goode' (1957) and 'Sweet Little Sixteen' (1957), Chuck Berry plays straight eighth notes on the guitar against swung triplet patterns in the piano and drum parts. In Berry's 'Carol' (1958) and Presley's 'Treat Me Nice' ambiguity between duple and triple subdivisions of the quarter-note persists among instrumental parts throughout the record. Ringo had a penchant for the in-between 'straight-shuffle' ride pattern, which gives a distinctive feel to a number of early songs, including 'She's a Woman', 'Help!', 'I'm a Loser', 'What Goes On', 'You Like Me Too Much', and 'Doctor Robert'.

    The Beatles' recording of 'Girl' from the *Rubber Soul* album provides an opportunity to hear the alternation between duple and triple subdivisions of the quarter-note. Most of the song features the 'shuffled' feel of triple quarter-note subdivisions, but the middle eight (at the lyric 'She's the kind of girl who puts you down ...') shifts to 'straight' duple subdivisions, particularly audible in the 'tit, tit, tit, tit' backing vocals.

4. In fact Ringo's ride technique was initially too idiosyncratic for George Martin's tastes. At the Beatles' first recording session with Ringo, the drummer took a novel approach to performing the ride pattern on 'Love Me Do', using a maracas instead of a stick to tap out the ride rhythm on the closed hi-hat cymbals in an attempt to thicken the hi-hat sound with that of the shuffling maracas (Lewisohn, 1992, p. 78). Unfortunately, with the primitive miking technique used at this session (employing a single drum microphone suspended high above the kit), both the maracas (a relatively hushed instrument) and the hi-hat (reduced in volume due to Ringo's unconventional maracas technique) are virtually inaudible. Martin deemed the tracks from this session unusable and, unimpressed with newcomer Ringo's studio debut, had the band re-record them a week later with session drummer Alan White sitting in for a dejected Ringo, who took up a tambourine on 'Love Me Do' and played maracas on 'P.S. I Love You'. The Beatles initially released the version of 'Love Me Do' with Ringo, whose drumming on the track is adequate, notwithstanding the inaudible ride patterns. The biggest differences between the two recordings of 'Love Me Do' is the presence of Ringo's tambourine on the Alan White version, which enhances the backbeat and – along with Lennon's harmonica lines – contributes to the rustic tone of the song. The Beatles

also recorded 'Please Please Me' at the Alan White session; however, White's track is marred by fluctuating tempos and a muffed drum fill (The Beatles, *Anthology 1*, Disc 1, Track 24, 1:06–1:08), and the band subsequently recorded the definitive version with Ringo.

Incidentally, the Beatles also recorded Mitch Murray's 'How Do You Do It' (later a number-one hit for Gerry and the Pacemakers) at the initial session with Ringo. George Martin wanted this, not 'Love Me Do', to be the first single but relented to the band's insistence on releasing only original songs as singles. Ringo's playing on 'How Do You Do It' – lively, fluid, and steady – is splendid, particularly the intricate rhythms played on the bell of the ride cymbal during the middle eight (The Beatles, *Anthology 1*, Disc 1, Track 23).

5.   Indeed, almost every song on *Help!* features prominent and well-arranged percussion parts, including the tasteful alternation between the tambourine and maracas on 'Hide Your Love Away', the close-miked shaker that abruptly shifts the feel during the middle eight in 'The Night Before' (at the lyric 'Last night is the night I will remember you by …') as Ringo effects rhythmic and timbral transpositions of his ride cymbal pattern, or the constant variation and close coordination between Ringo's inventive drumming and Lennon's tambourine on 'Ticket to Ride'. In 'Tell Me What You See', the dynamics and dramatic effect of the song depend largely on variations in the percussive register. Throughout the verses, as Lennon and McCartney softly recite a litany of promises, Ringo opts for a soft, tight sound. The ride pattern, played on tightly closed hi-hats with the tip of the stick, and the light rim-tap backbeat, are hardly audible under the other percussion instruments – a tambourine, claves, and a guiro. This sets up the dramatic drum entrance at the end of the chorus. Following the light drum sound of the verses, Ringo's hard-hitting solo entrance grabs the attention of the listener and contributes greatly to the rhetorical impact of the song. As the vocals alternate between the polite statements of the initial verse to insistent demands for attention, Ringo's tracks effectively do the same. Prominent percussion tracks help to differentiate the formal sections of the song on several additional tracks from *Help!* including Lennon's tambourine during the choruses of 'It's Only Love', cowbell quarter-notes in the choruses of 'I Need You', tambourine (overdubbed by Ringo) during the bridge and keyboard solo in 'You Like Me Too Much', and maracas (overdubbed by Ringo) on the choruses of 'I've Just Seen a Face'.

6.   Of course, Ringo was also capable of a lighter, more delicate touch as in the soft, tight hi-hat ride (played with the tip of the stick) and rim-tap backbeat on 'If I Fell', the restrained, staggered verse beat and understated cymbal bell patterns in the chorus of 'In My Life', and the gentle brushwork (integrated with apt maracas and tambourine parts) on 'You've Got to Hide Your Love Away', to name just a few early examples.

7.   This is not to suggest that other factors did not contribute to the Beatles' slower tempos after 1965. As others have suggested, the band's changing tastes in narcotics around this time may have strongly influenced the temporal character of their music. Len McCarthy (2001) has quantified the progressive slowing of tempos in rock music during the latter half of the 1960s, a trend for which he credits the Beatles.

8.   In 'Rain', Ringo's drum sound is further fattened by the use of variable speed recording. The drum tracks were recorded at a faster speed than they are actually heard on the final mix, lending them greater depth and thickness.

9.   In a similar testament to Ringo's impeccable sense of time, D. J. Fontana, drummer for Elvis Presley, relates the following encounter with the Beatles' drummer: 'I'll tell you a story about Ringo's drumming. We were jamming in the studio one night, and Ringo said "Do you mind if I play?" I said, "Are you kidding? Play!" I was playing the maracas or something behind him, just listening to him. I swear he never varied the tempo. He played that backbeat and never got off of it. Man, you couldn't have moved him with a crane. It was amazing. He played a hell of a backbeat man, and *that's* where it's at' (Weinberg, 1984, p. 127).

Chapter 10

The Beatle who became a man: *Revolver* and George Harrison's metamorphosis

Matthew Bannister

George Harrison was always the one who liked being a Beatle least, arguably because he had the least to gain by being one (Davies, 1968, p. 331). Two years younger than the others, he was often treated in a patronizing manner, as the 'baby' of the group (Martin and Pearson, 1994a, p. 123; Sheff and Golson, 1981, pp. 126-127; Davies, 1968, pp. 48, 91, 343). Sick of touring, he almost left the band in 1966: 'When the final show was over, Harrison said: "Well, that's it. I guess I'm not a Beatle anymore"' (Everett, 1999, p. 71). But touring was only one part of Harrison's problem.

This chapter will examine George Harrison's metamorphosis from Beatle to budding 'rock aristocrat' in terms of his *Revolver* contributions – their musical style, but also in terms of the kinds of genres invoked and the kind of subcultural associations made.

Context: George and the Beatles 1962–1966

Clearly George was essential to the Beatles as a live act, but by the time of the *Revolver* sessions (early 1966) the Beatles were reaching the end of their touring career. Moreover, from *Rubber Soul* onwards, the Beatles' increasing use of studio overdubbing meant that George's traditional contribution – a lead guitar part – could be (and often was) overdubbed by one of the other members (particularly McCartney – cf. 'Ticket to Ride', 'Another Girl', 'Michelle', 'Taxman'). The Beatles' later career was also marked by increasing experimentation with different instruments and sounds – so often there was little or no role for Harrison (apart from backing vocals). On many songs on *Revolver*, Harrison's guitar is absent ('Yellow Submarine', 'Good Day Sunshine', 'Eleanor Rigby' – and on 'For No One' he doesn't appear at all.

The Beatles pioneered the concept of the band as a self-contained creative unit: writing and recording almost entirely their own material. Accordingly, songwriters had a huge amount of power within the group. Aside from producing most of the group's material, they could also assert control over the recording process ('It's my song and I know what it needs') – and also made more money from royalties. George could hardly have been unaware of the example of Brian Jones of the Rolling Stones, another lead guitarist who was facing a decisive shift in the balance of the power against him as Mick Jagger and Keith Richards developed as a songwriting partnership, undoubtedly a factor in his gradual decline and fall.

Harrison had made significant technical and instrumental contributions to the Beatles' music: his adoption of the 12-string Rickenbacker on the soundtrack of *A Hard Day's Night* arguably inaugurated an entire genre: the west coast folk rock sound of the Byrds, which in turn became central to psychedelic music (Schaffner, 1977, p. 45). He was often the first to experiment with new sounds and technologies: Fender guitars ('Nowhere Man'), volume pedals ('I Need You; 'Yes It Is'), and of course Indian instruments, notably the sitar ('Norwegian Wood'), the use of which became a widely imitated innovation in western pop (Schaffner, 1977, p. 67). But the ideology of the auteur as evidenced in so many critical assessments of the Beatles' music tended to underline the centrality of the Lennon/McCartney songwriting 'team' to the Beatles' success, and to marginalize the contributions of others (Marcus, 1980; Mellers, 1973). Only through songwriting was it seen to be possible to gain the kind of financial and other recognition given to Lennon and McCartney.

As a songwriter, performer and in other terms, Harrison got notoriously short shrift from many of the other Beatles and their collaborators. Lennon made many disparaging remarks about Harrison, and then later somewhat disingenuously complained about being omitted from Harrison's autobiography *I Me Mine* (Sheff and Golson, 1981, pp. 126–127). George Martin remarked: 'When he brought a new song along to me, even before he had played it, I would say to myself, "I wonder if it is going to be any better than the last one?"' (Martin and Pearson 1994a, p. 124). Harrison's playing also came under critical scrutiny in the studio, particularly from Martin and McCartney – McCartney's 'pedantic insistence on having Harrison play every guitar line *just so* often caused tension' (MacDonald, 1994, p. 156). If Martin did not like Harrison's proposed lead part for a song, he would 'lead George to the piano, tinker a phrase and tell him to play that for a solo. Such was the origin of the guitar solo in "Michelle". "I was," Martin admits, "always rather beastly to George"' (Norman, 1981a, p. 252).

Before *Revolver*, five Harrison songs had been released on Beatles records: 'Don't Bother Me' (*With the Beatles*), 'I Need You' and 'You Like Me Too Much' (*Help*), and 'Think For Yourself' and 'If I Needed Someone' (*Rubber Soul*). All album tracks only, typically buried in the middle of sides and often dismissed by critics (MacDonald, 1994, pp. 115, 126), they were, nevertheless, also musically distinctive by contrast with contemporaneous Lennon/McCartney compositions. Their characteristic musical tone was less pop, more negative, sometimes minor ('Don't Bother Me'), marked by unorthodox, disorienting chord progressions ('Think For Yourself') and harmonic meanderings and ambiguities (MacDonald, 1994, p. 166). Clearly Harrison's rather poor singing (relative to Lennon and McCartney) also tended to reinforce 'negative' critical assessments of his work, as, for example, 'dour' (MacDonald, 1994, p. 75), 'melancholy' (MacDonald, 1994a, p. 115), 'bitter' (Everett, 1999, p. 40), a 'dark horse' (Martin and Pearson 1994a, p. 48), or just plain weak. Harrison's melodies also tend towards repetition, reticence and uncertainty: 'I've got no vocal range, so I've got to keep my songs simple' (Davies, 1968, p. 343). Habitually, his melodies employ long strings of syncopated crotchets, for example 'you don't get time to hang a sign on me' ('Love You To'); 'Let me tell you how it will be' ('Taxman'); 'And you've got time to rectify all the things that you should' ('Think For Yourself') (Everett, 1999, p. 48). The middle eight melodies of 'If I Needed Someone' and 'I Want To Tell You' feature the most sustained use of this device, Harrison's vocal consistently evading the strong beats in the bar, suggesting a certain reluctance to assert oneself.

Harrison's lyrics also tend to concern uncertainty and doubt (or projecting these same qualities onto a reviled Other) (e.g. 'Think For Yourself') and typically rely on negative or conditional constructions: 'Had you come some other day then it might not have been like this' ('If I Needed Someone'), 'So go away, leave me alone, don't bother me' ('Don't Bother Me'), and 'negative' terms have also been applied evaluatively to his vocal performances (MacDonald, 1994, pp. 51, 55). He also shows a tendency to avoid overtly romantic themes, apart from 'I Need You' (MacDonald, 1994, p. 142). His characteristic pessimism suggests the frustration and resentment of a reluctant underling who is nevertheless resigned to his lot. Clearly the 'sad sack' persona of Harrison as vocalist was reinforced by the songs Lennon and McCartney wrote for him (notably 'I'm Happy Just to Dance with You') and Harrison's real-life experiences in the recording studio with the other Beatles (Lewisohn, 1988, p. 81).

Harrison was legendarily a perfectionist in his guitar playing (Davies, 1968, p. 103), but the hectic schedules of early Beatles recording sessions often resulted in sloppy and half-formed Harrison solos being deemed 'rough enough', for example 'Slow Down', 'Everybody's Trying to Be My Baby', and 'Leave My Kitten Alone', the last of which surely would have been released if the guitar solo had been better. In contrast, his leads on most Beatles singles are excellent, as is most of his later recorded guitar work, presumably because he had more time to rehearse.

George's songs and parts were not accorded nearly as much time and attention in the studio as Lennon and McCartney's and this must have fuelled his resentment. 'One really got the impression that George was being given a certain amount of time to do his tracks whereas the others could spend as long as they wanted,' remarked Abbey Road engineer Geoff Emerick (Lewisohn, 1988, p. 81; MacDonald, 1994, pp. 116, 142, 166). George was not getting the credit he deserved for his musical contributions, and in the recording studio was risking becoming a sideman. What to do? Clearly Harrison needed to get more of his own songs on Beatles records. But competing with Lennon and McCartney on their terms was a formidable prospect. Harrison needed some way to differentiate his musical output from the others, but clearly it could not be solely through songwriting ingenuity. There was another possibility, however – creating cultural capital, or, in rock parlance, 'street cred', anticipating a trend or introducing the band to a new and important artist or genre, as Harrison had done with Bob Dylan (Miller, 1999, p. 226).

In the case of *Revolver*, two interconnected trends are relevant – first, the increasing interest in Oriental music and culture as an antidote to western materialism and spiritual sterility (Norman, 1981a, pp. 275, 295; MacDonald, 1994, pp. 5–6, 13–14). Harrison's interest had been sparked by the presence of Indian instruments on the set of *Help!*, the plot of which concerns an Indian 'cult' – only a year later, *Revolver* features Harrison's first full-blown attempt in the Indian idiom. Since none of the other Beatles could play Indian instruments, Indian music also gave Harrison the chance to control the recording process (Norman, 1981a, p. 268).

Second was the imminent rise of the rock counterculture, the underground and especially the US west coast hippie/psychedelic scene, which Harrison initially identified with, travelling to the Monterey Pop Festival, and citing the Byrds as the 'American Beatles' (Schaffner, 1977, p. 45). There could also be an element of self-interest here, as the Byrds/psychedelic sound was based around the jangling Rickenbacker twelve-string sound that Harrison had pioneered. On the Beatles' previous album, *Rubber Soul*, his 'If I Needed Someone' is a clear homage to the American group, with a guitar riff and chord progression based on their cover of 'Bells of Rhymney' and Byrds-style three-part harmonies. Harrison soon denounced hippies, but hip US musicians were another matter.

The year 1966 was a hugely fertile period for pop music, and all manner of musical genres and subcultures were proliferating. The competition was hotting up – Dylan was putting out records like *Blonde on Blonde* and had recently and controversially toured the UK with the Band. The Beach Boys had just produced *Pet Sounds*, and Californian psychedelic rock and its associated hippie lifestyle seemed to herald a new era of youth/music-based community. All the Beatles were interested by these developments (Davies, 1968, p. 285), but Lennon and McCartney perhaps in a more proprietorial way, as they also wished to preserve the Beatles' primacy in the pop/rock field. Harrison was presumably less concerned in this sense because he had less investment in the Beatles' collectivity, so could go further faster, perhaps finding the values of the counterculture accommodating in a way that the more sceptical Lennon and McCartney didn't. As a lead guitarist, he could identify with underground guitar 'heroes' like Eric Clapton and Jimi Hendrix (the former became Harrison's close friend). The celebrity all-star jam which was a recurrent feature of late-1960s and early-1970s rock culture was far more amenable to Harrison than the other Beatles (the bonus 'jam' LP included with *All Things Must Pass*, for example). Hence Ian MacDonald writes of Harrison's later composition 'While My Guitar Gently Weeps': '[it] enshrines, in its plodding sequence, rock's typical rhythmic overstatement ... the energetic topicality of pop is here supplanted by a dull grandiosity predictive of the simplified stadium music of the Seventies' (MacDonald, 1994, p. 242). We need not concur with MacDonald's judgement to recognize that the late-1960s 'progression' from pop to rock presented a golden opportunity for Harrison to define himself outside the Beatles. 'The most keyed-in of the Beatles ... he kept the right company, raved about the right records, and wrought the requisite changes on his own musical technique. He collaborated with the circle of Southern musicians who would lend their help to such milestones as *Layla and other assorted love songs* and Joe Cocker's *Mad Dogs and Englishmen*' (Harris, 2001, p. 68).

Harrison's contributions to *Revolver*

On *Revolver*, Harrison increases his share of composing credits to an all-time high of three (on the White Album he gets four, but that's a double album). Moreover, these are more prominently placed within the album. 'Taxman' is the first and only time a Harrison song achieves 'pole position'. Thematically it is continuous with the anti-romantic, accusatory tone present in his earlier songs – in this case the protest is directed at the British tax system, which also makes it the first 'political' Beatles song, antedating 'Revolution' by two years. That said, it's also very much a group effort – many of the 'best' lines ('My advice to those who die / Declare the pennies on your eyes') Lennon claimed as his contribution (Everett, 1999, p. 48), while musically Paul McCartney is all over the song, playing a distinctive, much imitated bassline and also the guitar solo (cf. 'Start', The Jam). It might seem rather surprising that Harrison did not play the solo on his own song, but he remarks, 'In those days, for me to be allowed to do my one song on the album, it was like "Great. I don't care who plays what"' (Everett, 1999, p. 49). Harrison's defensive deference is justifiable in light of the attitudes of other band members, like Lennon: 'I threw in a few one-liners to help the song along, because that's what he asked for. He came to me because he couldn't go to Paul, because Paul wouldn't have helped him at that period. I didn't want to do it. I thought, Oh no, don't tell me I have to work on George's stuff' (Sheff and Golson 1981, p. 127). However, at some point Lennon/McCartney's attitude must have changed, because their contributions loom large in the recording and it seems that Harrison again risks being sidelined, except this time, ironically, on his own composition.

But the song is also differentiated from earlier Beatles songs and allied with contemporaneous musical practices, Harrison's main source of creative empowerment. The trope of 'the Man', new to the Beatles, is continuous with black American and subsequently hippie culture's personification of an anonymous authority/Establishment figure as Other (e.g. Leadbelly's 'Midnight Special': 'You better not complain now, you'll get in trouble with the man', 'Drug Store Truck Drivin' Man', or the Small Faces' ironic paean to drug dealers 'Here Comes the Nice' – 'The man's gonna help you all he can'.)

The harmonic and melodic simplicity and repetitiveness of 'Taxman' (it only has three chords) is another differentiating factor, setting it apart from Lennon/McCartney's more traditional Tin Pan Alley-style harmonic complexity and embracing instead the emerging rock ethos of a more 'direct' blues-based harmonic approach as guarantor of authenticity. 'Taxman' clearly refers to contemporaneous developments in black R&B, with its soul devices (choked offbeat guitar, like Steve Cropper; staccato, blues-based bass riff, similar to James Brown; MacDonald, 1994, p. 160). 'Taxman' can also be viewed as a precursor of psychedelic rock, in which the use of raga-style eastern drones (as in Paul's solo) necessitates simple chords underneath. Some of Lennon's songs on *Revolver* also show this simplifying tendency – 'She Said She Said', for example, which is based on the same chords as 'Taxman' but features a more sustained pedal (on organ) and psychedelic worldview.

With its rhythmic abruptness, harsh sound and restricted harmonic palette, 'Taxman' was the Beatles' 'rockiest' song yet. This approach was empowering for Harrison, because it played to his strengths. The vocal melody, for example, typical of Harrison's syncopated crotchet style, and delivered in his usual acerbic manner, complements the nature of the subject matter and the genres referenced far better than in his earlier, more 'pop' work. The melody is also simple and repetitious enough not to 'tax' his vocal abilities. In a rock discourse that valued 'realism' over artifice, Harrison's gruff approach seemed suddenly relevant.

Just a day tripper?

'Love You To' was Harrison's first attempt to record in an authentic Indian style, making it the most radical departure to date from the accepted Beatles soundscape – none of the other Beatles were present on the track (Everett, 1999, p. 40). Melodically, the song is similar to 'Taxman' – repetitive and scalic – and lyrically it is ambivalent and saturnine in Harrison's usual style: 'I'll make love to you, if you want me to', an ambivalence underlined by the cryptic title. Also typical is the sour 'social comment': 'There's people standing round, who'll screw you in the ground' (Everett, 1999, p. 40). Again, while the lyrics can seem simplistic and crude, the us/them scenario typical in Harrison songs (as opposed to the you/me of pop) can have the effect of identifying the singer with a privileged subculture that views the straight world with a jaundiced eye, again an attitude which allies Harrison very much with the emerging rock counterculture.

The obvious criticism to level at George's eastern work is that it is a kind of Orientalism, a tourist's excursion into the realm of the Other. Edward Said defines Orientalism as 'the ontological and epistemological distinction between the "Orient" and the "Occident"' (Said, 1979, p. 1), a discourse of eastern 'Otherness' which '*is*, rather than expresses, a certain *will* or *intention* to understand, in some cases to control, manipulate, even incorporate, what is a manifestly different world' (Said, 1979, p. 12, author's italics). An obvious example in western music would be David Bowie's version of 'China Girl' (*Let's Dance* 1983, co-written by Iggy Pop) with its mock Asian guitar licks. A similar case might be made for the sitar on 'Norwegian Wood' in these terms, as adding a pleasingly exotic tinkle to what is otherwise a straightforward folk waltz. But it could equally be argued that it suited Lennon's ironic intent: to satirize the brittle pretensions of the bohemian demi-monde of the woman in the song.

The charge of Orientalism might make more sense if Harrison's song had employed eastern motifs only as ornament, but this does not seem to have been his approach. In terms of the Beatles' output of that time, and indeed western popular music in general, 'Love You To' was less an Oriental flirtation than a total immersion – a radical departure. And in countercultural terms, 'radicalism' is a desirable attribute. The affect of Harrison's eastern work can be alienating for the average western listener – clearly 'accessibility' was not Harrison's primary concern.

I won't attempt an analysis of the song's authenticity or otherwise to Indian music, as this analysis has been done well elsewhere (Everett, 1999, pp. 40–42). What is important to me is the way that the use of Indian culture (and arguably a philosophical viewpoint derived from eastern religion) sets Harrison apart from the other Beatles by identifying with an alternative set of musical and cultural values, introducing for the sensitive or 'hip' listener issues of cultural relativism (like racism) which complicate any direct (or uncomplimentary) comparison with other Beatles songs. By working with Indian music, Harrison thus cleared himself a 'space' where he could develop without being dismissed as a poor imitation of Lennon and McCartney. And those allied to the emerging rock counterculture, like Tom Wolfe, who dismissed the Beatles as too pop, could hardly level the same accusation at George (Marcus, 1980, p. 186; Norman, 1981a, p. 271). Interestingly, in Richard Goldstein's notorious panning of *Sgt Pepper*, 'How I Lost My Cool Through the New York Times' (Village Voice), George's 'Within You Without You' is singled out for praise, for its sincerity.

To the extent that it is possible to draw comparisons between Harrison's work and the other Beatles, the harmonic structure of the song (I ♭VII) echoes Lennon's 'Tomorrow Never Knows', and both feature a drone on the tamboura (played by Harrison; Martin and Pearson, 1994a, p. 79) which can be heard as both 'eastern' and psychedelic, and went on to feature a good deal on *Sgt Pepper* (MacDonald, 1994, p. 135).

> Psychedelic music ... aspires to a rushing roar of the sound, the primal OM. You can trace a thread through ... gamelan, didgeridoo music, raga ... the Velvet Underground, the Byrds ... minimal is maximal – simple patterns repeated can generate complexity and immensity ... drone music blurs the gaps between the notes to hint at the supramusical roar of the cosmos breathing. (Reynolds and Press, 1995, pp. 181–182)

If one follows Reynolds's line that psychedelia was about returning to the womb, then both Lennon and Harrison were reborn, as a human being and a heavenly avatar respectively. However, Lennon was only interested in eastern religion/ psychedelia/counterculture insofar as it supported his own eccentric individualism – ultimately, he said, 'I just believe in me' ('God', *Plastic Ono Band*, 1970). For Harrison it was an opportunity to identify himself with a new and different authority and to claim selfhood by submitting to it: 'Religion and God are the only things that exist' (Davies, 1968, p. 348). But also, by identifying with the anti-rational, anti-western values of psychedelia, and consequently with the acid-popping haphazardness of Lennon rather than the more cautious and controlling McCartney, Harrison aligns himself with a hip/progressive rock culture, that defines itself by opposition to the pop mainstream.

'I Want To Tell You'

> George Martin: 'What are you going to call it, George?'
> George Harrison: 'I don't know.'
> John Lennon: '… You've never had a title for any of your songs!'
> Engineer Geoff Emerick subsequently recorded the name of the song as 'I Don't Know' (Lewisohn, 1988, p. 81).

This sounds like an inauspicious birth for George's 'unprecedented' third contribution to the album, in circumstances which had more to do with Lennon's failure to come up with a new song (Everett, 1999, p. 57) than any newfound altruistic impulse within the group. Again, the song identifies both lyrically and musically with an emergent rock subculture: the distorted, descending guitar riff at the beginning portends the nascent heavy metal sensibility of Jeff Beck and the Yardbirds, reinforced by the 'heaviness' of the hammering beat and continuous thudding bass. This air of foreboding is exacerbated by the strongly dissonant piano, prefiguring perhaps John Cale's piano on the Velvet Underground's 'I'm Waiting for the Man' and the developing discourse of avant-garde or 'art' rock. Brian Epstein was an early champion of the New York group, and McCartney's piano on the track shows he was listening to the same modern classical composers as John Cale, Stockhausen, for example (Bockris and Malanga, 1983, pp. 83–84; Everett, 1999, p. 10). The ambiguity of the dissonance is so pronounced, it's as if the song harmonically was simultaneously pulling in two directions. Again this harmonic contradiction is reflected in the lyrics, which waver between different possibilities: 'I want to tell you … [but] when you're near, all those words … seem to slip away'. In the middle section, this paradox is slowly unravelled by re-envisioning 'reality' relatively, in terms of different levels of perception: 'It's only me and not my mind that is confusing things' (MacDonald, 1994, p. 166). Harrison's bumbling takes on a new relevance in relation to the 'rock' trope of inarticulacy, for example the Who's 'Can't Explain' or the stuttering 'My Generation'. If pop was about saying what you mean, for example 'I Want To Hold Your Hand', then rock was more about questioning the worth of saying it and articulating through abstract expressionism instead (possibly by trashing instruments).

Harrison's use of chord changes to express disorientation rather than as functional devices (MacDonald, 1994, p. 166; Everett, 1999, p. 58) anticipates and mirrors Lennon's harmonic experimentation on tracks like 'Strawberry Fields Forever' and 'I Am The Walrus'. Harrison's instrumental (guitar) contributions to *Revolver* can be viewed in this light – he plays a lot more on Lennon's than McCartney's songs. Much more than *Rubber Soul*, *Revolver* is dominated by electric rather than acoustic guitars, and the tone is typically distorted and harsh, often further manipulated by studio effects like ADT (artificial double tracking) and varispeeding which altered their timbral qualities. Harrison and the Beatles had begun such experiments with tone on *Rubber Soul*, the guitar solo on 'Nowhere Man' for example, with its super-trebly sound (Lewisohn, 1988, p. 13), but here that tone becomes ubiquitous (with the exception, again, of McCartney's songs). Harrison also experiments with backwards guitar ('I'm Only Sleeping') where his solo fills were played over the tape running in reverse. By contrast with *Rubber Soul*, *Revolver* is a much more self-consciously experimental, progressive 'rock' album, and this experimentation with different types of guitar sounds is broadly continuous with the emerging rock preoccupation with tonal extremities typically achieved by distortion, feedback or other kinds of technical manipulation – cf. Jimi Hendrix, Eric Clapton, Jeff Beck (MacDonald, 1994, pp. 142, 160).

In terms of lyrical personae, Harrison's introspective tone was now becoming very much du jour, as drug-induced self-examination, self-doubt and philosophizing took over from romance as privileged subject matter for rock, as opposed to pop. While McCartney continued to write in a broadly pop/romantic vein, or crafted dramatic vignettes ('Eleanor Rigby', 'For No One'), Lennon's writing was also becoming more introspective and esoteric ('She Said She Said', 'I'm Only Sleeping'). With their 'psychedelic' studio experimentation and general weirdness (backwards sounds, etc.), Lennon and Harrison's songs of this period are continuous with a slew of futuristic, speculative or 'drug' songs written by other bands in 1966–1967: the Small Faces' 'Itchycoo Park', the Kinks' 'See My Friend', the Yardbirds' 'Shapes of Things', the Beach Boys' 'Good Vibrations', Creation' 'How Does It Feel to Feel?', the Byrds' 'Eight Miles High', Jefferson Airplane' 'White Rabbit', the Supremes' 'Reflections', etc. All were characterized to some extent by ambiguous or explicit drugs references, musical exoticism (especially eastern or 'raga'), musical extremity, outlandish sound effects and unconventional song structures – in short, a new 'psychedelic awareness'. Such a new musical sensibility presented a challenge to the Beatles, but also an opportunity, especially for Harrison.

Beatles musical ideology and practice pre- and post-*Revolver*

The musical ideology of the Beatles up to 1966 had been very much about a syncretic and progressive absorption of influence from all areas of popular music and its crystallization into a new paradigm – the self-contained rock group, playing their own instruments, singing their own songs (Gloag, 2001, pp. 80–81). The central perception of the Beatles as songwriter/auteurs was that they were original and new, and that whatever influences were present in their music were transformed or ironized (hence 'Rubber Soul'). In a sense, this was a Romantic/modernist ideology of originality, which Lennon especially could have picked up at art school. Contemporary accounts of the Beatles' impact seem to confirm this 'newness', for example Bob Dylan: 'They were doing things nobody was doing ... Their chords were outrageous ... ' (Marcus, 1980, p. 179). The Beatles' unprecedented success can also be seen as enforcing an ideology of originality: the idea that there had never been a pop phenomenon like the Beatles slipped effortlessly into the perception that their music was similarly integrating and absorbing influence into 'something new'.

Revolver represented the first phase in the breaking down of this model of seamless originality, a process probably accelerated by LSD, which is known to have deleterious effects on the ego's construction of a unified self. Intra-group bickering reached an all-time high, and studio and songwriting practices also reflected increasing alienation within the group. By *Revolver*, Lennon and McCartney had virtually ceased writing as a team, and consequently the music started to sound more diverse than ever before. Compared with previous Beatles albums, *Revolver* sounds like a set of stylistically and sonically diverse compositions written and sung by different people rather than a group effort. The unity of the record lies in the overall excellence of composition and performance of each individual work, rather than in any stylistic continuity. This ongoing breakdown of the Beatles' musical regime into its separate components offered increasing opportunities for the previously oppressed Harrison to define his own space.

While the Beatles had always been inter-textual, quoting extensively from other music, previous to *Revolver* these practices had usually been tightly integrated into the group's overall sound. Harrison tended to be the exception to this rule, writing the Byrds-influenced 'If I Needed Someone' and playing lead parts that are more clearly influenced (by Chet Atkins and Carl Perkins) than other elements in the Beatles soundscape. From *Revolver* on, this soundscape gradually fractures and intertextuality becomes much more obvious, for example the pastiches of the White Album (for example, 'Yer Blues', 'Honey Pie', 'Why Don't We Do It In The Road?'). 'Tomorrow Never Knows' presents the first Beatle lyric that is cribbed from an outside source (Everett, 1999, pp. 34–35). It is also the first Beatles' recording to rely on a random, collage approach (the use of tape loops), while 'Yellow Submarine' is the group's first essay into the world of *musique concrète,* using found objects and sound effects, again in a collage-like manner. Many of the songs sound like parodies of other styles: soul music ('Got To Get You Into My Life') or classical high seriousness ('Eleanor Rigby'). Some are lyrically satirical – 'Doctor Robert', 'Taxman'. This heterogeneity was at once a reflection of the Beatles' increasing knowledge and use of the recording studio and also an increasing acknowledgement of the complexity of the outside world.

Conclusion

A huge stretching of the Beatles' musical canvas was taking place on *Revolver*, just as the Beatles' minds were also 'expanding' under the influence of acid. But the canvas could only stretch so far. According to MacDonald, the embracing of indeterminacy and resignation of personal responsibility that followed from psychedelic experience was ultimately responsible for the Beatles' social and artistic disintegration (MacDonald, 1994, p. 206). But it also produced some of their best work, and allowed the beleaguered Harrison to emerge from under the shadow of his seniors as a distinctive voice, achieved by exploiting his newfound freedom to not be 'a Beatle' but to locate his 'real' stylistic affiliations elsewhere in the emerging rock culture of the late 1960s and in Indian religion. Indeed Harrison enjoyed a newfound prominence: 'Within a year his fascination with Eastern philosophy was dominating the social life of the group' (MacDonald, 1994, p. 167). But more than that, Harrison could also increasingly identify with and form alliances with the emerging 'rock aristocracy', bringing in, for example, Eric Clapton, the first 'outside' rock musician to guest on a Beatles track ('While My Guitar Gently Weeps'), and later Billy Preston on the *Let It Be* sessions. In Harrison's contributions to *Revolver* we can discern signs of these 'things to come', in terms of their difference (especially the Indian influence) and their celebration of the nascent discourse of 'rock'. *Revolver*'s huge stylistic diversity gave Harrison the opportunity to be heard. But this same complexity and diversity also foreshadowed the eventual dissolution of the group into four disparate voices.

Chapter 11

Premature turns: thematic disruption in the American version of *Revolver*

Jim LeBlanc

On 20 June 1966, the Beatles' *Yesterday ... and Today* was released in the United States. Its cover, an innocuous snapshot of the four musicians posing in and around a large suitcase, was a last-minute choice by Capitol executives to replace a more controversial depiction of the band – one in which the four performers were clad in butcher's aprons and brandished slabs of meat and decapitated dolls: the infamous 'butcher sleeve'. The original jacket photo was rumored to represent the Beatles' reaction to Capitol's melding of previously released material with new work for this US album, thus mutilating their forthcoming offering, *Revolver*, which would not appear until August. Indeed, three songs from what would become the British version of *Revolver*, songs that would not appear on the American edition, were pre-released on *Yesterday ... and Today*: 'I'm Only Sleeping', 'And Your Bird Can Sing', and 'Doctor Robert', all penned primarily by John Lennon.[1]

Revolver was not, of course, the first US Beatles album on which the playlist varied from that on the Parlophone version. Capitol's predilection for including fewer tracks on its LPs than did its British corporate counterpart routinely resulted in different long-playing listening experiences on the North American side of the Atlantic, going all the way back to *Meet the Beatles* (which did not even bear the same *title* as its British edition, *With the Beatles*). In the case of *Revolver*, however, the pre-release of new Beatles material was particularly troubling because of the striking new sound of this album, much of which originates in Lennon's compositions (though certainly not exclusively).[2] The impact and exotic flavor of the record were undoubtedly diminished in the US by the release of 'Sleeping', 'And Your Bird', and 'Doctor Robert' nearly two months in advance of *Revolver*. In the words of Tim Riley:

> The result more than disrupts the intended flow of [the record] – it confines Lennon's presence to the last cut of each side. With five Lennon tracks on the Parlophone [i.e., British] sequence (instead of just two), his side endings sound less extremist, part of a larger process instead of a sudden swing to the surreal. (Riley, 1988, pp. 181–182)

Moreover, *Revolver* is not just another Beatles album. It has been widely maintained that this record may have been the band's best, or at least its most innovative and influential LP. Stuart Madow and Jeff Sobul, for example, call it a 'break-through album' (Madow and Sobul, 1992, p. 4) and Walter Everett remarks that 'the recordings were stunning … [*Revolver* was] fundamentally unlike any rock album that had preceded it' (Everett, 1999, p. 31). Wilfrid Mellers praises the LP as 'verbally and musically an extraordinary break-through' and goes on to point out that 'the songs complement one another without exactly forming a sequence' (Mellers, 1973, p. 69): the 'larger process' to which Riley refers.

It is the musical and textual thematics of this 'larger process' and their developmental distortion on the US version of *Revolver* that I wish to explore in the forthcoming pages, extending Riley's argument as well as reviewing and expanding on observations made by other critics. I hope to show that there was undoubtedly a certain fragmentation and weakening of the artistic integrity of *Revolver* as a result of the unfortunate pre-release of some of the material produced during the Beatles' spring 1966 recording sessions at EMI Studios. However, I will also suggest that the artistic corruption of the Beatles' magnificent set of early 1966 songs runs deeper than the *Yesterday … and Today* fiasco in the United States and that we may need to resituate, ever so slightly, the transformational moment in rock history that was heralded by *Revolver*'s release.

Most commentators seem to agree that 'Tomorrow Never Knows', the first recorded though last presented piece on the album, constitutes a kind of watershed in the Beatles' musical corpus. Madow and Sobul, for example, call it a 'pivotal song in the annals of rock & roll history' (Madow and Sobul, 1992, p. 12). Its prime position as concluding track on the album reflects the importance that George Martin as well as the Beatles themselves accorded it, and Mark Hertsgaard identifies it as 'the summit to which the entire album ascends' (Hertsgaard, 1995, p. 177). Appearing on both the British and American releases, 'Tomorrow Never Knows' incorporates nearly all of the technological innovations that were used or developed during the *Revolver* sessions. These include: tape reduction, artificial double-tracking (ADT), backward guitar solos, reversed tape loops, and the Leslie speaker that rotated Lennon's voice in an attempt to make him sound like a 'Dalai Lama singing on a hilltop' (Everett, 1999, pp. 36–38). In addition, *Revolver*'s concluding number resumes much of the album's thematic content. The electronic innovations themselves reflect the circularity implicit in the album's title, with solos and tape loops moving the music both forward and backward, and the Leslie speaker literally turning Lennon's vocals through a 360-degree rotation. Furthermore, there is the circle of life, death, and reincarnation which lies at the heart of the song's lyrics – based closely on Timothy Leary, Ralph Metzner, and Richard Alpert's psychedelic revision of the *Tibetan Book of the Dead* – in which dying (or 'not dying' in the case of the LSD experience and in Lennon's lyric) is merely a transitional journey towards rebirth and in which the game of existence is played out 'to the end / of the beginning'. Allusions to death and dying are unusually frequent on *Revolver* and words like 'die', 'died', 'dead', and 'dying' occur in seven tracks on both the British and

American editions, representing roughly 30 per cent of all Beatles songs in which such terms appear. References to unconscious, semi-conscious, and altered conscious states also occur throughout the album, and the drug theme is fairly evident in 'Tomorrow Never Knows', especially after one has discovered the origin of the song's words. The blissful, hypnotic condition described in Leary's text is echoed in 'Tomorrow''s mesmerizingly minimal harmonic structure, in which the only chord change (I-♭VII-I) seems almost to have derived from a remarkably fortuitous harmony between some of the reversed tape loops with the organ and vocal. Finally, the eastern roots of Leary's text surface texturally both in the drone of the Indian tamboura, which moans the tonic to open the piece, and in the South Asian colors of some of the tape loops.

Thus, life cycles, circularity in general, instances of reduced or altered consciousness, and South Asian influences all appear as prominent motifs in the album's concluding piece. These are all connected, of course, through the notion of rebirth in the *Tibetan Book of the Dead* – modulated for acidheads in Leary's work with the mantra: 'Whenever in doubt, turn off your mind, relax and float downstream' (Leary et al., 1964, p. 14).

The other John Lennon composition that appears on both the British and American versions of the album is 'She Said She Said'. It is interesting to note that this piece was the *last* to be recorded during the spring 1966 sessions. Like 'Tomorrow Never Knows', it graces the end of an album side. Though its production was less technologically complex than that of 'Tomorrow', it nonetheless echoes (or prefigures, depending how you look at it) the latter composition in several ways. Musically, for instance, we note a certain circularity in George Harrison's lead guitar responses to Lennon's vocal lines and in the song's rhythmically accelerated coda in which Harrison repeats Lennon's vocal at a measure's distance in a kind of simple round. Moreover, as Mellers has written (albeit disparagingly), the piece is musically 'totally without development, *rotating around itself*' (Mellers, 1973, p. 76; my emphasis). Here, too, death figures prominently in Lennon's lyrics, which reproduce a snippet of conversation that reputedly took place at a party in Benedict Canyon, California in 1965 – specifically, Peter Fonda's remark to Harrison that he [Fonda] knew 'what it's like to be dead' as a result of his heart having stopped beating three times during emergency surgery. At the age of ten he had shot himself in the stomach ('revolver' indeed!). Lennon's putative reply at the time was: 'You're making me feel like I've never been born. Who put all that shit in your head?' (Turner, 1994, p. 111). The preservation of the gist of this exchange in 'She Said She Said', as well as the song's bridge in which the composer reminisces about how 'everything was right' in his youth, bring the life cycle of birth, aging, and death into the tune in a kind of topsy-turvy manner: death suggesting never having been born (or reborn, perhaps) and the singer's nostalgic recollections of his boyhood suggesting a desire to move backwards through life. Finally, we should note that Fonda, Harrison, and Lennon were all apparently high on acid at the Benedict

Canyon affair, making 'She Said She Said' another song with hallucinogenic roots.[3]

And that's what we get from the pen of John Lennon on the American *Revolver*. To be fair we should note that the stylistic and thematic gulf between Lennon's closing tracks and the rest of the material on the American edition may not be as broad as Riley suggests. The electronic innovations, the musical themes, and the lyrical motifs that I've just presented do not occur exclusively in Lennon's material and there is still a great deal of thematic coherence on the US album, even without the three pre-released tracks. The use of tape reduction (that is, the condensation of a full tape of sound onto one or two tracks using the era's state-of-the-art four track recording technology) was rampant throughout the album and ADT was used in Harrison's 'Taxman' and 'I Want to Tell You', as well as in McCartney's 'Eleanor Rigby'. In 'I Want To Tell You', Harrison's lead guitar intro was rotated through a Leslie speaker, as was the countermelody McCartney sings near the end of 'Rigby' (giving it that distanced nuance). Minimal harmonic movement, with its characteristically hypnotic effect, is manifest in several songs. The first eight bars of 'Taxman''s verse, for example, are propelled by a harshly chromaticized tonic ($I^{7+\#9}$). The succeeding track on both editions of the album, 'Eleanor Rigby', is essentially a two-chord song (E-minor and C), and Harrison's 'Love You To' features the same I-♭VII-I progression that we hear in 'Tomorrow Never Knows'. As in the bridge of 'She Said She Said', childhood memories are recalled in McCartney's 'Yellow Submarine', the song that immediately precedes 'She Said She Said' on both versions of the album. The watery comfort of this children's song about a submarine also hints at one of Leary et al.'s trippy images in *The Psychedelic Experience*: 'You may feel yourself floating out and down into a warm sea' (Leary et al., 1964, p. 58). Death takes center stage in 'Eleanor Rigby', of course, and McCartney brilliantly evokes the death of love in 'For No One' – a piece that was originally titled 'Why Did It *Die*'. Finally, the eastern feel of 'Tomorrow Never Knows' is previewed in the lead guitar fade-out in 'Taxman' (played by McCartney), in the 'gamak-like ornaments' (Everett, 1999, p. 57) of the codal vocal part in 'I Want To Tell You' (again supplied by McCartney), and most explicitly of course in Harrison's Indic 'Love You To'. Cycles, circles, and circularity are less evident in the McCartney and Harrison numbers, however – with the exception perhaps of the 'turning guitar line' in 'I Want To Tell You' (Riley, 1988, p. 200) – and there are no other overt references to altered states of consciousness or unconsciousness on the American album (though some listeners have construed 'Yellow Submarine' to be a drug song and McCartney maintains that his 'Got To Get You Into My Life' is an 'ode to pot') (Miles, 1997, p. 190).[4]

On the other hand, the foregoing themes are significantly reiterated in the three Lennon compositions that were excised from the American *Revolver*, and in one of them in particular. 'I'm Only Sleeping' is the third cut on the A-side of the British album, and it is the first song on the record that is chiefly Lennon's. That it belongs on *Revolver*, rather than *Yesterday ... and Today* is articulated in Terence O'Grady's observation that: 'the hallucinatory tape effects [are] the song's most significant attribute ... and link it more closely to the experimental mood of the American *Revolver* than either of the other two [pre-released] Lennon compositions' (O'Grady, 1983, p. 95). Indeed, 'Sleeping' is packed with electronic hijinx: reversed guitar passages, ADT, and a varispeed recording technique through which the lead vocal was taped at 45 cps for playback at 50 cps creating, in Everett's words: 'a dreamy timbre that floats particularly well on the high sustained notes' (Everett, 1999, p. 50). There is a certain harmonic revolving in this piece as well, and Everett goes on to observe that: 'the underlying chords reverse themselves in circles' at certain points (at 0:21–0:28, for instance; Everett, 1999, p. 50). The fundamental lyrical motif of 'I'm Only Sleeping' addresses the cycle of sleeping and wakefulness. The 'brrrrring' of the song's opening minor chord, which seems to launch the sleeper into wakefulness like some jarring alarm, the 'yawning bass solo at the end of each refrain' (Riley, 1988, p. 185), and the similarly 'hypnotic, yawning effect' of the backwards guitar (Dowlding, 1989, p. 136) all serve to recreate musically the semi-conscious transition from the altered state of sleep to wakefulness. Moreover, the morning ritual of reawakening can be seen as a kind of rebirth. The 'only' of the song's title refrain is open to multiple interpretations, one of which is: 'Don't worry. I'm not dead (or narcotically comatose). It is not dying. I'm only sleeping.' Lennon's childhood pal, Pete Shotton, has remarked that this song 'brilliantly evokes the state of chemically induced lethargy into which John had ... drifted' in early 1966 (Shotton and Schaffner, 1983, p. 122), though Steve Turner counters that this tune is not about drugs, but simply reflects Lennon's heavy sleep habit of that era (Turner, 1994, p. 106). One way or the other, 'I'm Only Sleeping' presents the album's first homage to escapism. We should also note that the three reversed guitar bits bring an eastern element to the piece. As O'Grady puts it: 'the fluid, rapid ornaments and the hint of a pedal effect [in these passages] combine to suggest the Indian classical style' (O'Grady, 1983, p. 95).

Parallels between 'I'm Only Sleeping' and 'Tomorrow Never Knows', the record's signature piece, abound. There are the backward guitar parts, of course, which the Beatles used for the first time during the *Revolver* sessions (as they did reversed vocals, which we hear in 'Rain', the B-side of the non-album single that was released in June – more about 'Rain' in a moment). Then there's the mood of oneiric ethereality, created in 'Sleeping' through McCartney and Harrison's background vocals and in 'Tomorrow' through Lennon's Leslied lyrical delivery, which Madow and Sobul describe as communicating 'a feeling and illusion of floating dreamlike and weightless' (Madow and Sobul, 1992, p. 14). It is intriguing to note, though, that in 'Tomorrow Never Knows' one is invited to float 'downstream', while in 'I'm Only Sleeping' the semi-conscious dreamer floats 'upstream'. The original manuscript for 'Sleeping', jotted onto the back of a letter from the phone company, reveals that Lennon had originally written 'downstream', but then crossed out 'down' in favor of 'up' (reproduced in Shotton and Schaffner, 1983, p. 123). How does one float *up*stream? Certainly, the words 'float upstream' flow better acoustically in this context than the more dental 'float downstream', but this paradoxical reversal also serves to highlight the sharp contrast between unconscious, dream-filled sleep and the hyperconscious, psychedelic whitewater journey of the LSD trip. Indeed, the everyday escapism introduced in 'I'm Only Sleeping' acquires a juiced up, metaphysical dimension in the album's final cut.

Thus, 'I'm Only Sleeping' and 'Tomorrow Never Knows', Lennon's first and last tracks on the British *Revolver*, can be seen as companion pieces of sorts – the former introducing themes and effects that prepare the listener for the latter. This is perhaps the strongest point to be made against Capitol's decision not to include 'Sleeping' on the American *Revolver*, though we should not overlook the connections between this track and some of the other songs on the record, especially its immediate neighbors on Side A. For instance, both 'I'm Only Sleeping' and 'Eleanor Rigby', the cut that immediately precedes 'Sleeping' on the British LP, were recorded in E-minor, and the tonic that softly concludes McCartney's composition is boisterously reinvoked to open Lennon's piece – though as noted above, we hear the initial chord of 'I'm Only Sleeping' a semitone lower (as E♭-minor) than the pitch at which it was recorded. Both songs are moody, inward-looking compositions which, at the time, were unusual for the Beatles. Further, the backward guitar solo with which the Lennon song fades out anticipates the exotic sitar glissando that opens Harrison's 'Love You To', the next piece on the British edition, and the Indic sound of both passages creates a strangely similar harmonic and rhythmic effect on both sides of the silent groove which separates the two tracks. Mellers remarks that: 'It's interesting that this incipient dream-song ["I'm Only Sleeping"] immediately preceded the Beatles' first unambiguous exploration of orientalism' (Mellers, 1973, p. 73). Thus, 'Sleeping' is harmonically and thematically spliced, to some extent, to the McCartney and Harrison songs that surround it on the British LP, and this linkage is obviously lost on the American version. Finally, we should note that 'Yellow Submarine', like 'I'm Only Sleeping', was recorded using the varispeed technique that lowered the playback pitch of the instrumental tracks by one half-tone, while raising the vocals by the same interval.

As O'Grady implies, the parallels and similarities between these three 'core' Lennon compositions – 'I'm Only Sleeping', 'She Said She Said', and 'Tomorrow Never Knows' – and the other two Lennon tunes that were hacked from the American *Revolver* are not as evident. If the pace of 'I'm Only Sleeping' is tired and lethargic, and the atmosphere of 'She Said She Said' and 'Tomorrow Never Knows' is drug-drenched, the sound of 'And Your Bird Can Sing' and 'Doctor Robert', with the exception of the latter song's bridge, is crisp and bright. Nonetheless these two Lennon tracks still manifest relationships to other parts of the *Revolver* project that are worthy of note.

In later years, Lennon confessed a dislike for 'And Your Bird Can Sing', perhaps because it didn't quite fit the tone and thematic vision of his other work of this period. Indeed, 'Bird', like 'Doctor Robert', is comparatively lightly dosed with special effects, and it is the only one of his five contributions to *Revolver* that contains no allusions to altered states. Its linkage with other tunes on the LP is extensive, however. For instance, the downward harmonic swoop (bVII-IV) that supports Lennon's sustained vocal across the bar of the opening verse measures of 'She Said She Said' suggests a bird's gliding descent and previews the central image of the next Lennon track on the British edition.[5] Moreover, the avian motif of 'And Your Bird Can Sing' prefigures the squawking gull sounds in 'Tomorrow Never Knows'. The reluctant wakefulness of 'I'm Only Sleeping' is echoed in the phrase 'you may be awoken' in 'And Your Bird', and the doubled lyric 'I'll be "*round*"' alludes aurally, if obliquely, to the album's title. In addition, we should note the fanfare of circularity at the song's conclusion as the rapidly twirling carousel of McCartney and Harrison's lead guitar duet gives way to a quivering bass finale that creates the effect of light glimmering off a revolving silver sphere. Like 'I'm Only Sleeping', 'And Your Bird Can Sing' has intriguing ties to the songs that sandwich it on the British LP. Mellers remarks that the rising half-step modulation at the end of McCartney's 'Good Day Sunshine', the cut that immediately precedes 'Bird' on the British *Revolver*, 'generates a timeless, upward-lifting ecstasy' (Mellers, 1973, p. 76), the crowning touch on a tune that equates love with a sun-splashed day. On the British edition, this bright coda prepares the listener for the exuberant riff that opens 'And Your Bird Can Sing' (albeit a song that treats the theme of love gone sour). On the American LP, the happy modulation of 'Good Day Sunshine''s fade-out gives way to the somber, though beautiful 'For No One' – clearly a different experience for listeners on the western shore of the Atlantic. Neither 'Bird' nor the track that succeeds it on the British version, 'For No One', end on the tonic (but on IV and V^7, respectively), an harmonic characteristic that punctuates both songs with a whiff of irresolution. The original title for the tune, 'You Don't Get Me', and the lyrical motif of communication breakdown pave the way for Harrison's recapitulation of this theme, three tracks later on the British album, in 'I Want To Tell You'. Finally, 'And Your Bird Can Sing' is the sole Lennon cut on *Revolver* that deals even remotely with romance, a theme which is central to more than one of McCartney's tracks, including 'Here, There and Everywhere', 'Good Day Sunshine', 'For No One', and 'Got To Get You Into My Life.'

Musically lustrous like 'Bird', at least in its verse parts, 'Doctor Robert', the third of the pre-released numbers, is clearly the most overt drug song on the British *Revolver*. Said to depict the infamous New York physician Robert Freymann, who routinely dispensed vitamins, hallucinogens, and amphetamines to his patients, Lennon's lead vocal, spiked with ADT and taking on, in Tim Riley's analysis, 'the bleary, drugged-up feel of an addict' (Riley, 1988, p. 195), yields to some rather ethereal harmonies in the modulated bridge, which Everett has characterized as 'extraterrestrial' (Everett, 1999, p. 45). Thus, we encounter once again Lennon's interest in altered states, which has shifted from sleep and dreams in 'I'm Only Sleeping' to hallucinogenic distress in 'She Said She Said' to intoxicated well-being here in 'Doctor Robert', and which will reach its psychedelic apogee in the mystic monologue of 'Tomorrow Never Knows'. We should also note that the up- to downstream shift between 'I'm Only Sleeping' and 'Tomorrow Never Knows' surfaces as an up-and-down boogie shuffle in 'Doctor Robert': 'if you're *down*, he'll pick you *up*'. Like the three songs that precede it on the British LP, 'Doctor Robert' concludes on a harmony other than the one on which it began and, like 'Good Day Sunshine', its tonality sways between the keys of A and B, a recapitulation in 'Robert' of a harmonic gesture rare to rock and roll, which has just occurred three songs earlier on *Revolver* – though not on the American edition.

The foregoing analysis demonstrates how the American version of the Beatles' *Revolver* suffers extensively from the omission of the three pre-released Lennon numbers. The overall integrity of the album is severely compromised, and one might speculate that the impact of this trailblazing record was somewhat lessened in the US, because listeners there had already been exposed to some of this new material, including one of the more avant-garde pieces, as packaged with several 'oldies' on the *Yesterday ... and Today* LP. I'd like to argue, though, that this second contention may not be as significant as one might initially think – or rather, it may be significant, but we should think twice before pointing the finger of blame solely at Capitol's *Yesterday ... and Today*. For 'I'm Only Sleeping', 'And Your Bird Can Sing', and 'Doctor Robert' were not the only tracks from the *Revolver* sessions that were released prior to the August 1966 album. There were two others: 'Paperback Writer' and 'Rain'.

In the days before the Beatles, singles were what counted. Singles came first and, if successful, they were later repackaged in an album, along with other, usually mediocre songs. The LP was a vehicle intended primarily to resell the hit. With their prolific output of first-rate material, the Beatles did not need singles to justify an album. Moreover, they were reluctant to make their fans buy hit recordings for a second time as part of LPs, so often (though not always) they released singles that were not destined to appear on a forthcoming album. 'Paperback Writer' / 'Rain' was one of these. Recorded 13–16 April 1966, these songs were actually the fourth and fifth recorded during the momentous spring 1966 EMI sessions and, as we shall see, they are as musically and thematically linked with the rest of the collection as many of the songs that actually appear on the LP. Released on 30 May in the US and 10 June in the UK, 'Paperback Writer' and 'Rain' represent two more compositions that were prematurely cut from the whole of the *Revolver* sessions.

McCartney's 'Paperback Writer', marketed as the single's A-side, is characterized by much of the same technological gimmickry that infuses the album. Tape reductions allowed for more overdubs than would otherwise have been possible and ADT was applied to the lead vocal. In addition, McCartney's lead guitar was piped through a Leslie speaker. The composer even signed the song's manuscript 'Ian Iachimoe', an approximation of how he heard his name played back on a reversed tape (Everett, 1999, pp. 42–43). Unlike virtually all of the Beatles' earlier songs, but akin to much of the material on *Revolver*, the theme of 'Paperback Writer' contains no love interest. Moreover, it obliquely suggests the circular motif of the album in that: 'the song persuades ... through the circular notion that the attractively ingenuous would-be paperback writer [McCartney] sings of his main character, who himself wishes to be a paperback writer' (Everett, 1999, p. 43). Like 'Tomorrow Never Knows', 'Eleanor Rigby', and 'Love You To', 'Paperback Writer' is harmonically rather static, a two-chord song in fact, using only I^7 and IV. McCartney's active bass is striking and previews the more prominent role it will play on such *Revolver* tracks as 'And Your Bird Can Sing' and 'For No One', as well as on the single's B-side. Although the overall harmonic movement of the number is limited, the a cappella harmonies of the refrain are quite full and anticipate the richly textured bridge of 'Doctor Robert', recorded just a few days later. In the US, this last parallel is doubly lost on the listener as both 'Paperback Writer' and 'Doctor Robert' were released separately from *Revolver*, as well as separately from each other.

As is the case with 'She Said She Said', 'Tomorrow Never Knows', and the pre-released numbers on *Yesterday ... and Today*, it is Lennon's contribution to the 1966 single that seems most characteristic of the innovative nature of material produced during the *Revolver* sessions. In Riley's opinion, 'Rain' represents 'the first stirring of pop psychedelia' (Riley, 1988, p. 178).[6] In this sense, it is clearly the preamble, in terms of release date, to all five Lennon tracks on the British *Revolver*, especially 'I'm Only Sleeping' and 'Tomorrow Never Knows'. In common with these two pivotal *Revolver* cuts, 'Rain' presents (for the first time – again in terms of release date) a bit of reversed tape, producing the weirdly clipped vocal gibberish at the end of the piece. And as in 'I'm Only Sleeping' and 'Yellow Submarine', some of the instruments and Lennon's lead vocal are electronically manipulated using the varispeed technique, though in this case Starr's drums and Lennon's guitar were taped '*much* faster than heard' and the lead vocal (also doctored with ADT) was recorded a full major second lower than what we hear in the playback (Everett, 1999, p. 44; my emphasis). The chord progression underpinning 'Rain''s verse is a slightly modified I-IV-I, though the initial tonic strangely lacks its middle note, as the G-major chord is played as a G/D dyad – another example of the kind of reduced harmonics so common in the band's tunes of this period. Again like 'I'm Only Sleeping' and 'Tomorrow Never Knows', as well as 'Eleanor Rigby' and 'She Said She Said', 'Rain' is an inward-looking song, in which the singer maintains that the weather, fair or foul, is 'just a state of mind'. Furthermore, according to Turner, 'Rain' was the 'first Beatles' track to suggest new transcendental states of consciousness, not just in its lyric but in the music' (Turner, 1994, p. 102). Indeed, although 'Rain' contains no lyrical references whatsoever to hallucinogens, it may be one of the band's trippiest tunes. Everett observes that the slowed down instrumental track infuses 'a subtle but rich tone of queasy hesitation that could be likened to the nausea of an acid trip' and that the significantly sped up vocal results 'in the brilliant iridescence of an acid-streaked sunshine' (Everett, 1999, p. 44). 'Rain' is another Beatles tune in which death is invoked ('they might as well be *dead*'), bringing to eight the number of such songs recorded during the *Revolver* sessions and linking this track in still another way to the thematic fabric of the forthcoming album. Finally, the phrases 'I can show you' and 'Can you hear me' announce the plea for improved communication that will be restated in *Revolver*'s 'And Your Bird Can Sing' and 'I Want To Tell You'.

Thus, the two sides of the spring 1966 single, like 'Sleeping', 'Bird', and 'Doctor Robert', represent pre-released pieces from a 'breakthrough' collection, and it can be argued that their appearance, too, served to undercut the integrity and force of *Revolver*, both in the United States *and in Britain*. It is interesting to speculate on what might have resulted if 'Paperback Writer' and 'Rain' had been included in the British version of the album. With a few days remaining before they were due to embark on what would turn out to be their last few weeks of touring, the band still needed to come up with two more numbers to complete the fourteen-song set. McCartney brought forth 'Here, There and Everywhere' as his eleventh hour contribution to the collection, and Lennon brought a sketchy 'She Said She Said' to the studio. Would these compositions have appeared on *Revolver* if the two sides of the spring single had been included in the finished LP product? And if not, would they have ever been recorded at all? Lennon's last *Revolver* piece certainly bears the characteristic traits of the Beatles' collective avant-garde work of this period, but McCartney's ballad, while arguably one of the most beautiful love songs of the mid-1960s, is not typical of the rest of the album. Everett points out that: '"Here, There and Everywhere" presents the sparest and most relaxed texture of the LP' (Everett, 1999, p. 60). Madow and Sobul go even further: '"Rain" belonged on *Revolver*. It was perfectly suited for the album, especially when combined with "I'm Only Sleeping" on the British release. We feel the group should have substituted "Rain" for one of the titles on *Revolver*, most logically "Here, There and Everywhere"' (Madow and Sobul, 1992, p. 4). *Revolver* with 'Paperback Writer' and 'Rain', but without 'Here, There and Everywhere' and 'She Said She Said', might have been stranger, but would it have been even stronger?

It is also interesting to speculate further on the origin of *Yesterday ... and Today*'s original 'butcher sleeve'. According to Leary et al. in *The Psychedelic Experience*, failure to turn off one's mind, relax, and float downstream and attempts to impose egotistical interpretations on the 'vibratory waves of exter-nal unity' in the so-called 'fifth vision' of the LSD trip can result in the 'plastic doll phenomenon', in which: 'differentiated forms are seen as inorganic, mass-produced, shabby, plastic, and all persons (including self) are seen as lifeless

mannequins isolated from the vibrant dance of energy, which has been lost'
(Leary et al., 1964, p. 65). Perhaps it was this effect that informed the Beatles'
choice of decapitated dolls for inclusion in the original cover photo for
Yesterday ... and Today, on which three severed pieces from the *Revolver*
project made their premature appearance.

Notes

1.   The playlists for the British and US versions of *Revolver* are as follows, with each song's primary
     composer:

REVOLVER (BRITISH)	*REVOLVER* (AMERICAN)	
SIDE A	SIDE A	
Taxman	Taxman	(Harrison)
Eleanor Rigby	Eleanor Rigby	(McCartney)
I'm Only Sleeping	———	(Lennon)
Love You To	Love You To	(Harrison)
Here, There and Everywhere	Here, There and Everywhere	(McCartney)
Yellow Submarine	Yellow Submarine	(McCartney)
She Said She Said	She Said She Said	(Lennon)
SIDE B	SIDE B	
Good Day Sunshine	Good Day Sunshine	(McCartney)
And Your Bird Can Sing	———	(Lennon)
For No One	For No One	(McCartney)
Doctor Robert	———	(Lennon)
I Want To Tell You	I Want To Tell You	(Harrison)
Got To Get You Into My Life	Got To Get You Into My Life	(McCartney)
Tomorrow Never Knows	Tomorrow Never Knows	(Lennon)

The playlist for *Yesterday ... and Today* is as follows, with the British album on which each song
appears:

YESTERDAY ... AND TODAY (US ONLY)	
SIDE A	
Drive My Car	(*Rubber Soul*)
I'm Only Sleeping	(*Revolver*)
Nowhere Man	(*Rubber Soul*)
Doctor Robert	(*Revolver*)
Yesterday	(*Help!*)
Act Naturally	(*Help!*)
SIDE B	
And Your Bird Can Sing	(*Revolver*)
If I Needed Someone	(*Rubber Soul*)
We Can Work It Out	(*A Collection of Beatles Oldies*)
What Goes On?	(*Rubber Soul*)
Day Tripper	(*A Collection of Beatles Oldies*)

2. In citing composers for *Revolver* material, I will refer only to the songs' principal writers. It is well-documented that Lennon and McCartney usually wrote together, at least until the band's final years, though one or the other would normally arrive at the writing session with an idea, or even a melody plus a verse or two in hand.

3. Walter Everett has also remarked that several aspects of the song's instrumentation recall the LSD experience (Everett, 1999, p. 66).

4. Lennon claimed that the song was about acid (cited in Everett, 1999, p. 38).

5. Or maybe it's the other way around. Knowing what is to come on Side B, the listener may consciously or subconsciously associate the slide from ♭VII to IV with an image of a bird in descending flight – an imaginative leap that is unlikely without the foreknowledge of Lennon's next tune on the album. Either way, though, it's the presence of 'And Your Bird Can Sing' on the British edition that alters the listener's perception of the album in this way.

6. Madow and Sobul concur, calling it the 'first truly psychedelic song the Beatles released' (Madow and Sobul, 1992, p. 2).

Part IV

'Here, there, and everywhere'

Revolver's themes

Chapter 12

'Love is all and love is everyone': a discussion of four musical portraits

Sheila Whiteley

On 5 August, an LP appeared in the record shops which, were it not for the fact that approximately one million copies had been ordered in advance, might have seemed to stand little chance of being noticed on the shelves. Its cover, amid its rivals' Carnaby colours, was plain black and white: a collage of photo-fragments spiralling through what looked like palm fronds but proved on close inspection to be hair, encircling four silhouetted faces so instantly recognizable, it was not thought necessary to print their collective name. Who else in the world would announce themselves in graphics reflecting the smartest magazines? Who would call a record album simply *Revolver*, investing even that commonplace pun with the sleekness of some new-minted *avant garde*? Who but the Beatles would have the confidence colossal enough to be so chastely downbeat? (Norman, 1981, p. 263)

It is tempting to read Philip Norman's commentary on the launch of *Revolver* as a retrospective on the Beatles as the progenitors of art-rock – a generic which was to subsequently describe such innovatory bands as Pink Floyd, Yes, King Crimson, Led Zeppelin and Genesis. Creative experimentation, studio-layered instrumentation, sound collages, structural complexity, lush orchestration, and an emphasis on melody, harmony, more intricate rhythms, and lyrical sensitivity suggested a new artistic integrity. Who better than the Beatles, the darlings of Carnaby Street and King's Road, to promote the idea of pop as art, to produce a record as artistically 'credible as canvas or print' (Norman, 1981, p. 263)? Yet there is little doubt that *Revolver* did herald a new direction in popular music. Its fourteen songs are analogous to mini-portraits, some (like the cover itself) as probing as a black and white photograph, others like an exotic collage painted with an hallucinogenic brush, bright with technicoloured instrumentation or fluctuating with slow-burning, synaesthetic aromas comparable to those of Indian joss-sticks, 'mesmeric ... silky, dreamy ... weird and wonderful' (Martin, 1994, p. 79). It is funny, satirical, sentimental, poetic, lucidly non-sensical. 'In that one album, too, a mood and moment are caught as exactly as in the pithiest contemporary journalism', reflecting on the present while foreshadowing the summer of love, when the black and white swirls of Klaus Voorman's cover was suddenly overshadowed by Peter Blake's pop art design for *Sgt Pepper* (Norman, 1981, p. 263).

For many, however, *Revolver* stands out as the Beatles' most significant album. If *Rubber Soul* (1965) was analogous to 'the moment in *The Wizard of Oz* when Dorothy's world goes from black and white to technicolour', *Revolver's* cameos offer a balanced musicality which combines inventiveness with intelligence (DeRogatis, 1996, p. 23). As Wilfrid Mellers observed it is 'both verbally and musically an extraordinary breakthrough' (Mellers, 1973, p. 45), and nowhere is this more in evidence than in the haunting lyrics of 'Eleanor Rigby', a song which evokes memories of Liverpool's 'soot-black sandstone Catholic churches with the trams travelling past, the redbrick terrace houses with lace curtains and holy-stoned steps, the parchment-faced old spinsters … all the lonely people' (Melly, 1971, p. 85).

'Eleanor Rigby' is arguably one of the most famous of all Beatles' songs, and the first on which the group made no instrumental contribution. Tethered by an austere string arrangement by George Martin and with an acute sense of obser-vation which resonates with both pathos and social realism, the song invokes both a nostalgic and monochromatic portrait of loneliness:

'All the lonely people
Where do they all belong?'

The story of 'Eleanor Rigby' provides a specific insight into the 1960s concern for alienation. Career, family, education, morality and personal freedom were issues that had been fronted in the counterculture's stand against a prevailing ide-ology which was concerned, above all, with upholding the status quo of western capitalism. In the immediate post-war period (1945–1951), the British Labour Party had constructed a new form of consensus founded on the concept of reformed capitalism. Still based on a capitalist logic, its support for a mixed economy was to be tempered by the construction of a welfare state and an expan-sion in public ownership. The promise of a better future was appropriated by a reformed Conservative government where a continuing commitment to welfare and full-employment partly created the post-war boom under the slogan 'capital-ism for the people'. The class war, it was argued, was over, no longer necessary as the interests of the working people and their rulers were identical: capitalism was at last being politically managed to produce, for the great mass of ordinary people, 'a better life'.

Economic difficulties, humiliating defeats in foreign policy (not least the rejection of Britain's application to join the Common Market in 1963, the Suez catastrophe, and an increasing subordination to American interests), scandal (the Profumo affair) and satire (especially *Private Eye* and the radio programme *That Was The Week That Was)* rapidly eroded such naïve optimism. The Conservatives bowed out, but a renewed promise of growth by Harold Wilson's newly elected Labour government (1966) proved little more than Tweedledum to the Tories' Tweedledee. A wage freeze, cuts in public expenditure, a seaman's strike and a move to more coercive and punitive measures in the sphere of industrial relations led increasingly towards a harsh 'control culture'. This, in turn, was accompanied by a series of measures directed against the rising tide of permissiveness characterized, partly, by an emerging drug culture and a so-called increase in sexual promiscuity. The British working class, the only cause that had inspired a show of fighting spirit on its part during the 1960s (other than the standard run of wages and demarcation grievances), was increasingly characterized by its bloody-minded cry to drive the 'coloured' immigrants from the land.

It is not too surprising, then, that young people became increasingly concerned with the politics of consciousness – 'love, loneliness, depersonalisation, the search for the truth of the person' (Roszak, 1970, footnote, p. 65). Allied to a belief that popular music/rock could establish and articulate a particular location for self-identity, the mid-1960s witnessed a heady mixture of evangelical seri-ousness. As acknowledged leaders (in terms of musical experimentation, child-like scepticism and musical talent) it was no small wonder that the Beatles turned to the problems of alienation and anomie – and to their producer, George Martin, to concoct its evocative scoring and instrumental timbres.

What is immediately notable about the scoring of 'Eleanor Rigby', apart from its exclusive use of a string octet and Paul McCartney's plaintive vocals, is its overall simplicity. The harmonic scheme is largely based on alternating tonic and submediant chords and a thinly disguised repetition which draws the verse and chorus into a shared experience of individual and collective aloneness (Figure 12.1):

Figure 12.1 Repetitive structure of 'Eleanor Rigby'

It is also interesting to note that while there are subtle uses of nonharmonic tones which contribute to the poignancy of the melodic line (the C#, suggestive of the Dorian mode in the first two phrases of the verse; the C natural in the final phrase), these effect a natural flow to the almost incantatory vocal line, evoking memories of traditional church responsorials to produce a sense of objective distancing from the emotional quality of the words. This is enhanced by the 'matter-of-factness' of the lyrics where descriptions of the mundane ('writing the words of a sermon that no-one will hear', 'darning his socks in the night when there's nobody there') fill the two-bar phrases, culminating in a sense of resignation as the sustained final syllable is held over the next bar and followed by a pragmatic evaluation of personal worth ('nobody came', 'what does he care'). Life, like the melodic line itself, is thus shown as restricted: there is no richness of detail. Rather, it is analogous to the structure of the verse itself: a repeated five-bar phrase with little or no variation. The chorus is also repetitive (two four-bar phrases, again based primarily on chords I and VI), and provides what has been described as a second 'more subdued refrain' (O'Grady, 1983, p. 99) albeit that large vocal leaps create a dramatic context for the interrogative words that evoke the climactic of the sermon (Figure 12.2):

Where do—— they all— come— from?——
Where do—— they all— be - long?——

Figure 12.2   The chorus of 'Eleanor Rigby'

Overall, then, there is a sense of austerity and restraint and this is equally evident in George Martin's string arrangement. Repetition, as John Richardson observes, 'is a means of creating suspense … particularly when it is combined with other musical elements such as chromaticism and unresolved dissonances … In [Bernard] Herrmann's music, repetitive musical phrases are often spiked with highly dissonant passing tones … [and his] extensive use of repeated melodic/rhythmic figures, or ostinatos, as a means of creating suspense is perhaps his most significant trademark' (Richardson, 1998, pp. 167–168). Richardson's analysis of Herrmann's score for the Hitchcock movie *Psycho* and its comparison with Martin's arrangement for strings in 'Eleanor Rigby' provides a compelling argument for the way in which strings can be used in the repetitive context of popular music. As he points out, there is a clear textual/affective rationale for the choice of dysphoric as opposed to euphoric coding in this particular song. Not least, it is a song that seems unable to uproot itself from the past:

'Significantly, the verse of 'Eleanor Rigby' that contains the most overt references to death is that in which the influence of Herrmann's string writing is at its most pro-nounced. In the second half of the third verse, as McCartney sings 'Father McKenzie, wiping the dirt from his hands as he walks from the grave' we hear vigorous staccato bowing very similar to that in the murder scene of *Psycho*. In the chorus, moreover, a chromatically descending ostinato (D-C#-C-B), played as a countermelody in the violas, is very similar to the dysphorically coded ostinato patterns which characterise numerous Herrmann scores[1] … In the case of Eleanor Rigby the twice-repeated ostinato pattern becomes a microcosm of the narrative of the song: the descending chromatic lines mirror the irrevocable descent of Rigby herself at the same time as they invoke the death drive. (Richardson, 1998, p. 172).

I make no apology for quoting Richardson at some length. There is little doubt that Martin's scoring of the string octet plays the most significant part in the mini-drama of the song. Its stabbing ostinato moves the narrative, underlying both the remorseless logic of a Church which condemns a woman to a nameless grave, the symbolic of the priest 'wiping the dirt from his hands', and the stabs of conscience which draw the listener into the story of a woman who 'waits at the window', who 'died in the church'... and 'nobody came'. It invokes a quality of sober introspection – what the Catholic Church calls 'scrupulosity' – but clearly neither the song nor its subject matter solves the neurotic hurt of the problem. Rather, its lonely people seem analogous to Samuel Beckett's two sad tramps forever waiting under that wilted tree for their lives to begin.

Thirty years on the inclusion of a classical infrastructure within a popular song seems less than revolutionary. At the time, the socially-conscious lyrics and the innovative scoring gave 'Eleanor Rigby' a revolutionary freshness. Not least, Rigby's undeniable aloneness [2] associated her with the countless women who had neither family, friendship or – significantly – support from that bastion of respectability, the established Church. In particular, the refusal of the Catholic Church to reform its attitude towards birth control seemed little less than hypocrisy[3] given the increasing numbers of poor in the so-called developing countries of the third world and South America. In the UK and Southern Ireland, illegitimacy was still treated with a moral superiority that resulted in countless women being imprisoned in welfare nursing homes not too different from those of the Victorian poor houses of the nineteenth century. Birth control, backstreet abortions and unnecessary death were thus essential items on the feminist agenda[4] and while the liberalism of the early 1960s had borne legislative fruit in the spheres of abortion and divorce, for many such reforms either came too late or were considered less weighty than the dictates of the Church. Eleanor Rigby's drab and joyless destiny, it appears, was simply to be buried, along with her name – a sad indictment on a Church which is arguably the richest and most powerful in the Christian world.

While 'Eleanor Rigby' inhabits the black and white wasteland of spinsterhood, the pastel hues of 'Here, There and Everywhere' offer an altogether different portrait of love. Its acoustic simplicity is heightened by its position on the album. Sandwiched between George Harrison's 'Love You To' (the first Beatles' song to incorporate classical Indian music into a pop/rock format) and 'Yellow Submarine' (where sea sounds, gurgles, whistles, bells, a sub-aqueous two-bar brass solo and cockney commands from the bridge provide splashes of colour to the arguably hallucinogenic tale of 'a man who sailed the sea'), 'Here, There and Everywhere' is a sweetly balladic celebration of love. Where Harrison is bur-

dened by the tamboura drone of mysticism,[5] McCartney is liberated by the lumi-
nescence of romanticism. Musically, the song is retrospective. Its introduction
evokes memories of Lennon's 'If I Fell'[6] both in its chromatic inflections and in
its reflection on love. However, while the latter's twisting chromaticism underpins
a nagging uncertainty (Figure 12.3),

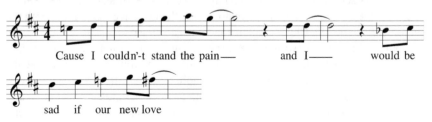

Figure 12.3   The twisting chromaticism of 'If I Fell'

the introduction to 'Here, There and Everywhere' is a reflective statement of
intent (Figure 12.4):

Figure 12.4   The introduction of 'Here, There and Everywhere'

While the expression of need is common to both songs, the more pervasive chromaticism in 'Here, There and Everywhere' provides a suffusing tonal colour to
McCartney's vocal line, linking the sentiments of the introduction to the bridge
which, in turn, provides an 'elegant and simple return to the major mode of the
verse' (O'Grady, 1983, p. 101) (Figure 12.5):

Figure 12.5   The bridge in 'Here, There, and Everywhere'

The introduction, verse and bridge are also linked through expansive leaps which colour the euphoric of romanticized love. This is enhanced by an extensive use of rhyme, which expands on the 'here, there and everywhere' through the commonplace of everyday experience ('running my hand thru' her *hair*', 'knowing that love is to *share*') while drawing more complex emotions into association ('each one believing that love never *dies*, watching her *eyes* and hoping that *I*'m always there.') In essence, then, the song is both 'naively celebratory' and conventional in its sentimentality (O'Grady, 1983, p. 101). Within the context of the 'swinging sixties', it also comes across as curiously conservative. However, it is arguably the case that the idealization of the woman as a fantasy figure and, more specifically, an earth mother was paradoxically central to countercultural philosophy.[7]

'Here, There and Everywhere' is but one of countless songs where the woman is inscribed as the provider, the forgiver, the healer. The image of the woman decked in flowers is common to 1960s iconography, and such songs as 'Mother Nature's Son' (Beatles, 1968) convey some sense of the conception of the woman as the 'receptive, seed-sheltering womb of a sweltering earth' (Dijkstra, 1986, p. 83). She is a symbol of nature, she is the earth, sexual but protective, always there for the masculine ego to inhabit when he wants to escape from the realities of life. She is both Madonna and Astarte, the eternal feminine, the one representing sexuality, matriarchal energy and death, the other a vision of idealized male-defined perfection.

The earth mother as Madonna can be traced to the nineteenth century. For Ruskin, 'the path of a good woman is strewn with flowers, but they rise behind her steps, not beneath them', an expression of both male sentimentality and their perception of the soul-healing power of the virtuous woman (Dijkstra, 1986, p. 269). 'A Hard Day's Night' (1964) jubilantly lauds the healing power of the woman: 'But when I get home to you, I know the thing that you do, will make me feel alright'. Four years later, 'Lady Madonna' (1968) conveys some of the understanding necessary for the contemporary earth mother as her lover 'Friday night arrives without a suitcase, Sunday morning creeping like a nun'. 'Hey Jude' (1968), one of the Beatles' greatest hits of all time, portrays the woman as mother, comforter and support: 'let her into your heart ... then you can make it better.'

While 'Here, There and Everywhere' initially suggests a somewhat sentimentalized and naïve ballad to an all-involving love, the question arises as to why romanticized femininity is problematic and how it relates to the fate associated with Eleanor Rigby's spinsterhood. Arguably, both songs draw on traditional definitions of femininity where such associations as 'gentleness, modesty, humility, supportiveness, empathy, compassion, tenderness, nurturance, intuitiveness, sensitivity, unselfishness' provide a common-place yet fiercely patriarchal basis for constructing appropriate codes for behaviour and identity (Tong, 1998, p. 3). 'To be feminine, according to an ordinary definition, is to be attractive, or to do one's best in being attractive and to attract' (Sontag, 2000, p. 121). The demonstrative of 'running my hand through her hair'[8] ('Here, There and Everywhere'), one of the key signifiers of femininity, contrasts with the stark passivity of 'wearing the face that she keeps in a jar by the door' ('Eleanor Rigby'). The former has no need to be named – 'she is everywhere'; the latter is singled out, the anonymity of her existence marking her as identifiably different, an unfulfilled woman, Eleanor Rigby. One has succeeded and her life is magically transformed as she fulfils her feminine destiny; the other has failed to meet these culturally defined criteria and is condemned to be alone in a nameless grave. For the politically aware, it would seem that beyond such front-line issues as the war in Vietnam, racial prejudice and hard-core poverty, the greater task of altering the *total* cultural context within which our daily politics take place was still the most challenging (Roszak, 1972, pp. 3–4).

My third musical portrait returns the listener to a more pragmatic portrait of love, this time dressed in the colourful robes of soul/Motown. As John Lennon commented, '"Got To Get You Into My Life" is the Beatles doing their Tamla Motown bit' (*Rolling Stones Interviews*, p. 196) and in common with the major-ity of McCartney-penned songs, the lyrics take the form of a mini-narrative. It is brashly optimistic, a holiday snapshot replete with brass and chorused 'ooohs'. At the same time, the opening words 'I was alone, I took a ride, I didn't know what I would find there' curiously presage the mundane narrative in 'A Day In The Life'[9] ('Woke up, got out of bed, dragged a comb across my head ...'). This time, however, there is no movement into an hallucinogenic dream-world. Rather, the song has certain characteristics in common with the verse melody of 'For No One' (McCartney) in its 'repeated-note, triad-based verse melody', while 'the harmonic alternation between tonic and subtonic chords over a tonic pedal' in the first eight bars recalls Harrison's 'If I Needed Someone' (1965) (O'Grady, 1983, p. 108). Perhaps this is not too surprising. Both songs relate, once again, to the concept of love; the first reflecting on lost love, 'a love that should have lasted years', the second resisting temptation because 'you see I'm too much in love'. There is also a passing reference to 'Eleanor Rigby' in the descending chromatic line of the bass guitar (Figure 12.6):

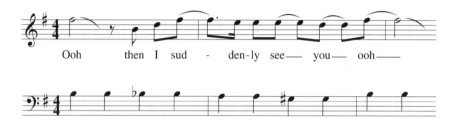

Figure 12.6   Bass line transcription

– a subtle reminder, perhaps, that loneliness is around the corner unless you grasp the moment.

Here, however, the comparison ends. 'Got To Get You Into My Life' is a lively up-tempo song which has the characteristics of a pub sing-along, albeit presaged by a brass riff. As George Martin recalls: 'Paul liked brass bands' (Martin, 1994, p. 64). He was also into the soul-jazz of Georgie Fame who he had heard at the London night-club 'Bag O'Nails'. Two of Fame's group 'The Blue Flames' (Eddie Thornton and Pete Coe) were hired for the horn section[10] which arguably dominates the texture, evoking both a soul feel and a sense of optimistic buoyancy. The chorus, in particular, is catchy, tuneful and raucous. Presaged by an assertive 'I need you ev'ry single day of my life', the chorus invites participation but it is quickly overtaken by the hard-hitting brass arrangement which both heightens the momentum and provides an edgy-rawness which is arguably English in its feel. Rather than the syncopated swing of contemporary American soul or, indeed, the more pervasive soul/jazz feel of The Blue Flames, its phrasing is more staccato, curiously reminiscent of a British Big Band horn section (Figure 12.7). There is an exactness, a sense of precision, not least in the final trumpet outro where the sustained concert G is suddenly taken up the octave. In England this is jokingly referred to as 'British Legion Bop' (left to right, right to left) and provides an evocative good-time feel which is comparable in effect to the music hall under-pinning for 'When I'm 64' (*Sgt Pepper's Lonely Hearts Club Band*, 1967).

Figure 12.7   Transcription to show difference between American and British style

'Got To Get You Into My Life' – despite its passing resemblance to soul and Motown (with its evenly accented quaver bass line and percussion and descending chromatic sequence) – thus comes across as curiously old fashioned. While the traditional interaction between audience and singer is replaced by brass, the sense of participation remains. It is essentially good-time music, uncomplicated and, like the sentiments of the song, unpretentious in its feel. A colour snapshot of a very new love – 'Got to get you into my life'!

In contrast, my final song, 'Tomorrow Never Knows', can be described as a deeply introspective self-portrait, albeit that it transcends the subjective and embraces the holistic of metaphysical experience. 'By 1966 Zen, Sufis, Hinduism, primitive shamanism, theosophy, left-handed tantra, Hindu temple bells' resonated with the counterculture's search for alternative lifestyles through spiritual and abstract thought (Roszak, 1972, p. 201). The concern for the metaphysical was complemented by the exploratory of drug-related experiences: both were a means to heightened consciousness. For many, the Beatles were the acid apostles of the new age and their LSD experiences are well documented.[11] My own research[12] focuses on the relationship between music and hallucinogenics and points to musical codings which suggest a certain homology with the experience of LSD. The techniques provide a musical analogy for the enhancement of awareness, the potentially new synthesis of ideas and thought relationships that can result from hallucinogens:

- an overall emphasis on timbral colour (blurred, bright, overlapping, associated with the intensification of colour and shape when tripping);
- upward movement in pitch (and the comparison with an hallucinogenic high);
- characteristic use of harmonies (lurching, oscillating and the relationship to changed focus);
- sudden surges of rhythm (the association with an acid rush) and/or a feel of floating around the beat (suggestive of a state of tripping where the fixed point takes on a new reality);
- shifting textual relationships (foreground/background, collages and soundscapes that suggest a disorientation of more conventionalized musical structures and that stimulate a sense of absorption with/within the sound itself).

Although much of my analysis was hypothetical in its matching of musical codings to a range of songs, Lennon's experimentation with, and increasing dependence on, hallucinogens is well documented.[13] Not least, his exploration of his mental 'inner space' through LSD and his absorbed reading of *The Psychedelic Experience* (Leary et al., 1964) – most specifically its paraphrasing of *The Tibetan Book of the Dead* – provided a personal authentication for the musical experiences of 'Tomorrow Never Knows'. Overdubbed tape loops, of which the most important are the heavy saturation and acceleration on a rising scalic sitar figure, and an oscillating B♭/C on the string setting of the Mellotron,[14] create cross-rhythms and shifting textual relationships. There is thus a sense of disorientation, an absorption with/within the sound itself through what is heard as a random patterning of colliding circles.[15] There is thus a curious resonance with the cover of *Revolver* itself – a further example of how hallucinogenic experience can effect a sense of synaesthesia – seeing what one hears, hearing what one sees. Rather than the more usual, extravagant colours of psychedelia, the black and white sobriety of the colliding circles of 'Tomorrow Never Knows' is introspective, a sensory metaphor of Leary's voluntary ego-death.

As Ian MacDonald observes, Lennon had 'become psychologically addicted to LSD, taking it daily and living in one long, listless chemically altered state'. At the same time, 'those who knew him in 1966 say his personality suddenly softened, his aggression giving way to a noticeably mellower mood' (MacDonald, 1994, pp. 153, 151). 'Tomorrow Never Knows' musically and lyrically resonates with his hallucinogenic experiences, encapsulating the Vedic teaching of 'Be Here Now'[16] – living in the present but conscious of both past and future – and the hippie maxim 'the world of the future will have no clocks'. Above all, the music encodes a sense of timelessness. Its eight-bar melody provides a musical analogy for stepping into the unconscious as the tonic chord slowly unfolds upon itself, repeatedly moving back to the tonic pitch via a flattened seventh (Figure 12.8).

Turn off your mind, re - lax and float down - stream—

Figure 12.8   Music showing a sense of timelessness

The sense of living in a never-ending present is heightened by looped effects which constantly move to the 'eternal' presence of the tonic (an orchestral chord on B♭ major; a Mellotron played on flute setting; another Mellotron oscillating in 6/8 over the 4/4 pulse of melody line, moving from B♭ [the flattened 7th] to C [the tonic] on its string setting), a musical metaphor for the tug between the conscious/unconscious of psychedelic experience. The sense of an hallucinogenic space is opened out by a brief, polyphonic string solo which merges into parts of McCartney's guitar solo for 'Taxman', slowed down, cut up and reversed. The effect is one of unpredictability. The 'known' has become unknown, confusing, strangely mesmeric, obsessive and absorbing. It is also apparent that 'Tomorrow Never Knows' relates, unequivocally, to *Lennon's* personal experience of LSD.

> The underlying personality, mood, attitudes, expectations and setting in which the drug is taken have proven to be far more important as determinants of the LSD experience than with drugs such as alcohol, marijuana, barbiturates, or amphetamines … Because of the intensity and complexity of the experience, it can … be disorganising and upsetting. (Fort, 1969, p. 183)

More specifically, 'the main dimensions of LSD experience are perceptual, cognitive (thought) and affective (mood) … Ordinary boundaries and controls between the self and the environment and within the self are loosened' (Fort, 1969, p. 182). The sense of perceptual change is at its most apparent in Lennon's voice which is initially double-tracked, then fed through the revolving speaker in the Leslie cabinet of a Hammond organ. It is well documented that Lennon wanted to sound like the Dalai Lama and thousands of monks chanting on a mountain top, and this fusion of the metaphysical with the hallucinogenic is what arguably makes the song uniquely introspective. The self becomes spiritually changed through expanded consciousness: 'It is knowing. It is believing ... it is not dying ... ', rather it is 'the end of the beginning'.

'Tomorrow Never Knows' is thus my final 'portrait of love'. From the mono-chrome loneliness of 'Eleanor Rigby', through the pastel tints of the romantic ballad of 'Here, There and Everywhere', and the brassy snapshot of 'Got To Get You Into My Life', Lennon finally demonstrates that the extra-ordinary of hallu-cinogenic experience allied to the metaphysical of spiritual quest could provide the pathway to self-negation and the knowledge that 'Love is all and love is everyone.'

Notes

1. Walt Everett observes that while George Martin did model his 'Rigby' scoring on some of Herrmann's work, it was *Fahrenheit 451* that he studied, not *Psycho*. Even so, it is agreed that the references to *Psycho* are valid.

2. As novelist A. S. Byatt observed, the image of 'keeping her face by the door' suggests that inside her home, behind her door, Eleanor Rigby is 'faceless, nothing'. Had it been kept in a jar by the mirror this would be less disturbing in its implications of makeup. (Talk on BBC Radio 3, 11 May 1993.)

3. And is arguably comparable to 'the moral Catholicism of the little boy who disciplines himself from masturbating and checks off his victorious days on the calendar' (Roszak, 1970, p. 190).

4. Called, at the time, Women's Liberation.

5. Harrison's personal search for identity and meaning through Indian mysticism is reflected in the abstract lyrics and use of sitar, tabla and tamboura. In common with songs that provide a metaphorical coding for hallucinogenic experience, 'Love You To' reflects the counterculture's idealist concern for a revolution of the spirit. Both are concerned with an opening of the self to experience, a freeing of the mind.

6. From the 1964 movie *A Hard Day's Night*.

7. For a more detailed discussion see Chapters 1, 2 and 3 in Whiteley, S. (2000), *Women and Popular Music: Sexuality, Identity and Subjectivity*, London: Routledge.

8. Throughout history, hair has signified political statements and cultural identity. Long, flowing hair has long been a signifier of femininity and is intrinsically linked to sexual desirability. In contrast, the shaved head (adopted by, e.g., Sinead O'Connor and Skin of Skunk Anansie) is problematic in its associations with the shaving of asylum inmates and prisoners, with martyr-dom (Joan of Arc), with the xenophobic nationalism of skinheads and, during the last war, with women who collaborated with the Nazis.

9. It is noted that, in 1980, John Lennon observed that he thought the lyrics referred obliquely to Paul McCartney's recent experience of LSD.

10. The others being freelance musicians.

11. See, for example, DeRogatis, J. (1996), *Kaleidoscope Eyes: Psychedelic Music from the 1960s to the 1990s*, London: Fourth Estate.

12. Whiteley, S. (1992), *The Space Between the Notes: Rock and the Counter-Culture*, London: Routledge.

13. See Russ Reising's chapter and to MacDonald, I. (1994), *Revolution in the Head: The Beatles Records and the Sixties*, London: Fourth Estate, pp. 148–153.

14. Walt Everett observes that the tape loops were made by McCartney at his home and that neither he nor John Lennon owned a Mellotron – Lennon purchasing his Mellotron months after *Revolver* was released. As such, it is considered that the Mellotron sound would have been dubbed off the radio.

15. As MacDonald (1994) observes, 'Colliding Circles was the title of an unused song which Lennon wrote for *Revolver*' (p. 152).

16. Alpert, R. (1971), *Be Here Now*, Lama Foundation.

Chapter 13

The Beatles, Postmodernism, and ill-tempered musical form: cleaning my gun; or, the use of accidentals in *Revolver*

Ronald Schleifer

Prelude: defining the modern

This chapter has its origin in the Beatles 2000 conference held in Jyväskylä, Finland during the summer of 2000. As part of preparing for my presentation, I had read Walter Everett's *The Beatles as Musicians* – just as, I think, the great majority of participants of the conference had consulted his book. The day before my presentation, I met Walter and mentioned a small typo I had seen in his book. There he notes – it's quoted below – 'the pitiable tritone-completing B♭' (Everett, 1999, p. 53) in 'Eleanor Rigby', and I pointed out that in *The Beatles Complete Scores* there simply isn't an instance of B♭ in the song. Walter thanked me for my observation, but the next day when I gave my talk, he pointed out that he had spoken too quickly and that the Beatles completed the tritone on a note somewhere between a B and a B♭. During the subsequent discussion, it became clear that the Beatles did not necessarily follow the well-tempered scale we are accustomed to; that in their music they followed their ears as sometimes string players do to this day.

The tempering of the scale is one, among many, of the great transformations that took place during the advent of Enlightenment modernism that have come down to us as a 'natural' way of organizing experience, what the Enlightenment called a 'transcendental' organization insofar as it transcended accidental differences of time and space. In a discussion of Bach's *Well-Tempered Clavier* examining precisely to what instrument 'clavier' refers, Hermann Keller notes that while 'there is music which can truly be brought to life only on the instrument for which the composer intended it' – he includes among his examples the fact that 'many pieces of Karl Philipp Emanuel Bach only [sound good] on the clavichord' and 'the piano sonatas of Beethoven only [sound good] on the pianoforte' – 'the special charm of *The Well-Tempered Clavier* exists precisely in the fact that a mere keyboard instrument, whether it be now the clavichord, the harpsichord, or the pianoforte, must serve as the medium for a music whose content is to be sought beyond the sound' (Keller, 1976, pp. 24–25). This 'transcendental' sense of music beyond its particular manifestation – a comprehension of 'absolute music', which 'means that it is the absolute, artistic *idea* expressed in the music that counts, not the technical way in which it is performed' (Bruhn, 1993, p. 11) – is a chief assumption of much of what we take to be the achievement of the Enlightenment and Enlightenment 'modernism'.

In important ways, this can help us understand the often vague term 'postmodern'. If modernism attempted to create first of all the general laws of science that 'transcend' and account for how the world works, but also to create the transcendental laws of 'universal' ethics and 'impersonal' aesthetics, then postmodernism attempts, among other things, to recover a sense of the power of local phenomena: how Beethoven's piano is necessary for his sonatas; how the particularities of gender or race or class need to be taken into account in relation to ethical questions; how the impersonal order of a beginning, middle, and end or of the seeming disappearance of the artist aren't the only ways to achieve aesthetic experiences. At its most outrageous, its critics think, postmodernism attempts to show that 'transcendental' scientific laws can *also* be understood in relation to their own history and to the ethical and political ends they serve or have served in discovering seemingly *disinterested* truths about the world. (This is most clear, I think, in attempts to create 'scientific' racism.) Certainly what is called postmodern often is a scandal to settled conceptions of art, the ethics of interpersonal relationships, and scientific 'truth' itself.

In any case, the well-tempered scale is one instance of the homogeneous, transcendental regularity of modernism that emerges in the early eighteenth century. It is opposed to a scale based upon the 'just' intervals of notes of particular scales, which are governed by the cycle of fifths. As Ralph Kirkpatrick notes,

> systems of tuning more closely attached to the pure fifths and thirds of the natural overtone series either require more intervals than the twelve-note octave of the ordinary keyboard afford, unless given special subdivisions, or they favor only certain tonalities. This explains the infrequency in older music of tonalities involving more than three or four sharps and flats. So-called pure intonation based on the natural intervals is still instinctive to every good musician and is still commonly practiced by string players and singers. Thus, for example, in pure intonation, a rising G-sharp functioning as a leading tone would differ from a descending A-flat. The conventional keyboard, however, gives the same sound for both notes, creating a compromise to which the sensitive musical ear has only reluctantly become accustomed. (Kirkpatrick, 1984, p. 7)

The benefit from this 'compromise', however, is not simply the wide range of possible keys and modulations created for keyboard instruments where they didn't exist before by means of the creations of an 'essential' A-flat that may exist under two names, but which possesses a 'transcendental' identity wherever it is sounded. Such a compromise, moreover, has profound *political* consequences that helped to reconfigure what we still take to be 'common sense'.

The tempering of the scale was first described by Andreas Werckmeister, who published *Musical Temperament / or clear and correct mathematical instruction / how to tune a clavier, particularly organs, positives, regals, spinets, and the like in equal temperament* in 1691. Twenty years later, Mattherson wrote a book of exercises that allowed students to play all twenty-four keys (twelve tones, major and minor). And in 1722 Bach composed the twenty-four preludes and fugues of Book I of *The Well-Tempered Clavier*, in, as he says, 'all tones and semitones, in major as well as minor, for the benefit and use of musical youth desirous of knowledge as well as those who are already advanced in this study' (cited in Kirkpatrick, 1984, p. 6). (Bach composed Book II about twenty years later [dated 1744]). This tempering takes its place alongside Samuel Johnson's 'tempering' of the English language with the publication of the *Dictionary* in 1754: henceforth, just as A-flats will always 'be' A-flat, so the spelling of words in English will always be self-identical no matter what their pronunciation. Moreover, as Toby Miller notes in appropriating Bach's title for a study of the political economy of contemporary citizenship, 'as a title and an intervention into musical technology, [*The Well-Tempered Clavier*] represents a move toward *politesse* and consistency over unruliness and difference, a move that was to typify the incorporation of music into popular education in the nineteenth century as part of a training in equable citizenship' (Miller, 1993, p. x).

Miller is examining the manner in which 'the hold that popular music can have on a politics of identity' is 'both different from and potentially unsettling for the project of government through culture exemplified by the pedagogic routine of *Das wohltemperierte Klavier*' (Miller, 1993, pp. x–xi). In this he is arguing that particular instances of popular music 'abjure', at least in moments, their 'attention to an even-tempered structure and style in the service of "the tissue of cultural values" [he is quoting Roland Barthes], preferring the directness … [of] a rawness … that transcends representational protocols, because it operates from a more elemental seduction and excess' (Miller, 1993, p. xi). That is, certain moments in popular music do not follow the 'representational protocols' of equal tempering, and this omission has the effect or result of serving other purposes, other ends. Miller goes on to cite the French philosopher, Jacques Derrida, who 'reminds us', he says, that 'moving out of tune is frequently rendered as a tonic delirium, "a social disorder and a derangement, [Derrida notes,] an out-of-tune-ness of strings and voices in the head parasitising the voice of reason that speaks equally in each"'. Such out-of-tune-ness, Miller concludes, breaches 'the unproblematic sweet reasonableness of *Das wohltemperierte Klavier* [that] is clearly akin to the ordered obedience of the desired subjects of civic culture' in the modern era (Miller, 1993, p. xi).

Taken from a postmodern point of view, the 'modernist' order of reason Miller is describing on the level of politics and which I have been describing on the level of aesthetics is thus neither universal nor transcendental, though one of its attributes is that it creates the impression that it is both. Moreover, what is striking for

Samuel Johnson and Bach – as it is for Galileo with his telescope, and even for Descartes with his invention of mechanical compasses to perform mathematical operations (Gaukroger, 1995, p. 94) – is that their 'discovery' of transcendental essences of spelling and sound are responses to historical and local technological innovations: widespread printing and keyboard music. It might well be that the transformation, in Enlightenment modernity, of each royal subject to a citizen equal, as Thomas Jefferson says, to every other citizen is also a function of growing standardizations of communication and consumption. In an analogous fashion, many of the innovations in the Beatles' music, as many of the contributions to this volume suggest, are responses to and the taking up of innovative means of creating, storing, and transmitting sound in their studio recordings: the Beatles, especially in *Revolver*, helped *identify*, as popular music does, communication and consumption. Even the transcribers of *The Beatles Complete Scores* (1993) – Tetsuya Fujita, Yuji Hagino, Hajime Kubo, and Goro Sato, as their names appear in eight-point type on the copyright page, or whoever anonymously produced the prelude to the score entitled 'A Guide to the Music' – note: 'a great deal of effort has been put into presenting these performances in musical notation that is as faithful as possible to the original recordings' (1993, p. 11). In the identification (or confusion) of communication and consumption – as in the confusion of aesthetics, politics (ethics), and the more general epistemology (understanding) whose clear and distinct demarcation was the work of Immanuel Kant's great critiques and, in fact, the work and source of much of the great and good achievements of Enlightenment modernity – the Beatles offer moments of postmodern, post-Enlightenment ethos (and understanding), power, and art.

Fuguing the postmodern

It is my contention that one might discern the postmodern, post-Enlightenment energy of *Revolver* in the seeming technological 'conventionality' – the representational protocol – of the *accidentals* of musical notation. (After all, the standardizing of tone and semitones – of G-sharps and A-flats – is precisely the work of the modernist 'tempering'.) Here, then, I examine the ways in which the Beatles use accidentals in *Revolver*. In its general meaning, 'accidents' are precisely the opposite to the essences of Enlightenment modernity: it is what the Enlightenment wants to forget, or at least to absorb within a system that accounts for them as essential to one extent or another. Accidentals can be seen, as Toby Miller notes, as a kind of 'tonic delirium' and 'derangement' as well as a 'moment' in the achievement of the tempered order or reason. That is, accidentals function like the title *Revolver* itself, a counterpoint of literal and figural meanings. The title refers to a gun – this is clear and almost immediate to those of us who come from the United States, where guns are rife, even if the Beatles themselves explicitly deny this meaning to their title. This *figurative* sense of 'revolver' as gun encompasses the manner in which rock and roll as a kind of music, with particular themes, styles, musical forms – in a word, with its particular 'signature' – will be exploded or at least threatened by this album. But the title also designates, *literally* and *materially*, the record itself, revolving on the turntable: it is this meaning, as Ringo notes, that governed the conscious choice of the title *Revolver*. In the same way, the accidentals of music – the imported sharps and flats of song and chord – explode (or at least threaten) the key signature of any particular piece they occur in and at the same time also articulate and present the material modality of the music, whether it be major or minor, Dorian or Lydian. Mode and key cross and interfere with one another; authentic or plagal modes underline the relationship (and counterpoint) between the simultaneous harmonies of key and the consecutive notes of musical scale. The same contrapuntal combination of meaning and materiality of the title *Revolver* or the keys and modes of music can be seen, as the *Dictionary of Music* notes, in the term 'key' itself, which is defined as '1. The tonal center of a composition. 2. The part of the *action* of a *keyboard* instrument that is touched by the fingers. [or] 3. A lever on a *woodwind instrument* that is moved by the fingers' (1976, p. 72). That the guitars and drums of the Beatles are without material keys and, instead, present the modification of keys – one might call the guitar fret a modified or 'accidental' key, so to speak – is interesting especially in the context of the double meaning of 'fret' itself.

In the same way that 'fret' – or 'revolver' for that matter – combines and contrasts two modes of meaning, one more or less literal (the movement of a record *revolving* on the record player) and one more or less figurative (the synecdochical description of a handgun, using the revolving bullet chamber to stand for the whole weapon), so *Revolver* combines the figurative meaning of music, its combinations and interrelations building up its transcendental musical 'sense', and its literal materialities in its soundings, the sensations and the *modal inflection* of sensation in another way of understanding 'sense'.[1] Mode is the 'accident' of key: literally it is realized in the presence and absence of accidentals in a scale, and figuratively it is the 'taming' (or 'tempering') of sound to key, a way of reincorporating accidents into meaningful system. If, as I have suggested, such 'taming' of emotion and meaning by means of *standardizations* of sense is one of the great achievements of our culture of Enlightenment modernity, then the emphasis on *accident* in the Beatles that I pursue situates their music within frameworks of what I described as 'postmodernity'. The double meanings I have presented – of 'revolver', 'fret', the material rhyming sounds of lyrics, and even the name 'Beatles' itself – underline the counterpoint of ('transcendental') meaning and ('local') materialism. Modernism resolves this contradiction in relation to transcendental meaning: near the turn of the twentieth century Paul Klee defined modern art as the quest to discover 'the essential nature of the accidental' (cited in Bradbury and McFarlane, 1976, p. 48); and James Joyce in *Ulysses* has Stephen Dedalus – who, perhaps, as a late member of that other 'beat' generation, the Symboliste poets of France, might have a claim to be an early, first 'Beatle' – Joyce, I say, has Stephen describe the artist as a person for whom there are no accidents: 'a man of genius', he says in the library chapter of *Ulysses*, 'makes no mistakes. His errors are volitional and are the portals of discovery' (Joyce, 1961, p. 190).

If these 'high' modernists aim at apprehending the accidental as essential – if they aim at *standardizing* the unexpected, fitting it within a system of meanings and expectations (as do J. S. Bach, René Descartes, and Samuel Johnson) – then the Beatles might be seen as low modern or 'postmodern' in their embrace of accidents as a theme in many songs and accidentals as a vehicle for the transformation of predictable formulas of popular music into the rich tapestry of their musical forms. Needless to say, I do not want to argue (or at least to *fully* argue) for the 'essential' postmodernity of the Beatles: the songs of *Revolver* do not offer the flatness of tone and affect that seems to me to most characterize postmodern art, even in 'I'm Only Sleeping', and besides, as I have suggested, at least some parts of the postmodern seek to call into question the Enlightenment notion of 'essence'. But still, there is a ubiquity of accidents in *Revolver*, both on the material levels of music and rhythm and on the cultural levels of lyric and reference, that does not too quickly resolve itself into either the easy postmodern idioms of kitsch and cliché or the difficult standardizations of high modernist profundity. What makes high modernism 'difficult', I think, is that it pursues transformations of mode rather than the repetitions of meaning found in cliché: Stephen Dedalus – or, for that matter, T. S. Eliot – can offer the kitschiest clichés (Odysseus' masculinist quest for wife and son, the 'end' of civilization in a pile of rubble or even the banality of Eliot's 'in my beginning is my end') in the mode of irony. In important ways, the Beatles in *Revolver* are without irony, or at least without the very quick assumption of mode into meaning that is the hallmark gesture of 'high' modernism.

In 'Eleanor Rigby', for instance, the ballad opens with Paul singing in E minor, and immediately in the second stanza the melody emphasizes a syncopated C sharp against the minor chord. (The violin even reinforces the syncopation in the last verse of the song.) The C sharp – which is the *only* accidental in the song's voice and, except for a D flat in the violin in the last chorus, the only accidental altogether – rings against the E minor chord, spelled out in the first line of the verse, and against the related major of echoing phrases, 'Lives in a dream', 'No one comes near', 'Nobody came'. Walter Everett describes this nicely (in a passage I have already quoted in my prelude) as 'a battle for priority [that] ensues between C and C♯; the former wins', he concludes, 'perhaps because in each refrain and chorus it enlists the help of the pitiable tritone-completing B♭' (Everett, 1999, p. 53). At the same time, with the C♯ the syncopated melody also rings a descending D major scale against the implicit E minor triads. Thus, the accidental transforms the modality of the music from minor to major in a manner that thoroughly complicates the simplicities of received rock music of the 1950s and early 1960s (Figure 13.1).

In addition to the music of 'Eleanor Rigby', its transformations of key and mode in the ringing of its accidental, the song also orchestrates rock and roll with a string quartet – really, a double string quartet – that emphasizes the accidental nature of solemnity gathering around the lives of Eleanor Rigby and Father McKenzie. The quartet – brilliantly orchestrated by George Martin – seems as out of place as the spinster and prelate, out of place the way that *these* people seem out of place in the solemnity of the church they work in. In this way, the song offers, pastiche-like, Romantic chordal harmonies and Baroque counterpoint within the two minutes of its cut. Moreover, both music and theme are especially out of place after 'Taxman', with its driving guitars and drum, imitating, as McCartney suggests, a Motown beat and sarcastic, articulate anger. Such pastiche, Fred Jameson has argued, is the signature of postmodernism, which is, he says, 'the imitation of a peculiar or unique, idiosyncratic style … . [in] a neutral practice of such mimicry, without any of parody's ulterior motives, amputated of the satiric impulse, devoid of laughter and of any conviction that alongside the abnormal tongue you have momentarily borrowed, some healthy linguistic normality still exists' (Jameson, 1991, p. 17).[2] Yet again, I do not want to suggest an essentialist definition of the postmodern, as I want to suggest a kind of slippage within it of the ruling assumptions governing the Enlightenment modernism, which includes the assumption that *everything* is recoverable and reducible to the abstract regularities and protocols of system.[3] Thus, the pastiche of 'Eleanor Rigby' is not so much an 'abnormal tongue' as a kind of accidental music, the kind of music that Eleanor Rigby might well hear without attending to in the church in which she works. There, it would be less an 'abnormal' voice, than an unheeded voice: 'Eleanor Rigby' keeps adding – almost 'fuguing' – voices as the song progresses, viola, cellos, the ghostly contrapuntal chorus in the last chorus, while it rings a Baroque quartet that is out of place in rock and roll. In this – hardly the tour de force harmonies of Bach's well-tempered fugues – it gathers together what would only be the *noise* of accident outside the noisy clichés of received rock music.

As this suggests, like the material and cultural music of this song, its inhabitants, Eleanor Rigby and Father McKenzie, themselves seem 'accidental': lives that are almost unlived – flat in tone and affect, neutrally practiced – and easily overlooked. Recall the song's narrative: Both Eleanor Rigby and Father McKenzie are associated with empty churches. For Eleanor Rigby it is the retrospective emptiness associated with the metonymic rice left by marriage already finished and underlined by the even more disturbing drumbeat of metonyms in 'Wearing the face that she keeps / In a jar by the door'. For Father McKenzie it is the prospective writing of sermons that, in the future, will never be heard, counterpointed by his futural work of darning socks for the next day. The power of these Father McKenzie lines – their pathos – is borne by the rhymes rather than (as in the first, Eleanor Rigby verse) the metonymic figures of rice and jar: in the McKenzie lines hear/near, there/care rhyme adverbs (what linguists call 'deictics') with affects in displacements that are not 'abnormal' in any sense Jameson might follow, but which still create the sense of senseless accident, a world in which place and affect have little common ground.

Let me explain this dense passage. The deictics of language are those words that *depend* upon the accidental situation of the speaker: 'near' only makes sense in relation to a place that is more or less idiosyncratic and accidental, the place of the speaker that is necessarily subject to change: what is *near* is always relative to where the speaker articulates the term. Thus the deictics of language, unlike a noun like 'rice', for instance, change with a change of speaker and therefore do not possess a 'transcendental' or 'abstract' meaning: what is near to me might well be far for you. This linguistic term will become more important in my second example from *Revolver*, 'Here, There and Everywhere', whose title literally strings together deictics. In 'Eleanor Rigby' the rhymes, hear/near, there/care, rhyme deictics and feelings, 'there' and 'care', but by connecting these dissimilar ideas only by means of the similarity of their material sound the rhyme emphasizes how they are 'accidental', out of place together (at least on the level of meaning).

In the last stanza, Rigby and McKenzie cross paths, accidentally, without meeting: Eleanor Rigby is buried by Father McKenzie, 'Along with her name / Nobody came', in a rhyme of noun and negatived verb, while Father McKenzie, metonymically, wipes 'the dirt from his hands / As he walks from the grave', and the song's narrative cannot quite rhyme 'grave' and 'saved'. (The particular – and pointedly 'non-transcendental' – moment of singing does create the strong effect of a rhyme, just as singing and strings, as Kirkpatrick suggests, often create the strong effect of 'just' rather than tempered scales.) If the first verse is retrospective, and the second prospective, the last presents the presence of death – an event explicitly unconnected with past or future – that has no salvation connected to it. If the modernist genius makes no mistakes, these are lives of quiet desperation that seem accidental through and through – like momentary deictics, *essentially* accidental, and, I might even say, *essentially* mistaken – revolving in meaningless repetition and pastiche, explosive in their emptiness and, if I can say so, their out-of-placeness.

The work of accidents can be seen in other ballads and songs of *Revolver* as well. I will examine one more. I would like to say that this example is random, chosen more or less arbitrarily from an album where the kind of emphasis on accidents that *cannot* be recovered for high art or high meaning in the modernist manner is repeated throughout. But really this choice of example is not that innocent, not so accidental. Rather, it is marked in its similarities to and differences from 'Eleanor Rigby' to allow for a kind of contrapuntal harmony to emerge from seeming accidental differences. That is, if 'Eleanor Rigby' is a ballad of emptiness orchestrated with eight strings, contrapuntal music, and a remarkable range of reference – narrative, affective, and a sense of displacement captured in the accidental materiality of rhyming sounds – then 'Here, There and Everywhere', as a ballad of fullness,

is its counterpoint and fulfilment. In the verse to 'Here, There and Everywhere' –
a wonderful ballad in G major – there are no accidentals. The melody rings its song
against voiced chords – the chorus of Beatles – with which it constantly agrees.
The chords themselves – G, A minor, B minor, C – sung by the chorus in ascending triads are full and round. Even the accident of F-sharp minor resolving itself
to a B7 – 'Changing my life with a wave of the hand / Nobody can deny / That
there's something there' – returns, with a feeling of propriety I should say, to A-
minor and the dominant seventh, D7 – B-minor's cognate – and back to the verse's
beginning, now 'there' rather than 'here'.

Opposed to this verse, is a strange introduction, ridden with accidentals, which
Everett describes as 'tonally mysterious and tempo-free' (1999, p. 60). (Figure
13.1)

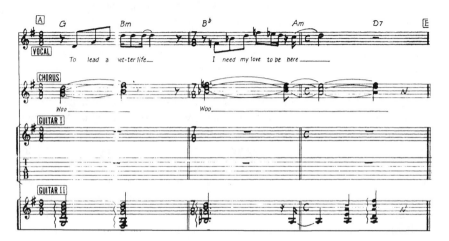

Figure 13.1   'Here, There, and Everywhere', bars 1–3 (1993, 392)

The score, in fact, marks its two bars as 8/8 and 7/8, but the effect it certainly
sounds, of being tempo free and virtually unresolvable tonally, is a function of the
seeming accidentals and accidents of sound. This is most clear, I think, in its non-
rhyming and, indeed, non-sensical statement: 'To lead a better life I need my love
to be here.' It is difficult (for me, at least) to grasp what can be meant by 'a better life' in this statement: the song as a whole pursues feeling rather than the
actions with which we usually associate *leading* a better life. Similarly, it is just
as difficult to grasp any direction in which the possible (not quite articulated)
descending chronological notes, G-F#-F-E, recoverable within its chords, might
take us. The magic of this song, like the pathos of 'Eleanor Rigby', resides in its
deictics, its 'here' which inhabits its '*there*' (the letters h-e-r-e in the word 'there')
and even inhabits its 'every*here*' through the accident of our spellings.

I'll return to this – it *is* the song's fullness – but first I'll turn to the bridge of the song. Here, also, is music rife with accidentals, pursuing but not quite achieving the standard four-chord pattern of traditional popular music, Bb, G-minor, C-minor, F7, and replacing the final chord with a D7 resolving to a G-minor, which is followed by a C-minor and D7 that resolves itself, unbelievably, into a G major chord. I say 'unbelievably' because bridges simply do not quote verses; bridges do not discover the verse – marked in this song by the choral triads – here, there, everywhere. All of this is effected by means of accidentals in the bridge melody – 'I want her everywhere / And if she's beside me / I know I need never care / But to love her is to need her everywhere' – which is emphasized and repeated in the accidentals in the two-bar background guitar riff that has replaced the chordal chorus as the accompaniment. The accidentals of the bridge *punctuate* the verse: literally, the bridge turns back into verse and chorus well before it's done just as it transforms love into need: 'But to love her is to need her everywhere.'

Both introduction and bridge are transformed through seeming accident to musical forms far shorter than the traditional introductions and bridges of rock and roll or popular music more generally: they are rendered accidental, absorbed, so to speak, in the fullness of the accident-free verse:

Here, making each day of the year
Changing my life with a wave of her hand
Nobody can deny
That there's something there –

There, running my hands through her hair
Both of us thinking how good it can be
Someone is speaking but she doesn't know he's there –

... everywhere –
Knowing that love is to share
Each one believing that love never dies
Watching her eyes
And hoping I'm always there – (1993, pp. 392–395)

That verse is simple declarative sentences – 'Here, ... there's something there'; 'There, ... Someone is speaking' – that somehow (in fact, through dangling participles) leave out the subject, leaving us with bodily gestures – a wave of the hand, running a hand through hair, and, finally, marking where 'there' is, seeing himself – hoping to see himself – always there, in her eyes. 'I want her everywhere', the bridge says, and resolves itself into 'to need her everywhere'. The song grasps us by singing desire and need together, making desire need, minor into major, filling out desire with need, need with desire, so that the seeming accident of need is assumed into the willfulness of desire. In this it seems to effect the modernist project of articulating the essential nature of the accidental:

the 'deictical' accident of place resolves itself in a 'transcendental' essence of meaning and meaningfulness.

Still, 'Here, There and Everywhere' does not fully achieve this aim precisely in the manner that it emphasizes the accidents of place and of material, corporeal existence. The accidents of the song, that is, are the bodies, the real places – 'Watching her eyes / And hoping I'm always there' – that persist in the resolution of 'I will be there and everywhere / Here, there and everywhere.' Real places are real deictics: this *here* place, where I'm talking, even though you're not listening, where I'm sitting, watching you, over *there*, seeing myself – this here self – reflected in those eyes, over there. The song transforms these real places to an unreal deictic: *everywhere*. 'I want her everywhere. I need her everywhere.' Love doesn't so much leave the accidents of material sounds, material places behind in opposition to the way that 'Eleanor Rigby' seems to enact how loneliness thrives on accident. Rather, love gathers up accident, weights it so to speak, carries it to major chords and carries it, in the verse, beyond the accidents of rhyme (hear/year, there/hair), to half-rhymes (thinking/speaking), and rhymeless statements. The most rhymeless statement of this lovely lovesong – which I hope, by the way, makes sense to all of us in its fugue of accident and necessity that inhabits love – is its final note, the dominant G over the choral C major chord. Paul's G hovers over the music the way that 'everywhere' hovers above the *here*'s and *there*'s of the song, the way that love seems to help us lead better lives, to think how good it can be, to imagine that, in our lives, 'there's something there', and to believe that love never dies even when people don't always know that we're speaking or that we're there.

The accidents of musical line, musical structure, and lyric call attention to themselves in *Revolver* and energize rather than temper its powerful sound. They enact, I think, a kind of cleaning that I articulate, almost accidentally, in the joke of my title, 'Cleaning My Gun', a refreshment of sound. This is what at its best might be called the post-Enlightenment postmodern cleansing of the modern: a kind of refreshment. In his essay, 'Note on the Meaning of "Post-"', Jean-François Lyotard tries to describe how the 'post' of postmodernism – or 'post-Enlightenment', as I call it (see Schleifer, 2000) – marks the confusion of the realms of (aesthetic) experience, (epistemological) knowledge, and (ethical) politics that Enlightenment modernity strove so hard to keep separate and 'pure' (e.g., Kant's 'pure reason') by gathering together opposites: accident and necessity, need and desire, body and spirit, emptiness and fullness. Such gathering creates the possibility (not the necessity) of refreshment, just as Bach, Johnson, and Descartes refreshed the world with new organizations of received phenomena. Thus, Lyotard argues in this article that the '"post" of "postmodern" does not signify a movement of *comeback*, *flashback*, or *feedback* – that is, not a movement of repetition but a procedure in "ana-"; a procedure of analysis, anamnesis, anagogy, and anamorphosis' (Lyotard, 1992, p. 68), a procedure or procedures to create new energies of attention. Such procedures, like the best of the Beatles' music, allow for 'postmodern' apprehensions – and even 'cleansings' – of what, of necessity, modernism couldn't attend to, such as 'deictical' knowledge, 'personal' politics, and even an aesthetics of emptiness as well as fullness. Certainly, the hovering love of 'Here, There and Everywhere' cleanses on the levels of place and person; but even the aesthetic pastiche of 'Eleanor Rigby' offers good health in its pathos, a kind of reality rarely found in the rock and popular musics of the 1950s, reducing, as they often do, high modernism to kitsch and simple cliché.

Notes

1. Needless to say, in many ways what I am describing is more complicated than this suggests. First of all, to call a record a 'revolver' is just as synecdochical as to call a gun a 'revolver', though the *reference* in the first case is figurative ('this album has the *power* of a weapon') while the reference in the second case is literal ('this album is simply a revolving record'). A second complication, however, is that the double meaning of 'fret' I describe is *modally* distinct from the double meaning of 'revolver'. 'Revolver''s two meanings exist on levels of the figurative and the literal, while 'fret''s two meanings stem from different linguistic histories: 'fret' as 'concern' derives from the Old English *fretan*, 'to devour', while the 'fret' of the guitar derives from Old French *frette*, 'a band or ferrule'. There is a third 'fret' as in the fretwork of architecture that derives, probably, from the combination of the Old French *frette* with the Old English *frætwa*, 'ornament'. The combination here of the two distinct linguistic traditions of English, Germanic and Romance languages, underlines the *traditional* differences between 'fret' and 'fret'. Most importantly, it underlines the *accidental* nature of this 'double meaning': the accident of the coincident of these words' *sounds* arbitrarily designating different *meanings*.

    Similarly, as Daniel Rosen has pointed out in a remarkably generous reading of an earlier draft of this chapter, the modality of minor keys are also more complicated than my discussion sometimes suggests: 'strictly speaking', he noted in a personal correspondence, 'any alterations noted in a key signature are considered accidentals. But I ordinarily refer only to pitches that are outside the tonic key as accidentals. And the accidentals within the minor key are not ordinarily included in the key signature, since it usually involves the use of flats and sharps simultaneously (i.e. g-minor, with two flats, requires an f-sharp as its leading tone). A tone outside the key is the meaning that I think you give to the term "accidental" in your definition. Now, C# is essentially within the key of e-minor. Remember, our system actually incorporates into its "mechanism" three forms of the minor mode – the natural, the harmonic, and the melodic. The C# is, of course, one of the scale tones in the melodic form of e-minor.'

2. By 'neutral practice' Jameson is describing what I called earlier a certain kind of flatness of tone and affect in much postmodern art.

3. I also do not want to suggest that the regularities of modernism – in political equality, aesthetic harmony, and scientific systematicity – are not great goods that have served humankind in important and humane ways. I do want to suggest, however, that the price of these achievements is often the too-quick overlooking of accidents of differences inhabiting equality, dissonances energizing harmony, and scientific abstractions that serve, in Bruno Latour's words, domination as well as emancipation (Latour, 1993, p. 10). For an extended discussion of these matters, see my *Analogical Thinking*.

Chapter 14

'It is not dying': *Revolver* and the birth of psychedelic sound

Russell Reising

> He fumbles at your Soul
> As Players at the Keys
> Before they drop full Music on –
> He stuns you by degrees –
> > – Emily Dickinson, 1862

Like Herman Melville, who dated the beginning of his actual life at age twenty-five, the beginning of his career as a writer, I date my alternative nativity, the transformative moment in my life, from my first encounter with *Revolver*. More specifically, the first time I heard 'Love You To', I knew something heavy had been dropped on me (long before I had 'dropped' anything heavy); the record introduced me to 'another kind of mind there' in that sound. As soon as the cut had finished playing, I called my two best friends and played it to them over the phone. Probably thinking me quite mad, one of them responded with disturbing indifference and the other by turning me on to a cut from the latest Ventures album. That was dying.[1] The acoustics of our conversation weren't all that inferior to my primitive 'hi-fi', so I've never believed that the song lost enough in telephonic translation to warrant the frigid reception from my two ex-best friends. That first encounter with *Revolver* revolutionized both my social priorities and my entire outlook on life, broke down something within me and ushered me into another kind of something there, something new, something exciting, something heavy, something I would spend an inordinate amount of the next three decades of my life enjoying and thinking about. That was *not* dying, but rather being reborn into some world I, along with millions of other music lovers could barely fathom at the time. Whether my doors of perception had been cleansed or I had broken on through to the other side, I had, in short, departed the comfortable world of Anglo-American pop music and entered the brave new world of psychedelia.

Revolver's impact on me cannot be attributed merely to some crisis in my own adolescence during which I was ripe for any kind of transformative experience.[2] In fact, this album invented musical expressions and initiated trends and motifs that would chart the path not only of the Beatles and a cultural epoch, but of the subsequent history of rock and roll as well. Let me requote the remark accompanying the VH1 ranking of *Revolver* as the Greatest Album of All Time: 'If pop music were destroyed tomorrow, we could re-create it from this album alone.' As I also note in my introduction and as many of the chapters in this volume demonstrate, *Revolver* introduced many conceptual and technical innovations to Anglo-American popular music, the significance and influence of which are still being felt and appreciated. For me, *Revolver*'s breakthroughs and the sources of its greatest impact reside in two distinct areas, both of which are central to the emergence and evolution of psychedelic music.

First, *Revolver* performs and elaborates on a complex interface between human consciousness and its accompanying technological environment, especially between the human voice and electronic musical effects, many of which are the first examples of sounds intended to reproduce or recall both the aural dimension and the altered perception of duration and continuity characteristic of psychedelic experience. The abrupt transition from, say, 'Eleanor Rigby' to 'I'm Only Sleeping' typifies the way *Revolver* jolts out of one perceptual frame into another, in a manner akin to the ways in which psychedelic experience affects attention span and can hurl us from blissful calm in one moment into frantic joy or anxiety in the next. The Thirteenth Floor Elevators capture something of this surging sense of reality in their early psychedelic classic 'Roller Coaster' and Pink Floyd albums regularly peel us from one tune to the next with disorienting transitional ruptures. The movements from one cut to the next throughout *Revolver* drama-tizes a wide range of musical possibilities and, while distinctly different from the seamless segues that mark many of the transitions from cut to cut on *Sgt Pepper's Lonely Hearts Club Band* or the second half of *Abbey Road*, nevertheless creates a language of coherence within musical variety, in many ways one of the hallmarks of psychedelic album composition, explored more fully by the Beatles on albums like *Sgt Pepper* and *Abbey Road*, by Pink Floyd on *Dark Side of the Moon* and *Wish You Were Here*, and by Yes on *Tales From Topographic Oceans*.

Second, in the complex skein of *Revolver*'s intra-album dialogue, an album's songs speak meaningfully to each other for the first time in rock and roll history. In so doing, *Revolver* articulates an evolutionary dialogue intended to encompass all of human experience and parallels the primary effects attributed to psyche-delic experience. As R. E. L. Masters and Jean Houston put it in their still influ-ential *Varieties of Psychedelic Experience* the same year that *Revolver* was released, 'the symbolic images experienced [at the deepest levels of psychedelic consciousness] are predominantly historical, legendary, mythical, ritualistic and "archetypal". The subject may experience a profound ... sense of continuity with evolutionary and historic process' (Masters and Houston, 1966, p. 147). While neither most Beatles' fans nor I comprehended this facet in 1966, *Revolver* pays musical testimony to these insights, both in the range of the heterogeneous musical forms that characterize the album's fourteen compositions and in the collection's rich lyrical content. Musically, no two of *Revolver's* cuts seems very clearly related to any other – each song seems to introduce an entirely new musical universe – but philosophically and thematically, the album twists, turns, stumbles, and surges toward the transcendent vision of 'Tomorrow Never Knows'.[3] In like manner, Jimi Hendrix arranges his tripartite guitar solo in 'All Along the Watchtower' so that each segment partakes of a different style and amplification mode, yet the solo holds together because of the family resemblances unifying the otherwise different psychedelically distorted sounds he explores. Of course, by the release of *Electric Ladyland* a mere two years later in 1968, his audience had already been sufficiently 'experienced' to process and appreciate his refinements. But in 1966, the idea of coherence lurking within the diversity of a collection of sounds pushed Beatles fans to another level of musical sophistication. To draw on my epigraph from Emily Dickinson, the Beatles intersperse musical and technological innovations by degrees throughout *Revolver*, preparing us for that 'Ethereal Blow' when 'they drop full Music on' in 'Tomorrow Never Knows'.

I believe that the Beatles are fully aware of, if not fully intent on, the theoretical dimension of *Revolver*. By originally calling 'Tomorrow Never Knows' (the first song recorded during the now famous 'Revolver sessions') 'Mark I', the Beatles signalled a new musical departure. As I will demonstrate in my discussion of 'Tomorrow Never Knows', that song recapitulates virtually every important thematic element introduced earlier on the album. While we can't argue definitively that the Beatles wrote and arranged the rest of the tunes in order to establish the prehistory of human evolution taken to such a quantum leap in the final cut, the coherence resulting from the complex interweaving of the album's lyrics suggests such a trajectory. But *Revolver* speaks eloquently to the entire prehistory of the Beatles' recording career in significant interalbum ways as well. That Harrison's countdown into 'Taxman' echoes the more exuberant such introduction to 'I Saw Her Standing There' has, of course, been duly noted by Beatles scholars. Other songs similarly position themselves vis-à-vis earlier tunes. In both the linguistic play of its title and its examination of romantic themes, 'Love You To', for example, recalls its innocent precursor 'Love Me Do' quite complexly. The way in which drinking from Doctor Robert's special cup results in our 'feeling fine' bears little resemblance to the way that being in love makes one feel in 'I Feel Fine'. 'Eleanor Rigby' offers a powerful counterpoint to all earlier songs with women's names for their titles, including the cover versions of 'Dizzy Miss Lizzy', 'Anna', and 'Long Tall Sally', and the gentle love song 'Michelle'. With a few notable exceptions, such as 'Martha My Dear', deeper and often darker songs follow in 'Lovely Rita', 'Polythene Pam', and 'Julia'. 'Tomorrow Never Knows' surely takes us beyond 'Yesterday', again both in terms of verbal reversals as well as in thematic transcendence. The dark explorations of 'For No One' might even signal the Beatles' looking back and repudiating the crudely commercial moment of their careers marked by the album *Beatles For Sale* by implying that their rejection of live performance only several months away signals their new commitment to uncompromising studio explorations: they will no longer sell out, or even perform live, for anyone.

Klaus Voormann's beautiful and, as Sheila Whiteley argues in a previous chapter, somewhat jarring cover art captures the album's emphasis on philosophical matters, on psychedelic coherence and mind expansion in his representation of the Beatles standing around, tangled within, perched upon, and peeking out of each other's heads (especially their ears and hair), suggesting that the symbiosis of this recording reached levels so profound as to minimize the distinctions among the four individual members of the band. Indeed, the fusion of photographic images with Voormann's drawings questions the distinctions between photograph and drawing, perhaps indicative of the Beatles' own problematization of the relationship of live performance and studio constructions, especially in the eeriness of what appear to be photographs of eyes lodged within the drawn facial features of each member. Moreover, the images Voormann selects for his photographic collage come almost exclusively from earlier manifestations of the Beatles' looks and styles, again suggesting that the group's latest manifestation signals a significant break from the literalness suggested in the photographs. Whether evoking images of summation or transcendence, these animated Beatles shuffled in with photos of their past glories register another kind of vision there. Just as his visual representations of the Beatles now freely exceed photographic documentation, the sonic and lyrical experiments characteristic of songs like 'Love You To', 'She Said She Said', and, of course, 'Tomorrow Never Knows' constitute fully realized musical breakthroughs within both their own corpus and rock and roll in general.

In its music and themes, *Revolver* represents psychedelic experience in a variety of ways. Most explicitly, 'Doctor Robert' pays homage to various medical practitioners who first introduced many luminaries to LSD. Specifically, the song virtually deifies Dr Robert Freymann, a New York physician famous for his mind-expanding concoctions, but Dr Max 'Feelgood' Jacobson, who provided psychedelic potions for Andy Warhol's New York circle before serving as John F. Kennedy's personal physician during his presidency, established himself as an equally influential dispenser of psychedelic experiences.[4] We know that each of the Beatles had his first LSD experience prior to the release of *Revolver*, with John, George, and their wives being turned on by George's dentist. John Lennon wrote two of his contributions, 'Tomorrow Never Knows' and 'She Said She Said' in the immediate wake of his earliest LSD trips. While 'She Said She Said', clearly recollects and revises one of Lennon's first psychedelic experiences, 'Tomorrow Never Knows' offers Lennon's theoretical take on the drug's possibilities, as well as his response to Timothy Leary, Ralph Metzner, and Richard Alpert's manual, *The Psychedelic Experience* (1964), based on the *Tibetan Book of the Dead*. Memory and pronouncement, immersion and detachment, such couplings of the immediate and experiential with the abstract and theoretical implied by these two compositions marks much of *Revolver*'s response to the Beatles' earliest psychedelic experiences, a phase during which Lennon, at least, was taking the drug on nearly a daily basis (DeRogatis, 1996, p. 25). Such symbiotic energies also characterize Lennon and McCartney's respective contributions to *Revolver*. McCartney's psychedelic offerings, 'Got To Get You Into My Life' and 'Good Day Sunshine', register the thrill and exuberance of psychedelic initiation. Whereas Lennon dramatizes the problematic communicative impasses and theorizes the psycho-philosophical dimension of psychedelia, McCartney domesticates his own initiations with love songs and images of sunny days and wild rides, maybe even hinting at Albert Hoffmann's famous bicycle ride during his accidental first ingestion of LSD.[5] Harrison documents the feeling of LSD in 'Love You To' as do Ringo Starr's vocals in 'Yellow Submarine', with each song bearing the unmistakable signature of its singer's personality and priorities. That each of the Beatles registers the impact of his inaugural LSD experiences in such diverse lyrical and sonic ways – including wild optimism, exotic sampling of other cultures, morbid introspection, and magisterial pronouncement – testifies, itself, to the heterogeneity and wide-ranging implications and impacts of psychedelic experience. But these four men still lived, thought, and functioned as 'the Beatles', and their identities, however diverse and ultimately irreconcilable, still meshed as one towering musical entity. Like the songs collected on *Revolver*, the group itself fused unity within diversity and expressed diversity through their unified compositions and recordings.

Perhaps more significant in the history of rock and roll, *Revolver* attempts to recreate what tripping actually *sounds* like. Gerald Marzorati might be right when he argued that for Beatles fans, outside of any lyrical beauty or content, 'what mattered was the *sound*, and the sound was something just this side of unimaginability' (Marzorati, 2000, p. 32). Marzorati's insight was true for what he calls 'the propulsive *yeahs*' from their earliest releases; how much truer for the work on *Revolver*. Walter Everett notes several other instances in which particular electronic effects reproduce phases from an LSD trip. Thus, on 'Rain', recorded during the *Revolver* sessions, both the drums and Lennon's guitar contribution are 'recorded much *faster* than actually heard, introducing the subtle but rich tone of queasy hesitation that could be likened to the nausea of an acid trip'. And, in 'She Said She Said', 'The LSD user's visual reverberations, or "trails", images similar to strobe photographs of moving objects, are heard in this music's various kinds of imitation', such as Harrison's guitar following several of Lennon's vocal lines at some distance. Similarly, 'the droning, cyclical ... harmonic pattern is a further type of repetition that may be related to the timeless quality of both an LSD trip and the mantra-based meditation in Indian practice' (Everett, 1999, pp. 44, 66). All of *Revolver*'s sonic boldness and experimentation signals the Beatles' response to their inaugural psychedelic trips, and cuts like 'Love You To' and

'Tomorrow Never Knows' set the agenda for rock and roll's psychedelicized sonic revolution for decades to come.

However, that does not necessarily mean that 'Tomorrow Never Knows' necessarily sounds good while tripping (one of the great conundrums of the trip is what works and what doesn't work as a musical accompaniment), but rather that it attempts to reproduce the aural dimension of the trip. 'Tomorrow Never Knows' encodes within the totality of its innovative musical and lyrical world what music, or even the world, in general might sound like during the height of a psychedelic experience, even if it were not characterized by some of the most remarkable, experimental sounds ever produced. Perhaps this is what Nick Bromell has in mind when he suggests that *Revolver* 'did not so much invite its still-innocent audience to "lose its time-sense in a brilliantly authentic evocation of the LSD experience" as offer extended immersion in denaturalized sound' (Bromell, 2000, p. 96). What he doesn't consider, however, is that the very denaturalization he identifies functions as a synecdoche, not a transparent representation, of the psychedelic state. In this respect, the Beatles offer *Revolver*'s final cut almost as a whirlwind education in psychedelia.[6] To summarize: *Revolver* represents those first thrills of insight and illumination felt after one's initial psychedelic experience, all filled with a sense of coherence, evolutionary transcendence, and newly liberated perceptions and perspectives. *Sgt Pepper's Lonely Hearts Club Band* already trivializes those insights by making them merely the playthings of technological innovation for the sake of mere sensory impressions. The continuity of *Revolver* is thematic, philosophical, and musical, whereas the continuity of *Sgt Pepper's Lonely Hearts Club Band* doesn't really reach beyond the fluidity of some of its musical segues. Even 'A Day In The Life', while potentially a song of summation and condensation, doesn't really speak to the other songs very clearly or synthetically.

But we should address the nature 'of the beginning'. In what follows, I will trace the boldness with which the Beatles structure their sonic revolution, paying attention not only to the thematics and significance of each cut, but also to the album's interstices and the thresholds of sound concluding one tune and beginning the next. Along the way, I will focus on lyrical and instrumental moments that strike me as the hallmarks of the Beatles' psychedelic initiation.

Revolver opens with George Harrison's voice emerging out of silent grooves along with some rambling swipes at a guitar. Immediately, as Tim Riley points out, *Revolver* frustrates the distinction between live performance and studio seclusion (Riley, 1988, pp. 182–183; see also Shaugn O'Donnell's chapter in this collection). Whereas Riley and others read this complex introductory scene as a problematic, even stumbling, moment in the Beatles' evolution, suggesting their frustration with live performances and the resulting tension aroused by their studio turn, I think we can view it equally as a statement of new beginnings, of possibility, wherein the Beatles' vocal presence enters into a new phase with their instrumentation and the technological experiments made possible by their migration from the stage into the studio. Again, Klaus Voormann's drawings slip beyond photographic literalism. I read this introductory chant as the first pulse in *Revolver*'s exploration of precisely those possibilities, an exploration that wanders the long and winding roads of the album's dialectic. Bromell offers a corrective over Riley's position when he comments that 'Tomorrow Never Knows' 'and so much of *Revolver* wreaks havoc with the distinction between the natural and the artificial' (Bromell, 2000, p. 96). Since it is not intended to evoke the intimate presence of the mop tops, Bromell concludes, *Revolver* can only distance and estrange us from the Beatles. But given the accomplishment of the very album in question, the distinction seems obsolete and archaic. On the other hand, Bromell's commentary on the electronification of the entire Beatles sound is very much to the point:

> The unearthly sounds that *Revolver* released into the world were at once the antithesis of the human and a provocative indication of the *mysterium tremendum*. They allowed the imagination to traverse the netscape of the future in which biology and technology would come full circle and touch. (Bromell, 2000, p. 98)

I agree completely. Mystery, technology, and the human presence at the heart of both are what *Revolver* is all about.

In any event, Harrison's countdown erupts in his wailed 'Oh' and the quartet's explosion in hard-edged unison. Hardcore to be sure, 'Taxman' establishes both the rhythmic pulse of *Revolver* and the album's first statement on the status of the contemporary individual, in this case in isolated opposition to some oppressive governmental apparatus. In, perhaps, the album's ultimate merging of the human and the technological, Paul's thumping, heartbeat bass provides a visceral foundation over which the rest of the instrumentation and vocals swirl around in varying degrees of intensity, humanizing *Revolver*'s entire theme. Together with *Revolver*'s innovative and uncanny blending of vocals with electronic effects, these mergings of the corporeal with the technological (constitutive, according to Sheila Whiteley, of the texturing and layering of sound that launches the psychedelic edge of some more obviously trippy music) close the gap between human and machine and realize the complementarity of human creativity with technology that is representative of psychedelic soundscapes. The outrage of 'Taxman' is monologic, but the song itself is the protest against the taxman, even though it is spoken from his hypothetical point of view, an experiment in ironic perspectivism that the Beatles will develop throughout the rest of their career, notably in songs like 'Paperback Writer' and 'She's Leaving Home'. The Beatles depict this particular form of oppression as but one mode, in this case a macro-institutional mode, among other forces capable of 'screw[ing] you in the ground', 'making [you] feel like you've never been born', and either wearing or bringing you 'down', all represented in *Revolver*'s other songs.

'Taxman' fades out to the tones of a solo electric guitar, giving way to the beginning of 'Eleanor Rigby'. The nearly perfect synchronization of Paul's voice with the strings enacts a virtual retreat from the rock mode, a break emphasized by the Beatles using two string quartets and by having no Beatles playing on 'Eleanor Rigby'. The cut thus represents the first of *Revolver*'s several attempts at withdrawal, abandoning the 'here and now' immediacy of 'Taxman''s complaint and harkening back to some traditional merging of human voice and acoustic instrumentation, characteristic, perhaps, of the musicological essence of a simpler and less technological culture (although not necessarily one immune to the corruption and exorbitant claims of the taxman). Lest we harbor any illusions about the coherence of such a culture, 'Eleanor Rigby' strands its small cast of characters in a shattered world of alienation and despair. Apparently the more 'organic' community, signaled by the acoustic mode, the quaint religious milieu, and occupations of picking up rice, writing sermons, or darning socks, provides no guarantee of human fullness or satisfaction. Eleanor Rigby's death signals *Revolver*'s first extended articulation of its dominant thematic: life and death, a meditation begun in 'Taxman' with George's 'advice to those who die' to 'declare the pennies on your eyes' and not resolved until the transcendent proclamation 'It is not dying' that opens 'Tomorrow Never Knows'.

Paul McCartney's vocal treatment in 'Eleanor Rigby' is noteworthy. At first, Paul's voice is slightly distanced through being reproduced on only the right channel. At the moment when he sings the first refrain of 'All the lonely people', Paul's voice takes on a rich depth as it sweeps across the entire stereo sound stage from the far right. I'm not aware of any such 'headphone' effect earlier in the Beatles' careers; this might be the first psychedelic effect achieved entirely through electronic manipulation. It is not the last.

After the strains of 'Eleanor Rigby''s string quartets fade out, 'I'm Only Sleeping' opens with the album's second consecutive example of a voice perfectly fused with its instrumental accompaniment, in this case with alarm clock abruptness in a wall of electrical sound, a thundering return to (and of) rock and roll, completely opposite of the acoustic mode of 'Eleanor Rigby'. Lennon's distanced voice, along with the fully fused electric background, suggests a possible musicological and technological transcendence of the impasse posed by 'Eleanor Rigby'. 'I'm Only Sleeping' also initiates the album's explicit psychedelic lyrical drift (and the first lyrical moment that will be requoted later on the record), with its line 'Stay in bed, float upstream (float upstream)', an anticipation of 'Tomorrow Never Knows' and its injunction to 'Turn off your mind, relax and float downstream'. One of the titles the Beatles considered for this album was *Magic Circles*, referring, perhaps, to the cyclical continuities embedded in intra-album relations such as this. Indeed, the dream-state evoked in 'I'm Only Sleeping' maintains the otherworldly tone of *Revolver*'s lyrics, lyrics that guide the Beatles through various attempts at transcendence. Apparently, the dream-state celebrated in 'I'm Only Sleeping' differs significantly from that of Eleanor Rigby, who 'lives in a dream', a dialectical reversal characteristic of *Revolver*'s evolutionary dynamic. Given that the oppression of 'Taxman' and the alienation of 'Eleanor Rigby' pose equally distasteful cul de sacs of modern existence, the dreamy state of withdrawal and observation from one's window tempts humanity with a more relaxed and distanced perspective.

In *Revolver*'s most innovative transitional moment, from 'I'm Only Sleeping' to 'Love You To', the ancient sounds of a slow, hypnotically, exotically, and almost morosely slow, sitar strum displace the Beatles' most experimental electric guitar riffs to date, a bracing movement encompassing a vast scale of sound, time, mind, and space, and one fully integrating the Beatles' Anglicized psychedelia with Asian influences. Fully coherent with the dreaminess of 'I'm Only Sleeping', the introduction of 'Love You To' casts the Beatles into Asiatic modes of sound and being, significantly more remote than the eighteenth-century milieu suggested by 'Eleanor Rigby', again as if seeking some other kind of engagement there, apart from the hurly burly of modern existence.[7] The sitar evokes soundscapes at least as ancient as its entry into India from Persia as the 'cihtar' in 1190, perhaps as far back as its pre-Islamic ancestry dating in the third millennium BCE (Sadie, 1984, pp. 353, 392, 518). In a remarkable act of space/time balancing, 'Love You To' contains and harmonizes both its exotic soundscape as well as the primitive surges provided by Harrison's growling guitar notes with the anachronistically futuristic sounds representative of *Revolver*. Art Kleps, one of Timothy Leary's contemporaries during the days of many gurus at the Hitchcock family's Millbrook estate in upstate New York, suggests that 'Indian music is perfect for stabilizing a high high because it in no way encourages you to notice the passage of time – or better, to notice that time has stopped passing and instead is sort of loitering around shooting the shit with space' (Kleps, 1975, p. 26). As I argue later, much of the lyrical significance of 'Tomorrow Never Knows' resides in its recapitulation of the entirety of *Revolver*'s thematics, in its suggestion of the virtual conflation of space and time. Kleps, and many other commentators, suggests that such destabilizations of one's experience of time marks the second stage of many psychedelic trips: 'this stage may be thought of as being "at the cellular level," and everything takes on a certain golden liquidity. One does not see events as occurring in a regular cause and effect or linear way but rather as being contained in some kind of "eternity capsule" outside of space-time (Kleps, 1975, p. 211). In *The Little Book of Acid*, Cam Cloud makes a similar point:

> The passage of time seems to slow down tremendously when under the influence of acid. A few minutes may seem like hours; a few hours may seem like days. This effect is known as 'time dilation'. At the peak of a very powerful trip it may seem as if time has come to a complete stop, plunging the tripper into a timeless, eternal realm. (Cloud, 1999, p. 1)

In one of the most remarkable psychedelic memoirs ever written, Malden Grange Bishop defined his own sense of time while under the influence: "'It's the epitology of time," I said aloud there in the silent room. "That's what I've been trying

to put into words. I was over time, I saw the top of time, or the end of time'"
(Bishop, 1963, p. 159). Indeed, the 'epitology', to use Bishop's coinage, or the
'timeless' realm of Indian music noted here thus functions doubly in 'Love You
To', as both atmospheric dreaminess of the particular cut and theoretical inter-
jection in which the Beatles speculate on the nature of time itself.

Already beginning *Revolver*'s synthetic work, 'Love You To' builds on the critique of those 'running everywhere at such a speed' in 'I'm Only Sleeping' and
similarly laments that sense that 'Each day just goes so fast / I turn around – it's
past', and opens up new possibilities for love rather than for solitary dreaming. In
doing so, 'Love You To' maintains a dialogue with the other cuts on *Revolver*,
while also constructing a dialogue within its own lyrics. The title responds to the
song's final couplet, 'I'll make love to you / If you want me to', with its simple
affirmation, redefining the craving suggested in 'want me to' with the relaxed
poise of 'Love You To'.

In the transition from 'Love You To' to 'Here, There, and Everywhere', the
Beatles enact yet another disorienting rupture, sliding the sitar and tabla fade-out
into a gentle electric guitar strum and the sweetest, most traditional of ballad
vocals. In a matter of seconds, they propel us many centuries ahead and juxtapose
their vision of Asian antiquity and exoticism with the mellow tones of a Paul
McCartney love song, in fact his favorite composition (MacDonald, 1994, p. 168).
In this rapid movement from present to distant past and back to the immediate
present, the Beatles conclude their first musical approximation of a psychedelic
state of mind, especially in the peculiarities of one's sense of time and one's attention span while under the influence of psychedelic substances.

Nor is this sonic shift out of sync with the song's lyrical direction. As if awak-
ening from the detached alternatives offered by 'I'm Only Sleeping' and 'Love
You To', 'Here, There, And Everywhere' returns the Beatles, *Revolver*, and the listener to the immediate present, domesticating the 'I'll make love to you' into the
familiarity of the modern love arrangement: 'To lead a better life I need my love
to be here'. In one remarkable transformation, 'Here, There, and Everywhere'
also recasts, in gentle, loving and tactile images, the idea of running out of desperation in 'I'm Only Sleeping' and 'Love You To' as 'There, *running* my hands
through her hair'. Moreover, the very concept of omnipresence suggested by the
title 'Here, There, and Everywhere' suggests the universalizing ambitions of
Revolver, both geographically, chronologically, and historically. In essence, then,
the lyrical content of 'Here, There, and Everywhere' functions both as an immediate return to the present from exotic otherness and as a thematic core of the
entirety of *Revolver*, which aims at nothing less than taking its audience here,
there, virtually everywhere popular music can travel. As William Burroughs
wrote to Alan Ginsberg after an experience with an Amazonian hallucinogenic
brew,

> The blood and substance of many races, Negro, Polynesian, Mountain Mongol,
> Desert Nomad, Polygot [sic] Near East, Indian – new races as yet unconceived and

unborn, combinations not yet realized passes through your body. Migrations, incredible journeys through deserts and jungles and mountains (stasis and death in closed mountain valleys where plants sprout out of the Rock and vast crustaceans hatch inside and break the shell of the body), across the Pacific in an outrigger canoe to Easter Island. The Composite City where all human potentials are spread out in a vast silent market. (Burroughs and Ginsberg, 1963, p. 44)

If existence really can be lived from the point of view of cosmic time and space, 'Here, There, and Everywhere' puts the individualistic grievances of 'Taxman' into another kind of perspective.

'Here, There, and Everywhere' departs just as it entered, in some of the most mellifluous tones on the album, a gentleness immediately disrupted by the slightly jarring tones of a heavy, jangling guitar strum, percussive effects, and, for the first time on the album, Ringo's voice. The sonic effects of 'Yellow Submarine' insinuate an entire new range of sound for *Revolver*, some of the first ambient effects in the Beatles' corpus. The undersea sonics of 'Yellow Submarine' anticipate not only the deep sea explorations of the Beatles' own 'Octopus' Garden', but also the aquatic soundscapes of Jimi Hendrix's '1983, A Merman I Should Turn To Be', Donovan's 'Atlantis', Emerson, Lake, and Palmer's 'Just Take a Pebble', Otis Redding's 'Dock of the Bay', Grand Funk Railroad's 'I'm Getting Closer to My Home', the Steve Miller Band's 'Song for My Ancestors', Paul Kantner and Grace Slick's 'Tetanic', Pink Floyd's 'Echoes', the ambitious introduction to Yes's monumental *Tales From Topographic Oceans* which stages the emergence of human life from its aquatic origins, and the Strawbs' 'Queen of Dreams', a veritable tour de force of the genre. To be sure, Jan and Dean, the Beach Boys, and others had surfed the waves of the west coast, and some young beauties got stranded in the water by virtue of the skimpiness of their 'Itsy, Bitsy, Teenie, Weenie, Yellow Polka-Dot Bikinis'. But psychedelia has explored a deeper fascination with oceanic venues. Dylan dances along the circus sands in 'Mr Tambourine Man' and Donovan opens his eyes to find himself 'by the sea' in 'Hurdy Gurdy Man'. But 'Yellow Submarine', in its persistent refusal to recognize any boundaries as stable or fixed, takes the full psychedelic plunge. Rock and roll was never the same, and that moment's ripples extend even to farcical pieces like 'Rock Lobster' by the B-52s.

While the song might initially sound a bit 'ridiculous', as Tim Riley characterizes it, 'Yellow Submarine' contributes significantly to *Revolver*'s overarching affirmative scheme with its many repetitions of the word 'life' (Riley, 1988, p. 188). Culminating this veritable orgy of affirmation, 'Yellow Submarine' fades out to the repeated chorus, 'We all live in a yellow submarine, yellow submarine, yellow submarine' (repeated in the song's final moments emphasizing 'We all live'), as if in implicit dialogue with the deathly atmospheres of 'Taxman' and 'Eleanor Rigby' as well as with the dreamy state of detachment of 'I'm Only Sleeping'. The other four occurrences of such words, '*Lived* a man who sailed the sea', 'Many more of them *live* next door', 'And we *lived* beneath the waves', and 'As we *live* a *life* of ease', all consolidate the tune's commitment to life. That the word 'life' appears only in two songs from *Rubber Soul*, and even then only in the limited senses of John's meditation on his past from 'In My Life' and in the viciously threatening 'Run For Your Life', suggests that the Beatles have a renewed commitment to another kind of life. We should recall that Paul McCartney originally conceived of 'Yellow Submarine' as a children's tune. Is it possible that the Beatles believed that unless ye become as a little child, you shall not enter the kingdom of heaven (or of the Beatles' genius)?[8] To write 'Yellow Submarine' off as merely light or to deny its importance because of its apparent childishness or silliness is, I believe, to fail to understand that silliness and profundity frequently cohabit very productively, albeit not always obviously to those inured to irony and cynicism.[9] 'Yellow Submarine' might even be said to advance the Asiatic philosophy first introduced sonically and thematically in 'Love You To' by, in Zen koan fashion, straining the boundary between the silly and the profound, albeit in the occidentalized fashion of a sea-faring tune.

Of course, the communal 'We all live' with brass band accompaniment does fade into the deeply distorted electric guitar effects and the morbidity of 'She said I know what it's like to be dead', a phrase that both opens and closes 'She Said She Said', one of the songs penned by Lennon in explicit reference to actual LSD trips. Not only does the instrumentation change dramatically, but the vocal delivery stages a transition from the choral unity of 'Yellow Submarine' to this fractured exchange of confusing and uneasy sparring. This remembered dialogue strands subjects in a world as bleak as that inhabited by Eleanor Rigby, Father McKenzie, and all the lonely people, but in this case the speaker finally transcends the futility and fatality of what 'She Said' by affirming 'I know that I'm ready to leave / Cause you're making me feel like I've never been born'. So, while it documents an exchange reminiscent of the interpersonal confusion recorded by R. D. Laing in *knots* (1970), 'She Said She Said' offers personal choice and an act of will as redemptive alternatives to the despairing situation. Apparently, the 'we all live' refrain from 'Yellow Submarine' has created a positive force field from which later songs develop, but that emergence 'don't come easy'.

The transition from 'She Said She Said' to 'Good Day Sunshine' marks the changing of the sides of the original British release of the *Revolver* album. 'Good Day Sunshine', positioned in its crucial place as 'Side Two, Cut One', not only sets the tone for the entire second side of *Revolver*, but also returns us to 'I'm Only Sleeping' with its exuberant wake-up call. Whereas the persona from 'I'm Only Sleeping' wanted to be left alone to his bed of dreams, 'Good Day Sunshine' strikes a chord of wakefulness and excitement in response to diurnal renewal, anticipating the similarly recuperative moment of 'Here Comes the Sun' opening Side Two of *Abbey Road*. That 'Here Comes the Sun' follows 'I want You' strikes me as a near-perfect revisiting of *Revolver*'s transitional scheme.[10] 'Good Day Sunshine' layers its heavy piano chords over the fading guitar effects and vocals ('I know what it's like to be dead. I know what it is like to be sad') of 'She Said

She Said', an effect lost with an album flip but restored by the seamless continuity of the CD. More importantly, the lyrics of 'Good Day Sunshine' offer a veritable feast of laughter, love, and exuberance, furthering the power of life-affirming optimism over the confusing discourses of death in 'She Said She Said'. The framing of 'She Said She Said' with 'Yellow Submarine' and 'Good Day Sunshine', then, situates confusion and negativity within episodes of choral communalism and love.

Yellow sunshine, orange sunshine, morning glory seeds – you could fill a whole bag of psychedelic tricks with the hallucinogens named for rising suns and tributes to morning. It was Henry David Thoreau who announced that 'Morning is when I am awake and there is a dawn in me', and psychedelic philosophers and chemists expanded his celebration of heightened consciousness into the psychedelic era, as marked by Donovan's 'Sunshine Superman'. Thus, 'Good Day Sunshine' initiates *Revolver*'s second side with double references to the life-affirming blaze of the sun and to the psychic and intellectual possibilities opened up by psychedelic experimentation. Side Two of *Revolver*, it should be noted, is one of the most explicitly psychedelic album sides in rock history, stringing out 'Good Day Sunshine', 'Doctor Robert', 'Got To Get You Into My Life', and 'Tomorrow Never Knows'. Even the less explicitly psychedelic tunes, 'For No One' and 'I Want To Tell You', take on greater psychedelic significance in the context of the predominant drift of *Revolver*'s final seven cuts.

The movement from 'Good Day Sunshine' to 'And Your Bird Can Sing' replaces the vocal repetitions of the phrase 'good day sunshine' with a hard-rocking jam foregrounding George's and John's guitars, while also reinstating the heartbeat pulse of Paul's bass line as the dominant rhythmic device of the album. This speaker remains unaffected by the various crises recounted, but this aloofness does not stage a return to the dreamy isolation of 'I'm Only Sleeping'. Even as he positions himself beyond the particular grievances of the song's implied auditor, this speaker reaffirms his presence *for* those who may lose their bearings as a result of material obsessions, world-weary ennui, and depression. In response to any of these crises, the vocalist reminds his audience, 'I'll be round'. I'll be a-round. I'll be 'round', like the round record *Revolver* spinning around and around on the turntable: 'And Your Bird Can Sing' thus partakes of *Revolver*'s thematics of circularity, of wholeness, of completeness, of the 'magic circles' that nearly formed its title. Round like the pennies you might put on the dead's eyes. Circular like the dialectic of floating upstream and floating downstream, or of sailing up to the sun until you find a sea of green. Round and whole as suggested by the deictic title 'Here, There, And Everywhere', or by the ability to call Doctor Robert anytime 'day or night', and maybe even like the rim of his special cup from which you can drink and feel fine.

'And Your Bird Can Sing' also pays oblique homage to *Revolver*'s overall sonic experiment in the line 'You tell me that you've heard every sound there is'. In one supreme example, the phase shift that alters the Beatles' choral singing that very line represents another of *Revolver*'s significant psychedelic vocal effects, suggesting that the Beatles pace the album's technological innovations, building up to 'Tomorrow Never Knows'. 'Eleanor Rigby' altered a single voice for a disruptive moment; 'And Your Bird Can Sing' stages something similar at a choral level, a return to the affirmative chorus 'We all live' from 'Yellow Submarine'.[11] Hyperbole, to be sure, but *Revolver* certainly has, even at this point of its unfolding, exposed its listeners to many other kinds of sounds.

Just as jarringly as the shift into and out of 'Love You To', 'And Your Bird Can Sing' slips from a guitar duet into the harpsichord/vocal introduction to 'For No One', another unearthing of nearly archaic musical remnants and a return to traditional instrumentation and styles later punctuated by Alan Civil's gorgeous horn solo. As in 'Eleanor Rigby' the archaic soundscape elicits a feeling of antiquity and doom, in this case of the collapse of a relationship, originally titled 'Why Did It Die?' (MacDonald, 1994, p. 164). However, in its own transcendence of the bleakness of loss, 'For No One' signals a fresh beginning, a realization that, perhaps, resulted in the song's title being changed. A new symbiosis of voice and instrument line emerges from Paul's bass-playing sometimes following his vocal progressions in near-perfect note-for-note unison, sometimes merging in a simple harmony with them. For all its sadness, then, 'For No One' nevertheless stages the triumph of its vocal/instrumental synthesis over the confusion and sadness of love gone wrong. Less than a year after recording 'For No One', the Beatles will announce 'all you need is love'. At this point, however, they suggest that all you need is music, and perspective.

The traditional sounds of harpsichord and horn provide the mellow closure that ushers 'For No One' into the space between the songs. The resulting silence is broken by the borderline country-western lead-in of 'Doctor Robert', a guitar sound reminiscent of *Rubber Soul* in general and 'What Goes On?' and 'Act Naturally' in particular. Doctor Robert might help you recover from the sadness of 'For No One', and the spectre of drugged distance recalls the dreamy escapism of 'I'm Only Sleeping', but the song makes us consider whether such avoidance constitutes a problem or a credible boon to consciousness. Moreover, the electrically altered and very lyrical chorus of 'Well, well, well, I'm feeling fine' pleads so eloquently for Doctor Robert's viability that it lends credence to his vision, or at least to the visions his 'special cup' can induce. As Janis Joplin ('Me and Bobby McGee') and Sgt Elias (in Oliver Stone's *Platoon*) insist, sometimes 'feeling good is good enough'. The repetition of 'Well, well, well' also suggests that we can all be well, at least potentially, if we're 'feeling fine'. With reference to earlier moments on *Revolver*, if you 'know what it's like to be dead', if 'your mind aches', if 'your bird is broken', or if 'your prized possessions start to wear you down', Doctor Robert will 'pick you up', providing all the good vibrations you need for a pharmacological good day of sunshine.

'Doctor Robert' fades out to the tones of a harmonious vocal-instrumental synthesis and gives way to the instrumental fade-in of 'I Want To Tell You'. The first of *Revolver*'s concluding trilogy of songs, one each by Harrison, McCartney, and Lennon, 'I Want To Tell You' sets the urgent tone of the album's philosophical and psychological epiphany in two ways. First, the Beatles 'want to tell you' something urgent, something new, something revolutionary. The urgency of this communiqué, expressed via a choral vocal mode, expands outward from the monolithic rhetoric of protest of 'Taxman' (replete with repetitive call and response warnings), as well as the interpersonal impasse of 'She Said She Said', and reaffirms the communal spirit of 'Yellow Submarine'. Perhaps most significantly, whatever urgency the Beatles express in 'I Want To Tell You' carries over into Paul's overtly psychedelic song, 'Got To Get You Into My Life', with the 'Got To' pushing the earlier 'I Want To' to a higher level of insistence and intensity. In this respect, 'I Want To Tell You' sets the stage for an important genre of psychedelic music, the messianic announcement of the wonders of psychedelic insight. The Thirteenth Floor Elevators' 'Kingdom of Heaven' is a good example, as is Kaleidoscope's 'I Found Out' (1968), which includes the lyrics 'I found out without a doubt what it's all about. And now I know in my soul just where to go'. Of course, John Lennon included his own 'I Found Out', albeit a more hostile version, on his first solo album, *Plastic Ono Band*. Certainty coupled with rhetorical hyperbole characterize these and similar pronouncements.

Second, 'I Want To Tell You' makes another significant contribution to *Revolver*'s psychedelic unity. The song's lyrics repeat the word 'mind' four different times, with three distinctly different meanings. 'Mind' alternately means one's being ('It's only me, it's not my mind / That is confusing things'), one's opinions ('Then I could speak my mind and tell you'), and one's caring or lack of caring ('I don't mind'). I take this flowering of many minds in 'I Want To Tell You' as a prelude to 'Got To Get You Into My Life' and its crucial opening stanza:

> I was alone, I took a ride,
> I didn't know what I would find there
> Another road where maybe I could see another kind of mind there.

The Beatles thus situate the very lyrical version of mind expansion and 'tripping' in the pivotal songs that give way to the revolutionary 'Tomorrow Never Knows'. I must again take exception with Tim Riley who declares 'Got To Get You Into My Life' as '*Revolver*'s most derivative cut' (Riley, 1988, p. 197), at least insofar as his perception fails to recognize that the blues-based instrumental presentation undergoes a powerful revision, in this particular deployment, by what John Lennon recalled as Paul's tribute to his early LSD experiences (Sheff and Golson, 1981, p. 191). Of course, we aren't sure whether this other kind of mind means another kind compared to the three earlier alternatives in 'I Want To Tell You', the fourth in an evolving surge of mind expansion, or some absolute anticipation of the ultimate transcendence of 'mind' as realized in the first line of 'Tomorrow Never Knows'. At any rate, the word 'mind', mentioned in only two other

Revolver songs, 'I don't mind, I think they're crazy' from 'I'm Only Sleeping' and 'Your day breaks, your mind aches' from 'For No One', virtually defines, in its seven repetitions, the final three cuts on the album, surely an indication of the Beatles' surging toward another kind of mind-expanding finale.

The actual transition from 'I Want To Tell You' to 'Got To Get You Into My Life' enacts perhaps the album's boldest transition, at least in terms of voice and technology. The vocal chorale fade-out features voices electronically altered to resemble brass instruments, leading into the pounding brass opening of 'Got To Get You Into My Life'. Functioning as a summation of *Revolver*'s several experiments in the interface between voice and instrument, this particular transition recalls the unified vocal/instrumental introductions to 'Eleanor Rigby' (acoustic) and 'I'm Only Sleeping' (electric). The brass section also recalls the solo horn from 'For No One', although they pump up the formal and contemplative solo horn into a jazzy brass section with brightness and surging intensity. As Walter Everett argues in this volume, Motown and its big band sound is more than a little on Paul McCartney's mind in this work on 'Got To Get You Into My Life', and the entire horn-based sound of groups like Blood, Sweat and Tears, Chicago, and others gained impetus from this expansive number. Nor should we ignore the possibility that the 'sunshine' to which Paul bids good morning is in fact the first pulse in the 'love song as coded paean to LSD' musical genre of which the Animals' 'A Girl Named Sandoz', Donovan's 'Mellow Yellow', and the Beatles' own 'Lucy in the Sky With Diamonds' are the best-known examples.

In terms of its own recollective placement on *Revolver*, 'Got To Get You Into My Life' prepares us for the revolutionary 'Tomorrow Never Knows', but also returns to the album's opening song. The wailed and despairing 'Oh' which opens 'Taxman' becomes the almost tipsily affirmative 'Ooh' repeated throughout 'Got To Get You Into My Life'. McCartney thus redeems the vocalizations of 'Taxman' and shores up the hope that *Revolver* struggles to consolidate throughout its song cycle. What a difference an 'O' makes, soothing the pain of 'Taxman', voicing the fine feeling of 'Doctor Robert', and perfecting the circular evolving of *Revolver* and its returning us near its end to the origins 'of the beginning'.

Of course 'Tomorrow Never Knows' opens with the injunction to 'Turn off your mind, relax and float downstream, / It is not dying, it is not dying', injecting one final affirmative pulse into the album's finale and evolving into its final vision of expansion and transcendence. As Jon Savage comments in his description of 'Tomorrow Never Knows' as the greatest British psychedelic song ever, '"Tomorrow Never Knows" takes you right into the maelstrom … it immediately impacted on pop culture' (Savage, 1997, p. 61). Indeed it does ascend into the maelstrom, but not without taking aboard its 'magic swirl ship' much of *Revolver*'s themes. Lennon's lyrics relate explicitly to the intensity of Harrison's 'I Want To Tell You' and McCartney's 'Got To Get You Into My Life'. Similar to the beginning injunction from Robert Frost's brilliant poem 'Directive' and its initial lines 'Back out of all this now too much for us', 'Tomorrow Never Knows', in essence, repudiates and transcends the insistence and immediacy of the lyrical drift of those two preceding songs, cutting *Revolver* loose from all forms of anxiety and stress with its own injunction to 'turn off your mind' and 'relax'. All three of these final songs return repeatedly to an opposition of being 'down' and being lifted 'up', also preparing us for the final injunction to:

Lay down all thoughts, surrender to the void,
It is shining, it is shining.

Timothy Leary captures the 'shining' element of psychedelic experience quite beautifully in *High Priest*, when he describes a particularly transcendent moment in a trip in the following way: 'I opened my eyes. I was in heaven. Illumination. Every object in the room was a radiant structure of atomic-god-particles. Radiating. Matter did not exist. There was just this million-matrix lattice web of energies. Shimmering. Alive. Interconnected in space-time. Everything hooked up in a cosmic dance. Fragile. Indestructible' (Leary, 1968, p. 328). It is quite likely such a shatteringly beautiful experience as this that powered John Lennon's creation of 'Tomorrow Never Knows'.

In a remarkable accomplishment of summation, 'Tomorrow Never Knows' recapitulates, in its own swirl of magic circles, virtually every motif articulated in *Revolver*'s earlier cuts. To return to my Emily Dickinson epigraph, whereas each of the earlier songs may have stunned us by degrees, 'Tomorrow Never Knows' is that moment when the Beatles 'drop full Music on' their listeners, setting the agenda for psychedelic music and for album-length experiments in lyrical coherence for decades to come. Virtually every word revisits and supercharges an earlier phrase from *Revolver*. The 'shining' of these lines refers us back to 'Good Day Sunshine', just as 'it is not dying' recalls the deaths recounted in 'Taxman', 'Eleanor Rigby', and 'She Said She Said'. 'Love is all and love is everyone' redeems the loneliness in 'Eleanor Rigby' and the loss of love in 'For No One' and reconfirms the drift of 'Love You To'. The notion of belief from 'it is believing' reaffirms 'each one believing that love never dies' from 'Here, There, and Everywhere'. 'It is knowing' reorients 'I know what it is like to be dead / I know what it is to be sad' from 'She Said She Said'. 'It is believing' rescues 'you don't believe her when she says her love is dead' from 'For No One'. 'It is not leaving' recuperates the earlier attempts at withdrawal and escapism from 'She Said She Said' and 'I'm Only Sleeping', while 'So play the game "Existence" to the end' redefines the 'games that begin to drag the speaker down' in 'Doctor Robert'. Finally, the line 'But listen to the colour of your dreams' revisits images of dreaming in both 'Eleanor Rigby' and 'I'm Only Sleeping'. Moreover, the return staged by 'Tomorrow Never Knows' is doubled by its final line, 'Of the beginning, of the beginning'.

The sonic effects of 'Tomorrow Never Knows' deepen that lyrical return to 'the beginning'. One of the song's most engaging effects is accomplished instrumentally by virtue of Paul McCartney's guitar solo from 'Taxman' being sampled, slowed down, cut up, and reversed in 'Tomorrow Never Knows' (MacDonald, 1994, p. 152), an instrumental accompaniment to the 'Ooh's of Got To Get You Into My Life' rounding out and redeeming the despairing 'Oh' from 'Taxman'. Even the tinny, dance hall piano at the song's conclusion refers back to the ragtime piano from 'Good Day Sunshine' and, looking forward, anticipates the end of 'Within You Without You' with its enigmatic laughter. The end literally revisits the beginning.

But rather than suggesting some pointless circularity, however, the Beatles return us to another kind of beginning, one reached by the historical and psychological journey through *Revolver* and its newly psychedelicized take on the human condition. In yet one final recapitulative moment, 'Tomorrow Never Knows' symbolically expands the geo-logic of *Revolver*, both in its re-referencing the eastern sounds of 'Love You To', and in John Lennon's original desire to have 1,000 Tibetan monks chanting in the background.[12] *Revolver's* exploration, then, plumbs the depths of the oceans in 'Yellow Submarine' and climbs to the top of the world for a view from Tibet. Here, there, and everywhere, indeed. But Lennon's perspective from mountain tops functions more than atmospherically and culturally. The Beatles, like Sly Stone, want to take us higher, and they do so gradually, as is suggested in the Dickinson epigraph, and not without complications occasionally interrupting its positive flow. Certainly, 'Tomorrow Never Knows' propels us beyond the confines of the individual ego which had delimited even the most optimistic songs on the album, and, while being the least subjective perspective offered on *Revolver*, returns us to the pulse of humanity taken up to highest levels by communal affirmations.

The negativity, alienation, and despair present in varying degrees on several of *Revolver's* cuts are all resolved, 'left', transcended within the psychedelic dialectic of its unfolding. It is in this respect that 'Tomorrow Never Knows' most complexly recapitulates psychedelic experience. 'It is not dying' dramatizes the symbolic 'death and rebirth' that many psychedelic journeys enable one to experience. It is not 'merely' dying, or being symbolically reborn, that forms the crux of these transformative experiences, but rather the sense of having been reborn into a life which, as one of Masters and Houston's psychedelic case studies put it, is 'a new life exactly like someone who has died and been reborn, leaving behind all the torments of the old life'.[13] The newness of 'Tomorrow Never Knows'' soundscape, then, mirrors the renewed appreciation of existence following the symbolic death of the psychedelic trip, which, in turn, emerges as a result of having transcended the troubles of loneliness, alienation, failed communication, and withdrawal, as represented throughout *Revolver's* fourteen songs.

Moreover, the concept of the album provided a vehicle and a philosophy capable of transcending the discrete units of songs usually packaged together to constitute a long-playing recording. Whereas albums prior to *Revolver* merely packaged thirteen or fourteen largely unrelated songs into the popular long-playing record format, *Revolver* gathered fourteen dialectically related statements on the human condition into a unified and coherent vision. The album progresses from its initial human vocal countdown to the highly technologized fade out of 'Tomorrow Never Knows', from static and repetitive individual protest to communal transcendence. In one sense it is popular music's first celebration of the human as technological and the technological as human. It also moves from anger and alienation through communal solidarity to redeem polarized individualism to the ecstatic merging into the transpersonal void. *Revolver* also ranges broadly throughout time and space, historically from invention of the sitar to the immediate present, geographically, from the Indian subcontinent to London, topographically from the ocean depths to the peaks of the Himalayas. No two transitions are the same, no two songs are musically the same (or even very closely related), and yet *Revolver* articulates a vision of human existence both evolutionary in its dynamic and unified in its themes. Unity within diversity and diversity punctuating unity: take your pick. Through its synthesizing ambitions, *Revolver* achieves something like the grand unification of experience that many regard as the hallmark of psychedelic experience itself. Jazz god John Coltrane, in one representative statement, reported that, during his first trip, he 'perceived the interrelationships of all life forms' (Lee and Schlain, 1985, p. 79). I would even venture that 'Tomorrow Never Knows' concludes *Revolver* with infinitely more sonic and lyrical coherence than 'A Day in the Life' sums up *Sgt Pepper's Lonely Hearts Club Band*.

Revolver's dynamism and much of its genius nestle along its borders, in the transitions from one song to the next, including the buffering silent spaces between the songs, between the notes, between the words. In its explosive dialectic with its silences, *Revolver* ushers popular music into another kind of world, one in which voices, sounds, and songs play out a musical and conceptual inquiry into the then and now as well as the here, there, and everywhere of human consciousness.

Notes

1. I must say, however, that Timothy Leary's decision in 1996 to have his cremated ashes sent up in a satellite to orbit earth, has made me reconsider the importance of the Ventures' homage to the satellite age and my friends' musical tastes!

2. For an account of psychedelics and rock music that addresses the impact, the endurance, and importance of the genre, see Nick Bromell's *'Tomorrow Never Knows': Rock and Psychedelics in the 1960s* (University of Chicago Press, 2000). Bromell's study is rich with cultural and psychological insights, although I disagree with what I see to be Bromell's ultimate characterization of psychedelics as little more than a passing fad of adolescence, as it trivializes both the accomplishments of psychedelic art as well as Bromell's own insights.

3. Tim Riley comments that *Revolver*'s transitions 'point toward the integration of song segues that makes *Sgt Pepper* a continuous stream of sound'. I would differ from Riley in suggesting that

Revolver's transitions fully realize both the coherence and the experimental edge that the Beatles' later reproduce on *Sgt Pepper*. Tim Riley, *Tell Me Why: The Beatles: Album by Album, Song by Song, The Sixties and After*, New York: Vintage, 1988, p. 196.

4. For information on Freymann, see Everett, 1999, p. 45 and the sources indicated in footnote 71 from that same page. For information on Dr Max Jacobson, see Lee and Schlain, 1985, p. 102.

5. Psychedelic rock lyrics pay frequent homage to Hoffmann's first, psychedelic ride by celebrating such magical forms of conveyance as Pink Floyd's 'Bike', the Moody Blues' see-saw, Steppenwolf's magic carpet, the Thirteenth Floor Elevators' roller coaster, the Who's magic bus, and, of course, the Beatles' own 'Yellow Submarine' and 'Magical Mystery Tour'. Not all trippers make it '2000 Light Years From Home' (Rolling Stones) or 'Eight Miles High' (Byrds), nor do they travel at speeds reaching '3/5 of a Mile in 10 Seconds' (Jefferson Airplane) or 'Interstellar Overdrive' (Pink Floyd), but the trip as metaphor has fueled these and many other mystical journeys.

6. See Madow and Sobul, 1992. Madow and Sobul offer little more than highly subjective and often repetitive remarks about the psychedelic phase of the Beatles' career, but their observations are occasionally interesting, and the scope of their study places *Revolver* in the context of later work.

7. 'Love You To' later becomes George Harrison's signature sound, playing at the moment he is introduced in the animated film *Yellow Submarine*.

8. We shouldn't forget that 'Yellow Submarine' was originally conceived of as a children's song. See Barry Miles, *Paul McCartney: Many Years from Now*, New York: Henry Holt & Co., 1997, pp. 286–287.

9. The novels of Tom Robbins are a case in point. Robbins's fictional project carries profoundly psychedelic and philosophical dimensions and regularly embodies the Tibetan notion of 'crazy wisdom', i.e., the belief that the silly can be profound and the profound silly.

10. Walter Everett points out that 'Good Day Sunshine' and 'Here Comes the Sun' also share choruses that are 'metrically relaxed, in a carefree manner', another characteristic suggestive of the exuberant feelings of optimism encoded within each song (1999, p. 58).

11. Of course, we might also regard the initial count-in on 'Taxman' and the dreamy quality engineered into John Lennon's voice on 'I'm Only Sleeping' as equally psychedelic. My point here is that in 'Eleanor Rigby' and 'And Your Bird Can Sing' these electronic effects jump out and distinguish themselves from the rest of the vocal treatments. Thanks to Jim LeBlanc for urging this clarification.

12. Ann Dyer's astonishing version of 'Tomorrow Never Knows' on *Revolver: A New Spin* emphasizes the Asiatic exoticism of the song with more explicitly Asiatic instrumentation and vocal effects.

13. Masters and Houston, 1966, p. 188.

Works Cited

'Every reference there is'

Alpert, Richard (1971), *Be Here Now,* Lama Foundation.
Anthology (2000), *The Beatles: Anthology*, London: Cassell.
'Beatle News' (1966), *The Beatles Monthly Book*, no. 33, April.
'Beatles Plus Jazzmen on New Album' (1966), *Melody Maker* 11 June.
Beatles, The (1989), *The Beatles' Complete Scores. Every Song Written and Recorded by the Beatles. Full Transcriptions from the Original Recordings*, transcription by Tetsuya Fujita, Yuji Hagino, Hajime Kubo and Goro Sato, London and New York: Wise Publications, 1993; originally published in 1989 by Shinko Music Publishing.
Beatles, The (1993), *The Beatles Complete Scores: Every Song Written and Recorded by the Beatles*, Milwaukee: Hal Leonard Publishing Corporation, 1993.
Beatles, The (2000), *Anthology*, London: Cassell; San Francisco: Chronicle Books.
Belmo (no date), *20ᵗʰ Century Rock and Roll: Psychedelia*, Burlington, Canada: Collector's Guide Publishing.
Berger, John (1972), *Ways of Seeing*, London: Penguin Books.
Bettens, Olivier (1998), '«Intonation juste» à la Renaissance: idéal ou utopie? Esquisse d'un modèle fondé sur la théorie de Zarlino', *Zarlino*, retrieved 12 April 2001, from the World Wide Web: http://www.virga.org/zarlino/.
Bisbort, Alan and Parke Puterbaugh (2000), *Rhino's Psychedelic Trip*, San Francisco: Miller Freeman Books.
Bishop, Malden Grange (1963), *The Discovery of Love: A Psychedelic Experience with LSD-25*, New York: Dodd, Mead & Company.
Bockris, Victor and Gerard Malanga (1983), *Up-tight: The Velvet Underground Story*, London and New York: Omnibus.
Bowman, Rob (1977), *Soulsville, U. S. A.: The Story of Stax Records*, New York: Schirmer Books.
Bradbury, Malcolm and James McFarlane (1976), 'The Name and Nature of Modernism', in *Modernism: 1890–1930*, ed. Bradbury and McFarlane, Harmondsworth: Penguin Books, pp. 19–55.
Bromell, Nick (2000), *'Tomorrow Never Knows': Rock and Psychedelics in the 1960s,* Chicago: University of Chicago Press.
Brown, Peter and Steven Gaines (1983), *The Love You Make: an Insider's Story of the Beatles*, New York: Signet Books.

Bruhn, Siglind (1993), *J. S. Bach's Well-Tempered Clavier: In-Depth Analysis and Interpretation*, Volume 1, Hong Kong: Mainer International Ltd.

Burroughs, William S. and Allen Ginsberg (1963), *The Yage Letters*, San Francisco: City Lights.

Butler, Judith (1990), *Gender Trouble: Feminism and the Subversion of Identity*, New York: Routledge.

Capuzzo, Guy (2001), 'Rotation as a Model for Rock Chord Progressions', *Second Biennial International Conference on Twentieth-Century Music*, Goldsmiths College, London, 30 June.

Clayson, Alan (1991), *Ringo Starr: Straight Man or Joker?*, London: Sanctuary Publishing.

Cloud, Cam (1999), *The Little Book of Acid*, Berkeley: Ronin Publishing Company.

Coates, Norma (1997), '(R)evolution Now? Rock and the Political Potential of Gender', in Sheila Whiteley (ed.), *Sexing the Groove: Popular Music and Gender*, New York: Routledge, pp. 50–64.

Coleman, Ray (1995), *Lennon: The Definitive Biography*, London: Pan Books.

Cotner, John S. (1999), '"Careful With That Axe, Eugene" (ca. 1968): A Study of Genre, Medium, Texture, and Structure', *Society for Music Theory Annual Conference*, Atlanta, 11 November.

Davies, Hunter (1968), *The Beatles*, London: Heinemann.

Davis, Edward E. (ed.) (1968), *The Beatles Book*, New York: Cowles Education Corporation.

Denisoff, Serge R. (1986), *Tarnished Gold: the Record Industry Revisited*, New Brunswick, New Jersey: Transaction Books.

DeRogatis, J. (1996), *Kaleidoscope Eyes: Psychedelic Music from the 1960s to the 1990s*, London: Fourth Estate.

Dijkstra, B. (1986), *Idols of Perversity: Fantasies of Feminine Evil in Fin-de-Siecle Culture*, New York: Oxford University Press.

Dowlding, William J. (1989), *Beatlesongs*, New York: Simon & Schuster.

Eerola, Tuomas (1998), 'The Rise and Fall of the Experimental Style of the Beatles', in Yrjö Heinonen, Tuomas Eerola, Jouni Koskimäki, Terhi Nurmesjärvi and John Richardson (eds), *Beatlestudies 1. Songwriting, Recording, and Style Change*, Jyväskylä: University of Jyväskylä (Department of Music, Research Reports 19), pp. 33–60.

Eisen, J. (ed.) (1969), *The Age of Rock: Sounds of the American Cultural Revolution*, Vintage Books: New York: Random House.

Emerick, Geoff (1988), 'Recording Techniques', in George Martin (ed.), *Making Music*, London: Barrie & Jenkins, pp. 256–265.

Everett, Walter (1994), 'An Update on the Current State of Schenkerian Research: Volumes Edited by Hedi Siegel and by Allen Cadwallader', *Theory & Practice* 19.

Everett, Walter (1997), 'Swallowed by a Song: Paul Simon's Crisis of

Chromaticism', in John Covach and Graeme M. Boone (eds), *Understanding Rock*, New York: Oxford University Press.

Everett, Walter (1999), *The Beatles as Musicians:* Revolver *through* The Anthology, New York: Oxford University Press.

Everett, Walter (2001), *The Beatles as Musicians: The Quarry Men through Rubber Soul*, New York: Oxford University Press.

Fast, Susan (1999), 'Rethinking Issues of Gender and Sexuality in Led Zeppelin: a Woman's View of Pleasure and Power in Hard Rock', *American Music* 17, pp. 245–299.

Fitch, Vernon (1999), *The Pink Floyd Encyclopedia*, 2nd edn, Ontario: Collector's Guide Publishing.

Fitzgerald, Jon (2000), 'Lennon-McCartney and the Early British Invasion, 1964–1966', in Ian Inglish (ed.), *The Beatles, Popular Music and Society. A Thousand Voices*, Houndmills: MacMillan, pp. 53–85.

Fort, J. (1969), *The Pleasure Seekers: The Drug Crisis, Youth and Society*, New York: Grove Press.

Forte, Allen (1995), *The American Popular Ballad of the Golden Era, 1924–1950*, Princeton, Princeton University Press.

Frith, Simon (1987), 'Towards an Aesthetic of Popular Music', in Richard Leppert and Susan McClary (eds), *Music and Society: the Politics of Composition, Performance, and Reception*, Cambridge: Cambridge University Press, pp. 133–149.

Garbarini, Vic (1980), 'The McCartney Interview', *Musician Magazine: Player and Listener Magazine*, August (also on record: EMI Records Ltd, Parlophone, 1980).

Gaukroger, Stephen (1995), *Descartes: An Intellectual Biography*, New York: Oxford University Press.

George, Nelson (1985), *Where Did Our Love Go?: The Rise and Fall of the Motown Sound*, New York: St Martin's Press.

Gillett, Charlie (1974), *Making Tracks: Atlantic Records and the Growth of a Multi-Billion-Dollar Industry*, New York: Sunrise.

Gloag, Kenneth (2001), 'The Beatles: High Modernism and/or Postmodernism?', *Beatlestudies 3: Proceedings of the Beatles 2000 Conference*, ed. Yrjo Heinonen et al., University of Jyväskylä, Finland, 79–86.

Goldstein, Richard (1966), 'On *Revolver*', *Village Voice*, **XI**, (45), pp. 23 –26.

Goodman, Joan (1984), 'Playboy Interview: Paul and Linda McCartney', *Playboy*, **31** (12) December.

Gordy Jr, Berry (1994), *To Be Loved: The Music, The Magic, The Memories of Motown*, New York: Warner Books.

Gore, Joe (1999), 'Bench Tests: Retro Replay', *Guitar Player*, **33**, May, pp. 107–108.

Green, Jonathon (1988), *Days in the Life: Voices from the English Underground 1961–1971*, London: Heinemann.

Harris, John (2001), 'A Quiet Storm', *Mojo*, July, pp. 66–74.

Harrison, Frederick W. (2001), 'West Meets East, or How the Sitar Came to Be Heard in Western Pop Music', *Soundscapes*, **4**, Spring, retrieved 12 April 2001, from the World Wide Web: http://beatles.soundscapes.ws/.

Harrison, George (1980), *I Me Mine*, New York: Simon and Schuster.

Helmholtz, Hermann L. F. (1862), *On the Sensations of Tone as a Physiological Basis for the Theory of Music*, New York: Dover Publications, 1954.

Henke, Jim and Parke Puterbaugh (1997), *I Want to Take You Higher: The Psychedelic Era: 1965–1969*, San Francisco: Chronicle Books.

Hertsgaard, Mark (1995), *A Day in the Life: The Music and Artistry of the Beatles*, New York: Delacorte.

Hodges, Nick and Jan Priston (1999), *Embryo: A Pink Floyd Chronology, 1966–1971*, London: Cherry Red Books.

James, Jamie (1993), *The Music of the Spheres: Music, Science, and the Natural Order of the Universe*, New York: Copernicus.

Jameson, Fredric (1991), *Postmodernism; or The Cultural Logic of Late Capitalism*, Durham: Duke University Press.

Johansson, K-G. (1999), 'The Harmonic Language of the Beatles', *STM-Online* (Svensk Tidskrift för Musikforskning), **2**, retrieved 12 April 2001, from the World Wide Web: http://www-hotel.uu.se/musik/ssm/stmonline/.

Jones, Cliff (1999), *Another Brick in the Wall: The Stories Behind Every Pink Floyd Song*, London: Carlton Books.

Joyce, James (1961), *Ulysses*, New York: Random House.

Julien, Oliver (1999), 'The Diverting of Musical Technology by Rock Musicians: The Example of Double Tracking', *Popular Music*, **28** (3), pp. 357–365.

Keller, Hermann (1976), *The Well-Tempered Clavier by Johann Sebastian Bach*, trans. Leight Gerdine, London: George Allen & Unwin.

Kirkpatrick, Ralph (1984), *Interpreting Bach's* Well-Tempered Clavier*: A Performer's Discourse of Method*, New Haven: Yale University Press.

Kleps, Art (1975), *Millbrook: The True Story of the Early Years of the Psychedelic Revolution*, Oakland: The Bench Press.

Kramarz, Volkert (1983), *Harmonie-analyse der Rockmusik. Von Folk und Blues zu Rock und New Wave*, Mainz: Schott.

Laing, R. D. (1970), *knots*, New York: Random House.

Latour, Bruno (1993), *We Have Never Been Modern*, trans. Catherine Porter, Cambridge: Harvard University Press.

Laurence, Paul (1978), 'I Was a Very Nervous Character: An Interview with George Martin', *Audio: The Equipment Authority*, May, pp. 46–60.

Leary, Timothy (1968), *High Priest*, Berkeley: Ronin Publishing.

Leary, Timothy, Ralph Metzner, and Richard Alpert (1964), *The Psychedelic Experience: A Manual Based on 'The Tibetan Book of the Dead'*, New Hyde Park, NY: University Books.

Lee, Al (1968), 'The Poetics of the Beatles', in Edward E. Davis (ed.), *The*

Beatles Book, New York: Cowles Education Corporation, pp. 99–127.

Lee, Martin and Bruce Shlain (1985), *Acid Dreams: The Complete Social History of LSD: The CIA, the Sixties, and Beyond*, New York: Grove Press.

Lennon, John and Paul McCartney (1966), 'Here, There And Everywhere', *Beatles Complete*, Warner Bros. Publications.

Lewisohn, Mark (1988), *The Beatles' Recording Sessions. The Official Abbey Road Studio Session Notes, 1962–1970*, New York: Harmony.

Lewisohn, Mark (1992), *The Complete Beatles Chronicle*, New York: Harmony Books.

Lewisohn, Mark (2000a), *The Beatles Recording Sessions: The Official Story of the Abbey Road Years 1962–1970*, New York: Prospero Books. (Previously published as *The Complete Beatles Recording Sessions* (1988), London: The Hamlyn Publishing Group PLC.)

Lewisohn, Mark (2000b), *The Complete Beatles Chronicle: The Only Definitive Guide to the Beatles' Entire Career*, London: Hamlyn.

Lyotard, Jean-François (1992), 'Note on the Meaning of "Post-"', in *The Postmodern Explained: Correspondence 1982–1985*, Minneapolis: University of Minnesota Press, pp. 64–68.

Mabbett, Andy (1995), *The Complete Guide to the Music of Pink Floyd*, London: Omnibus Press.

MacDonald, Bruno (1997), *Pink Floyd: Through the Eyes of the Band, its Fans, Friends and Foes*, New York: Da Capo Press.

MacDonald, Bruno and David Walker (1991), 'Another Brick in the Walrus', *The Amazing Pudding* (49), June, pp. 12–13.

MacDonald, I. (1994), *Revolution in the Head: The Beatles Records and the Sixties*, London: Fourth Estate.

Madow, Stuart and Jeff Sobul (1992), *The Colour of Your Dreams: The Beatles' Psychedelic Music*, Pittsburgh: Dorrance.

Marcus, Greil (1980), 'The Beatles', in Jim Miller (ed.), *Rolling Stone Illustrated History of Rock and Roll*, New York: Rolling Stone Pubs, pp. 179–189.

Martin, George (1988), 'Record Production', in George Martin (ed.), *Making Music*, London: Barrie & Jenkins, pp. 266–277.

Martin, George and Jeremy Hornsby (1979), *All You Need is Ears*, New York: St. Martin's Press.

Martin, George and William Pearson (1994a), *With A Little Help From My Friends: The Making of Sergeant Pepper*, Boston: Little, Brown.

Martin, George and William Pearson (1994b), *Summer of Love: The Making of Sgt. Pepper*, London: Macmillan.

Marzorati, Gerald (2000), 'Something New: More by The Beatles', *New York Times Magazine*, 19 November, Section 6, pp. 31–32.

Mason, Nick, David Gilmour, and Storm Thorgerson (1992), *Shine On: A Book to Accompany the CD Boxed Set*, London: Pink Floyd Music.

Masters, R. E. L. and Jean Houston (1966), *The Varieties of Psychedelic*

Experience, New York: Holt, Rinehart and Winston.

McCarthy, Len (2001), 'Slow Down! How the Beatles Changed the Rhythmic Paradigm of Pop and Rock', in Yrjö Heinonen, Marcus Heuger, Sheila Whiteley, Terhi Nurmesjärvi and Jouni Koskimäki (eds), *Beatlestudies 3. Proceedings of the Beatles 2000 Conference*, Jyväskylä: University of Jyväskylä (Department of Music, Research Reports 23), 2001, pp. 215–230.

Mellers, Wilfrid (1969), 'New Music in a New World', in Jonathan Eisen (ed.), *The Age of Rock: Sounds of the American Cultural Revolution*, New York: Vintage Books, pp. 180–188.

Mellers, Wilfrid (1973), *Twilight of the Gods: The Beatles in Retrospect*, London: Faber & Faber.

Melly, G. (1971), *Revolt into Style*, London: Penguin.

Miles, Barry (compiler) (1978), *Beatles in Their Own Words*, New York: Quick Fox.

Miles, Barry (1980), *Pink Floyd: A Visual Documentary*, New York: Quick Fox.

Miles, Barry (1997), *Paul McCartney: Many Years From Now*, London: Vintage.

Millard, Andre (1995), *America On Record: A History of Recorded Sound*, New York: Cambridge University Press.

Miller, James (1999), *Flowers in the Dustbin: The Rise of Rock and Roll 1947–77*, New York: Simon & Schuster.

Miller, Toby (1993), *The Well-Tempered Self: Citizenship, Culture, and the Postmodern Subject*, Baltimore: Johns Hopkins University Press.

Molenda, Michael (2000), 'Faith in Something Bigger: Throughout Tabloid Travails Noel Gallagher Keeps Oasis Rock Solid', *Guitar Player*, **34**, September, pp. 68–78.

Moore, Allan F. (1997), *The Beatles: Sgt. Pepper's Lonely Hearts Club Band*, Cambridge: Cambridge University Press.

Mulder, Juul (2000), *Beethoven Electrifies. Processing of Expressive, Dynamic Music as Measured in Non-musicians Using ERP's*, Leipzig: Max Planck Institute of Cognitive Neuroscience.

New Musical Express (1967), 'Life Lines of Pink Floyd', 19 August, p. 10.

Norman, Philip (1981a), *Shout ! The True Story of the Beatles,* London: Penguin.

Norman, Philip (1981b), *Shout: The Beatles in the Generation*, New York: MJF Books.

O'Grady, Terence J. (1975), 'The Music of the Beatles from 1962 to "Sergeant Pepper's Lonely Hearts Club Band"', Volume 1. PhD dissertation, University of Wisconsin at Madison.

O'Grady, Terence J. (1979a), '*Rubber Soul* and the Social Dance Tradition', *Journal of the Society for Ethnomusicology*, **23** January.

O'Grady, Terence J. (1979b), 'Rubber Soul and the Social Dance Tradition', in: Charles P. Neises (ed.), *The Beatles' Reader. A Selection of Contemporary Views, News, and Reviews of the Beatles in their Heyday*, Ann Arbor: Pierian

Press, 1984, pp. 47–55; original publication: Ethnomusicology, 1979, **23** (1), pp. 67–94.

O'Grady, Terence J. (1979b), 'The Ballad Style in the Early Music of the Beatles', in Charles Neises P. (ed.), *The Beatles' Reader. A Selection of Contemporary Views, News, and Reviews of the Beatles in their Heyday*, Ann Arbor: Pierian Press, 1984, pp. 79–88; original publication: College Music Symposium, 1979, **29** (1).

O'Grady, Terence J. (1983), *The Beatles: A Musical Evolution,* Boston: Twayne's Music Series.

Palisca, Claude V. (ed.) (1988), *Norton Anthology of Western Music, Vol. I*, 2nd edn, New York: W.W. Norton & Company.

Peyser, Joan (1969), 'The Music of Sound or, the Beatles and the Beatless', in Jonathan Eisen (ed.), *The Age of Rock: Sounds of the American Cultural Revolution*, New York: Vintage Books, pp. 126–137.

Pollack, Alan W. (1989–2001), 'Notes on ... Series', *The 'official' rec.music.beatles home page*, retrieved 12 April 2001, from the World Wide Web: http://kiwi.imgen.bcm.tmc.edu.

Porter, Steven (1979b), *Rhythm and Harmony in the Music of the Beatles*, Ann Arbor, Michigan: University Microfilms International.

Porter, Steven (1979c), '*Rubber Soul* and the Social Dance Tradition', *Journal of the Society for Ethnomusicology*, **23**, January.

Povey, Glenn and Ian Russell (1997), *In the Flesh: The Complete Performance History*, New York: Griffen.

Price, Charles Gower (1997), 'Sources of American Styles in the Music of the Beatles', *American Music*, **15** (2).

Quantick, David (2000), '*Revolver*' (50 Greatest British Albums Ever), *Q*, June, pp. 92–93.

Randel, Don Michael (ed.) (1986), 'Faburden', in *The New Harvard Dictionary of Music*, Cambridge, MA: The Belknap Press of Harvard University Press, p. 297.

Reck, David R. (1985), 'Beatles Orientalis: Influences from Asia in a Popular Song Tradition', *Asian Music*, **16** (1), pp. 83–149.

Reynolds, Simon and Joy Press (1995), *The Sex Revolts: Gender Rebellion and Rock'n'roll*, London: Serpent's Tail.

Richardson, J. (1998), 'Black and White Music: Dialogue, Dysphoric Coding and the Death Drive in the Music of Bernard Herrmann, The Beatles, Stevie Wonder and Coolio', in Y. Heinonen, T. Eerola, J. Koskimäki, T. Nurmesjärvi and J. Richardson (eds) *Beatlestudies I: Songwriting, Recording and Style Change*, Jyväskylä: University of Jyväskylä, Department of Music Research Reports 19.

Riley, Tim (1988), *Tell Me Why: The Beatles: Album by Album, Song by Song, The Sixties and After*, New York: Vintage.

Riley, Tim (2000), 'Drive My Car: 60s Soulsters Embrace Lennon-McCartney', in Yrjö Heinonen, Marcus Heuger, Sheila Whiteley et al. (eds), *Beatlestudies 3: Proceedings of the Beatles 2000 Conference*, Jyväskylä, Finland: University of Jyväskylä Press, pp. 15–25.

Romanowski, Patricia and Holly George-Warren (eds) (1995), *The New Rolling Stone Encyclopedia of Rock & Roll*, New York: Rolling Stone Press.

Roszak, T. (1970), *The Making of a Counter Culture. Reflections on a Technocratic Society and its Youthful Opposition*, New York: Faber and Faber.

Rowlands, Tom and Ed Simons (accessed 18 April 2001), 'Ask Tom and Ed', http://www.astralwerks.com/chemical/ask/musicresponse.html.

Roylance, Brian, Julian Quance, Oliver Craskke, and Roman Milisic (eds) (2000), *The Beatles Anthology*, San Francisco: Chronicle Books.

Rule, Greg (1997), 'Chemical Brothers: Water Into Acid – The Chemical Brothers Blow Up', *Keyboard*, **23** (6), June, pp. 30–34, 38–39.

Russcol, Herbert (1972), *The Liberation of Sound: an introduction to electronic music*, Englewood Cliffs, New Jersey: Prentice-Hall.

Sadie, Stanley (ed.) (1984), *New Grove Dictionary of Musical Instruments*, London: MacMillan.

Said, Edward (1979), *Orientalism*, New York: Vintage.

Savage, Jon (1997), '100 Greatest Psychedelic Classics', *MOJO*, **43**, June, pp. 56–67.

Schaffner, Nicholas (1977), *The Beatles Forever*, New York: McGraw Hill.

Schaffner, Nicholas (1988), 'Pink Floyd: Happy at Last', *Musician* **118**, August, pp. 70–80.

Schaffner, Nicholas (1991), *Saucerful of Secrets: The Pink Floyd Odyssey*, New York: Delta Books.

Schleifer, Ronald (2000), *Analogical Thinking: Post-Enlightenment Under standing in Language, Collaboration, and Interpretation*, Ann Arbor: University of Michigan Press.

Schulter, Margo (1998), 'Pythagorean Tuning and Medieval Polyphony', *Early Music FAQ*, retrieved 12 April 2001, from the World Wide Web: http://www.medieval.org/.

Scully, Rock and David Dalton (1996), *Living With the Dead: Twenty Years on the Bus with Garcia and the Grateful Dead*, Boston: Little, Brown and Company.

Sharp, Ken (1998), 'The Last Hurrah of the Fifth Beatle', *Goldmine*, **477** (6), November, pp. 14–19.

Sheff, David (2000), *All We Are Saying: The Last Major Interview with John Lennon and Yoko Ono*, in G. Barry Golson (ed.), New York: St. Martin's Griffin. (Previously published as *The Playboy Interviews with John Lennon and Yoko Ono* (1981), Playboy.)

Sheff, David and G. Barry Golson (1981), *The Playboy Interviews with John Lennon and Yoko Ono*, USA: Playboy.

Shillinglaw, Ann (1999), '"Give Us a Kiss": Queer Codes, Male Partnering, and the Beatles', in Patricia Juliana Smith (ed.), *The Queer Sixties,* New York:

Routledge, pp. 127–145.

Shotton, Pete, and Nicolas Schaffner (1983), John Lennon: *In My Life*, New York: Stein & Day.

Siegel, Jules (1966), 'Requiescat in Pace – That's Where It's At', *Village Voice*, **XI** (46) pp. 7, 14.

Simmons, Sylvie (1999), 'Danger! Demolition in Progress', *MOJO* **73**, December, pp. 76–95.

Simms, Bryan R. (1996), *Music of the Twentieth Century: Style and Structure*, New York: Schirmer Books.

Snyder, Jeff (accessed 19 April 2001), 'Musique Concrete', http://csunix1.lvc.edu/~snyder/em/schaef.html.

Snyder, Jeff (accessed 19 April 2001), 'Pierre Schaeffer: Inventor of Music Concrete', http://csunix1.lvc.edu/~snyder/em/schaef.html.

Sontag, Susan (2000), 'Amerikas døtre', *Henne,* No. 10: September/October, p. 118 (trans. J. Dennington).

Southall, Brian (1982), *Abbey Road*, Cambridge: Patrick Stephens and London: EMI Records.

Stewart, Allison. "Reviews: Standing on the Shoulder of Giants." January 8, 2002 at <http://www.cdnow.com/cgi-bin/mserver/SID=1971530343/pagename= /RP/CDN/FIND/a Ibum.html/artistid=OASIS/itemid=1159233>. Copyright February 9, 2000.

Thompson, Gordon (2001), 'Let Me Take You Down ... to the Subdominant. Tools of Establishment and Revealing the Establishment', in Yrjö Heinonen, Marcus Heuger, Sheila Whiteley, Terhi Nurmesjärvi and Jouni Koskimäki (eds), *Beatlestudies 3. Proceedings of the Beatles 2000 Conference*, Jyväskylä: University of Jyväskylä (Department of Music, Research Reports 23), pp. 283–291.

Thorgerson, Storm (1997), *Mind Over Matter: The Images of Pink Floyd*, London: Sanctuary Publishing.

Tillekens, Ger (1998), *Het Geluid van de Beatles* [The Sound of the Beatles], Amsterdam: Het Spinhuis.

Tillekens, Ger (2001), 'Words and Chords. The Semantic Shifts of the Beatles' Chords', in Yrjö Heinonen, Marcus Heuger, Sheila Whiteley, Terhi Nurmesjärvi and Jouni Koskimäki (eds), *Beatlestudies 3. Proceedings of the Beatles 2000 Conference*, Jyväskylä: University of Jyväskylä (Department of Music, Research Reports 23), 2001, pp. 97–111.

Turner, Steve (1994), *A Hard Day's Write: The Stories Behind Every Beatles Song*, New York: HarperCollins.

Uncut Magazine (2001), 'The Beatles: Their 50 Greatest Songs!', Take 50, July, pp. 28–64.

Valdez, Stephen (2001), 'Vocal Harmony as a Structural Device in the Commercial Recordings of the Beatles, 1962–1970', in Yrjö Heinonen, Marcus Heuger, Sheila Whiteley, Terhi Nurmesjärvi and Jouni Koskimäki (eds),

Beatlestudies 3. Proceedings of the Beatles 2000 Conference, Jyväskylä: University of Jyväskylä (Department of Music, Research Reports 23), 2001, pp. 243–253.

Van der Merwe, Peter (1989), *Origins of the Popular Style. The Antecedents of Twentieth Century Popular Music*, Oxford: Clarendon.

Wagner, Naphtali (1999), *The Beatles: The Seven Good Years,* Jerusalem: Magnes Press (Hebrew).

Wagner, Naphtali (2001), 'Tonal Oscillation in the Beatles' Songs', in Yrjö Heinonen, Marcus Heuger, Sheila Whiteley, Terhi Nurmesjärvi and Jouni Koskimäki (eds), *Beatlestudies 3. Proceedings of the Beatles 2000 Conference*, Jyväskylä: University of Jyväskylä (Department of Music, Research Reports 23), 2001, pp. 87–96.

Walker, Don (1985), *The Motown Story*, New York: Charles Scribner's Sons.

Watkinson, Mike and Pete Anderson (1991), *Crazy Diamond: Syd Barrett and the Dawn of Pink Floyd*, London: Omnibus Press.

Weinberg, Max (1984), *The Big Beat: Conversations with Rock's Great Drummers*, New York: Billboard Books.

White, Timothy (1990), 'Pink Floyd', *Rock Lives: Profiles and Interviews*, New York: Henry Holt and Company, pp. 507–523. Originally appeared in *Penthouse*, September 1988, as 'Pink Floyd: Roger Waters Exposes the Secrets of Rock and Roll's Most Self-Destructive Supergroup'.

Whiteley, Sheila (1992), *The Space Between the Notes: Rock and the Counter Culture*, London: Routledge.

Whiteley, Sheila (2000a), *Women and Popular Music: Sexuality, Identity and Subjectivity*, London: Routledge.

Whiteley, Sheila (2000b), 'No Fixed Agenda: The Position of the Beatles within Popular/Rock Music', *Beatles 2000*, Jyväskylä, 16 June.

Widders-Ellis, Andy and Jesse Gress (1994), 'Take a Rad Song and Make It Better. Exploded Views of Three Beatles' Classics', *Guitar Player*, **28** (9), pp. 95–104, 106, 108.

Winn, John C. (2001), 'Here, There & Everywhere', *Beatlology*, **3**, (4), March–April.

Wittgenstein, Ludwig (1963), *Philosophical Investigations* (first edition: 1953), translated by G. E. M. Anscombe, Oxford: Basil Blackwell.

Index

All entries to individual Beatles, Beatles songs, and Beatles albums and films are indexed alphabetically under 'Beatles, the,' beginning with individual Beatles, then individual songs not on *Revolver*, then albums. The same principle applies to entries for Pink Floyd. For *Revolver*, entries for the albums' themes appear first, followed by entries for the individual songs in the order they appear on the album.